Microsoft®

W9-AVY-166

Programming
ADO

David Sceppa

PUBLISHED BY
Microsoft Press
A Division of Microsoft Corporation
One Microsoft Way
Redmond, Washington 98052-6399

Copyright © 2000 by David Sceppa

All rights reserved. No part of the contents of this book may be reproduced or transmitted in any form or by any means without the written permission of the publisher.

Library of Congress Cataloging-in-Publication Data
Sceppa, David, 1972–
     Programming ADO / David Sceppa.
        p.   cm.
     Includes index.
     ISBN 0-7356-0764-8
     1. Database design.   2. Object oriented programming (Computer science)   3. ActiveX.
   I. Title.

     QA76.9.D26 S32 2000
     005.1'17--dc21   99-056529

Printed and bound in the United States of America.

1 2 3 4 5 6 7 8 9   QMQM   5 4 3 2 1 0

Distributed in Canada by Penguin Books Canada Limited.

A CIP catalogue record for this book is available from the British Library.

Microsoft Press books are available through booksellers and distributors worldwide. For further information about international editions, contact your local Microsoft Corporation office or contact Microsoft Press International directly at fax (425) 936-7329. Visit our Web site at mspress.microsoft.com.

Active Directory, ActiveX, FoxPro, FrontPage, Microsoft, Microsoft Press, MSDN, Outlook, Visual Basic, Visual C++, Visual FoxPro, Visual Studio, Windows, and Windows NT are either registered trademarks or trademarks of Microsoft Corporation in the United States and/or other countries. Other product and company names mentioned herein may be the trademarks of their respective owners.

The example companies, organizations, products, people, and events depicted herein are fictitious. No association with any real company, organization, product, person, or event is intended or should be inferred.

Acquisitions Editor: Eric Stroo
Project Editors: Alice Turner, Mary Barnard
Technical Editor: Jean Ross

Using the Companion CD

The CD included with this book contains many valuable resources, including sample files and additional documentation.

SAMPLE FILES

The companion CD for this book contains sample programs to help you learn more about ADO. All the samples are located in the Samples folder. You can view the samples from the CD, or you can install them onto your hard disk to run them and use them with your own applications.

> **NOTE** If you're unable to browse the files in the Samples folder, you might have an older CD driver that doesn't support long filenames. If this is the case, to browse the files you must install the sample files on your hard disk by running the setup program.

If you have the autorun feature in Microsoft Windows enabled, you'll see a splash screen when you insert the CD into the CD-ROM drive that will provide you with setup options. To start this screen manually, run StartCD from the root directory of the CD. Installing the sample files requires approximately 1.08 MB of disk space. If you have trouble running any of the sample files, refer to Appendix B or to the Readme.txt file in the root directory of the CD.

MDAC 2.5 REDISTRIBUTABLE SETUP

Another folder you'll find on the CD is MDAC25\Setup, which contains an executable file named mdac_typ.exe that will install Microsoft Data Access Components (MDAC) 2.5 libraries. After you've run this file, you'll find all the information regarding MDAC 2.5 in the MDACReadme.htm file on your hard disk in the \Program Files\Common Files\SYSTEM\ADO folder. You can also find information and updates to MDAC on Microsoft's Data Access Web site at *http://www.microsoft.com/data*.

MDAC 2.5 SDK

In the MDAC25\MDACSDK folder on the CD, you'll find the files for the Microsoft Data Access Components 2.5 SDK. Included with this SDK are documentation files, samples, and tools. You can install these files to your hard drive by running the Setup file contained in this folder. Refer to the Readme.txt or Readme.htm files in this folder for more information on the MDAC 2.5 SDK.

These SDK files are an excerpt from the data access portion of the Microsoft Platform SDK. If you prefer to see the entire package you can download the Platform SDK from *http://msdn.microsoft.com/downloads/sdks/platform/platform.asp*.

ELECTRONIC BOOK

In the Ebook folder on the companion CD is an electronic version of *Programming ADO* so that you can view and search the text on line. See the Readme.txt file in the root directory of the CD for information on using the electronic book.

SYSTEM REQUIREMENTS

The following is a list of system requirements necessary to run the files on this CD:

■ Microsoft Windows 2000, Microsoft Windows NT 4 Service Pack 4 or later, or Microsoft Windows 98

■ Microsoft Visual Basic 6

SUPPORT

Every effort has been made to ensure the accuracy of this book and the contents of the companion CD. Microsoft Press provides corrections for books through the World Wide Web at the following address:

http://mspress.microsoft.com/support/

If you have comments, questions, or ideas regarding this book or the companion CD, please send them to Microsoft Press using either of the following methods:
Postal Mail:

Microsoft Press
Attn: Programming ADO Editor
One Microsoft Way
Redmond, WA 98052-6399

E-mail:

MSPINPUT@MICROSOFT.COM

Please note that product support is not offered through the above mail addresses. For support information regarding Microsoft Data Access Components, see the Microsoft Data Access Web site at *http://www.microsoft.com/data*.

You can also call Standard Support at (425) 635-7011 weekdays between 6 a.m. and 6 p.m. Pacific time, or you can search the Microsoft Support Online at *http://support.microsoft.com/support*.

Contents at a Glance

Table of Contents

Table of Contents

Part II Working with the ADO Cursor Engine

Part III   Appendixes

Foreword

David and I had been swapping e-mail for several years when I was asked to write this foreword. Part of our daily routine involved hanging out on an internal Microsoft alias that deals with ADO issues—that's where we first met. All too often, it was David's sage advice that clarified an ADO issue I raised on this mailing list. Where David found the time to respond to the list given his other responsibilities is one of those mysteries of time and space that only Einstein could figure out.

When David's editors asked me to write this foreword, I was flattered but I knew that I would be working on my own ADO book for APress. I realized there might be a conflict of interest. Because David had selflessly provided so many great tips and techniques over the years, and because I had encouraged him to write a book in the first place, I couldn't turn him down. Now that I've read *Programming ADO*, I realize how well David's book complements my own books—both old and new.

I've been writing, teaching, and lecturing about Microsoft Visual Basic and data access since I started teaching Microsoft SQL Server at Microsoft University in 1988. Before that, I spent about a decade in the trenches, coding mainframe database systems and learning from other real-world developers. Because I'm no longer a front-line developer, I constantly have to communicate with developers and support people such as David to find out what's *really* working—and what's not. David's job brings him ear-to-ear—and often nose-to-nose—with some of the most difficult data access problems on the planet. He patiently listens to countless customers explain the symptoms of their problems. From these often-panicky accounts, David has to figure out what these customers have done to get ADO, ODBC, or OLE DB to behave (or misbehave) the way they're describing. I've found David's front-line experience invaluable—especially because David has a talent for guiding others to the "right" answer in a way that makes us feel smarter and better informed.

Programming ADO is much more than an ADO programmer's reference. Any serious developer will tell you that a thorough understanding of ADO requires more than just listing object names and their properties. ADO is a complex COM front end on an even more complex OLE DB data access layer connecting to an ever-growing number of providers. Understanding how these objects, interfaces, and providers interact is essential. While one really has to know how ADO behaves when things work as expected, it's even more important to know how ADO behaves (or misbehaves) when things go wrong. For example, error handling, and the messages ADO returns when "stuff" happens, is not one of ADO's most understandable aspects. David's explanation of ADO error management implementation, especially when updating Recordsets, is complete and easy to understand. I'm of the opinion that robust, comprehensive, and insightful error handling is what makes production programs successful. David's "What now?" approach clarifies a number of situations commonly encountered by those trying to code ADO. I also like David's "questions that *should* be asked more frequently" sections. These brief question/answer dialogues clarify a number of interesting points in a way that makes learning ADO far easier. David has compiled an invaluable, comprehensive guide for developers trying to get a handle on how to best create successful Visual Basic data access applications and components.

It's not only good or "right" code that makes successful applications—it's also good, well-planned designs. When we write about using low-level programming interfaces such as ADO, we must focus on using the practices that result in solid, scalable, and supportable applications—not necessarily applications that are easy to code. But without a clear and workable design, this process can be frustrating for developers and users alike. For example, I'm of the opinion that stored procedures can and do play an important role in scalable, high-performance SQL Server applications. While stored procedures are not necessarily easy to design, code, or access from ADO, it's important that developers understand how to access them from their applications and components. David's approach to design includes a comprehensive treatment of stored procedures: he provides a healthy section on the subject.

Some of the mysteries David's book delves into involve how ADO works with the Web through RDS and with shape and hierarchical data providers. Many readers find these new subjects a little murky when they depend solely on the Microsoft documentation—I know I did. As ADO takes on more and more functionality, the trick is knowing how to make the best of its new technology without letting this technology get the best of us.

David's writing style is thorough and easy to follow and understand. And while he doesn't include as many jokes as I do, I'm sure his readers will find this book a great resource despite this shortcoming.

Bill Vaughn
January 2000

Acknowledgments

First and foremost, I'd like to thank my mother and father for their constant support and patience.

I've been fortunate to have so many people point me in the right direction at exactly the right time, allowing me to take advantage of many opportunities throughout my programming career. As a first-time author, it's my duty to thank too many people, though I'm sure I'll unintentionally leave out some.

I'd like to thank Mary Sceppa and Hollis Graves for their encouragement and advice as well as for the computers I used throughout college. Thanks to Robert Welling for taking a chance and letting a scared little kid run his billing system. I'd also like to thank my extended family in the Seattle area, the Bramans, for helping me feel more at home out here.

Thanks to all the teachers, administrators, and professors who helped guide me through high school and college—especially James Pender, Judith Bolles, Tom Brown, Linda Mahler, and Robert Gunning.

So many people at Microsoft have helped me during the past few years in both technical and nontechnical situations. I'd like to thank Clay Stephens for getting my foot wedged firmly in the door and for getting me inside Microsoft. Thanks to my mentors, Greg Hinkel, Troy Cambra, and Jon Fowler. I must thank Bill Vaughn for the foreword of this book but primarily because *Hitchhiker's Guide to Visual Basic and SQL Server* [Microsoft Press, 1998] was my bible when I started in Microsoft Visual Basic database support. Thanks to Dave Stearns for some of the clearest answers to questions about Remote Data Objects (RDO) and the ODBC API. I hope this book will be as enlightening as the volumes of mail he's sent me. Thanks to Jim Lewallen and Greg Smith of the Microsoft ActiveX Data Objects (ADO) development team for answering so many questions about the goals and uses of specific features. I'd also like to thank Don Willits for helping me get this concept off the ground, Eric Schmidt for helping to put me in touch with so many people on the development team, and Sam Carpenter for keeping me (relatively) sane while I wrote this book.

Last of all, thanks to Mary Barnard, Alice Turner, Jean Ross, and the rest of the editing team for putting up with a first-time author. I'm sure you had no idea how much work you were signing up for.

Part I

Objects, Cursors, and Update Techniques

Chapter 1

Introduction

"I wish I'd known that before I started writing all this code."

You might be surprised at how often I've heard developers say something to this effect after I've explained to them how ADO works and what's going on under the covers.

For nearly four years I've been employed as a support professional—inexplicably, we're no longer called support engineers—in Microsoft Developer Support, working primarily with customers who are having trouble using Microsoft Visual Basic to build database applications. Lately, I've been surprised by the number of programmers who are having difficulty building applications with ADO. Discerning a pattern to the questions, I decided to write this book in the hope of sharing my knowledge of ADO with a greater number of programmers than I can speak to individually. If this book can help reduce the volume of support calls I handle in the process, that's a pleasant bonus.

WHERE ARE WE AND HOW DID WE GET HERE?

During the past five years, Microsoft has promoted Data Access Objects (DAO), and then Remote Data Objects (RDO), and now ActiveX Data Objects (ADO) as the primary data access technology for Visual Basic developers. It seems that Microsoft has been pushing a different data access technology with each successive version of Microsoft Visual Studio. Today, new versions of ADO are available on Microsoft's Web site and ship with other products and technologies, such as Microsoft Windows 2000, Microsoft Windows NT 4 Service Packs, Microsoft Internet Explorer versions 3 and later, Microsoft SQL Server 6.5 Service Pack 5 and SQL Server 7, Microsoft Office 2000, and even Microsoft Expedia Streets & Trips 2000.

One of the goals of ADO is to simplify data access. ADO is built upon some fairly complex technologies—OLE DB and ODBC (open database connectivity)—and is designed to allow you to programmatically access and modify data stored in a wide variety of databases. This broad reach is a departure from previous data access technologies. For the sake of comparison, let's take a quick glance at ADO's predecessors: DAO and RDO.

Data Access Objects

DAO was originally designed to interact with Microsoft Access databases. Although you can use DAO to access SQL Server and Oracle databases, many developers complain about DAO's performance with these large database systems. Others complain that DAO doesn't permit programmers to access some of the richer, more powerful features of SQL Server and Oracle, such as output and return parameters on stored procedures.

One of my coworkers likes to say that using DAO to work with an Oracle database is like performing brain surgery on yourself...without anesthetics...while wearing oven mitts. Extreme? Yes—but he does have a point. DAO is tuned to work with desktop databases, not client/server databases. Frustrated by DAO's performance and access limitations, developers who wanted to work with SQL Server and Oracle databases generally sought other options.

Remote Data Objects

Microsoft provided another option in RDO, which originally released with Visual Basic 4 Enterprise Edition. RDO's object model closely resembles the hierarchy of structures in the ODBC API. Programmers found that RDO provided much faster access to client/server database systems, such as SQL Server and Oracle, than DAO did. Although those familiar with the ODBC API quickly learned how to work with the RDO object model, developers lacking experience with that API, such as those who had been using DAO, found the RDO technology difficult to use.

The object model itself wasn't the problem for most programmers learning RDO: the nuances inherited from the ODBC API posed the greatest obstacles. Suddenly, programmers had to bone up on cursors and bookmarks. They had to learn many of the ins and outs of specific database systems. Does the error message "The connection is busy with results from another hstmt" ring any bells out there? If you try to do the impossible on an ODBC connection to your database, RDO won't save you. Instead, you'll get that error. DAO hid the problem from you by automatically creating another connection to your database to perform the action you requested.

Another challenge that RDO posed for programmers accustomed to writing DAO code was that RDO lacked many of DAO's features, such as sorting, searching, and filtering. Other DAO functionality unavailable in the RDO world includes data definition language (DDL) interfaces to ODBC API functions such as *CreateTable* and *CreateField*.

Best of Both Worlds: ActiveX Data Objects

Programmers clamored for a data access technology that combined the simplicity and relative ease of use of DAO with the speed, power, and control of RDO. Initially introduced as part of the Microsoft Internet Information Server 3 package, ADO was intended to be all things to all people. Of course, such lofty goals are rarely fulfilled.

While the initial release of ADO lacked many of RDO's features, I believe that ADO 2.0 offered comparable functionality. Certain RDO features, such as mixed cursors, have yet to be implemented in ADO, but these features are few and far between. In fact, I'm at a loss to name a single significant feature available in RDO that was not available in ADO 2.0 in one form or another. (I'm sure someone will tell me otherwise; a great way to find such features is to make a statement like that in a book like this.)

With the release of version 2.1, ADO and its supporting libraries began offering nearly all features available in DAO. DDL libraries were added to ADO in version 2.1 to provide functionality similar to functions available with DAO, such as *CreateTable*, *CreateField*, and *CreateIndex*. Microsoft Jet and Replication Objects (JRO) in ADO 2.1 offers much of the Jet-specific functionality available via the DBEngine object in DAO. ADO 2.1 also added functionality to simplify the retrieval of newly generated identity values. ADO 2.5 adds no new functionality to more closely match the capabilities of DAO and RDO, because perhaps the only place where ADO lags behind DAO is in its searching and filtering capabilities.

So ADO has most of the functionality of RDO and DAO as well as many helpful features not available in previous data access technologies. Great. Why, then, can't I get a moment's peace at work? Why are programmers having problems building applications with ADO?

Difficulties Using ADO

First of all, ADO is still a fairly new technology. The Microsoft Data Access SDK documentation that shipped with Visual Studio 6 (as part of MSDN Library Visual Studio 6) was for many programmers the primary source of information about ADO. Unfortunately, the information in the Data Access SDK is more reference-based than instructive—lacking samples, best practice information, and in-depth discussions about how the technology works.

One of the many reasons for the lack of detail in the documentation is that products are being released on Internet time. The team developing the data access components has been in "ship mode" for the past two years. Since these components are now included with many different Microsoft products—Internet Information Server 3 and 4, Internet Information Services 5, Visual Studio 6, SQL Server 7, Internet Explorer 4 and 5, Office 2000, and Windows 2000—the developers don't always have control over their own ship schedule. As with most products and teams under constant stress, something has to give, and in this case it's been the documentation. The development team has been operating in "ship now, document later" mode for too long.

Another reason programmers are having problems with ADO lies in its flexibility. While this flexibility is generally a strength, it has posed a challenge to the documentation team and been a source of confusion to programmers, because there is no "one way" to do things. For example, ADO offers many different ways to get data from your database into a Recordset object, yet much of the early documentation focused on only one of those methods; unfortunately, that method returned read-only data, not data that could be modified. For anyone who still hasn't been able to get an updatable Recordset object—we'll cover that topic in Chapter 4.

Lastly, building a multiuser database application with ADO, or with any other data access technology, isn't easy. Although tools such as Visual Basic 6 Data Environment Designer can save you a great deal of time, you should be wary of anyone who tells you that you can build a multiuser database application without having to write any code.

In many ways, ADO behaves like DAO in that it contains features that hide certain complexities from the programmer. I mentioned an RDO error message earlier—"The connection is busy with results from another hstmt"—that occurs when you try to use a connection that's already busy. ADO simplifies the programmer's task by establishing another connection rather than returning an error such as that. However, it's important to know what's going on behind the scenes and why: you wouldn't want to unwittingly create an application that establishes 8 or 10 connections per instance of your application. This book will discuss this and other such features in depth so that you don't stumble across them accidentally or employ them inappropriately.

WHAT WILL THIS BOOK DO FOR ME?

There is no substitute for a clear understanding of the requirements for the application you want to build or for experience with the tools you want to use to build that application. I can't stress this point strongly enough. While this book won't help you define the requirements, it will help you develop proficiency with ADO.

I don't believe there's a "best way" to use ADO. How you build your database applications will depend on what type of database you're accessing, the number of simultaneous users, the amount of code you're willing to write, and the amount of control you require over what's happening in your application, as well as your delivery schedule. This book will help you develop enough expertise with ADO so that you can decide what way is best for you, depending on the requirements of your application. It is designed to serve as an in-depth reference for the object model, as an explanation of much of the functionality of the cursor engine, and as a starting point for you to determine how to build your applications.

To begin Part I, we're going to cover the ADO object model. This material might already be familiar to those of you who have perused the ADO documentation that's included with many products and in the Data Access SDK, but I have a couple of reasons for not relegating it to an appendix. First, the simple act of reading through the list of features available in the ADO object model can help you come up with ideas. You never know when intuition will strike. Second, the properties, events, and methods that have caused the most confusion for developers are presented in more detail than in the ADO documentation.

After covering the object model in Chapters 2 through 6, we'll look at two more topics—cursors and update techniques—before closing Part I of the book. The type of cursor you use and how you plan to update your database are probably the two most important choices you'll make in how you use ADO, so we'll cover those topics in some detail.

Part II focuses on the ADO Cursor Engine. Chances are that when you develop your applications, you'll go one of two routes: either you'll depend primarily on the functionality made available by the ADO Cursor Engine, or you'll rely completely on your own code. Regardless of which path you choose, this material on the ADO Cursor Engine should be considered required reading.

Obviously, if you are going to use features of the ADO Cursor Engine, you should develop as much expertise with them as possible. The more you learn about how these features work, what their limitations are, and what's really going on behind

---

WARNING AND APOLOGY

The next few chapters are boring, especially if you're already familiar with the object model and the documentation. And for those who haven't done much programming with ADO, these chapters will still be boring. Regardless of which group you fall into, you can read Chapters 2 through 6 at your own discretion. They build character, and studies have shown they can cure insomnia.

the scenes, the less likely you'll be to code yourself into a corner. You'll also shorten your development time by leveraging features available in the ADO Cursor Engine.

Even if you plan on handling the task of updating your database by writing your own data access code, you can learn a lot from reading the chapters on the ADO Cursor Engine. You might decide that the features implemented by the ADO Cursor Engine are so logical and well thought out that you should do something very similar in your code. Perhaps when you read about the limitations in client-side recordsets, you'll understand the cause of those limitations, and therefore avoid such problems yourself. You may even come to the conclusion that the ADO Cursor Engine is the coolest thing you've ever seen and that you're going to use it rather than write large amounts of your own code. Hey, you never know.

There's even a middle ground. Some developers employ a mix of ADO features and their own code—using the ADO Cursor Engine to maintain their data and interact with the client application while using their own code to modify the contents of the database. Other programmers plan their applications so that they can initially rely on ADO features and then smoothly migrate to features they built themselves. Regardless of your plans, the information in Part II should prove useful.

Included as an appendix to this book is an introduction to Microsoft ActiveX Data Objects Extensions for Data Definition Language and Security (ADOX) and Jet and Replication Objects (JRO). These two libraries were implemented as part of ADO 2.1 to be used in conjunction with ADO.

ADOX is designed to mirror DAO's data definition features. You can use it to retrieve schema-type information about your database. In contrast to DAO, however, ADOX does more than retrieve this data in read-only mode. You can use ADOX to modify the structure of your database by adding and deleting tables, columns, and indexes. The ADOX object model also provides objects for managing security.

JRO adds Jet-specific features to ADO that were previously available only through DAO. As its name implies, you can use JRO to replicate Jet databases. JRO provides other Jet-specific features such as compacting databases and refreshing the Jet cache.

We'll cover ADOX and JRO in Appendix A.

WHERE'S THE CODE?

Since, as I mentioned before, there's no single "best way" to use ADO, I'm not going to focus on building a large sample application. While I think a large sample that shows off most of ADO's functionality is an attractive idea, I don't think it's appropriate for this text. Too often the material covered in a technical book focuses too heavily on the code and features used in the sample application. That's great—if your design goals meet those of the sample application. You're ultimately better off with a solid understanding of all of ADO's features rather than just the ones used in a large sample.

So instead, I've included some code on the companion CD that isn't so much a sample application as it is a set of tools to help you learn how to discover more about ADO. The more you learn about ADO and how the objects tend to behave, the more comfortable you'll become with determining what will happen in specific situations.

Probably the best example I can give of such a situation deals with conflict detection and resolution with the ADO Cursor Engine. Chapter 12 covers this topic in a fair amount of depth, but that information is not exhaustive by any means. The goal of the chapter is to help you understand what's going on behind the scenes and to show you what types of problems to look for (and how to handle them) when you're developing your application.

To help illustrate the issue of conflict detection, I've included on the companion CD a sample named Detecting Conflicts that I wrote to help me understand how to handle specific conflicts. You can modify that sample to work with your database and your query to determine what to do in your own application. But that's only one of the reasons I've included the sample.

As you learn more about ADO (and other technologies, database or otherwise), questions will naturally arise. You might see a particular method and ask yourself, "What happens to *my* data if...?" No book, training, or phone call to technical support will ever be able to answer all of your questions. What's much more valuable is learning how to answer those questions yourself, and this conflict detection sample shows you how.

Appendix B of this book contains a description of the sample applications and tools included on the companion CD. Use the samples to learn more about ADO, and take a look at the code in the samples, including the comments, to understand how to come up with your own tests and samples to answer your questions.

With a solid basic understanding of ADO (and with a slightly devious mindset), you can create well-built data access applications. You'll be able to answer your own questions and continue to develop more expertise without having to say, "I wish I'd known that before I started writing all this code." It is my hope that this book will help you develop that understanding.

Let's get started.

Chapter 2

A Brief Overview of the ADO Object Model

Those of you familiar with the Data Access Objects (DAO) and Remote Data Objects (RDO) object models might find the ADO object model somewhat of a departure. For example, ADO allows you to retrieve data from a database into a Recordset object without having to create a Connection object or any other object variables. You can create most of ADO's objects on their own without calling a function on another object to generate them.

ADO's creatable objects provide developers with a great deal of flexibility in how they build their applications; nevertheless, creatable objects can present a challenge to someone learning to use ADO. A developer who provides code in a magazine or Web site article to illustrate how he used ADO in his application doesn't usually explain why he chose to implement his solution that way. As a result, the reader of that article only picks up a small piece of the puzzle.

This chapter will briefly cover the three main ADO objects—Connection, Command, and Recordset—treating them initially as a hierarchy to show how they relate to each other. (See Figure 2-1.) Then we'll talk about how to avoid using the object hierarchy, and when it's appropriate to do so. (In subsequent chapters, we'll take a

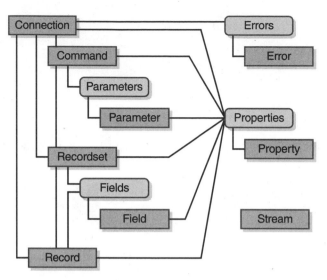

Figure 2-1 *The ADO object model.*

closer look at each of these objects and discuss ADO's use of dynamic properties.) After that, we'll explain the different ways you can create a disconnected recordset— one that is not connected to any database. Finally, we'll discuss ADO 2.5's additions to the object model: the Record object and the Stream object.

ADO OBJECT MODEL

The ADO object model can be separated into five parts, with each part focused on a different object: the Connection object, the Command object, the Recordset object, the Record object, and the Stream object. We'll cover the object model, focusing on these five objects, in more depth in Chapters 3 through 6. Here's a brief overview of the three core objects: Connection, Command, and Recordset.

Connection Object

As its name implies, the Connection object is your connection to the database; it manages the communication between your application and your database. (Both the Recordset and Command objects have an ActiveConnection property that you can use to refer to a Connection object.) Use the *Open* and *Close* methods of the Connection object to open and close the connection to your database.

The Connection object is at the top of the less-than-stringent hierarchy of ADO objects. It is comparable to the DAO Database object and the RDO rdoConnection object. ADO has no equivalent of DAO's DBEngine and Workspace objects or RDO's rdoEngine and rdoEnvironment objects. Unlike the DAO and RDO object models, ADO has no collection object in its object model containing all of the Connection objects.

Through its transactional methods—*BeginTrans, CommitTrans,* and *Rollback-Trans*—the Connection object allows you to manage the changes you make to your database in transactions. The *OpenSchema* method lets you view much of the metadata about your database. If you're using ADO's asynchronous features, events on the Connection object will fire to signify the completion of the asynchronous call. To determine why your query failed, you can evaluate the Errors collection of the Connection object.

Use the Connection object's *Execute* method to submit queries, including queries that generate Recordsets. The Connection object's *Execute* method also allows you to issue an action query to modify data, manipulate objects, or change database-specific settings on your database.

Command Object

The ADO Command object is designed to help you work with queries that you'll execute repeatedly or queries that will check the value of an output or return parameter on a call to a stored procedure. The Command object is similar to DAO's QueryDef object and RDO's rdoQuery object.

You can submit the query in your Command object to your database via the Command object's *Execute* method. As with the Connection object, you can issue an action query or a query that will return a Recordset. The ActiveCommand property on the Recordset object refers back to the Command object used to open that

---

ASYNCHRONOUS FUNCTION CALLS

Asynchronous calls pose an added challenge for programmers. Usually when you make an asynchronous call, there's code that you want to execute as soon as the call is completed. Events that signify the completion of an asynchronous call can greatly simplify your programming. Without these events, you need to use another thread to perennially check to determine when the call has completed. Programmers using ADO 1.5 could submit queries asynchronously but had to check the value of the Recordset object's State property to determine if the query had completed. Such code is suboptimal at best. ADO 2.0 simplified asynchronous programming for developers by firing events when asynchronous calls completed.

Recordset. Use the Command object's Parameters collection to work with parameterized queries and stored procedures. The ActiveConnection property on the Command object refers back to the Connection object.

Recordset Object

Here's where you get your data. The Recordset object contains the results of your query. These results consist of rows (called records) and columns (called fields) of data. Each column is stored in a Field object in the Recordset's Fields collection. The Recordset object is the equivalent of DAO's Recordset object and RDO's rdoResultset object.

You can use the *Open* method of the Recordset object to retrieve the results of a query either through the Command object or directly through the Connection object. You can also generate a Recordset object by calling the *Execute* method on either the Connection or Command object. Flexible, but confusing. The Recordset's ActiveConnection property refers to the Connection object that the Recordset uses to communicate with the database. Similarly, the ActiveCommand property refers to the Command object that generated the Recordset.

DYNAMIC PROPERTIES

Developers familiar with the DAO object model have probably had some experience with DAO's dynamic properties. DAO's Properties collection contains information about all of an object's defined properties (such as the DAO Recordset object's Updatable property). The Properties collection also allows you to retrieve information about user-defined properties.

ADO has a dynamic Properties collection, though it serves a different purpose than DAO's Properties collection. ADO's Properties collection contains Property objects that store information about database system features.

Different database systems expose different features. For example, secure Microsoft Access databases require a system database file (System.mdw). Microsoft SQL Server has options for using standard or integrated security. With RDO, you would need to provide database system information in the connection string or by making ODBC API calls to take advantage of the unique features of your particular database system. It would be impractical to attempt to make features such as these explicitly available through the ADO type library. Instead, ADO makes these features available through its object model by means of the dynamic ADO Properties collection, which is reserved for these database or provider-specific features. It does not contain information already available through the type library.

OUT OF THE ORDER CAME CHAOS

With DAO and RDO, it's fairly simple to explain to a programmer new to the object model how to connect to and query the desired database. In each case, you use the object model to create an object that represents a connection to your database. Then you use that object to retrieve the results of your query into another object.

As I explained earlier, you can follow the same pattern with the ADO object model. However, you can also open an ADO Recordset to retrieve the results of your query in a single call without using either a Connection object or a Command object. This flexibility makes the process of determining the "right" way to get your data more complicated.

There are times when you won't want to use all of the objects in the ADO hierarchy. For example, perhaps you have no intention of executing a query more than once, so you don't have any need to use the Command object. Or maybe your application will require only one Recordset object, and you don't plan to use the Connection object for any reason other than to retrieve the results of that one query. The following sections discuss these and other examples in detail.

Obtaining a Recordset Without a Command Object

If you are not going to execute your query more than once, or if you won't need Parameter objects, you probably don't need to use a Command object. As was shown in Figure 2-1 (on page 12), you can use a Recordset object with a Connection object without having to use a Command object. Here's an example:

```
strConn = "Provider=SQLOLEDB;Data Source=MyServer;" & _
          "Initial Catalog=Northwind;" & _
          "User ID=MyUserID;Password=MyPassword;"
Set cnNorthwind = New ADODB.Connection
cnNorthwind.Open strConn

strSQL = "SELECT * FROM Customers"
Set rsCustomers = New ADODB.Recordset
rsCustomers.Open strSQL, cnNorthwind
```

Connection Object: To Use or Not to Use

You might find that sometimes the only reason you use your Connection object is to open Recordset objects. Who would want to write the code shown in the previous section when you could use code that looks like this instead:

```
strConn = "Provider=SQLOLEDB;Data Source=MyServer;" & _
          "Initial Catalog=Northwind;" & _
          "User ID=MyUserID;Password=MyPassword;"
```

(continued)

15

```
strSQL = "SELECT * FROM Customers"
Set rsCustomers = New ADODB.Recordset
rsCustomers.Open strSQL, strConn
```

In this code snippet, we are opening the Recordset object without explicitly using a Connection object. Instead, we're passing a connection string, *strConn*, into the *ActiveConnection* parameter (the second parameter) on the *Open* method. This parameter (and the ActiveConnection property on the Recordset object) accepts a connection string or a Connection object. If a connection string is supplied instead of a Connection object, ADO will establish a connection to the database based on that connection string.

There is absolutely nothing wrong with the syntax of either example; each has its place. But proceed with caution! Before you decide that you'll always use the latter syntax, here's something to consider: do you want the ActiveConnection property on each of your Recordset objects to refer to the same Connection object?

If you choose to use the process demonstrated in the second snippet, you could wind up with code similar to the following:

```
Set rsCustomers = New ADODB.Recordset
rsCustomers.Open "SELECT * FROM Customers", strConn
Set rsOrders = New ADODB.Recordset
rsOrders.Open "SELECT * FROM Orders", strConn
```

Although each Recordset object was opened using the same connection string to communicate with the same database, you've created a separate Connection object for each Recordset. Each of the resulting Connection objects maintains its own physical connection to the database. For most database systems, physical connections are a precious resource and should not be consumed frivolously.

You can avoid generating additional Connection objects in two ways (or derivatives thereof). Your first alternative is to explicitly create a Connection object and use it with both Recordset objects:

```
Set cnNorthwind = New ADODB.Connection
cnNorthwind.Open strConn
Set rsCustomers = New ADODB.Recordset
rsCustomers.Open "SELECT * FROM Customers", cnNorthwind
Set rsOrders = New ADODB.Recordset
rsOrders.Open "SELECT * FROM Orders", cnNorthwind
```

The other method to ensure that you use only one Connection object, but without having to explicitly create one, is to utilize the ActiveConnection property on the initial Recordset object as shown in the following code:

```
Set rsCustomers = New ADODB.Recordset
rsCustomers.Open "SELECT * FROM Customers", strConn
Set rsOrders = New ADODB.Recordset
rsOrders.Open "SELECT * FROM Orders", _
            rsCustomers.ActiveConnection
```

Chapter 2   **A Brief Overview of the ADO Object Model**

Here we simply passed the ActiveConnection property from the initial Record-set, *rsCustomers*, into the *ActiveConnection* parameter on the *Open* method for the second Recordset, *rsOrders*.

Using the same Connection object for each of your Recordsets (even if you're not explicitly declaring a Connection object) will improve the performance of your queries and help control the number of actual connections you're making to the database. We'll discuss the reasons why one Connection object can generate multiple connections to your database in greater depth in Chapter 3.

Obtaining a Recordset Without a Database

Toward the end of the Bronze Age, Microsoft developed the ODBC cursor library. (OK, maybe the ODBC cursor library isn't that old, but given how quickly new technology is being released it seems like it might require carbon dating to determine when it was created.) Applications could use this library to store the results of a query while having to store only a small amount of the data within the application itself. Some saw this event as the beginning of database programming with rapid application development (RAD) tools and components. Programmers who loathe the idea of relying on anyone else's code believed it marked the beginning of the fall of civilization as programmers know it.

RDO 2.0 added its own cursor library. Microsoft Visual Basic 5 users could retrieve the results of a query into this library and actually disconnect from the database while still working with the query results. In fact, those users could modify the data and later reconnect to their databases to update them with that batch of changes.

ADO carries that concept of a disconnected recordset further. Early in ADO's lifetime, the Advanced Data Connector, a technology that was later renamed Remote Data Services (RDS), provided early versions of ADO with a cursor engine similar to RDO 2.0's client batch cursor library. This technology allowed ADO to pass a recordset across process boundaries. Rather than passing just a pointer to the object that contained the data, you could pass the data itself across the process boundaries. Beginning with ADO 2.0, recordsets can be persisted to a file and reopened later. You can also create your own recordset by taking a Recordset object variable and populating the Fields collection yourself.

Disconnecting a Recordset from a Connection

Prior to version 3.5 of DAO and version 2.0 of RDO, you couldn't work with a record-set without a live connection to your database. This restriction forced many programmers to maintain a live connection to the database for the lifetime of the application in order to continue to work with DAO and RDO objects, regardless of how infrequently that connection was used.

17

The other option was to retrieve the data from the DAO or RDO object and maintain that data within the application in some other fashion (Variant arrays, arrays of user-defined types, collections, and so forth). While this method of programming required a connection to the database only when necessary, it could require the developer to write a great deal more code than if she used DAO or RDO and maintained the database connection.

RDO 2.0 introduced the notion of disconnected recordsets. The operating principle here is that you should be able to open a connection to your database, retrieve data, close the connection, work with the data, and reopen the connection when you want to communicate with your database again.

You can use that same functionality in ADO 2.0 and later with client-side recordsets by setting the ActiveConnection property of the Recordset object to Nothing, as in the following example:

```
'Open a connection to your database.
Set cnDatabase = New ADODB.Connection
cnDatabase.CursorLocation = adUseClient
cnDatabase.Open strConn, strUserID, strPassword

'Make the query and retrieve the results.
Set rsData = New ADODB.Recordset
rsData.Open strSQL, cnDatabase, adOpenStatic, _
            adLockBatchOptimistic, adCmdText
Set rsData.ActiveConnection = Nothing

'Close your connection.
cnDatabase.Close

'Modify your recordset.
    :

'Reopen your connection.
cnDatabase.Open

'Point your recordset at your connection.
Set rsData.ActiveConnection = cnDatabase

'Submit the changes from the recordset to your database.
rsData.UpdateBatch
```

Figure 2-2 provides a summary of what's happening. Your application sends ADO a request for data. ADO asks the OLE DB provider or ODBC driver to establish a connection to the database. ADO then passes the query string to the provider/driver, the provider/driver retrieves the results from the database and passes them back to ADO, and ADO stores them in the ADO Cursor Engine. You can then close

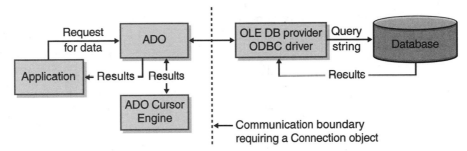

Figure 2-2 *The ADO Cursor Engine and disconnected recordsets.*

your connection. Using the ADO Cursor Engine's batch updating feature, you can modify the recordset and cache the changes until you want to submit them to the database.

Normally, when you call the *Close* method on the Connection object, all Recordset objects associated with that Connection object are implicitly closed as well. By setting the ActiveConnection property on the Recordset object to Nothing prior to closing the Connection object, you're asking the ADO Cursor Engine to dissociate the Recordset object from the Connection object.

After you've made all the desired changes to the Recordset object, reconnect to the database by calling the *Open* method of the Connection object, associate the Recordset with the Connection object, and submit the changes in the Recordset to the database by calling the *UpdateBatch* method on the Recordset.

Passing a Recordset Out of Process

The way in which Visual Basic handles objects might seem somewhat magical to developers who don't have a great deal of experience with COM. Visual Basic hides the complexities of COM from the developer. (I strongly recommend the books *Understanding ActiveX and OLE,* by David Chappell [Microsoft Press, 1996], and Dale Rogerson's *Inside COM* [Microsoft Press, 1996], to help you develop an understanding of working with COM objects across process boundaries.) For the benefit of the inexperienced, I'll attempt to explain the passing of COM objects across process boundaries without undue complexity.

You can create a function in Visual Basic that will return an object such as rdoResultset. If you call such a function locally, everything will behave exactly as you expect, just as if you'd returned simpler data such as a string or an integer. So long as you're using in-process libraries, your code will compile and run successfully. However, if your function passes the rdoResultset across process boundaries (such as from a Component Services component or from an ActiveX EXE), you're actually passing a pointer to the object; the object itself still resides on the server.

(See Figure 2-3.) (Component Services was previously known as Microsoft Transaction Server, or MTS.) The reason only a pointer is passed has to do with the default functionality of COM. Maintaining data in your Component Services or MTS objects in this fashion is strongly discouraged. These server technologies are designed to handle objects that maintain no state from the calling component. Returning a pointer to a COM object that resides in your Component Services or MTS business object requires maintaining state; this can lead to unexpected problems and generally results in poor performance and limitations on your ability to scale your application.

While there is code built into COM that passes simple data structures such as strings, integers, and even Variant arrays from one process to another, COM does not know how to pass complete objects. By default, COM will instead pass a pointer to the actual object. As a result, developers who want to build *n*-tiered applications using DAO or RDO make use of the *GetRows* function on the DAO Recordset and RDO rdoResultset objects. This function returns a Variant array with the results of the query rather than an object.

While code that passes Variant arrays instead of objects runs quickly and allows you to build stateless server components, you lose the ability to use many of the RAD features of DAO and RDO. For instance, you can't use bound controls such as text boxes, grids, list boxes, or combo boxes. (Although, some developers will tell you that not being able to use bound controls is a blessing in disguise.) You have to write code that interprets the contents of the Variant array, manages that data within your client application, passes that data back to your server component, interprets that information in your server component, and updates your database.

Keep in mind that passing a pointer to an object rather than passing the object itself is the default behavior for passing COM object information across process boundaries. While it's easy to understand how to pass an integer into another application, passing a COM object is more complicated. Let's look at the rdoResultset object again as an example. The COM libraries don't automatically know what information

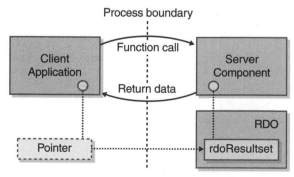

Figure 2-3 *Passing a pointer to an rdoResultset across a process boundary.*

RDO needs in order to take the information stored in the rdoResultset object on the server and create an rdoResultset on the client. If you're building your own COM object in C++, you can build custom marshaling libraries to pass the required information from the server to the client. Essentially, you're telling COM that rather than having COM pass a pointer to your object across process boundaries, you want to handle the marshaling process yourself. ADO saves you the trouble of having to build these libraries by providing a custom marshaling routine for Recordset objects. This routine is illustrated in Figure 2-4.

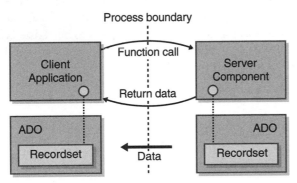

Figure 2-4 *Marshaling an ADO Recordset object across a process boundary.*

When you pass a Recordset object across process boundaries, ADO is loaded in both processes. All of the metadata for the Recordset—such as information about the Fields collection, including data types, which Field objects are updatable, and which Field objects are part of the primary key—as well as the contents of the Recordset are passed across the process boundary. The client application has its very own Recordset object, rather than a pointer to a Recordset object that resides on the server. With ADO, you can pass a Recordset object to another process on the same computer, to a process on another computer inside your network through Distributed COM (DCOM), or across the Internet through RDS and HTTP. If you're using ADO's batch updating feature, the client application can make changes to the Recordset that you can later submit to your database by passing the Recordset back to a server.

> **NOTE** Before you pass judgment too quickly and decide the preceding steps are too much work to go through, note that this approach allows you to have almost complete control of how the server and client manage the data in the application. If you want your client application to update a row in the table based on a timestamp by retrieving that timestamp value and merging it into the data already in the client application, you can write code to do just that. Time or budget constraints might impose the only limits to the functionality you can add to your application.

Persistence Can Pay Off

A salesman is going to call on a customer and needs to be able to generate order information, but since he's on the road, he won't have access to the database server once he leaves the office. It would be helpful if he could download customer, order, and product information and persist that data into a file or files on his laptop before he leaves. That way he could generate new orders while disconnected from the network and submit those orders when he returns.

In the past, you would have had to use a desktop database such as Access to maintain that data. ADO 2.0 introduced functionality that makes it possible to store database information on the desktop without having a desktop database. We discussed earlier how ADO can pass a Recordset object from one process to another. As you can see in the following code, the ADO Recordset object also has a *Save* method (as of ADO 2.0), which essentially takes the same data that ADO would normally pass across the process boundary from the client to the server and writes it to a file instead. You can later turn that file back into a Recordset object.

```
'Retrieve the results of your query
' and save them to a file. The path to the file
' and the filename are stored in the string
' strPathToOrdersFile.
Set cnDatabase = New ADODB.Connection
⋮
Set rsOrders = New ADODB.Recordset
rsOrders.Open strSQL, cnDatabase, adOpenStatic, _
            adLockBatchOptimistic, adCmdText
rsOrders.Save strPathToOrdersFile

'Retrieve the contents of the file into a Recordset,
' modify the Recordset accordingly, and then save the
' changes back to a file.
rsOrders.Open strPathToOrdersFile, , , _
            adLockBatchOptimistic, adCmdFile
rsOrders.AddNew
⋮
rsOrders.Update
rsOrders.Save strPathToOrdersFile

'Retrieve the contents of the file into a Recordset
' and submit the changes to your database.
rsOrders.Open strPathToOrdersFile, , , _
            adLockBatchOptimistic, adCmdFile
Set rsOrders.ActiveConnection = cnDatabase
rsOrders.UpdateBatch
```

Creating Your Own Recordset

Maybe you don't want to use a database at all, but you like using Recordset objects to store data in your application. You can then allow the user to interact with that data by means of a bound control such as a data grid.

ADO 2.0 introduced an *Append* method to the Fields collection for this very reason. You use this method to supply the structure for each field in your Recordset. Once you've provided this information about the fields, you call the *Open* method and start adding, editing, and deleting data, as shown in the following code snippet. The Recordset isn't actually updated until the *Update* method has been called.

```
'Retrieve the results of your query
' and store them in a file.
Set rsData = New ADODB.Recordset
rsData.Fields.Append "ID", adInteger, , adFldKeyColumn
rsData.Fields.Append "Description", adVarChar, 40
rsData.Open LockType:=adLockBatchOptimistic
rsData.AddNew
rsData.Fields("ID").Value = 1
rsData.Fields("Description").Value = "First Record"
rsData.Update
```

NEW OBJECTS IN ADO 2.5

ADO 2.5 extends the concept of universal data access into new areas with the Record and Stream objects.

Record Object

Not all data is rectangular like that in a Microsoft Excel spreadsheet. The Record object is designed primarily for interacting with document-based data-like file and directory structures. The Record object makes it possible for ADO to interact with data that resembles a hierarchical tree, such as the directories and files on a hard drive. A Record object can correspond to a row in a Recordset object, or it can represent an object in a hierarchy such as a file directory.

None of the "traditional" database providers or drivers included with Microsoft Data Access Components (MDAC) 2.5 support the Record object. In Chapter 6, we'll cover the Record object in more depth and show some examples of using the object with a couple of the providers that support it.

Stream Object

While the Record object can help you work with hierarchical directory structures, the Stream object lets you access the data stored in the hierarchy. For example, you can use the Record object to traverse through a file and directory structure on a hard drive via the OLE DB provider for Microsoft Active Directory Services. Then you can use the Stream object to retrieve the contents of the files that the Record object refers to.

However, it's not necessary to use the Record object and the Stream object together. The Record object is limited to a few nondatabase OLE DB providers with the release of MDAC 2.5, but you can use the Stream object with more traditional database applications. The Stream object exposes methods that make working with binary large object (BLOB) data such as SQL Server text and image fields much simpler than do the Field object's *GetChunk* and *AppendChunk* methods. (See Chapter 4 for more on these methods.) You can also use the Stream object to store Recordset objects rather than having to write them to your hard drive.

We'll discuss the Stream object in more depth in Chapter 6.

QUESTIONS THAT SHOULD BE ASKED MORE FREQUENTLY

Q. *Should I avoid using a Connection object if I'm not planning to use any of its properties and methods?*

A. There's no definite answer to this question, but I use a Connection object unless I'm going to open only a single Recordset in my application. My recommendation is to use a Connection object until you have your application working the way you'd like. If you then want to try opening your Recordsets without a Connection object, give it a shot and see if you've improved performance. Also check that you aren't creating additional physical connections to your database. Just be sure to back up your application before making such changes. There's nothing worse than breaking an application that was working fine, and then not being able to easily revert back to the working version.

Q. *Then should I generally use all of the other objects in the ADO object model as well?*

A. Let's not jump to conclusions. If I give you all the answers in the second chapter, what kind of book would this be? We'll talk about ADO objects in more detail in Chapters 3 through 6. You'll learn about the features available in each object, and you should end up with a good idea of when to use each one.

Chapter 3

The ADO Connection Object

If you're planning to use ADO in an application, chances are that you have a database you need to access. In the ADO object model, the Connection object is the link to your database.

This chapter will cover the ADO Connection object—its properties, methods, and events. We'll also talk about OLE DB providers and ODBC drivers, connection strings, and transactions.

ADO CONNECTION OBJECT PROPERTIES AND COLLECTIONS

Let's take a look at the properties and collections exposed by the Connection object, which are described in the following table.

CONNECTION OBJECT PROPERTIES AND COLLECTIONS

Property or Collection Name	Data Type	Description
Attributes	Long	Controls the behavior of the Connection object after *CommitTrans* or *RollbackTrans* has been called
CommandTimeout	Long	Sets the length of time that queries on this connection can run before timing out

(continued)

Connection Object Properties and Collections *continued*

Property or Collection Name	Data Type	Description
ConnectionString	String	Specifies how to connect to your database
ConnectionTimeout	Long	Sets the length of time that ADO will wait before an attempt to connect to your database times out
CursorLocation	Long	Sets the default value for the location of the cursor library for Recordsets opened on this Connection object
DefaultDatabase	String	When connecting to Microsoft SQL Server and other database servers that expose multiple databases, specifies which database on the server to use
Errors	Collection of Error objects	Each Error object contains information about an error that occurred on the Connection object
IsolationLevel	Long	Controls the level at which transactions for the database are isolated
Mode	Long	Sets the permissions for modification of the Connection object
Properties	Collection of Property objects	Stores information about provider-specific properties for the Connection object
Provider	String	OLE DB provider name
State	Long	Current state (open or closed) of the Connection object
Version	String	Version of ADO

Attributes Property

The Attributes property takes a value of type XactAttributeEnum and allows you to control the behavior of your Connection object after you've ended a transaction, as described in the following table.

XACTATTRIBUTEENUM VALUES

Constant	Value	Description
(No constant defined)	0	Default
adXactCommitRetaining	131072	Creates a new transaction when you call the *CommitTrans* method of the Connection object
adXactAbortRetaining	262144	Creates a new transaction when you call the *RollbackTrans* method of the Connection object

By default, the Attributes property is set to 0. This property is a bitmask and can be set to either of the values in XactAttributeEnum (adXactCommitRetaining or adXactAbortRetaining) or to the sum of those two constants. For more information on using this property, see the "Managing Your Transactions" section beginning on page 46.

CommandTimeout Property

Queries sometimes take longer to execute than expected. Your database server might be busy, or your network connection might be slow because of traffic. Maybe your query is extremely complex. Or maybe your query will return large amounts of data. In any case, you might want the query to fail after a given amount of time rather than letting it run ad infinitum.

The CommandTimeout property defines the length of time in seconds that your query will run before it times out and generates an error. The default value is 30 seconds. Once the database starts to return data from your query, the Command-Timeout value is ignored. For example, let's say that you've lost your mind and submitted a query that will return a hundred thousand rows of data into a client-side cursor. Chances are that it will take more than 30 seconds to retrieve that much data. As soon as the OLE DB provider signals to ADO that it has the first row of data from the query, the CommandTimeout value is ignored and ADO starts to retrieve the results of the query.

If you want to let your query run for as long as necessary without ever timing out, set the CommandTimeout property to 0.

ConnectionString Property

You use the ConnectionString property to define what database you'll connect to and how you'll connect to it. We'll describe building connection strings in more depth in the section "Using Data Links to Build Connection Strings" beginning on page 42, where we discuss the methods that use this property.

ConnectionTimeout Property

The ConnectionTimeout property is similar to the CommandTimeout property. You use it to define, in seconds, how long ADO will wait before it times out of its attempt to connect to your database. The default value for this property is 15 seconds. As with the CommandTimeout property, if you want the connection attempt to continue indefinitely, simply set this property to 0.

CursorLocation Property

This property determines how the results of your query will be stored. The Cursor-Location property for the Connection object has the same functionality as the same property for the Recordset object. For more information, see the "CursorLocation Property" section in Chapter 4.

DefaultDatabase Property

Some database servers, such as Microsoft SQL Server, expose multiple databases on a single server. When you install SQL Server 7, for example, you automatically get a Master database and two sample databases: Pubs and Northwind. If you're connecting to SQL Server and you don't specify the database that you want to use by explicitly setting this property or by defining the database in your connection string, you'll be connected to the Master database by default.

Errors Collection

The ADO Connection object exposes an Errors collection that contains information about the errors that occurred on that database connection. There are times when a single operation will return multiple error messages. Each message is stored in an Error object in the Errors collection.

> **NOTE**   This book will not cover the Error object in much depth. Perhaps ADO's greatest drawback is that it frequently generates error information that provides little to no help in determining the cause of the error. When an error occurs, the Errors collection often contains a single Error object whose Description property simply returns, "Errors occurred." Sad, but true.

The next time you use the Connection object, the previous contents of the Errors collection will be cleared.

IsolationLevel Property

You can use the IsolationLevel property to control the isolation level of the transactions on your Connection object. The property can be set to any one of the Isolation-LevelEnum values listed in the following table.

ISOLATIONLEVELENUM VALUES

Constant	Value	Description
adXactUnspecified	−1	Indicates that the provider is using an isolation level that cannot be determined
adXactChaos	16	Indicates that you cannot overwrite pending changes from more highly isolated transactions

Constant	Value	Description
adXactBrowse, adXactReadUncommitted	256	Allows you to view changes pending in another transaction
		Subject to nonrepeatable reads and phantom rows
adXactCursorStability, adXactReadCommitted	4096	Default; ensures that your transaction does not view any pending updates
		Subject to nonrepeatable reads and phantom rows, but immune to dirty reads (See the sidebar on page 49 for explanations of these terms.)
adXactRepeatableRead	65536	Ensures that your transaction does not view any pending updates and that rows you read are not modified by other transactions
		Subject to phantom rows
adXactIsolated, adXactSerializable	1048576	Specifies complete isolation from other transactions

Although the values might make this property look like a bitmask, you cannot set this property to the sum of two of these constants. Not all of these values are supported for all OLE DB providers, ODBC drivers, or databases. To learn more about using this property, see "Managing Your Transactions" beginning on page 46.

Mode Property

Use the Mode property to control the privileges (read-only, read/write) on your Connection object. You can set this property to any of the values available in Connect-ModeEnum, which are shown in the following table.

CONNECTMODEENUM VALUES

Constant	Value	Description
adModeUnknown	0	Default; uses the default permissions to your database
adModeRead	1	Connects to your database with read-only permissions
adModeWrite	2	Connects to your database with write-only permissions
adModeReadWrite	3	Connects to your database using read/write permissions
adModeShareDenyRead	4	Prevents other users from reading your database while your connection is open

(continued)

ConnectModeEnum Values *continued*

Constant	Value	Description
adModeShareDenyWrite	8	Prevents other users from modifying your database while your connection is open
adModeShareExclusive	12	Prevents other users from connecting to your database while your connection is open
adModeShareDenyNone	16	Allows other users to open the same Record with read and write permissions but prevents other users from using adModeShareDenyWrite or adModeShareExclusive

Administrators of client/server databases such as those implemented in Oracle and SQL Server might shudder at the thought of a property that a programmer can set in an application that limits database access to a single user at a time. However, those administrators don't need to lie awake at night worrying about such a property, since its capabilities are limited. Setting the Mode property to adModeShareExclusive before connecting to most databases won't prevent other users from connecting to the database. This property is designed for developers building applications for Microsoft Access databases and works only on Access.

You can read a value from or write a value to the Mode property while the Connection object is closed; when it's open, you can only read the value. Although the ConnectModeEnum values make this property look like a bitmask, it isn't. You can set the Mode property to only one of the values in ConnectModeEnum, or to the sum of constants in the enumerated data type if that sum equals another value in that type. For example, you can set the Mode property to adModeRead + adModeWrite because their values add up to the value of adModeReadWrite. You cannot, however, set the Mode property to adModeRead + adModeShareDenyWrite.

A write-only connection to an Access database is not possible, thus the adModeWrite and adModeShareDenyRead constants cannot be used on their own. These constants can be used only with their counterparts, adModeRead and adModeShareDenyWrite.

Properties Collection

ADO is designed to allow you to connect to all sorts of databases. Since no two database systems are exactly alike, exposing all their major features by means of a single object model is impractical, if not impossible. The standard properties, methods, and events of the Connection object allow ADO to expose a base level of functionality; additional functionality is exposed through the dynamic Properties collection. Some of the entries in the Properties collection, such as the Prompt property, apply to most OLE DB providers.

Actually, the Prompt property might appear familiar to RDO users. The rdoConnection object exposes similar functionality through the *OpenConnection* and *EstablishConnection* methods. You can set the Prompt property in ADO to any value in ConnectPromptEnum while the connection is closed:

```
cnDatabase.Properties("Prompt").Value = adPromptNever
```

After you've set either the Provider property or the ConnectionString property to specify the OLE DB provider you'll use to connect to your database, you'll see provider-specific items in the Properties collection. For example, if you set the packet size when you connect to SQL Server, the Packet Size property in the Properties collection will be set to that value. Similarly, you can set the Jet OLEDB:System Database property when you connect to an Access database, and that property will be set in the Properties collection.

If you want to learn more about provider-specific entries in the Connection object's Properties collection, take a look at the documentation on these OLE DB providers in the Microsoft Data Access SDK, programmatically navigate through the Properties collection on the Connection object after specifying the provider, or examine the All tab on the Data Link Properties property sheet. We'll talk more about using data links in the section "Using Data Links to Build Connection Strings" beginning on page 42, where we discuss connection strings in more depth.

Provider Property

This property contains the name of the provider that the Connection object uses to connect to your database. The Provider property is read/write when the Connection object is closed and read-only otherwise.

State Property

You can check the value of the State property to determine the current state of the Connection object. The Connection object has only three possible states: closed, open, or currently trying to connect to your database, as the following table shows.

OBJECTSTATEENUM VALUES
APPLICABLE TO THE CONNECTION OBJECT

Constant	*Value*	*Description*
adStateClosed	0	Indicates that the Connection object is closed
adStateOpen	1	Indicates that the Connection object is open
adStateConnecting	2	Indicates that the Connection object is currently trying to connect to your database

Version Property

The Version property is read-only and returns a string that you can use to determine the current version of ADO installed. If you build an application with one version of ADO and run that code on a machine with a newer version of ADO installed, the Version property will return the newer version number.

ADO CONNECTION OBJECT FUNCTIONS AND METHODS

Now let's examine each of the functions and methods exposed by the Connection object and listed in this next table.

CONNECTION OBJECT FUNCTIONS AND METHODS

Function or Method Name	Description
BeginTrans	Initiates a transaction
Cancel	Cancels an asynchronous attempt to connect to your database
Close	Closes the connection to your database
CommitTrans	Commits the current transaction
Execute	Submits a query to your database
Open	Opens a connection to your database
OpenSchema	Retrieves schema information from your database
RollbackTrans	Rolls back the current transaction

BeginTrans Method

The *BeginTrans* method initiates a transaction on your database. Actually, *BeginTrans* is a function that returns the nesting level of the transaction, but don't let the return value fool you. Currently, you can't nest ADO transactions. If you call *BeginTrans* more than once, you'll receive an error stating that only one transaction can be active on this session. *BeginTrans* takes no parameters.

The "Managing Your Transactions" section of this chapter provides more detailed information about this method.

Cancel Method

The *Cancel* method is intended to cancel an asynchronous query or an asynchronous attempt to connect to your database. *Cancel* takes no parameters.

Close Method

You can use the *Close* method to close an open connection. You might want to check the State property in your code before calling this method, to prevent generating an error. Calling the *Close* method on a Connection object that's already closed will generate an error. *Close* takes no parameters.

CommitTrans Method

The *CommitTrans* method commits the pending changes in the current transaction. *CommitTrans* takes no parameters. To learn more about using this method, see the "Managing Your Transactions" section later in this chapter.

Execute Method

You can use the *Execute* method to submit a query to your database. This method has three parameters, as shown here:

```
Connection.Execute CommandText, RecordsAffected, Options
```

The first parameter, *CommandText*, is a string that specifies the query you want to submit. This is the only parameter of the *Execute* method that is required. Here's an example:

```
cnDatabase.Execute "DELETE FROM MyTable WHERE ID = 7"
```

RecordsAffected, the second parameter, is an optional output parameter that you can use to determine how many rows were affected by your query. This parameter returns a value of type long and can come in handy if you're submitting action queries to update data:

```
strSQL = "DELETE FROM MyTable WHERE ID = 7"
cnDatabase.Execute strSQL, lngRecordsAffected
MsgBox lngRecordsAffected & " record(s) deleted"
```

The last parameter is the *Options* parameter, which also is optional and takes a long value. You can use this parameter with a value from CommandTypeEnum or one of the ExecuteOptionEnum values listed in the following table. For more information on specifying the command type and on the possible values for CommandTypeEnum, see the documentation on the CommandType property of the Recordset and Command objects in Chapter 4 and Chapter 5, respectively.

EXECUTEOPTIONENUM VALUES

Constant	Value	Description
adAsyncExecute	16	Executes the query asynchronously
adAsyncFetch	32	Fetches the results of the query asynchronously

(continued)

ExecuteOptionEnum Values *continued*

Constant	Value	Description
adAsyncFetchNonBlocking	64	Fetches the results of the query asynchronously without blocking
adExecuteNoRecords	128	Specifies that the query does not return records

Perhaps you're calling a stored procedure that will take a while to execute, or perhaps your query requires a great deal of processing by the server before it returns results. In that case, you can execute your query asynchronously by using the adAsyncExecute constant, and the rest of your code will continue to execute while ADO waits for the results of your query. (To determine when your query has completed, use the *ExecuteComplete* event on the Connection object.)

If you're using a client-side Recordset, you can use the adAsyncFetch constant to fetch the results of your query asynchronously. Once you submit your query and ADO has retrieved the number of rows specified in the Recordset object's CacheSize property, the adAsyncFetch constant specifies that your code continue to execute while ADO retrieves the rest of the results of the query asynchronously.

By default, the *Execute* method on the Connection object returns a Recordset object. If you use code such as the following to try to create an updatable Recordset, you will still have a read-only Recordset once the *Execute* method has completed:

```
'Create a new Recordset.
Set rsResults = New ADODB.Recordset
'Set the Recordset to use a keyset cursor and optimistic locking.
'These settings make the Recordset updatable.
rsResults.CursorType = adOpenKeyset
rsResults.LockType = adLockOptimistic
'Call Connection.Execute and retrieve a new, nonupdatable
' Recordset object.
Set rsResults = cnDatabase.Execute(strSQL)
```

The Recordset object is a return value, not an output parameter. The *rsResults* object variable in this example is not passed into the *Execute* method; the *Execute* method generates an entirely new Recordset object and returns it. This new Recordset object overwrites the old Recordset object referenced by the *rsResults* object variable.

> **NOTE**   While the fact that the Recordset object generated by the *Execute* method will overwrite the existing *rsResults* object variable might be obvious to many programmers, one of the most commonly asked questions on the external ADO newsgroups is, "Why is the setting I've assigned to the LockType/ CursorLocation/MaxRecords property ignored when I call the *Execute* method on the Connection and Command objects?"

The Recordset object returned by the *Execute* method inherits the default cursor type from the Connection object, based on the value of the Connection object's CursorLocation property. Because all client-side Recordset objects are static, if you use the *Execute* method with a Connection object whose CursorLocation property is set to adUseClient, you'll generate a static Recordset. If your Connection object's CursorLocation property is set to adUseServer (the default), the cursor type of the Recordset object returned from the call to the *Execute* method will be forward-only.

In short, if you want to maintain any control over the Recordset object generated by your query, use the *Open* method on the Recordset object rather than the *Execute* method of the Connection object. (See Chapter 4 for more information on using the Recordset's *Open* method.)

The best use of the *Execute* method is for action queries—queries that will not return a recordset. Just be sure to use the adExecuteNoRecords constant in the *Options* parameter. This will speed up the execution of your query because ADO will not attempt to fetch the query's results or generate a new Recordset object.

Another tip to improve performance is to use the appropriate value for the CommandTypeEnum in the *Options* parameter rather than letting ADO guess what type of query you're submitting.

Open Method

You use the *Open* method to connect to your database. The *Open* method on the Connection object has four parameters, all of which are optional:

```
Connection.Open ConnectionString, UserID, Password, Options
```

In the *Open* method, you can specify a connection string rather than setting the ConnectionString property prior to calling the method. The *UserID* and *Password* parameters are fairly self-explanatory; they accept string values that allow you to specify the user and password, respectively.

If you want to connect to your database asynchronously, simply use the adAsyncConnect constant (a member of the ConnectOptionEnum type) in the *Options* parameter. Your code will continue to run while ADO attempts to connect to your database. Once the attempt to connect completes (whether it succeeds or fails), the *ConnectComplete* event on the Connection object will fire. Not all OLE DB providers support asynchronous operations.

> **NOTE** I've noticed somewhat unexpected behavior when using the SQL Server OLE DB provider to connect asynchronously. The provider will try to locate the server synchronously. Once the provider locates the server, it will try to establish a connection asynchronously. Thus, the call to the *Open* method will not appear asynchronous if the server you're trying to connect to is unavailable.

If you're connecting to your database asynchronously, you might want to disable some of your application's functionality while you attempt the connection. For example, you would not want to try to submit a query to a Connection object that's still trying to connect. When the *ConnectComplete* event fires, you can determine whether the connection succeeded and enable the functionality in your application to submit the query, if appropriate.

OpenSchema Method

Perhaps your application allows the user to build queries at run time with a slick user interface. In that case, your application might need to retrieve metadata from your database. You'll want to provide a list of tables and the names of the fields in each table. You might even want to retrieve foreign key constraints to show relationships within the database. The *OpenSchema* method returns a Recordset object to help you retrieve this type of information:

```
Set Recordset = Connection.OpenSchema QueryType, Criteria, SchemaID
```

To use this method, you must specify a schema type in the *QueryType* parameter. Numerous values are available for the schema type and are contained in SchemaEnum. See the ADO Help files for a complete list of values. (Keep in mind that data access providers are not required to support all schemas.)

Generally, you want to put some restrictions on the schema that you're retrieving. For example, you might want to see the list of columns in a particular table. Simply specifying adSchemaColumns in the first parameter will retrieve information for all columns in all tables. The second parameter on the *OpenSchema* method, *Criteria*, is optional and takes a Variant array that defines the restriction you want to place on the schema. Each schema type has its own options for restrictions, and there are too many to list here. Your best bet is to look in the Microsoft Data Access SDK for the restrictions available for any particular schema type.

The current documentation for adSchemaColumns lists four available restrictions: TABLE_CATALOG, TABLE_SCHEMA, TABLE_NAME, and COLUMN_NAME. If you wanted to retrieve the columns for only the Customers table in your database, you could use code such as the following:

```
Dim rsSchema As ADODB.Recordset
Dim aRestrictions As Variant

aRestrictions = Array(Empty, Empty, "Customers", Empty)
Set rsSchema = cnDatabase.OpenSchema(adSchemaColumns, _
                              aRestrictions)
```

We created a Variant array with the same number of entries as the number of available restrictions for the schema. We used the desired entry in the Variant array and designated the other entries as Empty.

The *OpenSchema* method returns a Recordset object with the schema information. If you want to be able to sort or scroll through the resulting Recordset, set the CursorLocation property of the Connection object to adUseClient prior to calling *OpenSchema.*

The *OpenSchema* method has another optional parameter—*SchemaID*. The documentation states that you can set this parameter to a schema's globally unique identifier (GUID) if you've set the *QueryType* to adSchemaProviderSpecific.

RollbackTrans Method

This method rolls back the pending changes in the current transaction. *RollbackTrans* takes no parameters. To learn more about using this method, see the "Managing Your Transactions" section beginning on page 46.

ADO CONNECTION OBJECT EVENTS

The connection object raises the events listed in the following table.

CONNECTION OBJECT EVENTS

Event Name	*Description*
BeginTransComplete	Fires when the *BeginTrans* method completes
CommitTransComplete	Fires when the *CommitTrans* method completes
ConnectComplete	Fires when the attempt to connect to the database completes
Disconnect	Fires when the *Close* method completes
ExecuteComplete	Fires when the *Execute* method completes
InfoMessage	Returns informational error messages
RollbackTransComplete	Fires when the *RollbackTrans* method completes
WillConnect	Fires when the *Open* method on the Connection object is called, prior to the attempt to connect to the database
WillExecute	Fires prior to submitting a query to the Connection object with the Execute method or when the Open method is called on a Recordset associated with the Connection object

In order to create an object variable in Microsoft Visual Basic that exposes events, you'll need to use code such as the following:

```
Dim WithEvents cnDatabase As ADODB.Connection
```

You cannot use the New keyword in the Dim statement in Visual Basic and access the events for the object you've created.

BeginTransComplete Event

The *BeginTransComplete* event fires when you call the *BeginTrans* method on your Connection object. The event handler has four parameters:

```
BeginTransComplete TransactionLevel, pError, adStatus, pConnection
```

The first parameter, *TransactionLevel*, specifies the transaction level of the initiated transaction. This is the nesting level value that is returned by the *BeginTrans* method. The second parameter, *pError*, is a pointer to an Error object that contains error information. To determine whether an error has occurred, you can test to see whether this parameter is set to a valid Error object or you can check the value of the third parameter, *adStatus*. The *adStatus* parameter will return a value from the EventStatusEnum type. If *adStatus* is set to adStatusErrorsOccurred, errors have occurred and *pError* should be pointing to an object. The last parameter, *pConnection*, is a pointer to the Connection object that raised the event. Using this pointer can simplify the code in your event handlers.

If you want to prevent the event from firing again, set the *adStatus* parameter to adStatusUnwantedEvent.

CommitTransComplete Event

In the same way that the *BeginTransComplete* event fires when you call the *Begin-Trans* method, the *CommitTransComplete* event fires when you call the *CommitTrans* method. The *CommitTransComplete* event handler has the same parameters, for the same information, as the *BeginTransComplete* event handler, with the exception of *TransactionLevel*:

```
CommitTransComplete pError, adStatus, pConnection
```

Setting the *adStatus* parameter to adStatusUnwantedEvent will prevent this event from firing again.

ConnectComplete Event

The *ConnectComplete* event fires when ADO has completed its attempt to connect to your database. This event handler has three parameters, which are the same as the last three parameters in the event handlers for *BeginTransComplete* and *Commit-TransComplete*:

```
ConnectComplete pError, adStatus, pConnection
```

This event will fire immediately after you call the *Open* method of the Connection object, unless you attempt to connect to your database asynchronously. Setting the *adStatus* parameter to adStatusUnwantedEvent won't prevent this event from firing in the future.

Disconnect Event

When you call the *Close* method on the Connection object, the *Disconnect* event will fire. This event handler uses only two parameters:

```
Disconnect adStatus, pConnection
```

The first parameter, *adStatus*, returns a value contained in the EventStatusEnum type and indicates whether the *Close* method succeeded or failed. I've yet to receive any value other than adStatusOK in this event. If the server has shut down while the Connection object is open, the *Close* method still succeeds. If you have a transaction pending on the Connection object when you call the *Close* method, you'll generate an error that will prevent the Connection object from closing and the *Disconnect* event from firing. Setting the *adStatus* parameter to adStatusUnwantedEvent won't prevent this event from firing in the future.

If you disconnect from your database by letting the Connection object go out of scope or by setting the object pointer to Nothing, the *Disconnect* event will not fire.

ExecuteComplete Event

The *ExecuteComplete* event will fire when the query you executed on your connection completes. This event fires only with queries submitted by the *Connection.Execute*, *Command.Execute*, or *Recordset.Open* methods. If you call the *OpenSchema* method on the Connection object, the *ExecuteComplete* event will not fire.

After you submit your query, and before the query actually executes, the *Will-Execute* event fires. The *ExecuteComplete* event fires after the query has executed. Unless you have executed your query asynchronously, the *ExecuteComplete* event will fire before your code continues.

The *ExecuteComplete* event takes six parameters:

```
ExecuteComplete RecordsAffected, pError, adStatus, pCommand, _
                pRecordset, pConnection
```

The first parameter, *RecordsAffected*, returns the number of rows in the database affected by your query. This value is used if you submit an action query to modify rows in your database. If your query returns rows, this parameter is set to −1. The next two parameters, *pError* and *adStatus*, are used the same as in the events discussed previously.

The final three parameters are pointers to the Command, Recordset, and Connection objects being used, respectively. Even if you do not explicitly use a Command object, one is created for you. If you use the adExecuteNoRecords option on the *Execute* method of the Connection or Command object, the *pRecordset* parameter will be set to Nothing.

If you want to prevent this event from firing again, set the *adStatus* parameter to adStatusUnwantedEvent.

InfoMessage Event

Some database applications, such as SQL Server, raise informational messages that do not generate run-time errors but that might be helpful to trap in your application. When you connect to SQL Server through the SQL Server ODBC driver, you'll receive messages that state which database you're using (if you're not using the default Master database) and the programming language you're using. I'm not sure why, but these messages are not returned when connecting through the SQL Server OLE DB provider.

The *InfoMessage* event handler uses three parameters that might appear familiar to you by now if you've been reading this chapter straight through: *pError*, *adStatus*, and *pConnection*. You're probably better off walking through the Errors collection of the Connection object referenced by *pConnection* rather than relying on the Error object referenced by *pError*. If the database returns multiple informational messages based on the operation you perform, the *InfoMessage* event will fire only once. Only the first informational message will be available in the *pError* object, but all the messages can be accessed by means of the Errors collection on the *pConnection* object.

In my opinion, ADO doesn't do a great job of returning informational messages from stored procedures that return at least one recordset. Messages returned by your stored procedure after the first recordset might not be available. Apparently, this is because of limitations in the ODBC and OLE DB APIs. Hopefully this behavior will improve in a future release of ADO.

Despite what the documentation might say, setting the *adStatus* parameter to adStatusUnwantedEvent does not prevent the event from firing in the future.

RollbackTransComplete Event

The *RollbackTransComplete* event fires when you call the *RollbackTrans* method. The *RollbackTransComplete* event handler has three parameters:

```
RollbackTransComplete pError, adStatus, pConnection
```

See the earlier sections "*BeginTransComplete* Event" and "*CommitTrans-Complete* Event" for explanations of these parameters.

WillConnect Event

The *WillConnect* event fires once you've called the *Open* method on the Connection object. This event handler takes six parameters:

```
WillConnect ConnectionString, UserID, Password, Options, adStatus, _
            pConnection
```

The first four parameters map to the four parameters on the *Open* method of the Connection object. If you specify the user ID and/or password information in your connection string rather than through the *UserID* and *Password* parameters on the Connection object's *Open* method, these parameters will be blank in the *WillConnect* event. You can modify the *ConnectionString*, *UserID*, *Password*, and *Options* parameters within this event to change how you're connecting to your database.

If you set the *adStatus* parameter to adStatusCancel, the *Open* method on the Connection object will return with an error stating "Operation has been cancelled by the user."

Despite what the documentation might say, setting the *adStatus* parameter to adStatusUnwantedEvent does not prevent the event from firing in the future.

WillExecute Event

Similar to how the *WillConnect* event fires as you attempt to connect to your database, the *WillExecute* event fires as you submit a query to the database. As with the *ExecuteComplete* event, calling the *Execute* method of the Connection and Command objects as well as the *Open* method of the Recordset object generates this event. The *OpenSchema* method on the Connection object will not cause this event to fire.

The *WillExecute* event uses eight parameters:

```
WillExecute Source, CursorType, LockType, Options, adStatus, _
            pCommand, pRecordset, pConnection
```

The *Source* parameter refers to the query string. The *CursorType* and *LockType* parameters refer to the properties with the same name on the Recordset object.

Keep in mind that these parameters simply store the requested cursor type and lock type. What is actually returned might be different. If you set the CursorType and LockType properties on your Recordset object to invalid values (such as setting a client-side Recordset to a CursorType of adOpenDynamic and a LockType of adLockPessimistic), the invalid values will appear in the *WillExecute* event. Don't worry, we'll discuss these properties in more detail when we cover the Recordset object in Chapter 4 and cursors in Chapter 7.

The *Options* parameter holds the same value as the *Options* parameter used on the method call that submitted the query, such as *Connection.Execute*.

You can use the *adStatus* parameter to keep from submitting the query by setting it to adStatusCancel. If you want to prevent this event from firing again, set the *adStatus* parameter to adStatusUnwantedEvent.

The final three parameters on this event refer to the Command, Recordset, and Connection objects, respectively, used in the query. As described earlier in the *ExecuteComplete* event, if the adExecuteNoRecords value is used on the *Execute* method of the Connection or Command object, the *pRecordset* parameter in the *WillExecute* event will be set to Nothing.

ANATOMY OF A CONNECTION STRING

ADO is extremely flexible when it comes to connecting to databases and provides a variety of ways to build a connection string.

Using Data Links to Build Connection Strings

First let's spend a little time looking at how you create a connection to a database at design time, using Visual Basic 6. Whether you're using the DataEnvironment object, the DataView window, or the ADO Data Control (Microsoft ADO Data Control 6.0), you can access the same user interface, the Data Link Properties property sheet, to specify the OLE DB provider you want to use. Rather than including their own connection strings, each of these technologies uses the Data Link Properties property pages to let the user interactively build the connection strings.

Select the OLE DB provider on the Provider tab, as shown in Figure 3-1, and click Next to see the Connection property page, where you can specify the location of your database. You can even click the Test Connection button to test whether you can connect to the database you selected.

Perhaps the best way to learn about using connection strings is to create one. From a Visual Basic 6 project, simply reference the Microsoft OLE DB Service Component 1.0 Type Library and write code such as the following:

```
Dim objDataLink As MSDASC.DataLinks
Dim strConn As String

Set objDataLink = New MSDASC.DataLinks
strConn = objDataLink.PromptNew
MsgBox "The connection string you created is:" & _
       vbCrLf & strConn
```

When you run this code, it will display the same Data Link Properties property sheet interface used within Visual Basic 6. Once you click on the OK button for that set of property pages, you'll see a message box showing the connection string that you built. You can use the connection string returned from this simple snippet of code to learn how to build connection strings on your own. Another way of learning from existing connection strings is to pass a Connection object into the *Prompt-Edit* method on the DataLinks object, which will display the Data Link Properties property sheet with the properties for that Connection object. You can then edit that connection string.

NOTE You can display the Data Link Properties user interface in your applications if you distribute the Mdac_typ.exe file with your application to include the Microsoft Data Access Components.

A connection string consists of a series of name-value pairs delimited by semicolons:

```
strConn = "Setting1=Value1;Setting2=Value2;..."
```

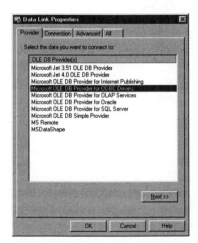

Figure 3-1 *Select your OLE DB provider on the Data Link Properties property sheet.*

Using Data Link Files

In version 2.0 of the Microsoft Data Access Components (MDAC), OLE DB provided functionality similar to that of ODBC DSN (data source name) through a feature called data links. This feature saves connection string information to a file with a .udl extension. Prior to MDAC 2.5, you could create a data link file by right-clicking in a folder or on the Desktop and selecting Microsoft Data Link from the New submenu. Although the ability to create data link files this way was removed in MDAC 2.5, you can still create a file with a .udl extension and it will be associated with data links.

Once you've created a data link file, right-click on the file, select Properties, and you'll see a user interface that is the same as the one described in the previous section (as shown in Figure 3-1 on page 43), only with a General tab added. You can view the contents of the file in a text editor such as Microsoft Notepad. To use this data link file in a connection string, you can use a name-value pair in the string, such as the following:

```
"File Name=MyDataLink.udl;"
```

If you do not specify a full path to the data link file, ADO will look in the current working directory for your application. You can also use relative paths in your connection string:

```
"File Name=Data\MyDataLink.udl;"
```

The OLE DB Provider For ODBC Drivers

ADO communicates with your database by means of an OLE DB provider, similar to how RDO communicates with your database through an ODBC driver. ADO 2.0 and later ship with native OLE DB providers for Access, SQL Server, and Oracle databases.

What if you don't have a native OLE DB provider to communicate with your database? As long as you have an ODBC driver that supports basic ODBC functionality, you should still be able to use ADO. The OLE DB Provider For ODBC Drivers makes ODBC API calls that ask the driver what functionality it supports. You might experience problems if the ODBC driver doesn't accurately state the functionality it supports.

In fact, the default OLE DB provider is the OLE DB Provider For ODBC Drivers. This provider acts as a translation layer between OLE DB and ODBC. In the connection string, this provider is listed as MSDASQL and is often referred to by its code name, Kagera. You can use this provider with an ODBC DSN—user, system, or file—or with a connection string that doesn't have a DSN. Here are some examples:

```
"Provider=MSDASQL;DSN=MyUserDSN;UID=MyUID;PWD=MyPwd;"

"Provider=MSDASQL;DSN=MySystemDSN;UID=MyUID;PWD=MyPwd;"

"Provider=MSDASQL;FileDSN=MyFileDSN;UID=MyUID;PWD=MyPwd;"

"Provider=MSDASQL;Driver={SQL Server};Server=MyServer;
    Database=MyDatabase;UID=MyUID;PWD=MyPwd;"
```

My recommendation is to use a native OLE DB provider if one is available.

The OLE DB Provider for Access Databases

If you're connecting to an Access database you can use the OLE DB provider for Access databases, Microsoft Jet 4.0 OLE DB Provider. To use this provider, specify the provider name and version and the location of your database in the connection string as follows:

```
"Provider=Microsoft.Jet.OLEDB.4.0;
    Data Source=C:\Path\To\MyDatabase.MDB;"
```

If you do not specify the entire path to your database, ADO will look for the database in your application's working path. You can also use relative paths. For example, if your database is in the Data subdirectory of your application, you could use the following connection string:

```
"Provider=Microsoft.Jet.OLEDB.4.0;
    Data Source=Data\MyDatabase.MDB;"
```

In the connection string, you can also specify the location of your system database, your database password, and a number of other options.

The OLE DB Provider For SQL Server Databases

If you're connecting to a SQL Server database, you can specify the native OLE DB provider, the location of your SQL Server, and the database you want to use, as well as security information:

```
"Provider=SQLOLEDB;Data Source=MyServer;
    Initial Catalog=MyDatabase;
    User ID=MyUID;Password=MyPassword;"
```

You can also specify the network library, packet size, and other attributes in the connection string.

The OLE DB Provider For Oracle Databases

Developers who want to use ADO with Oracle databases need to do a little more than just install ADO and build a connection string. Both the Microsoft OLE DB Provider For Oracle and the Microsoft ODBC Driver For Oracle communicate with Oracle's client components rather than directly with the Oracle database. In order to use ADO with Oracle, you have to install the appropriate version of the Oracle client utilities (SQL*Net) and create a database alias. Once you've done that, you can use a connection string such as this:

```
"Provider=MSDAORA;Data Source=MyDatabaseAlias;
    User ID=MyUID;Password=MyPassword;"
```

If you're looking to learn more about any of the above database provider options, see the documentation on these OLE DB providers in the Microsoft Data Access SDK, programmatically navigate through the Properties collection on the Connection object after specifying the provider, or examine the All tab on the Data Link Properties property sheet.

MANAGING YOUR TRANSACTIONS

There are times when you want to make a batch of changes to your database and you require that either all or none of the changes are made to the database; you can't allow partial transactions to complete. For example, imagine that you want to transfer money from your savings account to your checking account. The bank won't be happy if the withdrawal from your savings account fails but the deposit into your checking account succeeds. Similarly, you'll be less than thrilled if the converse occurs. If either task does not complete successfully, the other task should be canceled. In transactional programming, this all-or-nothing trait is called atomicity.

ADO offers a number of features to help you use transactions in your application.

BeginTrans, *CommitTrans*, and *RollbackTrans* Methods

You can use ADO's transactional methods to manage atomic units of work. Let's say that you're writing the software for an ATM machine. You could create code such as the following that makes use of ADO's transactional methods:

```
On Error Resume Next
'Start the transaction.
cnDatabase.BeginTrans
strSQL = "UPDATE Savings SET BalDue = BalDue - 50 " & _
        "WHERE AccountNumber = 123456789"
```

```
cnDatabase.Execute strSQL
If cnDatabase.Errors.Count > 0 Then
    'An error occurred, cancel changes.
    cnDatabase.RollbackTrans
Else
    strSQL = "UPDATE Checking SET BalDue = BalDue + 50 " & _
            "WHERE AccountNumber = 123456789"
    cnDatabase.Execute strSQL
    If cnDatabase.Errors.Count > 0 Then
        'An error occurred, cancel all of the changes.
        cnDatabase.RollbackTrans
    Else
        'No errors occurred, commit all of the changes.
        cnDatabase.CommitTrans
    End If
End If
```

Transactions are so simple to use they're almost dangerous: improper use of transactions can easily cause problems in your application. There are more don'ts than dos when using transactions in ADO, but don't let that scare you away from using them. For example, transactions should be isolated. Work performed on one transaction should not affect another transaction that's active at the same time. If you modify a row in one transaction, another user should not be able to modify that row in another transaction while your transaction is active.

Another point to remember is that you should close your transactions as quickly as possible. One way to accomplish this is to avoid requiring user interaction while your transaction is active. Imagine that you have designed an application that a number of salespeople are using to enter new orders. When they click on the button to submit an order, your code initiates a transaction and then enters the details for the order. If an item is out of stock, your code should handle that scenario gracefully by closing the transaction and presenting a message to the user. Do not leave the transaction active while your code presents the message box and the salesperson acknowledges receipt of the message that the order did not go through. End your transactions as quickly as possible to minimize potential locking conflicts.

Attributes Property

If the adXactCommitRetaining flag is turned on, a new transaction begins when you call *CommitTrans*. Similarly, if the adXactAbortRetaining flag is turned on, a new transaction starts when you call *RollbackTrans*. You can change the value of the Attributes property before opening your connection or after you've already established a connection to your database. The new value will take effect the next time you call one of the transaction methods (discussed in the previous section) on the connection.

Keep in mind that if you set the Attributes property to anything other than the default (0) and you begin a transaction, you might need to change this property value in order to close your Connection object. Calling the *Close* method on the Connection object will cause an error if a transaction is still pending. You can release the Connection object by setting the object to Nothing:

```
Set cnDatabase = New ADODB.Connection
cnDatabase.CursorLocation = adUseClient
cnDatabase.Attributes = adXactCommitRetaining + _
                        adXactAbortRetaining
cnDatabase.Open strConn, strUserID, strPassword

'Start a transaction.
cnDatabase.BeginTrans

    ⋮

'Commit the transaction.
cnDatabase.CommitTrans
'Because we've set the Attributes property to include
' adXactCommitRetaining, CommitTrans began another transaction.

'Reset the Attributes property to the default and call
' CommitTrans again before closing the transaction.
cnDatabase.Attributes = 0
cnDatabase.CommitTrans
cnDatabase.Close
Set cnDatabase = Nothing
```

IsolationLevel Property

If you're building a database application that will simultaneously handle transactions from multiple users, you need to know something about transaction isolation levels. Since entire books—such as *Principles of Transaction Processing for the Systems Professional,* by Philip A. Bernstein and Eric Newcomer [Morgan Kaufmann Publishers, 1996]—are dedicated to transaction processing, we'll introduce the topic only briefly here. Ideally you'll be convinced that you need to do further homework on this topic.

Most books on transactions state that each transaction should be isolated. Simultaneous transactions should not affect each other. This leads to very simple programming, at least in theory.

DEFINITIONS OF SOME TRANSACTIONAL TERMS

dirty read   When one transaction reads uncommitted changes from another transaction.

nonrepeatable read When data read in transaction A is modified by transaction B before transaction A completes.

phantom row   When transaction A examines the results of a query and then transaction B inserts a row that satisfies the criteria for transaction A's query before transaction A completes. This term comes from the fact that in this case, transaction A could run the same query twice and see a new row appear mysteriously (like a phantom) in the second set of results.

A truly isolated transaction should not be subject to dirty reads, nonrepeatable reads, or phantom rows. Isolating a transaction to this level, however, can lock large quantities of data on the server, leading to deadlocks or poor performance. In many cases, you'll find that you don't need to completely isolate your transactions.

SQL-92 is an ANSI standard for data access. SQL Server supports all four SQL-92 isolation levels, shown in the following table, and uses the Read Committed isolation level by default. You can set the ADO Connection object's IsolationLevel property to use any of the four SQL-92 isolation levels.

SQL-92 Isolation Levels	Dirty Read	Nonrepeatable Read	Phantom Row
Read Uncommitted	Yes	Yes	Yes
Read Committed	No	Yes	Yes
Repeatable Read	No	No	Yes
Serializable	No	No	No

A word of caution: Leave this feature alone unless you know what you're doing and you've discussed your plans with your database administrator. For example, say you want to see changes pending in another user's transaction, so you set the

IsolationLevel property to adXactReadUncommitted (or adXactBrowse), call *Begin-Trans*, and then execute a query to view that data. You will have no way of knowing which of the records you retrieved are marked as pending in another transaction, nor will you receive any notification if the data you read is no longer valid because that pending transaction rolled back.

COMPONENT SERVICES AND THE DISTRIBUTED TRANSACTION COORDINATOR

Earlier we presented a fairly simple example of a necessary transaction—the transfer of money from one account to another. Writing code to manage units of work on different databases in a single transaction is much more complex—unless you use Component Services (formerly named Microsoft Transaction Server).

Component Services uses a two-phase commit process to manage transactions across multiple databases. The standard example of a two-phase commit is a wedding ceremony. The minister asks both the bride and the groom if they do. If either party says that they don't, the marriage is off. That sounds simple enough. Now imagine that the wedding takes place over a transcontinental conference call, and the first party is cut off just after saying "I do" and before hearing the other party's response. At least one party doesn't know if he or she is married, which leaves the transaction incomplete.

If you're writing code to communicate to different database systems across a wide area network, you could have a similar problem. Imagine the code you would have to write to handle a transaction during which one database gets disconnected from another. Chances are, after you've written the code to manage that scenario once, you'd be able to reuse that code in your other applications.

The Component Services team has already written some of that code for you. They laid the groundwork, but they still can't know how to actually manage a specific database system's transactions. A database must support the two-phase commit protocol in order to support Component Services transactions. SQL Server 6.5 and later, as well as Oracle 7.3 and later, support Component Services transactions. Access databases and most other desktop databases (Microsoft FoxPro, Corel Paradox, Inprise dBase, and Pervasive Btrieve) do not.

Even if you're not going to use the Component Services transactional capabilities, you might want to use this service to manage your business objects if you're building a multitiered application.

If you want more information on Component Services, there are other books that cover Component Services (and Microsoft Transaction Server) in much more depth.

QUESTIONS THAT SHOULD BE ASKED MORE FREQUENTLY

Q.   *If I use only one Connection object, does that mean I'll have only one connection to my database?*

A.   No. If you ask ADO to accomplish a task and ADO determines that it cannot perform that task because the connection is busy, it will establish a temporary connection to your database in order to complete the task. This behavior is most likely to affect developers using SQL Server who encounter the limitation of one active query per connection. We'll talk about this more in Chapter 7 when we discuss cursors, but keep that distinction in the back of your mind. One Connection object does not equal one connection to your database.

Q.   *Should I rely on Visual Basic, COM, and ADO garbage collection, or should I close and release objects myself?*

A.   One memory leak can ruin your whole day. You should not need to worry about collecting your own garbage, but you should do it anyway. Close and release your ADO objects whenever possible.

Chapter 4

The ADO Recordset and Field Objects

Just as the Connection object is your link to a database, the Recordset object is your link to its data. When you submit a query to a database, ADO stores the results in the Recordset object. You can then use the Recordset object to examine the query results. The Recordset object also supports other functionality such as updating, sorting, and filtering. The Recordset object exposes a Fields collection, with each Field object corresponding to a different field in the results of your query.

ADO RECORDSET OBJECT PROPERTIES AND COLLECTIONS

Let's take a look at each of the different properties available on the Recordset object and listed in the following table.

RECORDSET OBJECT PROPERTIES AND COLLECTIONS

Property or Collection Name	Data Type	Description
AbsolutePage	Long	Identifies the page the current record of the Recordset is on
AbsolutePosition	Long	Identifies the position of the current record in the Recordset

(continued)

Recordset Object Properties and Collections *continued*

Property or Collection Name	*Data Type*	*Description*
ActiveCommand	Variant	Pointer to the Command object that created the Recordset object
ActiveConnection	String or Connection	Specifies the Connection object used to retrieve the results of your query
BOF	Boolean	Indicates whether you're currently at beginning of file (BOF), the position before the first record in your Recordset
Bookmark	Variant	Allows you to return to a particular record in the Recordset
CacheSize	Long	Specifies the number of records that ADO will cache from the server
CursorLocation	Long	Specifies the location of the cursor service (either client-side or server-side) that will maintain the results of your query
CursorType	CursorTypeEnum	Specifies the type of cursor used to access the results of your query
DataMember	String	Controls which Recordset in the data source you're binding to
DataSource	Object	Allows you to bind the Recordset to a data source
EditMode	EditModeEnum	Specifies the editing status for the current record in the Recordset
EOF	Boolean	Indicates whether you're currently at end of file (EOF), the position following the last record in your Recordset
Fields	Collection of Field objects	Pointer to the collection of Field objects that contain the results of your query
Filter	Variant	Allows you to filter your Recordset for particular records
Index	String	Controls the index currently in effect for a Record-set object
LockType	LockTypeEnum	Specifies how the contents of your Recordset can be locked and updated
MarshalOptions	Long	Controls which records are included in your Recordset when it is passed across a process boundary
MaxRecords	Long	Specifies the maximum number of records to be returned by your query
PageCount	Long	Returns the number of pages in your Recordset

Property or Collection Name	Data Type	Description
PageSize	Long	Specifies the number of records per page in your Recordset
Properties	Collection of Property objects	Collection of dynamic properties
RecordCount	Long	Returns the number of records in the Recordset
Sort	String	Allows you to reorder the data in your Recordset
Source	String or Command	Contains the query string used to build the Recordset
State	Long	Specifies the current state of the Recordset
Status	RecordStatusEnum	Returns the update status of the current record
StayInSync	Boolean	Controls whether references to child Recordsets will be kept in sync as you navigate through the parent Recordset

AbsolutePage, PageCount, and PageSize Properties

The PageSize property specifies the number of records per page in your Recordset. If you have a Recordset with 81 records and the PageSize property is set to 10 (its default value), the Recordset will have nine pages—the first eight pages containing 10 records each and the last page containing only one record. You can change the value of the PageSize property at any time. If the Recordset is currently open, the PageCount and AbsolutePage properties will be updated automatically.

The PageCount property is read-only and reflects the number of pages in the Recordset. If the Recordset does not support pages or bookmarks, this property will return −1.

The AbsolutePage property returns a long value. AbsolutePage will return the page number of the current record and is 1-based. You can use this property only if it's supported by the provider and if your record pointer is currently at a valid record. If your record pointer is not pointing to a valid record, AbsolutePage will contain a value in the form of a PositionEnum value constant. (See the following table.) If your record pointer is currently at BOF or EOF, the AbsolutePage property will return adPosBOF or adPosEOF, respectively. AbsolutePage will return adPosUnknown if the Recordset's current record is neither BOF nor EOF and the Recordset doesn't support bookmarks, or if the Recordset is empty.

If the Recordset supports bookmarks, you can set the AbsolutePage property to a long value, between 1 and PageCount, while the Recordset is open. You cannot set the AbsolutePage property to adPosBOF or adPosEOF. If you set the AbsolutePage property, ADO will move the current record pointer to the first record on that page.

POSITIONENUM VALUES

Constant	Value	Description
adPosUnknown	−1	The Recordset contains no data, the current position is unknown, or the property isn't supported for the current CursorType or provider.
adPosBOF	−2	The Recordset is at BOF, just before the first record.
adPosEOF	−3	The Recordset is at EOF, just after the last record.

As of ADO 2.1, the AbsolutePage property is supported for client-side Recordsets for all providers, and for server-side static and keyset Recordsets by means of the Microsoft OLE DB Provider For SQL Server and the Microsoft Jet 4.0 OLE DB Provider.

You can determine whether the Recordsets for your choice of OLE DB provider, cursor location, and cursor type will support the AbsolutePage property by using the *Recordset.Supports* method with the adApproxPosition constant.

AbsolutePosition Property

The AbsolutePosition property is similar to the AbsolutePage property, except that it refers to the record number within the Recordset rather than the page number. If your Recordset is at BOF or EOF, AbsolutePosition will return adPosBOF or adPosEOF, respectively. If the provider supports this property and your current record pointer is pointing to a record in the Recordset (neither BOF nor EOF), AbsolutePosition will return a number between 1 and the number of records in the Recordset.

For a Recordset that contains data and supports bookmarks, you can set this property to any number between 1 and the number of records in the Recordset to move to that specific record. You cannot set this property to adPosBOF or adPosEOF to move to BOF or EOF, respectively.

As of ADO 2.1, this property is supported for client-side Recordsets for all providers, and for server-side static and keyset Recordsets by means of the OLE DB Provider For SQL Server and the Jet 4.0 OLE DB Provider.

ActiveCommand Property

The ActiveCommand property contains the Command object that created the Recordset object. This property is read-only and is available even after the Recordset object has been closed.

ActiveConnection Property

For an open Recordset object, the ActiveConnection property is set to the Connection object used to retrieve your data. The property will not change once the Recordset object is closed. If your Recordset object was opened from a file, returned from another process, or created by populating the Fields collection yourself, this property will return Nothing, the default.

You can set the ActiveConnection property either to a connection string or to a Connection object while the Recordset is closed. You can also modify this property while the Recordset object is open, but only if you're using a client-side Recordset.

If you assign a connection string to the ActiveConnection property, ADO will create a new Connection object and attempt to connect to your database based on this string.

If you're using a client-side Recordset, you can set the ActiveConnection property to Nothing after opening the Recordset in order to disconnect the Recordset from your database. Once you've done that, the Recordset object will still contain the results of your query even after you close the Connection object.

BOF and EOF Properties

When you open a Recordset, you might want to programmatically loop through the records until you've reached the end of the Recordset. The BOF and EOF properties allow you to do this by letting you know when you've reached the beginning or end of the Recordset. Before the first true record in the Recordset, there is a placeholder that designates the beginning of the Recordset. Similarly, another placeholder designates the position following the last record in the Recordset. For example, you could use the following code to loop through the results of your query:

```
Dim strSQL As String
Dim rsCustomers As ADODB.Recordset
    ⋮
'Specify the query string.
strSQL = "SELECT * FROM Customers"

'Open a Recordset.
rsCustomers.Open strSQL, cnDatabase, adOpenStatic
'Check to see whether we've passed the last record in the Recordset.
'If we haven't, call DisplayCustomer and then move to the next record.
Do While Not rsCustomers.EOF
    DisplayCustomer
    rsCustomers.MoveNext
Loop
```

After you display the contents of the last record in the Recordset by means of the *DisplayCustomer* routine, the next call to the *MoveNext* method will move the current record pointer in the Recordset beyond the last record to EOF. At that point, the EOF property will be equal to True and you will exit the loop. If no records satisfy the results of your query, both BOF and EOF will be set to True.

Bookmark Property

Just as you use a bookmark to mark your place in a book, the Bookmark property allows you to mark a particular record in your Recordset. You can retrieve a bookmark for a particular record in a Recordset by using the Bookmark property. Setting the Bookmark property will set the current record pointer to the record at that bookmark.

Different OLE DB providers implement bookmarks in different ways. The actual value of the Bookmark property is unimportant. The property was not designed for you to keep track of the record number; it was designed so that you can access the contents of a particular record based on the value of the Bookmark property. The purpose of the property is to allow you to return to a particular record in the Recordset.

If you regenerate a Recordset by closing and opening it or by calling the *Requery* method, a new set of bookmarks is created—one for each record. As a result, a bookmark you retrieved before regenerating your Recordset might not point to the same record after you regenerate the Recordset. You might receive an error if you attempt to set the Bookmark property to a value retrieved prior to regenerating the Recordset. Even if you set the property without generating an error, you might find that you're looking at a different record than expected. The same is true if you pick up another edition of a particular book—there's no guarantee that the contents of page 45 will be the same in both editions.

The code that follows uses the *Find* method to try to locate a particular customer in the Recordset. If the search fails, we use the Bookmark property to return to the record that was current prior to the search.

```
Dim varBookmark As Variant
Dim rsCustomers As ADODB.Recordset
    ⋮
varBookmark = rsCustomers.Bookmark
rsCustomers.MoveFirst
rsCustomers.Find "CustomerID = 'XXXXX'"
If rsCustomers.EOF Then
    MsgBox "Customer not found. " & _
            "Returning to previous record."
    rsCustomers.Bookmark = varBookmark
Else
    MsgBox "Located desired customer."
End If
```

> **CAUTION**   Do not set the Bookmark property to a value in BookmarkEnum. Those constants are designed for the *Find* method, which we'll discuss a little later in this chapter.

CacheSize Property

If you're using a server-side Recordset, the CacheSize property specifies how many records ADO will retrieve from the OLE DB provider and store in its local cache. As you navigate through the Recordset, ADO will clear the cache and retrieve a new set of records from the OLE DB provider any time you navigate outside the currently cached records in the Recordset. This property defaults to 1, but setting this property to larger values might help decrease network activity. The CacheSize property can be modified even after the Recordset has been opened, but the change will not take effect until you move beyond the currently cached records.

CursorLocation Property

This property determines how the results of your query will be stored. You can set it to a value defined by CursorLocationEnum and shown in this table.

CURSORLOCATIONENUM VALUES

Constant	Value	Description
adUseServer	2	Default; uses the OLE DB provider and/or database to manage the results of your queries
adUseClient	3	Uses the ADO Cursor Engine to manage the results of your queries
adUseClientBatch	3	Hidden; equivalent of adUseClient
adUseNone	1	Hidden, undocumented, and unsupported (That warning should suffice.)

The default setting (adUseServer) uses server-side Recordsets, but you can set it to use client-side Recordsets by changing the setting to adUseClient. We'll talk more about the differences between server-side and client-side Recordsets in the coming chapters. Until that time, you can get by if you understand that setting CursorLocation to adUseClient causes the results of your entire query to be stored in the ADO Cursor Engine. Server-side Recordsets are managed by either the OLE DB provider or the database (depending on your database), with ADO storing a small portion of the data itself.

There are two hidden values in CursorLocationEnum, and the less said about these properties the better. Generally, hidden features are hidden for a reason—this is an object model, not a video game with hidden cheat codes and power-up features. The first value is adUseClientBatch. It exists for backward compatibility, and its use is identical to that of adUseClient. I am under strict orders not to talk about the last value, adUseNone. I asked about this value on an internal e-mail alias once and was sentenced to my cubicle for two weeks without caffeine. While this value looks like rdUseNone in Remote Data Objects (RDO), it isn't the same and is hidden for a reason to which I'm not privy.

Unless you set the Recordset's CursorLocation property, the Recordset will inherit the value of the Connection object's CursorLocation property if you used a Connection object to open your Recordset. If you do set the Recordset's CursorLocation property prior to opening the Recordset, ADO will use the value specified in the Recordset's CursorLocation property to determine the location of the results of your query. This property is read/write while the Recordset object is closed and read-only while the Recordset is open.

CursorType Property

The CursorType property contains a value that indicates the type of cursor used to store the contents of the Recordset. You can use this property to request a particular cursor type before you open the Recordset. The available values for the CursorType property appear in the following table.

CursorTypeEnum Values

Constant	Value	Description
adOpenForwardOnly	0	Default for server-side Recordsets; opens a Recordset that supports scrolling forward only
adOpenStatic	3	Default and only possible value for client-side Recordsets; supports scrolling forward and backward; changes made by other users are not visible
adOpenKeyset	1	Supports scrolling forward and backward; modifications and deletions by other users are visible
adOpenDynamic	2	Supports scrolling forward and backward; modifications, deletions, and insertions made by other users are visible

If you set the CursorType property to a value that the cursor location or provider doesn't support, you'll receive the closest available cursor type. The CursorType property is read/write while the Recordset is closed and read-only while the Recordset is open. You can set the CursorType property prior to calling the *Open* method, or you can set the *CursorType* parameter on the *Open* method, which will have the same effect.

Chapter 7 will go into much greater depth about cursors, their behavior, and their availability.

DataMember and DataSource Properties

Much like the Microsoft Visual Basic DataGrid control, the Recordset object can act like a complex data-bound control. You can set the DataSource property of the Recordset object to a data source such as the Visual Basic DataEnvironment or the Microsoft ADO Data Control, or to another Recordset object. If the data source you're binding the Recordset object to exposes multiple Recordsets, you can use the Data-Member property to specify the Recordset to which you want to bind:

```
Set rsDataBound = New ADODB.Recordset
rsDataBound.DataMember = "Command1"
rsDataBound.DataSource = DataEnvironment1
```

EditMode Property

The EditMode property is read-only and indicates the editing status for the current record. EditMode will return one of the values in EditModeEnum, shown in the following table.

EDITMODEENUM VALUES

Constant	Value	Description
adEditNone	0	Default; the record is not currently being modified.
adEditInProgress	1	The current record is being modified.
adEditAdd	2	The current record has been added to the Recordset with the *AddNew* method, but the *Update* method hasn't been called to commit the changes to the Recordset.
adEditDelete	4	The current record has been deleted.

If you're not editing the current record in the Recordset, the EditMode property will be set to adEditNone. If you modify one of the fields in the record or if you're in the process of adding a record to the Recordset, the EditMode property will return adEditInProgress until you call either the *Update* or the *CancelUpdate* method.

Calling the *Delete* method on the Recordset object will delete the current record from the Recordset but will not move to the next valid record. Until you move from the deleted record, EditMode will return adEditDelete.

Fields Collection

The Recordset object contains a Fields collection. Each object in this collection refers to a field in the results of your query. The Fields collection is the default property for the Recordset object, and the Value property is the default property for the Field object. There are many different ways to refer to a Field object in the Recordset's

Fields collection. The Fields collection is 0-based. In the following Visual Basic code, all lines are equivalent to each other, referring to the Value property for the CustomerID field in the *rsCustomers* Recordset object (assuming CustomerID is the first field in the Recordset):

```
rsCustomers.Fields("CustomerID").Value
rsCustomers.Fields(0).Value
rsCustomers(0).Value
rsCustomers("CustomerID").Value
rsCustomers!CustomerID.Value
rsCustomers.Fields("CustomerID")
rsCustomers.Fields(0)
rsCustomers(0)
rsCustomers("CustomerID")
rsCustomers!CustomerID
```

We'll discuss the Fields collection and the Field object later in this chapter, in the section "ADO Fields Collection" beginning on page 104.

Filter Property

The Filter property allows you to specify which records in your Recordset you want to view. This feature is designed for client-side Recordsets, but in most cases it also works with server-side Recordsets; just keep in mind that the ADO Cursor Engine is providing this functionality. Thus, if you're using a server-side Recordset, you're still retrieving all records that satisfy your query, but ADO is hiding the records that don't satisfy the criteria of the setting for the Filter property.

You can set the Filter property to a string to specify the filter criteria, to an array of bookmarks, or to any of the values in FilterGroupEnum (shown in the following table).

FILTERGROUPENUM VALUES

Constant	*Value*	*Description*
adFilterNone	0	Default; clears the current filter
adFilterPendingRecords	1	Displays only the records with pending changes
adFilterAffectedRecords	2	Displays only the records affected by the last call to *Delete*, *Resync*, *UpdateBatch*, or *CancelBatch*
adFilterFetchedRecords	3	Displays only the records currently stored in the cache
adFilterPredicate	4	Hidden, undocumented, and unsupported constant
adFilterConflictingRecords	5	Displays only the records that failed in the last batch update attempt

FilterGroupEnum constants

Here's a more detailed explanation of what the different constants in FilterGroupEnum are designed to do:

- **adFilterNone** This constant clears the current filter and makes all records in the Recordset visible. Setting the Filter property to an empty string has the same effect, because even if you set the Filter property to an empty string, ADO will actually set the property to adFilterNone. This means that you can reliably use the Filter property to see whether there is an active filter by testing for a value of adFilterNone.

- **adFilterPendingRecords** This filter value can come in handy if you're using the ADO Cursor Engine's batch updating functionality. When you set the Filter property to adFilterPendingRecords, only the records with pending changes will be visible in the Recordset. This includes records that you have modified, inserted, or deleted but whose changes have not yet been committed to the database. You can walk through the records visible in the Recordset object and check the Status property to determine how the record has been changed: by modification, deletion, or insertion. We'll talk more about this feature when we discuss using disconnected Recordsets and batch updates.

- **adFilterAffectedRecords** Setting the Filter property to this value displays only the records modified by the last call to the *Delete, Resync, UpdateBatch,* or *CancelBatch* method. To be honest, I've yet to find a scenario in which this filter value would be useful, but anything is possible.

- **adFilterFetchedRecords** This is another odd value. It's designed for server-side Recordsets and is related to the Recordset's CacheSize property. By setting Filter to adFilterFetchedRecords on a server-side Recordset, you'll see only the records currently stored in the cache. The advantage to this is that you can then navigate through the Recordset without invoking a network round-trip.

    Using this filter value with a client-side Recordset works a bit differently. Since all the data in a client-side Recordset is stored in the ADO Cursor Engine, there really isn't any cached data. Nevertheless, if you set the Filter property on the Recordset to this constant, only the number of records specified in the CacheSize property, counting from the current record, will be visible. If the number of records remaining, including the current record, is less than the value of the CacheSize property, only those remaining records will be visible.

- **adFilterPredicate**   At the time of this writing, this constant is hidden, undocumented, and unsupported. Perhaps it will become a viable feature in a future release of ADO. My attempts to use this constant generated an invalid page fault.

  NOTE   I have absolutely no idea why this constant exists. Don't trust anyone who claims to know what it's for, unless they can show you sample code that works.

    Throughout the rest of this text, I'll ignore this constant when discussing values from FilterGroupEnum, as should you.

- **adFilterConflictingRecords**   This constant hides all records in the Recordset except those that failed in the last batch update attempt. If you want to modify a record in your database but another user has modified that record between the time you retrieved it and the time you called *UpdateBatch*, ADO will mark that record as a conflict. Setting the Filter property on the Recordset to adFilterConflictingRecords will display only the records marked as conflicts in your last call to *UpdateBatch*. We'll talk more about this feature when we discuss using disconnected Recordsets and batch updates.

Setting the Filter property to a string

You can also set the Filter property of the Recordset to a string in order to specify which records you want to view. For example, if you retrieved the entire contents of your Orders table and wanted to view the orders only for a particular customer, you could use code such as the following:

```
rsOrders.Filter = "CustomerID = 'ALFKI'"
```

While ADO's filtering capabilities aren't as robust as those for the SQL Server and Jet database engines, they're still helpful. Bear in mind the following rules when setting the Filter property to a string:

- Each clause must use a field name in the Recordset, an operator (=, <>, <, >, <=, >=, or LIKE), and a value.

- If you use the LIKE operator to compare strings, you can use a wildcard (% or *) as the last character of the search string or as the first and last characters in the string.

- You can use multiple criteria, separated by AND or OR clauses. There is no precedence between AND and OR clauses. You can group clauses with parentheses, but you can only join groups of clauses with OR.

- If the field name you're referencing contains a space, you can delimit it with square brackets:

  ```
  rsAuthors.Filter = "[Year Born] = 1945"
  ```

■ You can delimit date values with single quotes or pound symbols, but it's not required unless you're specifying a date and a time. I'd still recommend using one of the delimiters.

■ You must delimit strings with either a single quote or a pound symbol. If there's a single quote in the string you're searching for, pound symbols might seem like the only choice. But here's a trick: you can delimit the string with single quotes if you change the single quotes in the embedded string to two consecutive single quotes. (Readers with some SQL Server experience might recognize this stratagem.) You don't need to do this if you delimit the string with pound symbols. However, if you need to use a pound symbol in the string you're searching for, you can't use two consecutive pound symbols. For example, if you were looking for the customer record with a CompanyName field value of Trail's Head Gourmet, you could use the following code:

```
strCriteria = "CompanyName = 'Trail''s Head Gourmet'"
rsCustomers.Filter = strCriteria
```

If you're prompting the user for the value to search for, do that person a favor and hide this level of complexity. After you receive the user's input, search for single quotes and replace them with two consecutive single quotes. Visual Basic 6 added a *Replace* function that makes this process simple:

```
strCriteria = "CompanyName = '" & _
              Replace(strCompanyName, "'", "''") & "'"
rsCustomers.Filter = strCriteria
```

Setting the Filter property to an array of bookmarks

You can set the Recordset's Filter property to an array of bookmark values. The following code retrieves the bookmarks from two records of the Recordset, then displays the two records that were active when the Recordset's Bookmark property was examined:

```
Dim aBookmarks(1) As Variant

aBookmarks(0) = rsCustomers.Bookmark
rsCustomers.MoveNext
aBookmarks(1) = rsCustomers.Bookmark
⋮
rsCustomers.Filter = aBookmarks
```

Visual Basic grids and filters

At the time of this writing, the DataGrid and HierarchicalFlexGrid controls that ship with Visual Basic 6 do not handle non-string-based filters very well. If you set the

Filter property on a Recordset to an array of bookmarks or to a value in FilterGroupEnum other than adFilterNone, the DataGrid control will still display all the records in the Recordset. The grid controls are also unable to display server-side Recordsets using string-based filters.

Hopefully, the complex data-bound controls (such as grids, list boxes, and combo boxes) that ship with the next version of Visual Basic will handle filtered Recordsets better.

Index Property

The basic idea behind the Index property is that you can use a table's index to control the order in which records in a table are displayed. You can then use the Recordset's *Seek* method, which we'll discuss later in this chapter, to search for a record based on its index value or values.

At the time of this writing, the only provider that supports the Index property is the Jet 4.0 OLE DB Provider, but only if you're using a Jet 4 and Access 2000–format database with a Recordset that has a CommandType setting of adCmdTableDirect. To determine whether your Recordset supports indexes, use the *Supports* method of the Recordset object with the adIndex constant.

If you're using a Recordset object that supports the Index property, you can set the Index property to a string that corresponds to the name of one of the indexes for the table that you've queried. You can set the Index property on a closed or open Recordset. If you set the Index property on an open Recordset that does not support indexes, you'll receive a trappable error.

Keep in mind that if you set the Index property on a closed Recordset, the Index property is supported only in a very specific scenario. From personal experience, I've found that you can set the Index property on a closed Recordset and then open the Recordset in a way that does not support indexes, without generating an error—which implies success. It appears that if you set the Index property prior to opening your Recordset, you'll receive an error only if the Recordset does support indexes and the specified index does not exist, or if you don't open your Recordset with the *CommandType* parameter on the *Open* method set to adCmdTableDirect.

The Index property is designed to provide functionality similar to the Index property on a Data Access Objects (DAO) Recordset object. The fact that it's currently supported for use only with Access databases is not a coincidence. It's a conscious attempt by the ADO development team to provide ADO with as much of DAO's functionality as possible. The scenario under which ADO's Index property is supported, as just described in the previous paragraph, is similar to the scenario in which DAO Recordsets support the Index property—using table-type recordsets. (See the DAO documentation for information on table-type recordsets.)

LockType Property

The Recordset's LockType property dictates whether and how your Recordset can be updated. This property is read/write when the Recordset is closed and read-only when the Recordset is open. You can also set this property by specifying the *LockType* parameter on the Recordset's *Open* method. You can assign any of the LockTypeEnum values shown in the following table to the LockType property.

LockTypeEnum Values

Constant	Value	Description
adLockReadOnly	1	Default; the Recordset is read-only.
adLockPessimistic	2	ADO relies on the OLE DB provider to ensure that your update attempt will succeed.
adLockOptimistic	3	The data is not locked until you call *Update*.
adLockBatchOptimistic	4	Modifications to your data are cached until you call *UpdateBatch*.

Locking options

The following is a brief explanation of the different locking options available to you in ADO. We'll discuss updating your database with ADO in more depth in Chapters 8, 10, and 12.

■ **adLockReadOnly**   Read-only Recordsets need little explanation. If you know you're not going to update the data you're retrieving, request read-only Recordsets. You'll get your data back faster.

■ **adLockPessimistic**   The idea behind pessimistically locked Recordsets is fairly simple: make sure that attempts to update succeed. This means that attempts to edit will fail in order to prevent multiple users from simultaneously trying to edit the same record. Such attempts are considered "pessimistic" because you're expecting that multiple users will try to update the same data at the same time.

> **NOTE**   Pessimistic locking is falling further and further out of favor. In upcoming chapters, we'll take a look at why and then focus on optimistic locking.

■ **adLockOptimistic**   While optimistically locked Recordsets might require more code, they are much more appropriate than pessimistic locks for multiuser applications. Two users can simultaneously edit the same record of data. Whoever commits their changes first will successfully update that record, and the second user's attempt to update that data will fail. There's nothing wrong with a failed attempt to update data; you just have to handle such failures elegantly.

■ **adLockBatchOptimistic** Batch optimistic updates are more optimistic than normal optimistic updates. In batch updates, ADO caches the updates until you call the *UpdateBatch* method on the Recordset object. This feature is primarily designed for client-side Recordsets, but it can also work with server-side Recordsets if the OLE DB provider and/or database supports having multiple records with pending changes. For example, SQL Server cursors support this functionality, while Microsoft Access cursors do not.

If you request a LockType that is not supported for the combination of provider, cursor location, and cursor type, you'll receive the closest available LockType.

MarshalOptions Property

In Chapter 15, we'll talk about passing a Recordset object across process boundaries. You can pass a Recordset object from a business object to a client application across a process boundary. The MarshalOptions property, which is read/write at all times, is designed to improve performance in this type of multitiered application using ADO's batch updating feature. If the client application modifies data and you want to pass that data from the Recordset back to the business object to update the database, passing the unmodified records across the process boundary is likely a waste of time and bandwidth. You can designate whether all records will be passed, or only those that have been updated, by setting the MarshalOptions property to one of the MarshalOptionsEnum values shown in the following table.

MARSHALOPTIONSENUM VALUES

Constant	Value	Description
adMarshalAll	0	Default; ADO will pass all records in the Recordset across process boundaries.
adMarshalModifiedOnly	1	ADO will include only records that contain pending changes when the Recordset is passed across process boundaries.

MaxRecords Property

How much data will your queries retrieve? Are you building your own queries, or does your application build queries based on interaction with the user? How do you know that the query you're about to execute won't return thousands upon thousands of records?

The MaxRecords property is designed to limit the number of records returned by a query. By default this property is set to 0, which means that ADO won't place any restrictions on the number of records returned by the query. You can set this property to a long integer prior to opening the Recordset object to limit the number of records returned by your query:

```
strSQL = "SELECT * FROM Customers"
Set rsCustomers = New ADODB.Recordset
rsCustomers.MaxRecords = 100
rsCustomers.Open strSQL, cnDatabase, adOpenStatic
```

ADO doesn't actually implement this feature, however. Instead, ADO passes this information along to the OLE DB provider, and it's up to the provider to support this functionality. At the time of ADO 2.5's release, this feature was implemented for the OLE DB Provider For SQL Server and the SQL Server ODBC driver, as well as for the OLE DB Provider For Oracle and the ODBC driver for Oracle.

If you're using an Access database, you'll find that the MaxRecords property does not affect the number of records your query returns. The OLE DB provider and ODBC driver for Access databases support similar functionality by allowing you to change your query string to include this information in the query itself:

```
strSQL = "SELECT TOP 10 * FROM Customers"
Set rsCustomers = New ADODB.Recordset
rsCustomers.Open strSQL, cnDatabase, adOpenStatic
```

Properties Collection

Like the Connection object, the Recordset object exposes a Properties collection. When you assign the Recordset a valid connection to your database—by either opening the Recordset or setting the ActiveConnection property—ADO populates the Properties collection with provider-specific properties.

ADO also adds entries to the Properties collection that are specific to the ADO Cursor Engine if the Connection object the Recordset is using has its CursorLocation property set to adUseClient, or if the Recordset's own CursorLocation property is set to adUseClient.

If you'd like to learn more about what properties are exposed in the Properties collection for your database connection, examine the Properties collection and check the documentation in the Data Access SDK and/or the documentation provided for your specific OLE DB provider. We'll discuss many of the dynamic properties specific to the ADO Cursor Engine in later chapters of this book.

RecordCount Property

You can use the RecordCount property to determine how many records exist in your Recordset. RecordCount will return −1 if the provider or cursor doesn't support bookmarks. You can also use the *Supports* method of the Recordset object with the adBookmarks constant to determine whether your provider supports this feature so that your Recordset can return a valid value for RecordCount. Checking the value of this property while the Recordset is closed will generate a run-time error.

In general, you can obtain a valid value from the RecordCount property if you're using a Recordset based on a static or keyset cursor. We'll discuss cursors in greater depth in Chapter 7.

Sort Property

You can use the Sort property to control the order of records in your Recordset. This feature is implemented by the ADO Cursor Engine and works with only client-side Recordsets. Set the Sort property to a single field name or multiple field names separated by commas; if the field name contains a space, delimit it with square brackets. You can control whether ADO sorts in ascending or descending order for a particular field by using the ASC or DESC keywords after the field name in the sort string, as shown in the following code. By default, ADO sorts in ascending order.

```
strSQL = "SELECT * FROM Authors"
rsAuthors.CursorLocation = adUseClient
rsAuthors.Open strSQL, cnDatabase, adOpenStatic
rsAuthors.Sort = "[Year Born], Au_ID DESC"
```

To unsort your Recordset, set the Sort property to an empty string.

When you sort on a field for the first time, the ADO Cursor Engine automatically builds a temporary index. This temporary index is deleted when you clear the Sort property. You can build the temporary index yourself before using the Sort property by setting the dynamic Optimize property on the desired Field object to True:

```
rsAuthors("Year Born").Properties("Optimize") = True
```

Source Property

The Source property contains information about the query used to build your Recordset. You can set the Source property to a string or a Command object when the Recordset is closed, but the Source property will return only a string value. If you use a CommandType property value other than adCmdText to submit your query, the Source property will contain the actual query string submitted to the provider. For example, if you specify only the table name in the query and use the adCmdTable constant for CommandType, the Source property will return the string "select * from *TableName*". If you use a parameterized query, the Source property will contain the parameter markers but not the values for those parameters submitted in the query.

State Property

You can check the value of the State property to determine the current state of your Recordset object. There are four possible values for the State property on a Recordset object, defined by the constants in ObjectStateEnum shown in this next table. The first two values are relatively straightforward: when the Recordset object is closed the State property is set to adStateClosed, and when it's open the State property is set to adStateOpen.

OBJECTSTATEENUM VALUES

Constant	Value	Description
adStateClosed	0	The Recordset object is closed.
adStateOpen	1	The Recordset object is open.
adStateConnecting	2	Not applicable to the Recordset object.
adStateExecuting	4	The Recordset object is executing your query.
adStateFetching	8	The Recordset object is fetching the results of your query.

The other two values of the State property applicable to the Recordset object come into play when you're using ADO's asynchronous query features. If you execute your query asynchronously, the Recordset's State property will be set to adStateExecuting. The ADO Cursor Engine also supports fetching the results of your query asynchronously. If you use this feature, the State property will be set to 9 (adStateOpen + adStateFetching) while ADO continues to fetch data.

Status Property

The Status property on the Recordset object describes the status of the current record and is particularly useful when you're working with ADO's batch updating feature. You can use the Status property to examine records that contain pending changes and determine whether the records have been changed by insertion, deletion, or modification. Some developers use this information to modify the database on their own by means of a stored procedure or an action query (INSERT, DELETE, or UPDATE). The Status property can contain a combination of the values in RecordStatusEnum, shown in the following table.

RecordStatusEnum Values

Constant	Value	Description
adRecOK	0	The record has not been modified or was successfully updated.
adRecNew	1	The record corresponds to a new pending record that has not been submitted to the database.
adRecModified	2	The record has been modified. This value is not used for deleted or inserted records, only for existing records that have been modified.
adRecDeleted	4	The record has been deleted from the Recordset.
adRecUnmodified	8	There are no pending changes for this record.
adRecInvalid	16	The record was not saved, because its bookmark is invalid.
adRecMultipleChanges	64	The record was not saved, because it would have affected multiple records.
adRecPendingChanges	128	The record was not saved, because it refers to a pending insert.
adRecCanceled	256	The record was not saved, because the operation was canceled.
adRecCantRelease	1024	The record was not saved, because of existing locks.
adRecConcurrencyViolation	2048	The record was not saved, because optimistic concurrency was in use.
adRecIntegrityViolation	4096	The record was not saved, because the user violated integrity constraints.
adRecMaxChangesExceeded	8192	The record was not saved, because there were too many pending changes.
adRecObjectOpen	16384	The record was not saved, because of a conflict with an open storage object.
adRecOutOfMemory	32768	The record was not saved, because the computer has run out of memory.
adRecPermissionDenied	65536	The record was not saved, because the user has insufficient permissions.
adRecSchemaViolation	131072	The record was not saved, because it violates the structure of the underlying database.
adRecDBDeleted	262144	The record has been deleted from the data source.

You'll also want to use the Status property to determine why conflicts occurred when you called the *UpdateBatch* method on your Recordset. Since ADO relies on the OLE DB provider to determine the cause of the conflict, you might not receive the identical value for the Status property when the same problem occurs with different databases. Your best bet is to create the expected conflicts yourself and observe the results. We'll cover batch updating and conflicts in more detail in Chapter 12.

Keep in mind that this property is a bitmask and that you should use bitwise comparisons. In Visual Basic, you'd do this with the AND operator rather than the = operator.

I've been unable to come up with scenarios that will cause ADO to set this property to one of the more exotic constants, such as adRecObjectOpen, for the Status property.

StayInSync Property

The StayInSync property helps control the behavior of your hierarchical Recordset as you navigate through it. This property is set to True by default, which means that as you navigate through a Recordset, references to child Recordsets are automatically kept in synchronization.

Say you have a customers/orders hierarchical query, and you open the customers-level Recordset. If the customers-level Recordset's StayInSync property is set to True when you reference the orders-level Recordset, the data in the orders-level Recordset will remain synchronized with the current record in the customers-level Recordset as you navigate through the latter. If the StayInSync property on the customers-level Recordset is set to False when you reference the orders-level Recordset, the contents of that reference won't change as you navigate through the customers-level Recordset.

Changing the value of the StayInSync property of a Recordset object will have no effect on references you've already made to child Recordsets.

ADO Recordset Object Functions and Methods

Now let's take a closer look at the functions and methods available on the Recordset object. The following table offers a brief description of each available function and method.

RECORDSET OBJECT FUNCTIONS AND METHODS

Function or Method Name	Description
AddNew	Adds a new record to your Recordset
Cancel	Cancels an asynchronous query
CancelBatch	Cancels pending changes in a Recordset that uses batch optimistic updates
CancelUpdate	Cancels pending changes on a record currently being edited
Clone	Creates a new reference to your Recordset that allows independent navigation
Close	Closes the Recordset object, releasing its contents
CompareBookmarks	Compares two bookmarks in the same Recordset
Delete	Deletes the current record from your Recordset
Find	Searches your Recordset for a record based on a string criteria
GetRows	Returns data from your Recordset in a two-dimensional Variant array
GetString	Returns data from your Recordset in a string
Move	Moves the position of the current record in your Recordset
MoveFirst	Moves to the first record in your Recordset
MoveLast	Moves to the last record in your Recordset
MoveNext	Moves to the next record in your Recordset
MovePrevious	Moves to the previous record in your Recordset
NextRecordset	Retrieves the results of the next query in your batch query
Open	Opens the Recordset
Requery	Reexecutes the query that generated the Recordset
Resync	Retrieves the current data for the records in the Recordset from your database
Save	Writes the contents of the Recordset to a file
Seek	Searches the Recordset for a specified string
Supports	Specifies whether the Recordset supports a particular type of functionality
Update	Writes pending changes to the Recordset
UpdateBatch	Submits pending changes in a Recordset that uses batch optimistic updating to the database

AddNew Method

Use the *AddNew* method to insert new data into the Recordset. This method accepts the following optional parameters:

- ■ ***FieldList*** This parameter accepts a Variant array containing the names of the fields you want to populate.

- ■ ***Values*** This parameter accepts a Variant array containing the values for the fields you want to populate.

There are two ways to use this method. You can call *AddNew*, populate the Value property of the desired Field objects, and then call the *Update* method:

```
rsCustomers.AddNew
rsCustomers.Fields("CustomerID").Value = "NewID"
rsCustomers.Fields("CompanyName") = "New Customer"
rsCustomers.Fields("Address").Value = "23 Highview St."
rsCustomers.Fields("City") = "Westwood"
rsCustomers.Fields("State") = "MA"
rsCustomers.Fields("Zip") = "02090"
rsCustomers.Update
```

You can also perform all these actions in a single function call using the two optional parameters on the *AddNew* method, each of which accepts a Variant array. The first Variant array contains the names of the fields to populate, and the second contains the values to insert into those fields.

```
varFields = Array("CustomerID", "CompanyName", _
                  "Address", "City", "State", "Zip")
varValues = Array("NewID", "New Customer", _
                  "23 Highview St.", "Westwood", _
                  "MA", "02090")
rsCustomers.AddNew varFields, varValues
```

If you're in immediate update mode (with a LockType of adLockOptimistic or adLockPessimistic), the provider will attempt to write the new record to the database as soon as you have completed the insertion (immediately after the call to *Update* in the first example, and after the call to *AddNew* in the second example). If you're using batch optimistic updating, this newly inserted record will be marked as a pending insert in the Recordset (with a Status value of adRecNew) until you call the *UpdateBatch* method to submit the changes to the database.

Cancel Method

The *Cancel* method allows you to terminate the execution of an asynchronous query. Although I've used this feature with server-side Recordsets, I've yet to successfully use it on a client-side Recordset. Before relying on this feature in your application, be sure to test the State property on the Recordset before (to see if the Recordset is open) and after (to see if the Recordset is closed) issuing this method to ensure that *Cancel* is behaving as expected.

CancelBatch Method

Use the *CancelBatch* method when you want to cancel pending batch changes in an optimistically locked Recordset. The *CancelBatch* method has one parameter, which controls the records in your Recordset for which you want to roll back changes:

- **AffectRecords**   Controls which records will be affected by the *CancelBatch* method. This optional parameter takes its value from AffectEnum. See the sidebar for more information on the behavior associated with each constant.

AFFECTENUM VALUES

Constant	Value	Description
adAffectCurrent	1	Affects only the current record.
adAffectGroup	2	Affects only the records currently visible based on whether the Filter property is set to an array of bookmarks or to a value in FilterGroupEnum other than adFilterNone.
adAffectAll	3	Default, but hidden in the type library; affects all records in the Recordset, except for other levels of a hierarchy or other chapters at the same level. If a string-based filter is used, only those records visible through the filter will be affected.
adAffectAllChapters	4	Affects all chapters at the same level of the Recordset, regardless of the current filter.

THE STRANGE TALE OF AFFECTENUM

The ADO development team devised a wonderful way to control the records that a method such as *UpdateBatch* affects: they offered the optional parameter *AffectRecords*. Depending on the value you specify for this parameter, the method will affect only the current record, all the currently visible records, and so on. To me, this is much more elegant than providing separate methods such as *UpdateBatchCurrent* or *UpdateBatchAll*. Simply provide a value from the AffectEnum enumeration in the *AffectRecords* parameter, and voila!

For several reasons, which I'll try to explain without performing a "career-limiting move," the behavior associated with some of the constants is somewhat counter-intuitive.

The behavior associated with the adAffectCurrent value is simple to understand. Use this constant when you want to affect only the current record. Things get more complex when explaining the behavior of the rest of the constants.

Different types of filters exist. The first type is the one that most programmers traditionally envision—one such as *rs.Filter = "Country = 'Germany'"*. I refer to this type of filter as string-based because we're setting the Filter property to a string. As we discussed earlier in the chapter, the Filter property also accepts an array of bookmarks and any of the visible constants from FilterGroupEnum. Internally, ADO handles the string-based filters differently than the other filters.

The adAffectGroup constant affects the currently visible records, but only if the Recordset's filter property has been set to an array of bookmarks or to one of the constants in FilterGroupEnum other than adFilterNone. If you have either no filter or a string-based filter and you use adAffectGroup as the value in the *AffectRecords* parameter, you'll receive a trappable error.

If you use the adAffectAll constant, you'll affect all records in the Recordset. Sort of. If the Recordset's Filter property is set to a string-based filter, only the records visible through the filter will be affected. (Prior to ADO 2.0, adAffectAll affected all records when a string-based filter was in use, including those not visible through the filter.) However, if you're using an array of bookmarks or one of the values from FilterGroupEnum, you'll affect all records, including those that aren't visible through the filter. Also, if you're using a hierarchical Recordset, only the currently visible records will be affected if you use adAffectAll. I'm not sure why the adAffectAll constant is hidden in the type library, but it works just fine and in many cases is the default value for the *AffectRecords* parameter.

We'll talk about hierarchies in more depth in Chapter 14. Until then, this quick overview of how hierarchies and AffectEnum work should suffice. Hierarchies contain elements called "chapters." In a customers/orders hierarchy, a chapter in the orders level of the hierarchy represents the orders associated with the current customer. If you want to affect only the current chapter, use the adAffectAll constant. But if you want to affect all chapters in the current level of the hierarchy, use adAffectAllChapters.

Say you've modified all the customers and all the orders in the hierarchy. If you call *UpdateBatch* on the orders Recordset and use adAffectAllChapters, you'll submit pending changes for all orders—but you won't submit any of the pending changes in the customers Recordset. If you use adAffectAll instead of adAffectAllChapters, *UpdateBatch* will affect only the orders for the current customer.

One last note. Even if you're not using a hierarchical Recordset, adAffectAllChapters might come in handy. If you have a string-based filter on a normal, nonhierarchical Recordset but you want to affect all the records rather than only those visible through the filter, use the adAffectAllChapters constant.

If this seems confusing to you, join the club. It took me a long time to feel like I understood the behavior associated with each constant. The behavior is confusing, but it works.

CancelUpdate Method

The *CancelUpdate* method is similar to the *CancelBatch* method in that it's used to cancel changes made to the Recordset. The *CancelUpdate* method, however, cancels changes for only the current record and is designed for use while the record is being edited. Say you're programmatically adding or modifying a record in optimistic updating mode and you decide that you no longer want to make those changes to the record. If you call the *CancelUpdate* method prior to calling *Update* on the Recordset, the changes you've made will be canceled.

If you find that the *CancelUpdate* method isn't having the effect you anticipated, be sure to check the EditMode property prior to calling *CancelUpdate*. Some bound controls implicitly call the *Update* method on the Recordset, so the *CancelUpdate* method can't undo those changes. Contrary to what's stated in the product documentation, the *CancelUpdate* method will not generate an error if the current record has not been edited.

Clone Method

There may be times when you want to maintain two separate references to the same Recordset. For example, you might want to display two separate grids that contain the same data on the same form at the same time and allow the user to navigate through the grids separately. The *Clone* method is designed to handle this type of scenario.

You can call the *Clone* method to generate a new Recordset object variable. The one parameter on the method can be used to set the LockType of the new Recordset object variable:

- ■ **LockType**   Controls the LockType for the new Recordset object. This optional parameter accepts a value from LockTypeEnum.

By default, the new Recordset object variable will be created with a LockType value of adLockUnspecified, meaning the clone will receive the same value for the LockType property as the value the original Recordset object variable received. You can also use the *LockType* parameter to request that the new Recordset object variable be read-only by setting the parameter to adLockReadOnly.

This method is available only for Recordsets that support bookmarks. The bookmarks are interchangeable between a Recordset and its clones. Attempts to use the *Clone* method on a Recordset that does not support bookmarks (forward-only or dynamic cursors) will generate an error.

Cloned Recordset object variables refer to the same data in memory. Changes made in one Recordset object variable are visible in other variables that refer to the same Recordset. When you're done using a clone of a Recordset, you can call the *Close* method without affecting the original Recordset or the other clones.

Close Method

Speaking of the *Close* method... Calling the *Close* method on the Recordset object releases the Recordset's resources. If you have multiple references to the same Recordset object, the *Close* method will close all references to that Recordset unless you used the *Clone* method to obtain those references. This is demonstrated in the following code. When the *Close* method is called on the *rsOriginal* object, *rsOriginal* and *rsDuplicate* are closed, but *rsClone* remains open.

```
rsOriginal.Open strSQL, cnDatabase, adOpenStatic
Set rsDuplicate = rsOriginal
Set rsClone = rsOriginal.Clone
rsOriginal.Close
```

If you have multiple references to the same Recordset object and don't want to use the *Clone* method, don't use the *Close* method to release your object variable. Instead Visual Basic users can simply let the object variable go out of scope or explicitly set the object variable to Nothing. Setting the last object variable referencing a Recordset to Nothing will implicitly close the Recordset object.

CompareBookmarks Method

If you have the values of two bookmarks, you can use the *CompareBookmarks* method to compare them. This method takes two parameters—the bookmarks you're comparing—and returns a value from CompareEnum, as described in the table that follows.

■ **Bookmark1** This parameter accepts a CompareEnum data type constant. It is the first bookmark to compare.

■ **Bookmark2** This parameter accepts a CompareEnum data type constant and is the second bookmark to compare.

COMPAREENUM VALUES

Constant	Value	Description
adCompareLessThan	0	The first bookmark is before the second.
adCompareEqual	1	The bookmarks are equal.
adCompareGreaterThan	2	The first bookmark is after the second.
adCompareNotEqual	3	The bookmarks are not equal.
adCompareNotComparable	4	The bookmarks cannot be compared.

There are some ground rules for using this method. First, the Recordset must support bookmarks. Second, you should compare bookmark values from the same

Recordset object or its clone. There is no basis of comparison for examining bookmarks from different Recordsets, even if they're two Recordsets based on the same query string. For example, client-side Recordset bookmarks are usually equal to the AbsolutePosition property for that record. If you run the same query twice, there is no guarantee that you'll retrieve the same data: records might have been added, modified, or deleted between the execution of your queries. As a result, even if you're looking at the nth row of each Recordset, you're not guaranteed that those two rows contain the same data.

I mentioned that client-side Recordsets generally use bookmarks that correspond to the record number in the Recordset. This allows ADO to determine which of the two bookmarks appears first in the Recordset if the two bookmarks are not equal. However, there is no requirement that bookmarks be ordered by record number. As a result, you might find that comparing two unequal bookmarks returns adCompareNotEqual, rather than adCompareGreaterThan or adCompareLessThan.

It is worth repeating that you should not compare bookmarks from different Recordset objects (unless they're clones of each other), even if the Recordsets are based on the same query string. If either bookmark you pass into the *Compare-Bookmarks* method does not correspond to a record in the Recordset object whose *CompareBookmarks* method is called, you'll receive a run-time error. However, if you open two client-side Recordsets based on different query strings and compare the bookmarks for the initial record in each Recordset, the *CompareBookmarks* method will return adCompareEqual. Why? The bookmarks both contain the value −1.

Delete **Method**

Use the *Delete* method to delete records from your Recordset. The *Delete* method has one parameter:

- **AffectRecords**   This parameter controls which records will be affected by the *Delete* method. It takes its value from AffectEnum and is optional.

As of ADO 2.5, the only value for *AffectRecords* that I've been able to use successfully is the default—adAffectCurrent. (Why create an optional parameter that accepts no value other than the default? Your guess is as good as mine.) This feature might be more thoroughly implemented in a future release. Until then, if you want to delete more than a single record at a time you can use the *Delete* method within a loop.

After you call the *Delete* method, the deleted record remains current until you move to the next available record. Unless you're using client-side batch optimistic updating, the deleted record is no longer available. Attempting to reference this record will generate an error.

If you're using client-side batch optimistic updating, the record is deleted only within the Recordset until you call the *UpdateBatch* method. You can locate pending deletions such as these by saving bookmark values prior to deleting records. You can also use the Filter property on the Recordset by setting it to adFilterPendingRecords and searching for records with a Status property value of adRecDeleted. Once you've located a pending deletion, you can check the OriginalValue property on each Field object to determine which record you deleted. (See the discussion of Field object properties beginning on page 107.)

Find Method

You can use the *Find* method on the Recordset to locate a record based on a search string. This feature works with client-side and server-side Recordsets, but only if the Recordset supports bookmarks (static or keyset). If the *Find* method is called on a server-side Recordset, ADO walks through the contents of the Recordset to locate the appropriate record. With client-side Recordsets, ADO builds an internal index on the field referenced in the search criteria. This method accepts the following parameters:

- **■** *Criteria* This parameter accepts a string data type. The criteria specifies the field name, value, and operator used to search your Recordset.

- **■** *SkipRecords* This parameter accepts a long data type. It controls how many records to skip before beginning your search and is optional.

- **■** *SearchDirection* This parameter takes its value from SearchDirection-Enum and is optional. It controls the direction in which ADO will search your Recordset.

- **■** *Start* This parameter takes a Variant data type and is optional. It accepts a bookmark to specify where in your Recordset the search will begin.

The *Criteria* parameter is a string—the search criteria. You can specify one field and one value in the string. You can compare the field and the value with these operators: =, <, >, <=, >=, <>, or LIKE. If you use the LIKE operator, you can use a wildcard (*, %, or _) either at the end of the string value or at the beginning and end of the string value. If no records satisfy the criteria, the Recordset will point to BOF or EOF.

You can use the second parameter, *SkipRecords*, to specify how many records you want to skip relative to the current record. This optional parameter accepts a long value, which defaults to 0, and can prove handy if you don't want to include the current record in your search. For example, if you want to loop through all the customers from Germany, you could use code such as the following:

```
strCriteria = "Country = 'Germany'"
rsCustomers.Find strCriteria
Do While Not rsCustomers.EOF
    rsCustomers.Find strCriteria, 1
Loop
```

Of course, if this was your goal, you could have used the Filter property instead.

The third parameter, *SearchDirection*, is also optional and accepts one of the two SearchDirectionEnum constants shown in the following table.

SEARCHDIRECTIONENUM VALUES

Constant	Value	Description
adSearchForward	1	Default; searches forward through the Recordset from the record specified
adSearchBackward	−1	Searches backward through the Recordset from the record specified

The final parameter on the method, *Start*, accepts a Variant and is used to control where the search starts. This optional parameter can accept a bookmark or one of the BookmarkEnum constants shown in this next table.

BOOKMARKENUM VALUES

Constant	Value	Description
adBookmarkCurrent	0	Default; begins the search at the current record
adBookmarkFirst	1	Begins the search at the first record in the Recordset
adBookmarkLast	2	Begins the search at the last record in the Recordset

Generally speaking, you'll want to use this parameter if you have a bookmark value other than the current record at which you want to begin the search, or if you want the search to begin with the first or last record in the Recordset.

One final note on the *Start* parameter. I was surprised to see that the adBookmarkFirst and adBookmarkLast values in this enumeration are positive integers. Why? In the discussion of the Bookmark property on the Recordset, I pointed out that client-side Recordsets use record numbers to denote their position. So how does the *Find* method determine the difference between adBookmarkLast and the bookmark for the second record in a client-side Recordset? Variants. The value of the

Bookmark property for the second record in a client-side Recordset is 2, but it's stored as a double (don't ask me why) in a Variant. The *Find* method determines the data type of the data passed into this parameter to determine whether you're handing it a value from a Bookmark property or a value from BookmarkEnum. I don't know what made me decide to investigate this, but I found it interesting and thought I'd pass it along. A tip of the hat to whoever wrote that ADO code.

The *Find* method was a welcome addition to ADO (it was added in ADO 2.0) and contains much of the same functionality of the DAO Recordset's *Find* methods. ADO's search functionality, however, is not as robust as DAO's. Perhaps it will be more comparable in future versions. But remember that DAO does more than submit queries and handle the results. Unlike ADO, DAO is also a database engine that generates the results of Jet queries, which means it must have some fairly advanced searching routines.

ADO will probably never have the advanced search features of a database system such as SQL Server, Access, or Oracle, but that's not one of its primary purposes. If you really need advanced search capability, write your own code to walk through the contents of the Recordset to locate the desired record. If you even start to complain that ADO isn't able to handle your search with the *Find* method, imagine the code it takes to parse, analyze, and implement complex search criteria.

GetRows Method

Here's a helpful method that gets a lot less attention than its RDO and DAO counterparts did. *GetRows* returns a two-dimensional Variant array that contains data from your Recordset. Because neither DAO nor RDO could pass their objects out of process, this method was used a great deal in multitiered applications. Plus, by storing the results of your queries in Variant arrays, you had complete control over how you handled your data—for example, when you queried your database and how you updated your data (through action queries or stored procedures).

This approach is still perfectly valid and extremely powerful in ADO. If you use precious little of ADO's functionality, your chances of running into any compatibility problems from one version of ADO to the next are almost negligible. However, storing your data in Variants this way isn't sexy. It doesn't make use of functionality provided in rapid application development (RAD) tools such as ADO, and it doesn't sell products because there's little chance you'll use new features. The major drawback to this approach is that you have to write all your code yourself.

Back to the *GetRows* method. This method takes three parameters:

■   ***Rows***   This parameter accepts a GetRowsOptionEnum data type constant and is optional. It specifies how many rows ADO will place in the Variant array returned by the *GetRows* method.

■ **Start**   This parameter accepts a string or a Variant data type and is optional. It accepts a bookmark value to control where ADO will begin reading records for the resulting Variant array.

■ **Fields**   This optional parameter accepts a Variant data type. It accepts a Variant array specifying names of the fields in the Recordset to place in the resulting Variant array.

The *Rows* parameter determines how many records ADO will place in your Variant array. This parameter takes a GetRowsOptionEnum value and defaults to adGetRowsRest (−1), which happens to be the only constant in the data type.

The second parameter, *Start*, accepts a string or a Variant to control where ADO should start placing data into your array. You can pass a bookmark value, adBookmarkFirst, or adBookmarkLast, just as you can with the *Start* parameter on the *Find* method.

You can use the third parameter, *Fields*, to control which fields appear in the two-dimensional Variant array that is returned from this method. The *Fields* parameter is optional and accepts a Variant array of field names, similar to the *FieldList* parameter of the *AddNew* method.

The *GetRows* method on the Recordset object does not require that the Recordset support bookmarks, unless you use the *Start* parameter. If you specify a value for the *Start* parameter that you retrieved from the Recordset's Bookmark property, the Recordset must support bookmarks (static or keyset cursor). If you specify adBookmarkFirst or adBookmarkLast, the Recordset needs to support only scrolling (static, keyset, or dynamic cursor).

After you've called the *GetRows* method, the current record in the Recordset is the first record not used in the Variant array. If there are no more records in the Recordset, EOF will be set to True.

GetString Method

The *GetString* method is similar to the *GetRows* method except that it builds a string rather than a Variant array. Although this method has five parameters (all optional), it's not as complex as you might think.

■ **StringFormat**   This parameter takes its value from StringFormatEnum. It specifies the format used to generate the string.

■ **NumRows**   This parameter accepts a long data type. It specifies how many records will be placed in the resulting string.

■ **ColumnDelimiter**   This parameter accepts a string data type. It specifies the value that ADO will use to delimit the columns in the resulting string.

- **RowDelimiter** This parameter accepts a string data type. It specifies the value that ADO will use to delimit the records in the resulting string.

- **NullExpr** This parameter accepts a string data type. It specifies how ADO will represent a Null value in the resulting string.

The first parameter, *StringFormat*, defaults to adClipString (2). In fact, this is the only available value for the parameter. Originally, the plan was to add functionality to build HTML table strings by means of this parameter, but the more thought the development team gave to this feature, the less appealing it became. They felt that only a small percentage of users would want to use a base HTML table with no built-in formatting or font features. If you want to build a relatively simple HTML table, you can use the *ColumnDelimiter* and *RowDelimiter* parameters. For a more complex HTML table—"I want negative balances to appear red, bold, and italic"—you'll need to loop through the Recordset and build the string by hand.

Use the second parameter, *NumRows*, to control how many records are used to build your string. This parameter accepts a long value and defaults to adGetRowsRest (−1).

The third and fourth parameters on the *GetString* method, *ColumnDelimiter* and *RowDelimiter*, control how the fields and records are delimited in your string. By default, these parameters are set to the tab and carriage return, respectively. These defaults are handy if you want to display the contents of your Recordset in one of the Visual Basic FlexGrids or in a Microsoft Excel spreadsheet. As just mentioned, you could build an HTML table by using the HTML table delimiters in these parameters.

The fifth and final parameter on this method is *NullExpr*. Null values don't translate easily to strings, and many programmers forget this when trying to display the contents of fields on a form. Null values in your Recordset are converted to the value in the *NullExpr* parameter, which defaults to an empty string.

Move Method

The *Move* method moves the cursor from one record to another within a Recordset. This method uses two parameters:

- **NumRecords** This parameter accepts a long data type. It specifies the number of positions that ADO will move the current record pointer.

- **Start** This optional parameter accepts a string or a Variant data type that contains a bookmark to control where the navigation will commence.

The first parameter, *NumRecords*, is required and accepts a long value to determine how many records to move from the current position. If you specify a negative value for this first parameter, ADO will move backward that number of records. Note, however, that you can't specify a negative value if the cursor is forward-only, unless you remain inside the currently cached records.

If you specify a number that would move the Recordset beyond its boundaries, the Recordset will be set to BOF or EOF, depending on the direction you're moving. It's worth mentioning that *Move 0* in ADO does not behave the same way as it does in RDO. In fact, calling *Move 0* in ADO does nothing whatsoever.

The *Move* method also accepts an optional parameter, *Start*, which controls where ADO will begin to move from. You can use this parameter only if your Recordset supports bookmarks (static or keyset cursor). This property defaults to adBookmarkCurrent, and you can set it to adBookmarkFirst, adBookmarkLast, or any valid bookmark value.

MoveFirst, MoveLast, MoveNext, and *MovePrevious* Methods

The *MoveFirst* method moves to the first record. *MoveLast* moves to the last record. *MoveNext* moves forward to the next record in the Recordset, and *MovePrevious* moves back one record. If you're using a Recordset that supports only scrolling forward, calling *MoveFirst, MoveLast,* or *MovePrevious* will generate a run-time error.

If you call the *MoveNext* method while you're currently examining the last record in your Recordset, the EOF property will be set to True. Trying to check the value of any of the fields in your Recordset while at EOF will generate a run-time error. Similarly, if you call *MovePrevious* while examining the first record in your Recordset, the BOF property will be set to True.

The following code uses the *MoveNext* method to move through the Recordset and print the contents of the CustomerID field for all records:

```
strSQL = "SELECT * FROM Customers"
rsCustomers.Open strSQL, cnDatabase, adOpenForwardOnly
Do While Not rsCustomers.EOF
    Debug.Print rsCustomers.Fields("CustomerID").Value
    rsCustomers.MoveNext
Loop
```

If you have changes to a record pending (you've modified the current record but haven't yet called the *Update* or *CancelUpdate* method), ADO implicitly calls the *Update* method to commit those changes when you call one of these *Move* methods.

NextRecordset Method

Some database systems (such as Oracle and SQL Server) support batch queries, which allow you to submit multiple query strings at once. You can then process the results, one set at a time. In ADO, the *NextRecordset* method allows you to move from one set of results to the next set.

The *NextRecordset* method takes one parameter:

■ ***RecordsAffected*** This output parameter will contain the number of records affected if the query modifies data in your database. It is a long data type and is optional.

If you wanted to execute a number of action queries and retrieve the number of records affected by each query, you could use code such as the following:

```
strSQL = "DELETE FROM [Order Details] " & _
            "WHERE OrderID = 10251; " & _
         "DELETE FROM Orders WHERE OrderID = 10251"
Set rsData = cnDatabase.Execute(strSQL, _
                                   lngRecordsAffected)
MsgBox lngRecordsAffected & " Order Detail(s) deleted."
Set rsData = rsData.NextRecordset(lngRecordsAffected)
MsgBox lngRecordsAffected & " Order(s) deleted."
```

Because these are action queries, the only data returned is the number of records affected by the query; no records or fields are returned. If you were to check the State property of the Recordset object, you'd see a value of adStateClosed, so don't stop retrieving Recordsets when you receive one with this State value. Test until the returning Recordset is set to Nothing. Just make sure that you don't dimension the Recordset in Visual Basic using the keyword New. With this keyword, every time you check the object variable it will be set to a new Recordset object if the Recordset was set to Nothing. For example, look at the following code. The Do While loop in this code snippet is an infinite loop.

```
Dim rsData As ADODB.Recordset

strSQL = "SELECT * FROM Customers; " & _
         "DELETE FROM Customers WHERE 1 = 0; " & _
         "SELECT * FROM Orders"
Set rsData = New ADODB.Recordset
rsData.Open strSQL, cnDatabase, adOpenForwardOnly
Do While Not (rsData Is Nothing)
    Set rsData = rsData.NextRecordset
Loop
```

In each of the code snippets we've used to demonstrate this method, we've stored the Recordset object returned from the call to *NextRecordset* in the same object variable we used to call *NextRecordset*. However, using the same object variable is not mandatory; you could return the next Recordset into a different one:

```
strSQL = "SELECT * FROM Customers; " & _
         "SELECT * FROM Orders"
rsCustomers.Open strSQL, cnDatabase, adOpenStatic
Set rsOrders = rsCustomers.NextRecordset
```

If you're using a server-side Recordset, the data for the initial Recordset is lost as soon as you call *NextRecordset*. However, if you're using client-side Recordsets, you can scroll through the contents of each of these Recordsets. In the previous code example, the data in the *rsCustomers* Recordset is still available after the *NextRecordset* method is called. You also cannot pass the initial Recordset out of process and then call the *NextRecordset* method in the other process. This functionality might be available in a subsequent release.

ADO does not parse the query string that you pass to it. It simply passes this query string along to the OLE DB provider. It's up to the OLE DB provider and/or database system to parse and process the query or queries. ADO doesn't actually submit each query in a batch query separately, but it could in a future release.

The *NextRecordset* method is not available on client-side Recordsets when using Remote Data Service (RDS).

It's worth noting that action queries in a batch process or a stored procedure might return a closed, empty Recordset. SQL Server users can prevent retrieving unwanted Recordsets by using SET NOCOUNT ON and SET NOCOUNT OFF to control this behavior. Check your SQL Server documentation for more information on this feature.

Open **Method**

The *Open* method is the most powerful and versatile method of retrieving data from your database. You can set the ActiveConnection, Source, LockType, and CursorType properties on the Recordset prior to using the *Open* method, or you can supply this data in its parameters, all of which are optional:

- **Source** This parameter accepts a Variant. You can use the *Source* parameter to specify the query string or Command object you want to use. If you do use a Command object in this parameter, be sure to leave the *ActiveConnection* parameter on this method blank. Instead, set the ActiveConnection property on the Command object. This parameter can also contain a table name, a stored procedure call, a URL, a filename, or a Stream object.

- **ActiveConnection** This parameter accepts a Variant in the form of a connection string or an open Connection object, just like the ActiveConnection property.

- **CursorType** This parameter accepts a CursorTypeEnum value. (See page 60 for a list of CursorTypeEnum values.)

- **LockType** This parameter accepts a value from LockTypeEnum. (See page 67 for a list of LockTypeEnum values.)

■ ***Options*** This parameter accepts a CommandTypeEnum value and/or a combination of asynchronous ExecuteOptionEnum constants, as respectively shown in the following two tables.

COMMANDTYPEENUM VALUES

Constant	Value	Description
adCmdText	1	ADO will pass the query string as is to the OLE DB provider.
adCmdTable	2	ADO will assume that the query string is the name of a table and attempt to modify the query string appropriately.
adCmdStoredProc	4	ADO will assume that the query string is the name of a stored procedure and attempt to modify the query string appropriately.
adCmdUnknown	8	ADO will try to execute the query string in a variety of ways.
adCmdFile	256	ADO will open the Recordset from a file.
adCmdTableDirect	512	ADO will attempt to use an optional interface on OLE DB providers to retrieve the contents of the table.

EXECUTEOPTIONENUM VALUES

Constant	Value	Description
adAsyncExecute	16	ADO will execute the query string asynchronously.
adAsyncFetch	32	ADO will fetch the results of the query asynchronously.
adAsyncFetchNonBlocking	64	ADO will fetch the results of the query asynchronously without blocking the main thread.
adExecuteNoRecords	128	No records are returned from the query. (This option isn't available on the Recordset object.)

We've discussed most of these parameters earlier in this chapter in terms of their use as properties. We'll also talk more about cursors and updating your database in later chapters. For now, let's talk about the *Options* parameter and using values from CommandTypeEnum and ExecuteOptionEnum. The *Options* parameter is a bitmask, so you can use the sum of constants, such as adCmdTable + adAsyncExecute, as shown in the following code:

```
rsCustomers.Open "Customers", cnNorthwind, _
                adOpenStatic, adLockReadOnly, _
                adCmdTable + adAsyncExecute
```

In an attempt to make ADO friendlier, the concept of a CommandType was introduced. You can specify a table name or a stored procedure name, and ADO will try to execute that query string on its own, as well as trying to retrieve the contents of a table with the same name or execute a stored procedure of the same name. While this functionality is helpful for the novice developer, it means that ADO might need to pass multiple query strings to your OLE DB provider before it finds a query string that executes successfully.

Although I appreciate this attempt to simplify things, I would never ask ADO to figure out what type of query I'm executing unless absolutely necessary. Besides, it's not always as simple as it sounds. When you pass ADO a table name and specify adCmdTable in the *Options* parameter, ADO simply prepends "select * from " to the query string. If the table you want to query contains a space in its name, this query will fail if you did not delimit the table name yourself. This point is illustrated by the following code:

```
'This will fail.
rsOrderDetails.Open "Order Details", cnNorthwind, _
                adOpenStatic, adLockReadOnly, _
                adCmdTable

'This will succeed.
rsOrderDetails.Open "[Order Details]", cnNorthwind, _
                adOpenStatic, adLockReadOnly, _
                adCmdTable
```

Don't get me wrong—there are times when I use this functionality; I just grin (or grouse) and bear it when it doesn't work the way I'm expecting it to. I suggest using the adCmdText constant for your CommandType, but I'll admit I do use the adCmdFile constant when I want to reopen a Recordset that I had previously persisted to a file:

```
rsCustomers.Open "C:\Customers.rst", Nothing, _
                adOpenStatic, adLockReadOnly, adCmdFile
```

We'll talk about this feature more in Chapter 13, when we discuss persistence.

ADO 2.5 allows you to use a Stream object that contains Recordset data (stored by using the Recordset's *Save* method) in the *Source* parameter.

The other constant that I use from time to time in the *Options* parameter is adCmdTableDirect. This command type closely resembles DAO's table-type Recordset.

Some OLE DB providers will implement an optional feature that can provide better performance when retrieving all records and columns from a table. If you need to retrieve the entire contents of a particular table, you might want to try using this constant and find out whether your OLE DB provider supports it and whether it will improve the performance of your application.

You can also use the *Options* parameter on the *Recordset.Open* method to utilize ADO's asynchronous functionality. If you specify adAsyncExecute, the query will be executed asynchronously.

The adAsyncFetch and adAsyncFetchNonBlocking options apply to client-side Recordsets only. Once ADO has retrieved an initial number of records, the rest of the records are fetched on a background thread. If you attempt to move to a record that has not been fetched and you use the adAsyncFetch constant, the main thread will be blocked while ADO continues to retrieve data. Once that record is available, the main thread will resume. With the adAsyncFetchNonBlocking constant, if you move beyond the records that have been fetched, you'll move to EOF instead and the main thread will not be blocked.

Requery Method

The *Requery* method on the Recordset object reexecutes the query that created the Recordset object. It has the following parameter:

■ ***Options*** This optional parameter accepts an ExecuteOptionEnum value. (See page 89 for a list of ExecuteOptionEnum values.) You can call the *Requery* method asynchronously by setting this parameter to adAsyncExecute.

You can use this method on server-side or client-side Recordsets. This method is very useful if you want to repeatedly execute the same parameterized query. Simply change the value of the appropriate Parameter object or objects, and then call the *Requery* method on the Recordset object. We'll talk more about parameterized queries in Chapter 5, when we discuss the Command object.

When you call the *Requery* method, you're rerunning the query—similar to calling the *Close* and then *Open* methods on the Recordset object. Although your data will be fresher than it was before you called the *Requery* method, the contents of your Recordset might have changed dramatically. Changes made by other users (modifications, insertions, and deletions) will affect your query. Records that were in your Recordset prior to calling *Requery* might not appear in the Recordset after the call. For these reasons, you should not rely on bookmark values retrieved prior to calling *Requery*. In many cases, using a previously retrieved bookmark for a server-side Recordset will result in a run-time error.

Resync Method

The *Resync* method is similar to the *Requery* method: you use it to refresh the data in your Recordset. It has the following two parameters:

- **AffectRecords** An optional parameter, it accepts a value from AffectEnum. Use this parameter to control which records you want to resynchronize. This parameter defaults to adAffectAll.

- **ResyncValues** This parameter is optional and accepts a value from ResyncEnum. Use this parameter to control where ADO stores the newly retrieved data. This parameter defaults to adResyncAllValues.

The *Resync* method differs from the *Requery* method in that it does not reexecute the query that generated the Recordset object. Instead, ADO examines the record you want to refresh and executes a separate query to retrieve the current contents of that record in the database. For example, if you created your Recordset with the query

```
SELECT CustomerID, CompanyName, BalanceDue FROM Customers
```

calling the *Resync* method would cause ADO to execute the following query for each record, where x is the value of the CustomerID for each record in the Recordset:

```
SELECT CustomerID, CompanyName, BalanceDue FROM Customers
    WHERE CustomerID = x
```

Since you're not actually reexecuting the query that you originally submitted to generate the data in your Recordset, new records that might satisfy the results of your query will not be retrieved when calling the *Resync* method.

This method is not available for server-side Recordsets. If you call the *Resync* method on a server-side Recordset, you'll generate a run-time error. Prior to ADO 2.0, calling *Resync* on a server-side Recordset did not generate an error; ADO executed the *Requery* method instead.

You can use the *Resync* method only on client-side Recordset objects that are not marked read-only. If the Recordset is read-only, the ADO Cursor Engine does not need to retrieve much metadata for your Recordset, such as which fields constitute the primary key or which fields are updatable. Without this metadata, ADO cannot create the queries to retrieve the most up-to-date data for the records in your Recordset.

You can use the first parameter, *AffectRecords*, to control which records you want to resynchronize. By default, this parameter is set to adAffectAll. For more information on the behavior associated with the different possible values for the *AffectRecords* parameter, see the sidebar on pages 76–77 about the AffectEnum enumeration in the *CancelBatch* method.

The second parameter, *ResyncValues*, is designed to help manage batch updates that fail as a result of modifications made by other users. By default, ADO will store the newly retrieved data in the Value property of the Field objects in your Recordset. If you're attempting to determine why some batch updates failed, you probably don't want to overwrite the information you currently have stored in the Value property. When you specify adResyncUnderlyingValues in the optional *ResyncValues* parameter, ADO will store the newly retrieved data in the UnderlyingValue property of the Field objects instead of in the Value property. We'll discuss these properties in more depth as we cover how to handle optimistic updating conflicts in Chapter 12.

Save Method

You can call the *Save* method to save the contents of a Recordset to a file and re-open it later. This method accepts two parameters:

■ **Destination**   This is an optional parameter. It accepts a string containing the filename where you want to save the recordset or a Stream object.

■ **PersistFormat**   This optional parameter accepts a value from Persist-FormatEnum; it controls the format for the recordset file. *PersistFormat* defaults to adPersistADTG but can be set to adPersistXML as of ADO 2.1.

The first time you save a recordset, you must specify a filename in the *Destination* parameter. Only the records currently visible will be stored in the file. If you specify a filename that already exists, you'll generate a run-time error. Once you've opened your recordset from a file, you can resave its contents to that file and overwrite the old data by omitting the *Destination* parameter.

The *Save* method was added in ADO 2.0, and the only available format was adPersistADTG—the same format used when passing a Recordset object out of process. As of ADO 2.1, you can also save a Recordset to an XML file through the adPersistXML constant. Although the ability to write to an XML file is part of ADO 2.1 and later, the ability to turn an XML file back into a Recordset is actually implemented through the Microsoft Internet Explorer XML parser. If you do not have the parser that is included with Internet Explorer 5 on your machine, you will not be able to open the Recordset you saved into an XML file.

Seek Method

At the time of this writing, the only OLE DB provider that supports the *Seek* method is the Jet 4.0 OLE DB Provider, but only when used with Jet 4 and Access–formatted databases and server-side Recordsets with a CommandType of adCmdTableDirect. This method is similar to the *Find* method, but the OLE DB provider, rather than the

ADO Cursor Engine, does the searching. To determine whether your OLE DB provider supports this functionality, use the *Supports* method on the Recordset object with the adSeek constant. The *Seek* method has two parameters:

■ **KeyValues** This parameter is required. It accepts a Variant array of the key values—one value per field in the current index. If the index in use is based on a single field, you can omit the Variant array and simply supply the key value you want to locate.

■ **SeekOption** This parameter is optional and accepts one of the values from SeekEnum shown in the following table. It defaults to adSeekFirstEQ.

SEEKENUM VALUES

Constant	Value	Description
adSeekFirstEQ	1	Seeks the first key matching the criteria
adSeekLastEQ	2	Seeks the last key matching the criteria
adSeekAfterEQ	4	Seeks the first key that matches the criteria; if none are found, seeks the key following the position where the key would be found
adSeekAfter	8	Seeks the key following the key in the criteria
adSeekBeforeEQ	16	Seeks the first key that matches the criteria; if none are found, seeks the key prior to the position where the key would be found
adSeekBefore	32	Seeks the key prior to the key in the criteria

The code that follows is an example of how to use the *Seek* method with an Access 2000 database:

```
Set rsCustomers = New ADODB.Recordset
rsCustomers.Open "Customers", cnNorthwind, adOpenStatic, _
                adLockReadOnly, adCmdTableDirect
rsCustomers.Index = "City"
rsCustomers.MoveFirst
rsCustomers.Seek Array("London")
```

Supports Method

You can use the *Supports* method on the Recordset object to understand what functionality is available based on your choice of OLE DB provider, CursorLocation, CursorType, and LockType. It takes one parameter:

■ **CursorOptions** This parameter is required and accepts one of the values from CursorOptionEnum, shown in this next table.

CursorOptionEnum Values

Constant	Value	Functionality Your Recordset Supports
adAddNew	16778240	*AddNew* method
adApproxPosition	16384	AbsolutePage and AbsolutePosition properties
adBookmark	8192	Bookmark property
adDelete	16779264	*Delete* method
adFind	524288	*Find* method
adHoldRecords	256	Very similar to bookmarks
adIndex	8388608	Index property
adMovePrevious	512	*MovePrevious, MoveFirst, Move,* and *GetRows* methods
adNotify	262144	Events
adResync	131072	*Resync* method
adSeek	4194304	*Seek* method
adUpdate	16809984	*Update* method
adUpdateBatch	65536	*UpdateBatch* and *CancelBatch* methods

If you're building an application that allows the user to generate ad hoc queries, you might want to use the *Supports* method to determine which functionality is available in the Recordset you've just opened.

To be truthful, I don't know the purpose of adHoldRecords. The documentation implies that you can navigate through the Recordset and retrieve more data without having to commit pending changes, but the function returns True on read-only Recordsets when using this constant.

Update Method

Use the *Update* method to commit changes to the current record. When you call the *Update* method, the changes are submitted to the database as well as to the Recordset unless you're using batch updates (LockType = adLockBatchOptimistic). In that case, the changes in the modified records are cached until you call the *UpdateBatch* method. The *Update* method has two optional parameters:

- **Fields** This parameter accepts a Variant array of field names that you want to update.

- **Values** This parameter accepts a Variant array of values that correspond to the fields you want to update.

You can use the *Update* method in one of two ways. You can modify the Value property of Field objects and then call the *Update* method, or you can call the *Update* method and use the optional parameters as shown:

```
rsCustomers.Update Array("CompanyName", "BalanceDue"), _
                   Array("New Name", 100.00)
```

This code is equivalent to:

```
rsCustomers.Fields("CompanyName").Value = "New Name"
rsCustomers.Fields("BalanceDue").Value = 100.00
rsCustomers.Update
```

Note that there is no *Edit* method on the Recordset object. If you want to modify a record, you can start by modifying the Value property on the desired Field objects, or you can use the optional parameters on the *Update* method as was shown.

If you call the *Update* method on a client-side Recordset that is not using batch updates and does not have a connection to the database, ADO will not generate a run-time error and will mark that record as if it had successfully updated a database.

UpdateBatch Method

If you're using batch updates, call *UpdateBatch* to submit the cached changes in the Recordset to your database. This method has one parameter:

- **AffectRecords**   This is an optional parameter that accepts a value from AffectEnum. It defaults to adAffectAll and determines which records' pending changes you want to submit to the database.

You can use the *AffectRecords* parameter to control which records' changes will be submitted to the database. (See the "*CancelBatch* Method" section in this chapter on page 76 for more information on the behavior associated with each of the AffectEnum values.)

If you call the *UpdateBatch* method on a client-side Recordset that doesn't have a connection to the database, ADO will not generate a run-time error and will mark the applicable records as if they were successfully updated in a database.

ADO RECORDSET OBJECT EVENTS

ADO introduced events in version 2.0. They can greatly help you organize your code and respond to actions on your Recordset objects. Documenting all the different ways the events could fire, however, would be an overwhelming and nearly impossible task. Instead, we'll cover the basics of each event, as described in the following table. If you're looking for a list of events and parameter values for a specific scenario—

"What if a user modifies a field in the grid and then clicks on another record?"—your best bet is to put code into each of the event handlers, create the desired scenario, verify the events that fire, and check the value of the parameters in those events.

RECORDSET OBJECT EVENTS

Event Name	Description
EndOfRecordset	Fires when you navigate beyond the last record of data in your Recordset
FetchComplete	Fires when the ADO Cursor Engine retrieves the last of the data in your Recordset that uses asynchronous fetching
FetchProgress	Fires after the ADO Cursor Engine retrieves a batch of records for your Recordset that uses asynchronous fetching
FieldChangeComplete	Fires after you've modified the value for a field
MoveComplete	Fires after the current position of the Recordset changes
RecordChangeComplete	Fires after you modify a record
RecordsetChangeComplete	Fires after the Recordset object has changed
WillChangeField	Fires before the contents of a field change
WillChangeRecord	Fires before the contents of a record change
WillChangeRecordset	Fires before the Recordset object changes
WillMove	Fires before the current position in the Recordset changes

EndOfRecordset Event

This event fires when you move beyond the last record in your Recordset. There's a property you can set on most Visual Basic navigation controls that enables the control to automatically add a record to the end of your Recordset when you reach EOF. With this event, you can provide similar functionality in your application. The *EndOfRecordset* event supports three parameters:

■ *fMoreData* This parameter accepts Boolean operators. Set it to True if you appended a new record to the end of your Recordset in the event handler.

■ *adStatus* This parameter returns a value from EventStatusEnum, as shown in the table on the following page.

■ *pRecordset* This parameter is a pointer to the Recordset object that fired the event.

You can also use the *EndOfRecordset* event simply to determine when you've reached the end of your Recordset.

EVENTSTATUSENUM VALUES

Constant	Value	Description
adStatusOK	1	The operation that caused the event was successful.
adStatusErrorsOccurred	2	The operation that caused the event failed because of an error or errors.
adStatusCantDeny	3	The event cannot request cancellation of the pending operation.
adStatusCancel	4	Requests cancellation of the operation that caused the event to occur.
adStatusUnwantedEvent	5	Prevents subsequent notifications of the event.

If you do not want this event to continue to fire, you can set the *adStatus* parameter to adStatusUnwantedEvent.

FetchComplete Event

This event fires only if you're using asynchronous fetching with a client-side Recordset. After the final *FetchProgress* event fires, *FetchComplete* will fire. The *FetchComplete* event has three parameters:

- **pError**   If *adStatus* is set to adStatusErrorsOccurred, this parameter is a pointer to an Error object.

- **adStatus**   This parameter takes its value from EventStatusEnum, as shown in the table above.

- **pRecordset**   This is a pointer to the Recordset object that fired the event.

Setting *adStatus* to adStatusUnwantedEvent will not prevent the event from firing in the future. We'll talk more about ADO's asynchronous fetching feature and events at the end of this chapter.

FetchProgress Event

Like the *FetchComplete* event, the *FetchProgress* event fires when you use asynchronous fetching with the ADO Cursor Engine. It has four parameters:

■   *Progress*   This parameter accepts a long value.

■   *MaxProgress*   This parameter accepts a long value.

■   *adStatus*   This parameter takes its value from EventStatusEnum, as shown in the table on the preceding page.

■   *pRecordset*   This parameter is a pointer to the Recordset object that fired the event.

The *Progress* and *MaxProgress* parameters are designed to help you determine what percentage of the fetching has completed thus far. To date, I've retrieved only a value of 1 from the *MaxProgress* parameter and 0 for *Progress* until the final time the event fires.

Two dynamic properties on client-side Recordsets can help determine how often this event fires: Initial Fetch Size and Background Fetch Size. They default to 50 and 15, respectively. These properties are available as soon as you set the Recordset's CursorLocation property to adUseClient. Once ADO has retrieved the number of records specified in the Initial Fetch Size property, the *ExecuteComplete* event on the Connection object will fire. From that point on, after ADO retrieves the number of records specified in the Background Fetch Size property, it will fire the *FetchProgress* event. The *FetchProgress* event will also be fired if ADO reaches the end of the Recordset without retrieving the number of records specified by Background Fetch Size. After *FetchProgress* fires for the final time, *FetchComplete* will fire.

Setting *adStatus* to adStatusUnwantedEvent will prevent the event from firing again.

WillChangeField and *FieldChangeComplete* Events

Whenever you change the Value property of Field objects in your Recordset, the *WillChangeField* and *FieldChangeComplete* events will fire. These events use the following syntax:

```
WillChangeField cFields, Fields, adStatus, pRecordset
FieldChangeComplete cFields, Fields, pError, adStatus, pRecordset
```

The following is a list of the combined parameters for both *WillChangeField* and *FieldChangeComplete*:

■   *cFields*   This is a long data type parameter that specifies the number of fields modified.

■   *Fields*   This parameter accepts a Variant array of Field objects.

■   *pError*   This parameter is a pointer to the Error object if an error occurred.

- **adStatus** This parameter takes its value from EventStatusEnum, as shown in the table on page 98.

- **pRecordset** This parameter is a pointer to the Recordset object that fired the event.

If you want to determine which fields have been or will be modified, you can use code as follows in the event handler for either event:

```
Dim lngCounter As Long

For lngCounter = 0 To cFields - 1
    Debug.Print Fields(lngCounter).Name
Next lngCounter
```

If an error occurs, you can use the *pError* parameter in the *FieldChangeComplete* event handler to determine the cause.

You can set the *adStatus* parameter to adStatusUnwantedEvent to prevent either event from occurring in the future. You can set this parameter to adStatusCancel if you want to prevent the Field from being updated. In the *FieldChangeComplete* event, this parameter will be set to adStatusErrorsOccurred if an error occurs.

As far as I can tell, there is no way to use the *WillChangeField* event to examine the change that will be made to the Field.

WillChangeRecord and RecordChangeComplete Events

You can use the *WillChangeRecord* and *RecordChangeComplete* events to keep track of changes to the records in your Recordset. These events will fire as a result of calls to the *Update*, *Delete*, *CancelUpdate*, *AddNew*, *UpdateBatch*, *CancelBatch*, or *Resync* methods on the Recordset. The events will also fire the first time you modify the value of a field. When the event fires, the only records visible through the filter are those affected by the action that caused these events to fire. You cannot change the Filter property in either of these events. The *WillChangeRecord* and *RecordChangeComplete* events use the following syntax:

```
WillChangeRecord adReason, cRecords, adStatus, pRecordset
RecordChangeComplete adReason, cRecords, pError, adStatus, pRecordset
```

The following is a list of the combined parameters for both these events:

- **adReason** This parameter accepts certain values from EventReasonEnum.

- **cRecords** A long data type parameter, it specifies the number of records modified.

■   ***pError***   This parameter is a pointer to the Error object if an error occurred.

■   ***adStatus***   This parameter accepts a value from EventStatusEnum, as shown in the table on page 98.

■   ***pRecordset***   This parameter is a pointer to the Recordset object that fired the event.

The *adReason* parameter can help you understand why the event fired. Changing the current record in different ways will cause the *adReason* parameter to contain different values, as detailed in the following table.

EVENTREASONENUM VALUES AVAILABLE TO *WILLCHANGERECORD* AND *RECORDCHANGECOMPLETE*

Constant	Value	Description
adRsnFirstChange	11	The record was modified for the first time. Subsequent modifications to the record prior to submitting those changes to the database will not cause the events to fire.
adRsnAddNew	1	The record was added by using *AddNew*. Subsequent modifications to the record prior to submitting those changes to the database will not cause the events to fire.
adRsnDelete	2	The record was deleted.
adRsnUpdate	3	The pending changes in the record were submitted to the database by *Update* (for LockTypes of adLockOptimistic or adLockPessimistic), or by *UpdateBatch* (for a LockType of adLockBatchOptimistic).
adRsnUndoUpdate	4	A pending modification was canceled by *CancelUpdate* or *CancelBatch*.
adRsnUndoAddNew	5	A pending insertion was canceled by *CancelUpdate* or *CancelBatch*.
adRsnUndoDelete	6	A pending deletion was canceled by *CancelBatch*.
adRsnResynch	8	The record was changed by calling the *Resync* method.

Setting the *adStatus* parameter to adStatusUnwantedEvent will prevent the event from firing in the future. If you want to cancel the operation that caused the event, you can set the *adStatus* parameter to adStatusCancel in the *WillChangeRecord* event handler so long as the parameter was not equal to adStatusCantDeny when the event fired. Setting the *adStatus* parameter to adStatusCancel will cause the function that fired the event to return an error.

WillChangeRecordset and RecordsetChangeComplete Events

These events can fire as a result of changing the Filter property or by calling *Requery*, *Close*, or the different navigation methods on the Recordset. They use the following syntax:

```
WillChangeRecordset adReason, adStatus, pRecordset
RecordsetChangeComplete adReason, pError, adStatus, pRecordset
```

The following is a list of the combined parameters for these events:

- **adReason**   This parameter takes certain values from EventReasonEnum.

- **pError**   This parameter is a pointer to the Error object if an error occurred.

- **adStatus**   This parameter accepts a value from EventStatusEnum, as shown in the table on page 98.

- **pRecordset**   This parameter is a pointer to the Recordset object that fired the event.

The *adReason* parameter can help you understand why the event fired. Changing the current record in different ways will cause the *adReason* parameter to contain different values. (See the following table.) For example, if your Recordset does not support bookmarks (server-side forward-only and dynamic cursors), these events will fire when ADO refreshes the cache. This can happen the first time you examine the data in the Recordset object; by navigating outside the currently cached records by calling the *Move*, *MoveNext*, or similar methods; or by setting the Filter property. If you call the *Requery* method on a Recordset that doesn't support bookmarks, these events will fire with an *adReason* of adRsnMove.

EVENTREASONENUM VALUES AVAILABLE TO WILLCHANGERECORDSET AND RECORDSETCHANGECOMPLETE

Constant	Value	Description
adRsnRequery	7	An operation requeried the Recordset.
adRsnSynch	8	The query has been resynchronized with the database.

Constant	Value	Description
adRsnClose	9	Calling the *Open* or *Requery* method (whether your Recordset supports bookmarks or not) will cause the *RecordsetChangeComplete* event (but not the *WillChangeRecordset* event) to fire with this value for the *adReason* parameter.
adRsnMove	10	*Requery* has been called on a Recordset that doesn't support bookmarks.

Setting the *adStatus* parameter to adStatusUnwantedEvent will prevent the event from firing in the future. If you want to cancel the operation that caused the event, you can set the *adStatus* parameter to adStatusCancel in the *WillChangeRecordset* event so long as the parameter was not equal to adStatusCantDeny when the event fired. Setting *adStatus* to adStatusCancel will cause the function that fired the event to return an error.

WillMove and *MoveComplete* Events

The *WillMove* and *MoveComplete* events fire when you navigate through your Recordset. These events use the following syntax:

```
WillMove adReason, adStatus, pRecordset
MoveComplete adReason, pError, adStatus, pRecordset
```

They support the following parameters:

- **adReason**   This parameter takes certain values from EventReasonEnum.

- **pError**   This is a pointer to the Error object if an error occurred.

- **adStatus**   This parameter accepts a value from EventStatusEnum, as shown in the table on page 98.

- **pRecordset**   This parameter is a pointer to the Recordset object that fired the event.

The *adReason* parameter can help you understand why the event fired. Changing the current record in different ways will cause the *adReason* parameter to contain different values, as explained in the following table.

EventReasonEnum Values
Available to *WillMove* and *MoveComplete*

Constant	Value	Description
adRsnRequery	7	The *Requery* method was called. Currently, calling *Requery* will cause the *WillMove* and *MoveComplete* events to fire twice, first with an *adReason* of adRsnRequery and then with an *adReason* of adRsnMove.
adRsnMove	10	Calling the *Move* or *Requery* method, or moving to another record by setting the AbsolutePage, AbsolutePosition, Bookmark, Filter, or Index property, will cause these events to fire with this value in the *adReason* parameter.
adRsnMoveFirst	12	The *MoveFirst* method was called.
adRsnMoveNext	13	The *MoveNext* method was called.
adRsnMovePrevious	14	The *MovePrevious* method was called.
adRsnMoveLast	15	The *MoveLast* method was called.

Setting the *adStatus* parameter to adStatusUnwantedEvent will prevent the event from firing in the future. If you want to cancel the operation that caused the event, you can set the *adStatus* parameter to adStatusCancel in the *WillMove* event as long as the parameter is not equal to adStatusCantDeny when the event is fired. Setting *adStatus* to adStatusCancel will cause the function that fired the event to return an error.

ADO Fields Collection

The ADO Fields collection contains the Field objects for your Recordset. Like all collections, the Fields collection exposes a Count property and an Item property (the default). With the Item property, you can return a particular Field by name or index.

ADO 2.5 has introduced some new methods to the collection: *CancelUpdate*, *Resync*, and *Update*. These methods provide functionality that's similar to that of the methods with the same names on the Recordset object. They're designed to be used on the Fields collection of the Record object because it directly exposes such methods. Calling these methods—or entering certain parameters when calling some of the methods—on the Fields collection of the Recordset object will generate a run-time error.

Let's take a look at the methods exposed by the Fields collection and listed in this next table.

FIELDS COLLECTION METHODS

Method Name	Description
Append	Adds a new Field to the collection
CancelUpdate	Cancels the pending changes for a record
Delete	Deletes a Field from the collection
Refresh	Refreshes the Fields collection
Resync	Resynchronizes the current record
Update	Submits the pending changes in a record

Append Method

You can use the *Append* method on the Fields collection to create your own Recordset object without using a database. You can populate the Fields collection with Field objects in this fashion and then call the *Recordset.Open* method to start adding records to your Recordset. If you're not trying to communicate with a database but would like to maintain your data in a Recordset object, this method is for you. Its parameters are as follows:

- **Name**   This parameter accepts a string that represents the name of the new field.

- **Type**   This parameter can take a byte value from DataTypeEnum and designates the data type for the new field.

- **DefinedSize**   This parameter accepts long type data and is optional. It is the defined size for the new field.

- **Attributes**   This optional parameter accepts long type data. It sets attributes for the new field.

- **FieldValue**   This optional parameter accepts a Variant containing the value of the new field.

The *DefinedSize* parameter is helpful when using variable length strings and binary data. You don't need to use this parameter with data types that have a predefined size, such as integers. If you're using a numeric field, you can set the NumericScale and Precision properties on the Field object after creating the field with the *Append* method but prior to opening the Recordset by calling the *Open* method.

You can set attributes for the field you're creating by using the *Attributes* parameter on the *Append* method. You can use a combination of values from FieldAttributeEnum (shown on page 108) in this parameter.

Although you can use any entry in DataTypeEnum (see ADO Help) for the data type for your new field, you should refrain from using certain data types in this fashion. You should avoid types such as adVariant, adIUnknown, and adIDispatch in creatable Recordsets. I won't go into too much detail about why here. Suffice it to say that these data types could be used to store COM objects, but knowing how and when to decrement the reference counter for these objects can be tricky. To simplify this dilemma, ADO never decrements the reference counter. Thus, if you're trying to use a creatable Recordset to maintain COM objects, you're liable to encounter behavior that looks like a memory leak. In other words, don't do it. Your best bet is to stick with the data types that ADO uses to store data from your database.

You can also call the *Append* method on the Fields collection of a Record object, if the Record allows it. The *FieldValue* parameter accepts a Variant for the value of the new field. This parameter was added in ADO 2.5 and is designed for the Fields collection on the Record object. As mentioned before, if you use this parameter on the Fields collection of a Recordset object, you'll generate a run-time error.

CancelUpdate Method

This method is similar to the *CancelUpdate* method on the Recordset object. You can use it to cancel the pending changes in the Fields collection of a Record object. Calling this method on the Fields collection of a Recordset object will generate a run-time error.

Delete Method

You can use the *Delete* method to remove a Field object from the Fields collection. The *Delete* method accepts a single required parameter, as follows:

■   ***Index***   This parameter specifies the Field you want to delete.

The *Index* parameter accepts a long integer or a string so that you can specify the Field you want to delete by name or by number.

You can call the *Delete* method on the Fields collection of a creatable Recordset object that you have yet to open. You can also call the *Delete* method on the Fields collection of a Record object to delete a record-specific field, if you have permission to do so.

Refresh Method

Call the *Refresh* method to refresh the Fields collection. This method has no visible effect on the Fields collection of the Record or Recordset object.

Resync **Method**

The Fields collection exposes a *Resync* method similar to the *Resync* method on the Recordset object and is designed to supply similar functionality for the Record object. This method forces ADO to refetch the contents of the Record from your data store. Calling the *Resync* method on the Fields collection of a Recordset object will cause a run-time error.

The *Resync* method accepts one optional parameter, as follows:

■ ***ResyncValues***   This optional parameter is of type ResyncEnum and defaults to adResyncAllValues. It can be used to control where the newly fetched data is stored—in the Value property or in the UnderlyingValue property of each Field.

For more information, see the discussion of the *Resync* method on the Recordset object on page 92 in this chapter.

Update **Method**

The *Update* method on the Fields collection is designed to let you submit the changes stored in the Fields collection of a Record object to your data store. This method is similar to the *Update* method on the Recordset object. Calling this method on the Fields collection of the Recordset object will generate a run-time error.

ADO FIELD OBJECT PROPERTIES

Let's take a closer look at the properties of the Field object. This next table offers a preliminary description of each property.

FIELD OBJECT PROPERTIES

Property Name	Data Type	Description
ActualSize	Long	Returns the actual size of a field's value
Attributes	Long	Describes characteristics of the field
DataFormat	Object	Can be used to format your data
DefinedSize	Long	Returns the defined size for a field
Name	String	Contains the name of the field
NumericScale	Byte	Indicates the numeric scale for numeric data
OriginalValue	Variant	Contains the original value for the field
Precision	Byte	Indicates the precision for numeric data

(continued)

Field Object Properties *continued*

Property Name	Data Type	Description
Properties	Collection of Property objects	Collection of dynamic properties
Type	Byte	Returns the data type for the field
UnderlyingValue	Variant	Indicates the most recently retrieved value from the database for the field
Value	Variant	Contains the current value for the field

ActualSize Property

The ActualSize property tells you how much data actually exists in your field. This property is read-only and is primarily intended for variable length strings or binary data. For example, if you define an Address field to hold up to 64 characters, you can check the ActualSize property to find out how much data actually exists in the field without having to examine the contents of the Value property. The ActualSize property is also helpful when dealing with long variable and binary data types.

As of ADO 2.1, it is possible for the ActualSize property to be larger than the DefinedSize property. If you're using a Unicode data type, the DefinedSize property will return the number of Unicode characters that the field can hold. The ActualSize property will return the length of that string in bytes. Thus, the ActualSize property value is twice the number of Unicode characters.

Attributes Property

The Attributes property contains metadata about the field, such as whether it's updatable or nullable. The property is a bitmask and is the sum of one or more values from FieldAttributeEnum, as shown in the following table.

FIELDATTRIBUTEENUM VALUES

Constant	Value	Description
adFldMayDefer	2	The data is retrieved separately from the other fields in your Recordset. This behavior is common for long text or binary fields with server-side Recordsets that support scrolling.
adFldUpdatable	4	The field is updatable.
adFldUnknownUpdatable	8	The provider cannot determine if the data is updatable.

Constant	*Value*	*Description*
adFldFixed	16	The field contains fixed-length data such as an integer.
adFldIsNullable	32	The field accepts Null values.
adFldMayBeNull	64	The field can contain Null values.
adFldLong	128	The field contains long string or binary data. You can use the *Append-Chunk* and *GetChunk* methods.
adFldRowID	256	The field contains a row identifier.
adFldRowVersion	512	The field contains some kind of time or date stamp used to track updates.
adFldCacheDeferred	4096	The provider caches field values, and subsequent reads are done from the cache.
adFldIsChapter	8192	The Field corresponds to a chapter in a hierarchical Recordset.
adFldNegativeScale	16384	The field has a negative value for its numeric scale. (For example, 12,000 with a numeric scale of −3 would be stored as 12.)
adFldKeyColumn	32768	The field is part of the primary key.
adFldIsRowURL	65536	For fields exposed by the Record object; the value of the field corresponds to the location of the Record.
adFldIsDefaultStream	131072	For fields exposed by the Record object; the field contains the default stream of data for the Record.
adFldIsCollection	262144	For fields exposed by the Record object; the field contains a collection of data.

DataFormat Property

You can use the DataFormat property on a field to control how the data is retrieved or displayed. This feature is fairly well explained in the Visual Basic documentation. The DataFormat property is also exposed on most Visual Basic controls that you can bind to a field, such as a TextBox. The property is basically a pointer to a DataFormat object, which extends the functionality available in the Visual Basic *Format* function.

Possibly the best use of this feature is to display True, False, and Null values. In order to use the DataFormat property on a Field object, you must reference the Microsoft Data Formatting Object Library (MSStdFmt.dll) and use the StdDataFormat object. The following code uses a StdDataFormat object on a bit field in the Products table of the Northwind database:

```
Dim fmtDiscontinued As StdFormat.StdDataFormat
  ⋮
strSQL = "SELECT * FROM Products"
rsProducts.Open strSQL, cnNorthwind, adOpenStatic

Set fmtDiscontinued = New StdFormat.StdDataFormat
fmtDiscontinued.Type = fmtBoolean
fmtDiscontinued.TrueValue = "Discontinued"
fmtDiscontinued.FalseValue = "Currently Produced"
Set rsProducts!Discontinued.DataFormat = fmtDiscontinued
```

Checking the Value property of the Discontinued field will now return "Currently Produced" or "Discontinued" instead of True/False or 0/1.

DefinedSize Property

The DefinedSize property contains the defined size for a field. This property is a long data type and is read-only. Generally, this information is helpful when you're using a variable-length string or binary field. The ADO documentation implies that the property returns the size of the field in bytes.

As of ADO 2.1, the DefinedSize property returns the number of characters a variable length string field supports rather than the number of bytes. Thus, both ANSI (single-byte) and Unicode (double-byte) string fields that accept the same number of their respective characters have the same value for the DefinedSize property. This behavior is different from that of the related property, ActualSize. With that property, the returned value is the number of bytes in the string, rather than the number of characters.

Name Property

The Name property contains the name of the Field object in string format. Generally, this property will refer to the name of the column in the table that you're querying. With most OLE DB providers, you can use an AS clause to choose a different name if you don't want to use the column name.

USING THE NAME PROPERTY WITH JOIN QUERIES

If you're using a Recordset based on a join query, the behavior of the Name property will depend on how the OLE DB provider or ODBC driver returns data about the columns in the results of your query. Using ADO 2.5 and the OLE DB Provider For SQL Server as a test, I submitted a join query that retrieved data from the Customers and Orders tables, basing the relationship on the CustomerID field:

```
strSQL = "SELECT * FROM Customers, Orders WHERE " & _
        "Customers.CustomerID = Orders.CustomerID"
```

I found that as I examined the Name property of each Field object, there were two fields with the same name—CustomerID. Keep in mind that you'll see the same behavior with the SQL Server query tools. I then used the Jet 4.0 OLE DB Provider, and the two fields came back with different values for the Name property—Customers.CustomerID and Orders.CustomerID. Compare this to using RDO with SQL Server, which returned two rdoColumn objects of different names—CustomerID and CustomerID1.

If you're going to use Recordsets based on a join, test to see whether your query returns multiple Field objects with the same value for the Name property. If that's the case and it poses a problem, your best bet is to use AS clauses in your query to ensure unique column names in the results.

NumericScale Property

Used for numeric data, the NumericScale property returns the scale of the numeric values for the field. This property contains a byte value and indicates the number of digits to the right of the decimal point that you can store in the field. For example, if you used a numeric data type in your database to store monetary units and did not store fractions of a cent, then NumericScale would be 2.

It's possible for a database to use a negative value for a numeric scale, though I'm not aware of any databases or providers that implement this functionality. There is a value in FieldAttributeEnum called adFldNegativeScale that would (we hope) be used to indicate that a field has a negative value for its numeric scale. This could come in handy for large numbers with limited precision. For example, if you wanted to keep track of the past lottery jackpots and decrease the amount of data to store, you could store 5 with a NumericScale of −6 to represent $5 million.

OriginalValue Property

When you're editing the Recordset, the OriginalValue property contains the data for the Value property of the Field object before it was edited. This property is read-only and returns a Variant.

If you're using a LockType of adLockOptimistic or adLockPessimistic, the OriginalValue property contains the value for the field prior to editing. If you call *CancelUpdate* while editing the current record, the Value property on each field will be set to the OriginalValue property. Once you modify the value of a field and successfully update that record with the *Update* method on the Recordset object, the OriginalValue property on the Field is set to the newly submitted value.

In batch optimistic update mode, using *CancelUpdate* to cancel changes to a record while that record's EditMode is adEditInProgress resets the Value property on each Field to the OriginalValue property. Because calling the *Update* method in this mode caches only the pending changes in the Recordset rather than actually modifying the data in your database, the OriginalValue property is not updated until you call *UpdateBatch*. After you've called the *Update* method, canceling the pending changes in a record by calling *CancelBatch* will reset the Value property on the Field objects to the OriginalValue property.

We'll talk more about this property in Chapter 10, when we examine how the ADO Cursor Engine submits changes to your database.

Precision Property

The Precision property returns the maximum number of digits that the field can store, including digits to the right of the decimal point. This property is read-only and contains a byte value.

Properties Collection

Like most ADO objects, the Field object exposes a Properties collection. The contents of the collection will depend on the OLE DB provider, CursorLocation, CursorType, and LockType. We'll discuss many of the dynamic properties specific to the ADO Cursor Engine in Chapters 10 and 12 of this book.

Type Property

The Type property on a Field object contains a byte value from DataTypeEnum. For more information on the contents of DataTypeEnum, please see the ADO documentation in the Microsoft Data Access Components (MDAC) SDK and Platform SDK. This property is read-only. See the discussion of creatable Recordsets on page 106 for more information on how to use the Type property.

UnderlyingValue Property

You can use the UnderlyingValue property to check the current field's value in your database. This property is not available for read-only Recordsets. With some OLE DB providers, this property will contain live data when using a server-side Recordset. If you're using a client-side Recordset, this data is not live and can be retrieved by using the *Resync* method. The UnderlyingValue property can also be updated by a failed optimistic update attempt on a client-side Recordset if you're using the Update Resync dynamic property with the adResyncConflicts constant.

The UnderlyingValue property is read-only and contains a Variant. We'll discuss this property in more depth when we discuss conflict detection in Chapter 12.

Value Property

The data you retrieved from your query is stored in the Value property. This property is the default property on the Field object, so you generally do not need to explicitly call the Value property when you want to examine the contents of a field. The Value property contains a Variant and is read/write only if your Recordset supports updates.

ADO supports setting and returning long string and binary data with the Value property.

ADO FIELD OBJECT METHODS

The two methods available on the Field object are *AppendChunk* and *GetChunk* and are described in the following table. These methods are designed to help you work with large string and binary data type fields.

FIELD OBJECT METHODS

Method Name	*Description*
AppendChunk	Appends data to a large string or binary field
GetChunk	Retrieves data from a large string or binary field

Before we talk about using these methods, let's talk a little bit about the large string and binary data types. These data types have different names depending on what documentation you're reading. ADO uses adLongVarChar to designate long strings, adLongVarWChar for long Unicode strings, and adLongVarBinary for long binary fields. SQL Server uses the names text, ntext, and image for the same data types, respectively. These fields can store large amounts of string or binary data, which is usually stored separately from the rest of the data in your table. They're often called BLOB fields (for binary large objects, not because they slither through air ducts to attack teenagers at movie theaters).

Similarly, the string or binary data is often retrieved separately from the rest of the data in the results of your query. Traditionally, you don't know how much data is contained in such a field. Retrieving this data separately allows you to save time and bandwidth by not retrieving the contents of BLOB fields that you won't ultimately examine in your code. To retrieve this data separately from the rest of the data in your query, you need to make sure the table's primary key is part of your query and that the BLOB fields are the last fields referenced in your query string.

Before visions of BLOBs dance in your head, remember that databases are not file servers. If you want the best possible performance from your database system, don't use it to move large pieces of data that could be better handled by your operating system. Instead, use your database to store the name and location of the file that contains the desired data. Yes, storing this data in your database can simplify your data access code and make backups easier, but that's no excuse for choosing poor performance.

Unfortunately, the code samples that demonstrate the use of long binary data that are included with Access versions 2, 95, 97, and 2000, and with SQL Server 7, further confuse most developers. The Northwind database that has shipped with Access for the past few versions contains bitmaps in the Photo field of the Employees table. To make it easier to use this data, Access wraps this data in its own proprietary header format that allows you to simply double-click on a field marked as an OLE Field, and Access launches the appropriate application that will display and edit the data in that field. Unfortunately, the structure of these headers has never been documented.

Visual Basic users have placed large amounts of data into Access OLE Fields only to find that they could not retrieve this data as easily as they'd hoped. There's a small sample application called RemoveAccessHeaders on the CD included with this book that can strip the OLE headers in Access from data stored as an OLE Field and store the contents of the file instead. It's effective, but painful and inelegant.

SQL Server 7 also shipped the Northwind database as a sample database. The structure is almost identical to that of the Northwind database in Access, but the Photo field in the Employees table contains the same Access header. Maybe this is a good thing. Developers who want to store files in their database might try to build an application that retrieves these images, not realizing that the data is a bitmap wrapped in an Access header and consequently they won't be able to view the image in their application. With any luck, this discovery will encourage them to store the filename in their database instead of the contents of the file.

Let's return to the *AppendChunk* and *GetChunk* methods. If you're using a server-side Recordset, the BLOB data won't be retrieved until you request it. If you're using a client-side Recordset, the ADO Cursor Engine retrieves all BLOB fields when you open the Recordset. By retrieving all this data ahead of time, you can close your connection to the database and still access the contents of the BLOB fields. With most OLE DB providers, you should be able to use the Value property on the Field object to retrieve and modify its contents rather than using *GetChunk* and *AppendChunk*.

If you want to determine which fields you can use the *AppendChunk* and *GetChunk* methods on, examine the Attributes property of each Field object and test for adFldLong.

> **NOTE** ADO 2.5 introduced a Stream object that can simplify the process of moving data from files to databases and back. If you've decided to store the contents of files in your database (despite my recommendation against doing so), you can avoid the cumbersome *AppendChunk* and *GetChunk* methods by using the Stream object. Chapter 6 contains some fairly simple sample code that shows how to use the Stream object in such a scenario.

AppendChunk Method

Use the *AppendChunk* method to place data into a BLOB field. This method has one parameter:

■   ***Data***   This parameter accepts Variant type data you want to append to the desired field.

The initial call to the *AppendChunk* method will overwrite the current contents of the field. Successive calls to the method without moving off the current record will continue to add data to the field.

GetChunk Method

The *GetChunk* method retrieves data from a field and returns it to a Variant. It accepts one parameter:

■   ***Length***   This parameter is a long data type. It accepts the number of bytes of characters you want to retrieve.

To determine how much data there is to retrieve in a particular field, check the ActualSize property of the field prior to calling *GetChunk*. If you request more data than remains in the field, ADO will return only the data remaining. So, if the ActualSize property returns −1 and there is no way to determine how much data exists in your BLOB field, you'll have to retrieve the data in chunks and examine what has been returned. Testing the size of the variable that holds the data returned by the *GetChunk* method and comparing that size to the amount of data requested will help you determine when you've retrieved all available data for the field.

It's worth noting that as of ADO 2.1, when you retrieve string data the ActualSize property returns the number of bytes rather than the number of characters in the field, while the *Length* parameter of the *GetChunk* method designates the number of characters to return rather than the number of bytes.

QUESTIONS THAT SHOULD BE ASKED MORE FREQUENTLY

Q. *Do you really need every record in your table?*

A. So many customers call to complain that the applications they built suddenly started to perform poorly once they moved into production. The most common cause? Queries that retrieve all records and all fields from a table. Of course the query's performance will degrade when you move from a small test database to a full production database. It will continue to degrade as you add more data to the table.

Q. *Do you really need every field in your table?*

A. Even if you do need to retrieve every record, do you really need to retrieve every field? Too many programmers use *SELECT * FROM MyTable* simply out of laziness. Others use this simple query because it's the only way they ever learned to query tables. Books and documentation tend to show simple, concise code primarily because a single line of code that takes up multiple lines on a page doesn't look nice, and too much detail can often make an example confusing. As a result, many queries that you'll see in online documentation or in books such as this will use *SELECT * FROM MyTable*. You'll see a number of queries of this type in this book, but now you know why.

Even if you do need every column from your table, you would probably see better performance if you avoided the wildcard character (asterisk) and listed each field instead—unless the query string is so long that the OLE DB provider or ODBC driver chokes on it.

Q. *How do I know when my asynchronous query has completed?*

A. Unfortunately, the answer isn't quite as simple as the question. If you're simply using the adAsyncExecute constant in your *Recordset.Open* call, the *ExecuteComplete* event will fire when your query completes. If you're using the ADO Cursor Engine's asynchronous fetching feature, things get a little more complex.

In this chapter, we covered the *FetchProgress* and *FetchComplete* events for the Recordset object. These events fire when you fetch your data asynchronously. Usually.

Actually, these events fire (as of ADO 2.5) only if your query returns at least the number of records specified in the Initial Fetch Size dynamic property in the Recordset object's Properties collection. What to do if your query returns fewer records? Well, here's some code for the *ExecuteComplete* and *FetchComplete* event handlers that works pretty well for me.

The initial test makes sure that the *pRecordset* object exists. (If you used *adExecuteNoRecords* as one of the parameters when you created your Recordset object, this *pRecordset* object is set to Nothing.) The Recordset object's State property is set to adStateOpen or adStateClosed if the query has completed. If the State property returns adStateOpen + adStateFetching, there's still more data for ADO to fetch. Once ADO has fetched the remaining data, the *FetchComplete* event on the Recordset object will fire.

```
'The ExecuteComplete event handler
Private Sub cn_ExecuteComplete(...)
    If Not pRecordset Is Nothing Then
        If pRecordset.State = adStateOpen Or _
           pRecordset.State = adStateClosed Then
            Debug.Print "cn_ExecuteComplete -- Query has completed"
        Else
            pRecordset.State = adStateOpen + adStateFetching
            Debug.Print _
                "cn_ExecuteComplete -- Wait for rs_FetchComplete"
        End If
    Else
        Debug.Print "cn_ExecuteComplete -- Query has completed"
    End If
    If Not pError Is Nothing Then
        Debug.Print pError.Description
    End If
End Sub

'The FetchComplete event handler
Private Sub rs_FetchComplete(...)
    Debug.Print "rs_FetchComplete -- Query has completed"
End Sub
```

Actually, this code won't tell you exactly when you've fetched all your data if you're running a hierarchical query, but we'll talk more about hierarchical queries in Chapter 14.

Chapter 5

The ADO Command and Parameter Objects

The Command object can help simplify your programming and can improve your application's performance. This object's primary use is for repeated execution of a single query or multiple similar queries. The Command object exposes a Parameters collection, with each Parameter object corresponding to a parameter in a query.

ADO COMMAND OBJECT PROPERTIES AND COLLECTIONS

Let's take a closer look at the properties and collections of the Command object.

COMMAND OBJECT PROPERTIES AND COLLECTIONS

Property or Collection Name	Data Type	Description
ActiveConnection	String or Connection	Specifies the Connection object used to communicate with your database

(continued)

Command Object Properties and Collections *continued*

Property or Collection Name	Data Type	Description
CommandText	String	Contains the query string or the name of the table, view, or stored procedure you want to execute
CommandTimeout	Long	Controls the number of seconds the query will run before timing out
CommandType	CommandTypeEnum	Specifies the type of Command to execute
Name	String	Contains the name of the Command object
Parameters	Collection of Parameter objects	Contains parameter information for the query
Prepared	Boolean	Specifies whether the Command will be prepared and stored in the database
Properties	Collection of Property objects	Contains dynamic properties for the query
State	Long	Indicates the current state of the Command object

ActiveConnection Property

This property is similar to the ActiveConnection property on the Recordset object (described in Chapter 4). You can set this property either to a Connection object or to a connection string. If you set the ActiveConnection property to a string, ADO will create a new Connection object and attempt to connect to the database based on this string.

CommandText Property

The CommandText property contains the query string you want to execute. You can use simple query strings such as

```
SELECT CustomerID, CompanyName, BalanceDue FROM Customers
    WHERE CustomerID = 7
```

as well as parameterized queries such as

```
SELECT CustomerID, CompanyName, BalanceDue FROM Customers
    WHERE CustomerID = ?
```

This property is possibly the heart of the Command object, yet it's one of the simplest and most straightforward properties.

CommandTimeout Property

Queries can hang for a number of reasons, including high network traffic, data-locking issues, and extreme complexity. In many cases, you'll want to cancel your query after a certain length of time. The CommandTimeout property allows you to do so.

The CommandTimeout property takes a long integer that specifies the number of seconds that ADO will wait for your query to complete before timing out and canceling the query; it defaults to 30 seconds. If you want your query to run indefinitely without timing out, set CommandTimeout to 0.

Not all queries time out the same way. A query that generates a client-side Recordset might run longer than the CommandTimeout setting. The reason is that the CommandTimeout property controls how long ADO will wait for the query to begin to return results. Once the OLE DB provider starts to return data, ADO retrieves the rest of the results of your query regardless of the CommandTimeout setting. With a server-side Recordset that uses a static cursor, you might be more likely to time out because the database's query processor might generate the results for the entire query before returning the records that ADO requested.

If the database takes more time than you've specified in the CommandTimeout property, ADO will cancel the query and generate an error. If you have enough expertise with your particular database, you should be able to test this scenario by generating a query whose results take longer to return than you've specified. For example, I'll lock data in my Microsoft SQL Server database by modifying it within a transaction, and then I'll submit a query on another connection that should retrieve that same row of data to see whether the query will time out.

CommandType Property

The CommandType property represents an attempt to simplify data access by letting you simplify your query. You can specify what type of query you're submitting to ADO by using the CommandType property. For example, you can simply supply a table name as your query string and specify a CommandType of adCmdTable. The following table shows the CommandTypeEnum values you can use with this property.

COMMANDTYPEENUM VALUES

Constant	*Value*	*Description*
adCmdText	1	The query will not be modified by ADO.
adCmdTable	2	ADO will append "select * from " to the query.
adCmdStoredProc	4	ADO will format the query as a call to a stored procedure; for example: *{? = CALL MyProc (?)}*.

(continued)

CommandTypeEnum Values *continued*

Constant	Value	Description
adCmdUnknown	8	Default value; ADO will try different methods of executing the query until the query succeeds.
adCmdFile	256	Indicates that the CommandText property refers to a filename. Not applicable to the Command object. Applicable to the *Open* method on the Recordset object.
adCmdTableDirect	512	ADO will use an optional but advanced set of OLE DB API calls to retrieve all rows and columns from the table name specified. Not applicable to the Command object. Applicable to the *Open* method on the Recordset object.

Wouldn't it be nice to simply supply an object name—a table name, or the name of a stored procedure or view—instead of having to type out the entire query, and to simply let ADO determine what to do with that information? Maybe, maybe not.

I talk a little bit about why I avoid using the adCmdTable constant in the discussion on the Recordset's *Open* method in Chapter 4 (beginning on page 88).

The default value for CommandType is adCmdUnknown. What happens if you use this value with your query? As the name of the constant implies, ADO does not know what type of query you're submitting. So ADO guesses based on some internal algorithms that we won't discuss here. Let's look at an example and see how ADO handles a Command object whose CommandType is adCmdUnknown:

```
Set cmdCustomers = New ADODB.Command
Set cmdCustomers.ActiveConnection = cnNorthwind
cmdCustomers.CommandText = "Customers"
Set rsCustomers = New ADODB.Recordset
rsCustomers.Open cmdCustomers
```

Yes, this code will work. It will successfully retrieve the contents of the Customers table into the Recordset object. I ran similar code against SQL Server and used the SQL Server Profiler to watch the Transact-SQL commands that ADO submits. This is what I saw in the log:

```
exec Customers
Customers
select * from Customers
```

ADO had to go through three iterations of what the query could be before it found the right one. This is an example of why I avoid using the default value, adCmdUnknown, as the CommandType value.

Quite a few programmers use the adCmdStoredProc constant. It's similar to the adCmdTable constant except that it lets you specify only the stored procedure name in the CommandText property rather than the table name. However, this constant doesn't allow much control over the way ADO handles the parameters associated with the stored procedure. For example, you might want to call a stored procedure and provide some values as part of the call rather than as ADO Parameter objects. (We'll talk about the Parameter object in the second half of this chapter.)

Let's see what happens to the CommandText property for the Command object when you use the adCmdStoredProc value. In the following code, we'll examine the contents of the CommandText property after each call:

```
With cmdStoredProc
    'Specify that the Command object will call a stored procedure.
    .CommandType = adCmdStoredProc
    'Specify the stored procedure name.
    .CommandText = "MySP"
    'CommandText property now contains "{ call MySP }".
    'Populate the Parameters collection.
    .Parameters.Append .CreateParameter("@RetVal", adInteger, _
                                        adParamReturnValue)
    .Parameters.Append .CreateParameter("@Param1", adInteger, _
                                        adParamInput)
    .Parameters.Append .CreateParameter("@Param2", adInteger, _
                                        adParamInput)
    'CommandText property now contains "{ ? = call MySP (?, ?) }".
End With
```

ADO will take the value specified in the CommandText property and format it to the ODBC standard for stored procedure calls, *{ call MySP }*. If you populate the Parameters collection, ADO will build that information into the CommandText property. Although this is an efficient, appropriate, and impressive algorithm, I'd rather simply specify the query string the way it should be formatted. In the preceding case, I would use the following code instead:

```
With cmdStoredProc
    'Specify that the Command object will use a text string.
    .CommandType = adCmdText
    .CommandText = "{? = CALL MySP(?,?)}"
    'Populate the Parameters collection.
    .Parameters.Append .CreateParameter("@RetVal", adInteger, _
                                        adParamReturnValue)
    .Parameters.Append .CreateParameter("@Param1", adInteger, _
                                        adParamInput)
    .Parameters.Append .CreateParameter("@Param2", adInteger, _
                                        adParamOutput)
End With
```

This code specifies parameters, but the values must be provided elsewhere. However, by using adCmdText and maintaining full control over the query string that ADO will submit as we've done here, you can modify this code to supply some parameter values in line. Suppose your sample stored procedure took an input parameter followed by an output parameter. If you know the value you want to submit for the input parameter, you can build it into your code this way:

```
With cmdStoredProc
    .CommandType = adCmdText
    .CommandText = "{? = CALL MySP(" & intParam1 & ",?)}"
    .Parameters.Append .CreateParameter("@RetVal", adInteger, _
                                        adParamReturnValue)
    .Parameters.Append .CreateParameter("@Param2", adInteger, _
                                        adParamOutput)
End With
```

You don't need to use a Parameter object for the input parameter if you plan to call this stored procedure only once. With the adCmdStoredProc constant, you don't have this level of control.

In short, you should avoid using adCmdUnknown (the default), adCmdStoredProc, and adCmdTable for the CommandType property.

Name Property

The Command object exposes a Name property, which stores a string. This property is set to an empty string by default. The Name property is read/write prior to setting ActiveConnection, at which point it becomes read-only.

The Name property serves two purposes. First, it helps you better trap for asynchronous events. The Command object doesn't expose events, so if you execute commands asynchronously, you might need to use events exposed by the Connection and Recordset objects to check the status of the operation. Since you'll probably execute more than one query on a particular Connection object, you need to be able to determine which query fired the event you're currently trapping.

Here's an example: The Connection object's *ExecuteComplete* event uses a *pCommand* parameter to specify which query generated the event. Rather than having to use the Microsoft Visual Basic Is operator or examine a lengthy string in the CommandText property on the *pCommand* parameter, you can choose to examine the Name property instead, assuming you set this property earlier in your code.

There's a second use for the Name property, which I file under "Just because you can, that doesn't mean you should." Once you set the Name property on the Command object and set the ActiveConnection property to a Connection object, you can execute the command as if it were a method on the Connection object, as shown in the following code:

```
strSQL = "SELECT OrderID FROM Orders WHERE OrderDate >= ? AND" & _
         " OrderDate <= ?"
'Create the Command object.
Set qryOrderRange = New ADODB.Command
With qryOrderRange
    'Set the Name of the qryOrderRange command to OrderRange.
    .Name = "OrderRange"
    .CommandText = strSQL
    'Create the parameters to insert into the query string.
    .Parameters.Append .CreateParameter("@Start", adDBTimeStamp, _
                                        adParamInput)
    .Parameters.Append .CreateParameter("@EndDate", adDBTimeStamp, _
                                        adParamInput)
    'Set the Command object's ActiveConnection property.
    .ActiveConnection = cnNorthwind
End With
Set rsOrders = New ADODB.Recordset
rsOrders.CursorLocation = adUseClient
'Use the Name of the qryOrderRange object to access the query
' through the Connection object.
cnNorthwind.OrderRange #8/1/1996#, #8/31/1996#, rsOrders
```

While it's a neat trick, code like this uses late binding, so it runs slower than code that uses the *Execute* method on the Command object (see page 127) or the *Open* method on the Recordset object.

Parameters Collection

The Command object exposes a Parameters collection, which we'll discuss a little later in this chapter.

Prepared Property

Some database systems allow you to compile a query once and execute it multiple times with different parameters. Essentially, this feature is similar to a temporary stored procedure. The Command property exposes this functionality through the Prepared property. The Prepared property stores a Boolean value and defaults to False.

To determine whether setting this property to True will improve the performance of your application, your best bet is to run your own tests. I've yet to see any definitive statistics that explain under what circumstances Prepared should be set to True. Through my own testing, I've found that using this property with SQL Server 7 actually decreases performance even when executing the same query repeatedly. Your mileage can vary.

Properties Collection

Like most ADO objects, the Command object exposes a Properties collection whose contents depend on your choice of OLE DB provider. Unlike with the Connection, Recordset, and Field objects, however, there's generally no need to use these properties with the Command object.

State Property

Just like the Connection and Recordset objects, the Command object exposes a State property. The State property takes an ObjectStateEnum type, but only two values from ObjectStateEnum apply to the Command object: adStateClosed and adStateExecuting. If you execute the command asynchronously (with either the *Command.Execute* or the *Recordset.Open* method), the State property of the Command object will return adStateExecuting while ADO awaits the results of the query. Once the Connection object's *ExecuteComplete* event fires, this property is reset to adStateClosed.

If you're also using the ADO Cursor Engine's asynchronous fetching feature, the Command object's State property is set to adStateClosed once the ADO Cursor Engine has retrieved the initial set of rows. I don't recommend using the Command object again until ADO has fetched all the results for the query. Wait for the Recordset object's *FetchComplete* event to fire, or make sure the Recordset's State property is set to 1 (adStateOpen) and not 9 (adStateOpen + adStateFetching).

ADO COMMAND OBJECT METHODS

Now let's take a look at the methods available on the Command object.

COMMAND OBJECT METHODS

Method Name	Description
Cancel	Cancels an asynchronous query
CreateParameter	Creates a Parameter object for the Command object's Parameters collection
Execute	Executes your query

Cancel Method

The *Cancel* method allows you to terminate the execution of an asynchronous query. Keep in mind that if you execute the query using the asynchronous fetching option, canceling the query after the *ExecuteComplete* event of the Connection object has fired will have no effect.

CreateParameter Method

The *CreateParameter* method returns a Parameter object. If you're using a parameterized query, you can populate the Parameters collection for the Command object by using the *Append* method on the Parameters collection combined with the *CreateParameter* method on the Command object. Here are the parameters that the *CreateParameter* method supports:

- **Name**   This optional parameter accepts a string that represents the name of the parameter.

- **Type**   This optional parameter accepts a value from DataTypeEnum for the parameter's data type. For information on DataTypeEnum values, see the ADO documentation in the Platform SDK Help.

- **Direction**   This optional parameter accepts a value from ParameterDirectionEnum. (See the table on page 131 for ParameterDirectionEnum values.) It specifies the direction (input or output) for the parameter.

- **Size**   This optional parameter accepts a long value to specify the maximum size of the parameter.

- **Value**   This optional parameter accepts a Variant that specifies the value for the parameter.

The parameters on the *CreateParameter* method correspond to most of the properties on the Parameter object that you're liable to set. I'll describe these parameters in more detail later in the chapter when we cover the Parameter object. Perhaps the only properties you might need to set on the Parameter object that aren't available as parameters on the *CreateParameter* method are the NumericScale and Precision properties.

Execute Method

As its name implies, the *Execute* method executes the query your Command object contains. By default, this method will return a Recordset object with the results of your query. It has the following parameters:

- **RecordsAffected**   This optional parameter accepts a long value that returns the number of records affected by the query.

- **Parameters**   This optional parameter accepts a Variant array that specifies the parameters for the query.

■ ***Options*** This optional parameter accepts a long value. You can supply a value from CommandTypeEnum and/or values from ExecuteOptionEnum.

The initial parameter, *RecordsAffected*, will contain a long integer that indicates the number of records affected by your query. If you're using action queries to update data in your database, you'll probably want to know how many records your query modified.

The *Execute* method also takes a parameter, *Parameters*, that you can use to supply values for the parameters of your query without having to use the Parameters collection. This parameter on the *Execute* method accepts a Variant array of values and/or variables that correspond to the items in your Command object's Parameters collection. Values supplied in *Parameters* will override the values in the Parameters collection.

Just as with the *Options* parameter of the *Recordset.Open* and *Connection.Execute* methods, you can use this final parameter of the *Execute* method with constants from CommandTypeEnum (see page 121) and/or ExecuteOptionEnum (see page 89 in Chapter 4). The parameter is a bitmask, so you can combine appropriate constants such as adCmdText + adExecuteNoRecords. You can also specify a value or values from ExecuteOptionEnum in this parameter to execute your command asynchronously.

ADO PARAMETERS COLLECTION

Each Command object exposes a Parameters collection that you can use for parameterized queries. The Parameters collection exposes most of the same properties and methods as all standard collections, but there are two methods on the Parameters collection worth discussing—*Append* and **Refresh*. Each of these methods can be used to populate the Parameters collection. Generally, you'll use either one or the other in your applications.

IMPORTANT METHODS OF THE PARAMETERS COLLECTION

Method Name	*Description*
Append	Appends a Parameter object to the Parameters collection
Refresh	Refreshes the Parameters collection

Append Method

Use the *Append* method to add a Parameter object to the Parameters collection. By populating the Parameters collection on your own, you can achieve better performance than if you have ADO ask the OLE DB provider to supply that information. *Append* takes one parameter:

■   ***Object***   This value specifies the Parameter object that you want to append to the Parameters collection.

There are two main ways to use the *Append* method on the Parameters collection. You can use a Parameter object variable as the *Object* parameter:

```
Set param = cmd.CreateParameter(...)
cmd.Parameters.Append param
```

However, I prefer to combine the two lines of code and avoid using the object variable:

```
cmd.Parameters.Append cmd.CreateParameter(...)
```

We'll talk more about populating the Parameters collection on your own at the end of the chapter.

Refresh **Method**

If you call the *Refresh* method on the Parameters collection, ADO will ask the OLE DB provider for parameter information about the query that the Command object will execute. The information includes the number of parameters as well as their data type, direction, and size. This functionality is optional for OLE DB providers: some provide all or part of this information; others provide none.

ADO PARAMETER OBJECT PROPERTIES AND COLLECTIONS

The purpose of the Parameter object is to enable you to reuse a query while changing a small piece of the query. For example, you could build a query such as the following to select a single customer record based on the value of the CustomerID field, and then execute that query multiple times, changing only the value of the CustomerID each time the query is executed:

```
SELECT * FROM Customers WHERE CustomerID = ?
```

If you're using a parameterized query, you can change the value without having to rebuild the entire query string. In short, the Command object can use parameters the same way a function can use parameters. The following table shows the properties and collections of the Parameter object.

PARAMETER OBJECT PROPERTIES AND COLLECTIONS

Property or Collection Name	Data Type	Description
Attributes	Long	Describes some of the characteristics of the Parameter object
Direction	ParameterDirectionEnum	Indicates which type of parameter you're using—input, output, input/output, or return
Name	String	Contains the name of the Parameter object
NumericScale	Byte	Indicates the numeric scale for numeric data
Precision	Byte	Indicates the precision for numeric data
Properties	Collection of Property objects	Contains dynamic properties
Size	Long	Returns the defined size for a field
Type	DataTypeEnum	Returns the data type for a field
Value	Variant	Contains the current value for a field

Attributes Property

The Attributes property describes some of the properties of the parameter, such as whether it accepts Null values. The Attributes property uses a long integer to store the sum of values from the ParameterAttributesEnum enumeration shown in this next table. This property is read/write.

PARAMETERATTRIBUTESENUM VALUES

Constant	Value	Description
adParamSigned	16	The data type of the parameter is signed; it applies to numeric data types.
adParamNullable	64	The parameter accepts Null as its value.
adParamLong	128	The parameter accepts long string or binary data.

Direction Property

Most programming languages have different parameter types that control whether data is passed to and/or from a procedure. Many databases also utilize these concepts. ADO uses the Direction property on the Parameter object to denote the direction in which data will be passed.

Not all databases support all the settings available in ADO. You might need to supply parameter direction information even if you're using the *Refresh* method on the Parameters collection to retrieve information about your parameters. For example, SQL Server lets you use the OUTPUT keyword to specify that the parameter can return data. However, there is no way to specify whether the parameter is used for output only or for both input and output.

The SQL Server OLE DB provider (or ODBC driver) will assume that the parameter is for both input and output. If you neglect to supply a value for the parameter before executing the query, you'll receive an error. You can set the Direction property to any of the values in ParameterDirectionEnum, shown in the following table. If you want the parameter to be output-only, you'll need to manually set the Direction property on the Parameter object to adParamOutput. Of course, you're better off populating the Parameters collection to begin with, so this shouldn't be an issue for you, right?

PARAMETERDIRECTIONENUM VALUES

Constant	*Value*	*Description*
adParamUnknown	0	Direction is unknown.
adParamInput	1	Default; parameter is input-only.
adParamOutput	2	Parameter is output-only.
adParamInputOutput	3	Parameter is input/output.
adParamReturnValue	4	Parameter is the return value for a stored procedure.

Name Property

The Name property can help you locate the Parameter object in the Parameters collection and improve the readability of your code. Beyond that, you don't need to use it. As long as the parameters on your SQL Server stored procedures have names, you do not need to set the Name property of your Parameter objects to the same value.

NumericScale and Precision Properties

Like the Field object (discussed in Chapter 4), the Parameter object exposes Numeric-Scale and Precision properties. If you're using variable-length numeric data types, you'll want to set the NumericScale and Precision properties accordingly. These are probably the only properties on the Parameter object that you might want to set that aren't available on the *CreateParameter* method of the Command object. For more information on these properties, see the discussion of the Field object on pages 111 and 112 in Chapter 4.

If you're having trouble setting these properties correctly, here are a couple of suggestions for finding the correct settings:

- If the property corresponds to a field in one of your tables, query that table and examine the settings for the NumericScale and Precision properties on the Field object in the returned Recordset.

- Call *Parameters.Refresh* once (if your OLE DB provider or ODBC driver supports that functionality), and check the value of the NumericScale and Precision properties.

Use the values you retrieve from either of these suggestions to set these properties in your code.

Properties Collection

Like most ADO objects, the Parameter object also exposes a Properties collection. I have yet to see this collection populated, but if a provider wanted to expose some provider-specific properties, that information could be available in this collection.

Size Property

The Parameter object's Size property corresponds to the Field object's DefinedSize property (discussed on page 110 in Chapter 4): it applies to variable length string and binary data types. For ANSI and Unicode strings, the value of this property determines the number of characters, rather than the number of bytes, that the Parameter object can store.

Type Property

The Type property for the Parameter object corresponds to the Type property for the Field object. If you're unsure of the data type to use for a parameter, use one of the two guidelines listed above for the NumericScale and Precision properties (but query the Type property, of course).

Value Property

The Value property stores the value of the parameter in a Variant, similar to the Value property on the Field object. Like the Field object, the default property on the Parameter object is the Value property.

ADO PARAMETER OBJECT METHOD

Let's take a look at the lone method on the Parameter object, *AppendChunk*.

PARAMETER OBJECT METHOD

Method Name	Description
AppendChunk	Adds chunks of string or binary data to the Parameter object

AppendChunk Method

The Parameter object's *AppendChunk* method functions just like that of the Field object (discussed on page 115 in Chapter 4). Use it to add chunks of string or binary data to a Parameter object that uses a long string or binary data type.

QUESTIONS THAT SHOULD BE ASKED MORE FREQUENTLY

Q. *Should I always use a Command object?*
A. In short, no. The Command object can be extremely handy, but it's primarily designed for two-tiered client-server applications, which, these days, aren't as fashionable as multitiered applications. If you're building a query that will run in a Component Services (formerly known as Microsoft Transaction Server) component or in Active Server Pages (ASP), there's really no reason to use a Command object.

Q. *Should I always use Parameter objects in my query?*
A. Again, in short, no. If you're executing your query only once, there's usually little reason to use a parameterized query.

If you know ahead of time that you're going to retrieve information about a particular customer, but you're accepting input from the user to decide which customer, you might be tempted to use this information in a Parameter object. While that's a perfectly acceptable reason for using a Parameter object, bear in mind that you could also simply build your query string and include that information prior to submitting the query.

Many developers will use parameterized queries because they're receiving input from the user and don't want to worry about delimiting the string or date. You'll understand why if you've ever had to build a query like the following:

```
SELECT * FROM Authors WHERE Au_LName = 'O''Leary'
```

Q. *Why should I use* **Parameters.Append** *instead of* **Parameters.Refresh?**

A. Unless you're building an ad hoc query tool, you should avoid calling *Parameters.Refresh* in your application at all costs.

When you call *Parameters.Refresh*, you're asking the OLE DB provider to supply parameter information that you should already have available to you. If you're not dealing with an ad hoc query tool, you should know what the data type and direction for your parameters are.

There's a natural tendency to believe that writing less code means your application will run faster. While that's true in general, your application will often run faster if you populate the parameters collection yourself. Why? Asking the OLE DB provider to supply information about the parameters for your query incurs network round-trips that could easily be avoided by writing a little more code.

Also, for large database systems, it's actually the database system that has to generate the information that's handed back to ADO. Collecting information about the parameters is often a costly query that examines system tables. Many developers using Visual Basic, Remote Data Objects (RDO), and Oracle complained about poor performance on parameterized queries because the more tables and stored procedures they added to their database, the longer it took to retrieve the parameter information. This is one of the reasons the ADO developers added the *Append* method to the Parameters collection.

Finally, many OLE DB providers are unable to supply all the information you need for your Parameter objects anyway. SQL Server has no way of indicating whether a parameter is input/output or output-only. Even if you call *Parameters.Refresh*, you'll need to modify the Direction property of your Parameter object if you want it to be an output-only parameter. The Microsoft Jet 4.0 OLE DB Provider has difficulty determining the length of character-based parameters, and you might need to set the Size property yourself even after calling *Parameters.Refresh*. (If this information seems overwhelming, revisit the previous two questions.)

Q. *What's the deal with Microsoft Access QueryDefs with ADO?*

A. The answer to this question could fill an entire book, but I'll give a brief answer here. There is a difference between how the Jet 4.0 OLE DB Provider and the Jet ODBC driver handle QueryDefs (query definitions). Part of the reason for this difference in behavior is that a Jet QueryDef is somewhere between a view and a stored procedure. The other part of the reason is that the OLE DB provider and the ODBC driver were developed by entirely different teams, and the provider and driver libraries each directly access the Access database.

To make a long story short, the Jet 4.0 OLE DB Provider treats a QueryDef as a view, and the Jet ODBC driver treats a QueryDef as a stored procedure. Say that you built a parameterized QueryDef named GetAnOrder for the query *SELECT * FROM Orders WHERE OrderID = ?*. The Jet 4.0 OLE DB Provider treats the QueryDef like a table. You would use the following code to run the query with the Jet 4.0 OLE DB Provider:

```
With qryGetOrder
    .CommandText = "SELECT * FROM GetAnOrder"
    .CommandType = adCmdText
    .Parameters.Append .CreateParameter("pOrderID", adInteger, _
                                        adParamInput)
    Set .ActiveConnection = cnNorthwind
End With
```

The ODBC driver for Access treats that same QueryDef like a stored procedure. To run the QueryDef using the ODBC driver for Access, you would use the following code:

```
With qryGetOrder
    .CommandText = "{CALL GetAnOrder (?)}"
    .CommandType = adCmdText
    .Parameters.Append .CreateParameter("pOrderID", adInteger, _
                                        adParamInput)
    Set .ActiveConnection = cnNorthwind
End With
```

You're also likely to see inconsistencies if you compare schema information returned by the OLE DB provider and the ODBC driver, or if you look at QueryDefs in the Visual Basic DataView window.

Chapter 6

The ADO Record and Stream Objects

ADO 2.5 introduces two new items to the ADO object model—the Record object and the Stream object—expanding ADO into a more universal data access model. These two objects make ADO an effective data access technology for more than just traditional data stores such as Microsoft SQL Server, Microsoft Access, and Oracle. Before we discuss the objects themselves, let's take a look at some of the available OLE DB providers that let us use these new objects.

> **NOTE** As I write this chapter, Microsoft Data Access Components (MDAC) 2.5 is in its final stages of development. The Record and Stream objects might have changed slightly between the time I wrote this book and the time ADO 2.5 (as part of MDAC 2.5) is released. Be sure to check Microsoft's online Knowledge Base, as well as the ADO Web site at *http://www.microsoft.com/data/ado*, for the latest and greatest information.

WHICH OLE DB PROVIDERS SUPPORT THE ADO RECORD OBJECT?

As of the release of MDAC 2.5, few OLE DB providers support the Record and Stream objects. In fact, none of the OLE DB providers that are scheduled to ship with MDAC 2.5 support them. The documentation included with MDAC 2.5 focuses on the OLE DB Provider For Internet Publishing because that's the most widely available and useful provider that supports these objects.

OLE DB Provider For Internet Publishing

The full install of Microsoft Internet Explorer 5 ships with an OLE DB provider designed to communicate with web servers such as Microsoft Internet Information Services (IIS) 5. There's a growing standard among web servers called Web Distributed Authoring and Versioning (WebDAV), which defines a method of interaction with the files maintained by the web server. This standard set of interfaces allows web development tools such as Microsoft FrontPage to post new or modified files to your web site.

The OLE DB Provider For Internet Publishing lets you use WebDAV to communicate with your web site by using ADO. You can use this provider and ADO to interact with your web site the same way that FrontPage does.

OLE DB Provider For Microsoft Exchange Server

The Record and Stream objects are designed to make working with "document" data stores (such as file systems and message stores) simpler for programmers. One OLE DB provider that's currently in the works and demonstrates this commitment to "nondatabase" data is the OLE DB Provider For Microsoft Exchange Server. You could use such a provider to communicate with your mail server by using ADO instead of the Messaging Application Programming Interface (MAPI) to build e-mail applications like Microsoft Outlook.

Future OLE DB Providers

I see the Record and Stream objects as a step forward by the ADO team to promote ADO (and OLE DB) as a truly universal data access technology. In some ways, the OLE DB Provider For Internet Publishing is an example of how developing an OLE DB provider can simplify interacting with your data store. Perhaps more programmers will develop OLE DB providers as a result.

ADO RECORD OBJECT

Traditional database programmers will not find the Record object useful (because the OLE DB providers for traditional relational databases don't support it), but they're not the programmers for whom the ADO development team built this object. The name of this object might make you think that it's used to interact with a single record in a Recordset object. Although this is probably the easiest way to envision the Record object, the object does a lot more than simply hold a record's worth of data that is already available in a Recordset.

Hierarchical Data

Many data stores expose data in hierarchies. File systems, for example, contain files and directories. While a file might resemble a row in a table in a traditional relational database, a directory resembles both a row in a table and a table. The Record object is designed to handle data in a similar manner. Call a Record object's *GetChildren* method, and you'll receive a Recordset object that contains the child data (the records) associated with that Record object.

Nonrectangular Data

In some cases, you can use the Record object to access more information than what's accessible through the Recordset object. Imagine the records in a Recordset as a grid: each record (row) contains the same set of fields (columns). This rigid, rectangular structure can prevent you from accessing certain data—creating, if you'll pardon the pun, gridlock.

Once again, take data in a directory as an example. Files and subdirectories have some of the same attributes, such as the name and the date created, but they also expose unique attributes. For example, files generally have an application associated with them, and directories generally contain information about whether they're visible as a network share. Because this structure of files and subdirectories within a directory exposes different attributes, the attribute data is considered nonrectangular.

If you were to look at the files and subdirectories of a particular directory in terms of a Recordset object, you'd see only the common attributes (columns of data) that are exposed by both the files and subdirectories. Examining a file and a subdirectory as individual Record objects will expose all the attributes of both structures. Therefore, the Count property of the Fields collection might be larger when you look at a record of data in a Record object than when you look at that same record in a Recordset object, as shown in Figure 6-1.

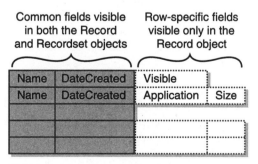

Figure 6-1 *Fields available in a Recordset object and a Record object.*

I've explained this concept to a number of programmers. Some "get it," and others don't. Chances are, if you can't think of any cases in which this functionality would be useful, it's because you haven't encountered a scenario that required access to nonrectangular data. If that's the case, don't strain yourself trying to envision handy uses for this functionality. Just know it's available in case you need it.

ADO RECORD OBJECT PROPERTIES AND COLLECTIONS

Let's look at the properties and collections exposed by the Record object and shown in the following table.

RECORD OBJECT PROPERTIES AND COLLECTIONS

Property or Collection Name	Data Type	Description
ActiveConnection	Variant	Specifies the Connection object used to retrieve the data for the Record object
Fields	Collection of Field objects	A pointer to the collection of Field objects that contain data in the Record object
Mode	ConnectModeEnum	Specifies the permissions for modification of the Record object
ParentURL	String	Indicates the parent URL for the Record object
Properties	Collection of Property objects	Collection of dynamic properties for the Record object
RecordType	RecordTypeEnum	Indicates the type of the Record object
Source	Variant	Specifies the source of the data contained in the Record object
State	ObjectStateEnum	Indicates the state of the Record object

ActiveConnection Property

The ActiveConnection property on the Record object contains the connection information that ADO will use to connect to your data store. You can set the ActiveConnection property to a valid connection string or to an open Connection object. The Active-Connection property will return a Connection object.

Use the Record object's ActiveConnection property in the same way you'd use the ActiveConnection property on the Recordset and Command objects. (See Chapters 4 and 5, respectively.)

Fields Collection

Like the Recordset object, the Record object exposes a Fields collection. As mentioned earlier in this chapter, when you examine a record in a Record object its Fields collection might contain more entries than if you examine the same record in a Recordset object. For more information on the Fields collection, see Chapter 4.

Mode Property

The Mode property indicates the permissions for modification of the Record object. This property contains a long value that represents a bitmask of values in Connect-ModeEnum, as the following table describes.

CONNECTMODEENUM VALUES

Constant	*Value*	*Description*
adModeUnknown	0	Uses the default permissions to your Record object
adModeRead	1	Default; opens the Record object with read-only permissions
adModeWrite	2	Opens the Record object with write-only permissions
adModeReadWrite	3	Opens the Record object using read/write permissions
adModeShareDenyRead	4	Prevents other users from reading the contents of your Record object while it's open
adModeShareDenyWrite	8	Prevents other users from modifying your Record object while it's open
adModeShareExclusive	12	Prevents other users from connecting to your Record object while it's open
adModeShareDenyNone	16	Allows other users to open the same Record object with read and write permissions but prevents other users from using adMode-ShareDenyWrite or adModeShareExclusive

You can set this property only on a closed Record object; the value of the Mode property is read-only when the Record is open. Although the Record's Mode property accepts the same values as the Connection object's Mode property, in functionality it closely resembles the Recordset object's LockType property.

ParentURL Property

The ParentURL property is read-only and contains a string indicating the location of the Record object's parent Record. The documentation for ParentURL states that this property will be set to Null if the Record represents the root in a hierarchy or if the type of data stored in the Record does not support URLs (such as a record in a Recordset). While testing with the beta versions of ADO, I found that the root Record's ParentURL property returns the URL for that Record, rather than Null or an empty string.

Properties Collection

Like most ADO objects, the Record object exposes a Properties collection whose contents depend on your choice of OLE DB providers. In the samples I've written to test the Record object's Properties collection using the OLE DB Provider For Internet Publishing, the Properties collection is always empty. However, as more OLE DB providers support the Record object, this collection is where those providers will expose provider-specific attributes for the Record object.

RecordType Property

The RecordType property indicates the type of data stored in the Record object. It's read-only and returns one of the values from RecordTypeEnum listed in the following table.

RecordTypeEnum Values

Constant	Value	Description
adSimpleRecord	0	Indicates a simple record (does not contain child nodes)
adCollectionRecord	1	Indicates a collection record (contains child nodes)
adStructDoc	2	Indicates a special kind of collection record that represents COM structured documents

Source Property

Like the Source property on the Recordset object, this property stores a Variant that directs ADO to the location where the Record's data is stored. While the Record object is closed, this property is read/write. While the Record object is open, this property is read-only.

You can set the Source property to a string or to a Record object. The Source property corresponds to the *Source* parameter on the Record's *Open* method. For more information, see the *Open* method documented later in this chapter beginning on page 146.

State Property

The Record object's State property indicates the current state of the Record. Like the State property on the Recordset object, this property returns a long value that represents a bitmask of values available in ObjectStateEnum. The following table lists these values.

OBJECTSTATEENUM VALUES APPLICABLE TO THE RECORD OBJECT

Constant	Value	Description
adStateClosed	0	The Record object is closed.
adStateOpen	1	The Record object is open.
adStateExecuting	4	The Record object is being opened asynchronously.

The OLE DB Provider For Internet Publishing does not support opening Record objects asynchronously. If you use a provider that does support asynchronous operations with the Record object, be sure to perform bitwise operations rather than checking for specific values when testing the State property. For example, if the Record object is being opened asynchronously, the State property will return a value of 5 (adStateOpen + adStateExecuting).

NOTE ObjectStateEnum also contains the value adStateFetching, but this value currently is not applicable to the State property of the Record object.

ADO RECORD OBJECT FUNCTIONS AND METHODS

Now let's examine the functions and methods exposed by the Record object and shown in the following table.

RECORD OBJECT FUNCTIONS AND METHODS

Function or Method Name	Description
Cancel	Cancels an asynchronous action on the Record object
Close	Closes an open Record object
CopyRecord	Copies the Record object to another location
DeleteRecord	Deletes the Record object
GetChildren	Retrieves the child data associated with the Record object
MoveRecord	Moves the Record object to another location
Open	Opens an existing Record object or creates a new Record object

Cancel Method

Use the *Cancel* method to cancel a pending asynchronous call on the Record object. This method can cancel calls to the *Open, CopyRecord, DeleteRecord,* and *MoveRecord* methods on the Record object, which can all be called asynchronously if the OLE DB provider supports asynchronous operations. The *Cancel* method takes no parameters.

Close Method

The *Close* method closes an open Record object. Like the *Close* method on a Recordset object, a Record object's *Close* method does not remove the object from memory. The *Close* method takes no parameters.

CopyRecord Method

The *CopyRecord* method copies a Record and its contents to another location. This method accepts six parameters:

```
Record.CopyRecord Source, Destination, UserName, Password, _
                  Options, Async
```

The *Source* parameter is optional and accepts a string to denote the Record you want to copy. If you omit this parameter, the data referenced by the current Record object will be copied. The *Destination* parameter is marked as optional in the ADO Help files, but it's actually required. This parameter accepts a string value to specify the location where you want to create a new copy of the Record object.

The *UserName* and *Password* parameters are optional and can be used to authorize the user to copy the Record to the specified destination. You can use the optional *Options* parameter to specify which of the attributes available in CopyRecordOptions-Enum (and listed in the following table) you want. The *Options* parameter can accept the sum of multiple values from CopyRecordOptionsEnum.

COPYRECORDOPTIONSENUM VALUES

Constant	Value	Description
adCopyUnspecified	−1	This is the default.
adCopyOverWrite	1	Overwrites whatever data is currently stored in the location specified by the *Destination* parameter. The *CopyRecord* method will fail if you attempt to copy over existing data without specifying this option.
adCopyNonRecursive	2	Copies the Record object but none of the child data associated with it. For example, *CopyRecord* copies the directory but not the files and subdirectories contained in it.

Constant	*Value*	*Description*
adCopyAllowEmulation	4	Requests that the provider attempt to simulate the copy (using download, upload, and delete operations) if the attempt to copy the Record object fails, because the destination URL is on a different server or serviced by a different provider than the source. Note that specifying this option can cause increased latency and/or data loss because of different provider capabilities when moving resources between providers.

The optional *Async* parameter accepts a Boolean value that indicates whether you want to call the *CopyRecord* method asynchronously. By default, this parameter is set to False. (Be aware that not all OLE DB providers that support the Record object allow asynchronous operations on the Record object.)

DeleteRecord Method

Use the *DeleteRecord* method to delete the Record and its contents. The *DeleteRecord* method accepts two optional parameters, as shown here:

```
Record.DeleteRecord Source, Async
```

The *Source* parameter accepts a string to denote the Record you want to delete. If you omit this parameter, the data currently referenced by the Record object will be deleted. The *Async* parameter accepts a Boolean value and indicates whether you want to call the *DeleteRecord* method asynchronously. By default, this parameter is set to False. (Note that not all OLE DB providers that support the Record object allow asynchronous operations on the Record object.)

GetChildren Method

The *GetChildren* method returns a Recordset object, as shown:

```
Set Recordset = Record.GetChildren
```

The returned Recordset object contains the child data associated with the current Record. You can call this method on Record objects that have a RecordType property value of adCollectionRecord. Depending on the functionality that your OLE DB provider supports, you might be able to call this method on a Record object whose RecordType is adStructDoc.

MoveRecord Method

The *MoveRecord* method copies a Record object and its contents to another location, and then deletes it from its current location. This method accepts the following six parameters:

```
Record.MoveRecord Source, Destination, UserName, Password, _
                  Options, Async
```

All the parameters behave the same as the parameters for the *CopyRecord* method, with the exception of the *Options* parameter. Rather than taking a value from CopyRecordOptionsEnum, the *Options* parameter for the *MoveRecord* method accepts values from MoveRecordOptionsEnum, shown in the next table. The *Options* parameter can accept the sum of multiple values from MoveRecordOptionsEnum.

MoveRecordOptionsEnum Values

Constant	Value	Description
adMoveUnspecified	−1	This is the default.
adMoveOverWrite	1	Overwrites whatever data is currently stored in the location specified by the *Destination* parameter. The *MoveRecord* method will fail if you attempt to move data onto existing data without specifying this option.
adMoveDontUpdateLinks	2	Modifies the default behavior of the *MoveRecord* method by not updating the hypertext links of the source Record object. The default behavior depends on the capabilities of the provider. The move operation updates links if the provider offers this capability. If the provider cannot fix links or if this value isn't specified, the move succeeds even when links have not been fixed.
adMoveAllowEmulation	4	Requests that the provider attempt to simulate the move (using download, upload, and delete operations) if the attempt to move the Record object fails because the destination URL is on a different server or serviced by a different provider than the source. Note that specifying this option can cause increased latency and/or data loss because of different provider capabilities when moving resources between providers.

Open Method

Use the *Open* method to open an existing Record or create a new one. The *Open* method has seven parameters, all of which are optional:

```
Record.Open Source, ActiveConnection, Mode, CreateOptions, _
            Options, UserName, Password
```

The *Source* parameter accepts a string or a Recordset and indicates the location of the data in your data store. You can use this parameter to override the current setting of the Record object's Source property. If you omit this parameter, ADO will use the current setting for the Source property.

The *ActiveConnection* parameter accepts a connection string or a Connection object to indicate the location of your data store. Omitting this parameter will cause ADO to use the current value of the Record object's ActiveConnection property to connect to your data store. Using this parameter overrides the current setting for the ActiveConnection property on the Record object.

The *Mode* parameter accepts values from ConnectModeEnum and corresponds to the Record object's Mode property to specify the access mode used to communicate with your data store. The *CreateOptions* parameter accepts values available in RecordCreateOptionsEnum, listed in the following table.

RECORDCREATEOPTIONSENUM VALUES

Constant	Value	Description
adFailIfNotExists	−1	Default; results in a run-time error if the value in the *Source* parameter points to a nonexistent node
adCreateNonCollection	0	Creates a new Record object with a RecordType value of adSimpleRecord
adCreateCollection	8192	Creates a new Record object with a RecordType value of adCollectionRecord
adOpenIfExists	33554432	Specifies that if the Record object at the location used in the *Source* parameter exists in your data store, the *Open* method will open that Record object rather than create a new one
adCreateOverwrite	67108864	Specifies that if the Record object at the location used in the *Source* parameter exists in your data store, the *Open* method will overwrite that data with a new Record
adCreateStructDoc	−2147483648	Creates a new Record object with a RecordType value of adStructDoc instead of opening an existing Record

You can use the *Options* parameter to supply a combination of values from RecordOpenOptionsEnum for further options upon opening your Record, as this next table shows.

RECORDOPENOPTIONSENUM VALUES

Constant	Value	Description
adOpenRecordUnspecified	−1	This is the default.
adOpenAsync	4096	Indicates that you want to open the Record object in asynchronous mode.
adDelayFetchStream	16384	Specifies that the default stream associated with the Record object need not be fetched initially.
adDelayFetchFields	32768	Specifies not to fetch the fields associated with the Record object initially, but to fetch each field at the first attempt to access that field.
adOpenSource	8388608	Indicates that if the value in the *Source* parameter points to a node containing an executable script (such as an .asp script file), a Record containing the source is opened rather than the executed contents of the script. Only valid with noncollection Record objects.

You can specify the *UserName* and *Password* parameters to authorize the user to open or create the Record.

ADO STREAM OBJECT

In addition to the Record object, ADO 2.5 introduces the Stream object to the ADO object model. Although you can use the Stream object in conjunction with the Record object to access document-based data, the Stream object can also be used independently in ways that traditional database programmers and web programmers alike will find useful.

Working with Document Data

While the Record object allows you to interact with the structure of documents, the Stream object lets you access the contents of those documents. You can use the Stream object's *Open* method to access the default stream of data associated with the Record. From there, you can read and modify the contents of the document through the Stream object's properties and methods. The code that follows uses a Stream object to store the contents of a file in a Record object:

```
Stream.Open Record, adModeReadWrite, adOpenStreamFromRecord
Stream.Position = 0
Stream.LoadFromFile strPathToFile
Stream.Flush
```

Working with Persistent Data

In ADO 2.5, the Recordset object's persistence features have been enhanced to work with Stream objects. You can persist data to a Stream rather than to a file by using the Stream object's *Save* method. To turn that data back into a Recordset object, simply use the Stream object as the *Source* parameter on the Recordset's *Open* method.

Working with BLOB Data

Writing code to access and modify BLOB (binary large object) data (long string and binary fields) in your database has never been easy. Programmers using ADO and its predecessors have had to rely on the Field object's *GetChunk* and *AppendChunk* methods...until now.

BLOB fields often contain the contents of files. The Stream object greatly simplifies the process of interacting with this data. You don't need to access the data in small chunks or determine how much data you're about to access. For example, to retrieve the contents of the ImageField field and store that data in a file, you could use the following code:

```
Stream.Type = adTypeBinary
Stream.Write Recordset.Fields("ImageField").Value
Stream.SaveToFile strPathToFile
```

To move the contents of the file back to the database, you'd use this code:

```
Stream.Type = adTypeBinary
Stream.LoadFromFile strPathToFile
Recordset.Fields("ImageField").Value = Stream.Read
```

ADO STREAM OBJECT PROPERTIES

Here's a list of the properties available on the Stream object.

STREAM OBJECT PROPERTIES

Property Name	Data Type	Description
Charset	String	Specifies the character set for the text stream
EOS	Boolean	Indicates whether the current position is at the end of stream (EOS)
LineSeparator	LineSeparatorEnum	Specifies the character or combination of characters used as the line separator in the text stream
Mode	ConnectModeEnum	Indicates the permissions for modifying data in the Stream object

(continued)

Stream Object Properties *continued*

Property Name	Data Type	Description
Position	Long	Specifies the current position in the stream
Size	Long	Indicates the size of the stream of data
State	ObjectStateEnum	Indicates the current state of the Stream object
Type	StreamTypeEnum	Indicates the type of data stored in the Stream object

Charset Property

The Charset property contains a string that specifies the character set used to store string data in the Stream. You can set this property to any of the registered character sets available in your local registry under the key HKEY_CLASSES_ROOT\MIME\ Database\Charset. The Stream object's Position property must be set to 0 before you can set the Charset property. If the Stream is set to store binary data, this property is ignored.

The Stream object stores text data in Unicode format, no matter what the value of the Charset property is. If you're going to work with text data that uses a different character set, you should set the Charset property to reflect that character set so ADO can translate the data to the correct format as it's read into and out of the Stream object. Say you're working with ANSI data and you want to store that data in a Stream object and then save it to a file. If you leave the Charset property with its default setting, the data will be saved to the text file in Unicode format. However, you can set the Charset property to the appropriate character set so your data will be stored to the text file in the desired format. For example, if you want to specify that you're using ANSI data, set the Charset property as shown here:

```
Stream.Charset = "iso-8859-1"
```

Remember that this property affects how ADO accepts and returns string data, so you're best off setting this property when the Stream object is closed. You can modify the Charset property after you've already stored text in your Stream, but this will only affect how ADO translates the string data when it's returned.

EOS Property

The EOS property is similar to the EOF property on the Recordset object. It stores a Boolean value that indicates whether you're positioned at the end of the data stored in the Stream object. You can call the *SetEOS* method to denote the end of the data.

LineSeparator Property

Use the LineSeparator property on the Stream object to control the character or characters that ADO will use to separate lines of text. This value can be set to any of the values available in LineSeparatorEnum, shown in the following table. You can set the LineSeparator property on the Stream object at any time, regardless of whether the Stream is open or closed.

LINESEPARATORENUM VALUES

Constant	Value	Description
adCRLF	−1	Default; a combination of the carriage return and line feed characters will be used to separate lines of text.
adLF	10	The line feed character will be used to separate lines of text.
adCR	13	The carriage return character will be used to separate lines of text.

Mode Property

The Mode property indicates the permissions for modifying the Stream object. This property contains a long value that represents a bitmask of values in ConnectModeEnum. (See "Mode Property" under the Record object discussion earlier in this chapter for a list of values.) The Stream object's Mode property functions similarly to the Record object's Mode property.

Position Property

The Position property contains a long value that specifies the current byte position (0-based) in the stream of data. This property is read/write while the Stream object is open. If you attempt to check the Position property on a closed Stream, you'll receive a run-time error.

When using a Stream to store Unicode data or other multibyte string data, be sure to set the Position property to an even number because each character uses 2 bytes of space.

Size Property

The Size property is read-only and returns a long value that indicates the size, in bytes, of the data stored in the Stream object. Checking the value of this property on a closed Stream will generate a run-time error. The Size property will return −1 if the data in the Stream object is an undetermined size. If the data is too large to be stored in a long integer, the Size property will be truncated.

State Property

The Stream object's State property has the same functionality for a Stream object as the Record object's State property has for a Record. See "State Property" under the Record object discussion earlier in this chapter (page 143) for a description of the State property and its possible values.

Type Property

The Type property indicates the type of data stored in the Stream object. This property will take one of the values in StreamTypeEnum, as listed in the following table. You can set the Type property on a closed Stream object or on an open Stream object whose Position property value is 0.

STREAMTYPEENUM VALUES

Constant	Value	Description
adTypeBinary	1	The Stream object contains binary data.
adTypeText	2	Default; the Stream object contains text data.

ADO STREAM OBJECT FUNCTIONS AND METHODS

Let's examine the functions and methods available on the Stream object and shown in the following table.

STREAM OBJECT FUNCTIONS AND METHODS

Function or Method Name	Description
Cancel	Cancels a pending asynchronous call to a Stream object
Close	Closes an open Stream object
CopyTo	Copies data from the Stream object to another Stream object
Flush	Flushes the contents stored in the Stream object's buffer
LoadFromFile	Loads the contents of a file into the stream
Open	Opens the Stream object
Read	Reads binary data from the stream
ReadText	Reads text data from the stream

Function or Method Name	Description
SaveToFile	Persists data from the Stream object to a file
SetEOS	Sets the current position as the end of the Stream object
SkipLine	Moves to the beginning of the next line of data in a text stream
Write	Appends binary data to the stream
WriteText	Appends text data to the stream

Cancel Method

You can call the *Cancel* method to terminate a pending asynchronous call to the Stream object's *Open* method. This method takes no parameters.

Close Method

The *Close* method closes a Stream object and releases the data associated with that Stream object. This method takes no parameters.

CopyTo Method

You can use the *CopyTo* method to move data from one Stream object to another. The *CopyTo* method takes two parameters as shown here:

```
Stream.CopyTo DestStream, NumChars
```

The first parameter, *DestStream*, is required and accepts an open Stream object. The second parameter, *NumChars*, is optional and accepts a long integer specifying the number of characters or bytes (starting at the current position) to copy to *DestStream*. The default value for this parameter is –1, which specifies that all data, from the current position to EOS, should be copied. If you specify a value that's larger than the remaining number of characters or bytes in the source Stream, this method will copy only the remaining characters or bytes and no error will occur.

If you're using a Stream of type adTypeBinary, the *NumChars* parameter actually specifies the number of characters to copy, regardless of whether you're using Unicode or ANSI strings. After ADO copies the data from the source Stream to the destination Stream, the current position in the source Stream will be the byte or character that follows the last byte or character copied.

Flush Method

Call the *Flush* method to send the data buffered in the Stream object to that object's underlying source to ensure the contents have been written. You should not need to call *Flush* prior to closing your Stream because calling the *Close* method will implicitly flush the buffered data. If you need to write the data stored in the buffer while keeping the Stream object open, that's a good time to call the *Flush* method. The *Flush* method takes no parameters.

LoadFromFile Method

If you want to load the contents of a file into a Stream object, call the *LoadFromFile* method. This method takes a single string parameter that contains the name and location of the file you want to load:

```
Stream.LoadFromFile FileName
```

The *FileName* parameter can contain any valid pathname and filename in Universal Naming Convention (UNC) format. If the specified file doesn't exist, a trappable error occurs.

When you use the *LoadFromFile* method, the contents of the file overwrite the contents of the Stream. When the *LoadFromFile* method completes, the Stream object's Position property will be set to 0—the beginning of the Stream.

Open Method

The *Open* method opens a Stream object from a Record object or a URL. The *Open* method accepts five optional parameters, as shown here:

```
Stream.Open Source, Mode, OpenOptions, UserName, Password
```

The *Source* parameter specifies the source of the data to retrieve into the Stream object. This parameter accepts an open Record object or a string that contains a valid URL. You can also specify an empty string for the *Source* parameter, to open an empty Stream object. If you omit this parameter, the value of the Source property will be used.

The *Mode* parameter accepts a value from ConnectModeEnum and corresponds to the Stream object's Mode property. (See page 141 for a list of the values in ConnectModeEnum.) If you omit this parameter, the value of the Mode property will be used. The *OpenOptions* parameter accepts values from StreamOpenOptionsEnum, shown in the following table.

STREAMOPENOPTIONSENUM VALUES

Constant	Value	Description
adOpenStreamUnspecified	−1	Default; opens the Stream object with default options.
adOpenStreamAsync	1	Opens the Stream object in asynchronous mode.
adOpenStreamFromRecord	4	Specifies that the *Source* parameter contains an open Record object. The default stream associated with that node is opened.

The *UserName* and *Password* parameters contain strings that authorize the user to open the Stream.

Read Method

Use the *Read* method to retrieve binary data from the Stream object. This method accepts a long integer and returns a Variant:

```
Variant = Stream.Read NumBytes
```

The *NumBytes* parameter specifies the number of bytes to return, starting with the current position in the Stream. If you specify a number that's larger than the number of bytes remaining in the Stream, the *Read* method will return only the remaining data; no error will occur. If you omit this parameter, this method will return all the data from the current position through the end of the Stream. *NumBytes* can also accept the value adReadAll from StreamReadEnum, the values from which are shown in the following table.

STREAMREADENUM VALUES

Constant	Value	Description
adReadAll	−1	Default; reads all remaining characters in the Stream object
adReadLine	−2	Reads until the end of the current line

ReadText Method

The *ReadText* method is similar to the *Read* method, except that it retrieves text data rather than binary data from the Stream object. *ReadText* takes a single parameter, *NumChars*, and is shown here:

```
String = Stream.ReadText NumChars
```

In addition to a long integer value, *NumChars* can accept either of the values in StreamReadEnum.

Whether the Stream object contains single-byte characters (such as ANSI) or multibyte characters (such as Unicode), *ReadText* will return the number of characters specified rather than the number of bytes. The Stream object's Charset property specifies the type of character data stored in the Stream.

SaveToFile Method

To save the contents of the Stream to a file, call the *SaveToFile* method. This method takes two parameters as follows:

```
Stream.SaveToFile FileName, SaveOptions
```

The *FileName* parameter is required and accepts a fully qualified name for the file to create. This parameter is a string data type and accepts UNC paths. The *SaveOptions* parameter is optional and accepts one or both of the values from Save-OptionsEnum, shown in the following table.

SAVEOPTIONSENUM VALUES

Constant	Value	Description
adSaveCreateNotExist	1	Default; creates a new file. Raises a trappable error if the file already exists.
adSaveCreateOverWrite	2	Overwrites the existing file if it exists.

When the *SaveToFile* method completes, the Stream object's current position will be at EOS.

SetEOS Method

SetEOS designates the current position as the end of the stream of data. All data from that position onward will be lost. This method takes no parameters.

SkipLine Method

The *SkipLine* method skips to the beginning of the next line of text in your Stream. If your text data has no more remaining line separators, the position will be set to the end of the Stream—the Stream object's EOS property will return True and its Position property will return the same value as its Size property.

Write Method

Use the *Write* method to append binary data to your Stream. The *Write* method accepts a single parameter, shown here:

```
Stream.Write Buffer
```

The *Buffer* parameter is required and accepts a byte array containing the data to append to the Stream.

After the *Write* method completes, the current position of the Stream will be the byte following the data appended to the Stream. If you aren't positioned at the end of the Stream prior to calling *Write*, you'll overwrite data in the Stream with the data in the *Buffer* parameter.

WriteText Method

Use the *WriteText* method to append text data to your Stream. The *WriteText* method accepts two parameters, shown here:

`Stream.WriteText` *Data, Options*

The *Data* parameter is required and accepts a string containing the data to append to the Stream. The *Options* parameter is optional and accepts one of the two values in StreamWriteEnum, which the following table describes.

STREAMWRITEENUM VALUES

Constant	Value	Description
adWriteChar	0	Default; appends only the string in the *Data* parameter to the Stream object
adWriteLine	1	Appends the string in the *Data* parameter, as well as the line separator specified by the LineSeparator property, to the Stream object

After the *WriteText* method completes, the current position of the Stream will be the character following the data appended to the Stream. If you aren't positioned at the end of the Stream prior to calling *WriteText*, you'll overwrite the existing data in the Stream with the data in the *Data* parameter.

QUESTIONS THAT SHOULD BE ASKED MORE FREQUENTLY

Q. *Do you have a sample that shows how to use the Record object and the Stream object to work with document data?*

A. Why yes, I do. The My Web Site sample included on the companion CD uses the Record and Stream objects in conjunction with the OLE DB Provider For Internet Publishing to interact with a web site. You can upload and download files as well as copy, move, and delete files and folders. For more information, see Appendix B.

Q. *I'm a database programmer, and I work with databases such as SQL Server, Oracle, and Access. I've read all about the Record object, but I still don't see what value it offers me. Am I missing something?*

A. Not really. The Record object is valuable for programmers who want to access document data, such as files and e-mail messages, through OLE DB providers that support the Record object. Don't try to force the Record object into your applications.

Q. *I'm having problems connecting to my web site using the OLE DB Provider For Internet Publishing. Any suggestions?*

A. Keep an eye on the online Knowledge Base on Microsoft's Web site. As more programmers begin to use this OLE DB provider, you'll likely see a FAQ that covers possible connection problems. Web server setup, WebDAV, and security are not my forte.

Q.   *In Chapter 5, you recommended storing files in the file system rather than in the database. Now that the Stream object makes interacting with BLOB data simple, do you recommend storing the contents of files in databases?*

A.   No. Although the Stream object definitely simplifies interacting with BLOB data (I'll never call *AppendChunk* or *GetChunk* again!), I still recommend storing files in the file system rather than in the database. While keeping the contents of your files in your database might be simpler from the standpoints of programming, backup, and security, you'll still achieve much better performance by storing filenames in the database and using the operating system to move files between the client and the server.

Chapter 7

Cursors, Foiled Again

In Chapter 4, we briefly discussed the CursorType property of the Recordset object. In this chapter, we examine cursors in more depth.

WHAT IS A CURSOR?

A cursor is a data structure that stores the results of your query. In ADO, you can think of the Recordset object as a COM object that simplifies accessing data in a cursor. The cursor type determines the functionality available to a specific Recordset object: different types of cursors support different levels of functionality. Some cursors allow you to view changes that other users have made to the records that make up the results of your query. Some cursors only let you move forward through the results of your query, while other cursors allow you to move forward and backward.

This chapter describes the different types of cursors and explains the functionality available to the Recordset objects defined by each type. Will you see changes made by other users? Will you be able to determine the number of records returned by your query? Will you be able to bookmark a particular record and move back to it later? What happens when the cursor type you requested isn't available?

DEFINITIONS OF CURSOR TYPES

Many different types of cursors exist, and each has its own unique set of characteristics. Some cursors allow updating, and some allow you to view changes made by other users. Let's take a look at the features of each type of cursor in some depth.

Forward-Only Cursors

The forward-only cursor is the simplest type of cursor. As its name suggests, and as shown in Figure 7-1, you can only move forward through the records in this cursor. After you move beyond a record, it is no longer available in the cursor. Although this level of functionality might seem limiting, it is extremely fast.

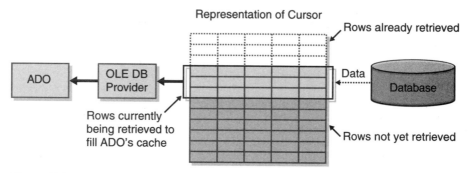

Figure 7-1 *The forward-only cursor.*

Most client/server developers prefer the forward-only cursor because of its speed and the minimal stress it places on the database system. This cursor allows developers to retrieve the data from the cursor (in the case of ADO, the Recordset) and manage the results of the query on their own—in a Variant array or a collection, for example.

The adOpenForwardOnly constant, a CursorTypeEnum type, corresponds to this type of cursor. It is the default value for a Recordset object's CursorType property when you use the default value (adUseServer) for the Recordset object's Cursor-Location property. ADO retrieves from the cursor up to the number of records specified by the CacheSize property, and then when you navigate beyond the data in the cache, ADO retrieves the next set of records.

You can use the Recordset's *MoveNext* method to navigate forward through the Recordset, but using the *MovePrevious*, *MoveFirst*, or *MoveLast* methods will generate an error stating that the cursor does not support fetching backward. You can use the *Move* method with a negative number to move backward as long as you do not navigate outside the records currently held in the cache.

Some database systems support updatable forward-only cursors, some do not.

Firehose Cursors

There is a special type of cursor often called a firehose cursor. It's a forward-only cursor that is read-only and returns data one record at a time. The data comes out extremely fast—like water coming out of a fire hose—and it's up to you to figure out what to do with it. Some databases and OLE DB providers support only this type of cursor because of its performance and simplicity. Most database systems use this scenario (forward-only, read-only, and one record at a time) as the default way to return the results of a query, and those systems use no cursor-like structure to store these results. Therefore, a firehose cursor is sometimes not considered a cursor.

In order to use a firehose cursor in Remote Data Objects (RDO), you have to use an rdoQuery object and set the RowsetSize property (similar to the CacheSize property on the ADO Recordset object) to 1 or set the CursorDriver property to rdUseNone. Using firehose cursors with ADO is simpler because this is the default type of cursor used by ADO. If you want to use a non-firehose forward-only cursor, you'll need to set the Recordset's CacheSize property to an integer larger than the default of 1.

Microsoft SQL Server is optimized for this type of query. If you decide to use a firehose cursor with SQL Server, you'll see excellent performance, but with one important caveat: SQL Server can support only one active query on a connection. If you open a firehose cursor and do not fetch all of the data, and then close that cursor, you've tied up that connection. Programmers familiar with RDO might remember the error message "Connection is busy with results from another hstmt." You received this error if you tried to use a connection that was busy, such as in the case just described.

For better or for worse, OLE DB—the technology on which ADO is based—simplifies things for the programmer. Rather than generate an error message, the OLE DB provider will simply request another connection. Thus, if you use code like the following, you'll be using the default firehose cursor type and will open up three separate connections to your SQL Server database:

```
Set cnNorthwind = New ADODB.Connection
cnNorthwind.CursorLocation = adUseServer
cnNorthwind.Open strConn
Set rsCustomers = cnNorthwind.Execute("SELECT * FROM Customers")
Set rsOrders = cnNorthwind.Execute("SELECT * FROM Orders")
Set rsProducts = cnNorthwind.Execute("SELECT * FROM Products")
```

If you use any other type of cursor, the connection is available as soon as SQL Server returns data from your query. The following code specifies that we want to retrieve the results of our queries into static cursors.

```
Set cnNorthwind = New ADODB.Connection
cnNorthwind.CursorLocation = adUseServer
cnNorthwind.Open strConn
Set rsCustomers = New ADODB.Recordset
rsCustomers.Open "SELECT * FROM Customers", cnNorthwind, adOpenStatic
Set rsOrders = New ADODB.Recordset
rsOrders.Open "SELECT * FROM Orders", cnNorthwind, adOpenStatic
Set rsProducts = New ADODB.Recordset
rsProducts.Open "SELECT * FROM Products", cnNorthwind, adOpenStatic
```

DEALING WITH MULTIPLE CONNECTIONS

The behavior in which an OLE DB provider establishes added connections when needed is part of the OLE DB specification. The development team felt that this behavior would simplify programming by avoiding error messages such as "Connection is busy with results from another hstmt." This change is wonderful for programmers developing applications that will be accessed by a small number of simultaneous users.

For applications that need to handle large numbers of concurrent users, however, this change in behavior has met with a bit of frustration. Some developers notice the automatic addition of connections only when they deploy their applications and see a much higher than expected number of connections to their database.

What can you do to avoid a similar fate? My advice is to use a utility that displays the connections to your database. SQL Server 7 users can use SQL Server Profiler or, as it was called in previous versions, SQL Trace. Run your application and see if your code generates added connections. If it does, determine why your code might require the added connections.

The most likely causes for added connections are

- Using a connection that still has pending results from a firehose cursor

- Using a connection that has an asynchronous operation still running

Some OLE DB providers can help you to prevent multiple connections from being established. The OLE DB Provider For SQL Server exposes a dynamic property through the Connection object that you can set to make the provider generate an error rather than create an additional connection. The following code will generate an error when you attempt to retrieve the results of the second query:

```
Set cnNorthwind = New ADODB.Connection
cnNorthwind.CursorLocation = adUseServer
cnNorthwind.Open strConn
cnNorthwind.Properties("Multiple Connections") = False
Set rsCustomers = cnNorthwind.Execute("SELECT * FROM Customers")
Set rsOrders = cnNorthwind.Execute("SELECT * FROM Orders")
```

Unfortunately, the error message you'll receive—"Object was open"—doesn't do a great job of explaining the reason the error occurred, but at least you'll keep the OLE DB provider from generating unexpected connections to your database. If you change the code to retrieve the results of the initial query before submitting the second query, as shown below, the code will run without generating an error.

```
Set rsCustomers = cnNorthwind.Execute("SELECT * FROM Customers")
Do While Not rsCustomers.EOF
    rsCustomers.MoveNext
Loop
Set rsOrders = cnNorthwind.Execute("SELECT * FROM Orders")
```

Hopefully other OLE DB providers will implement a similar feature. Perhaps it will even become a part of the next set of OLE DB specifications.

Static Cursors

A static cursor—shown in Figure 7-2—is similar to a forward-only cursor except that the static cursor supports scrolling forward *and* backward. The query processor builds the results of the query and populates the entire cursor. You can navigate back and forth through the cursor as long as you'd like, and the data won't change. As the cursor name implies, the data is static.

Representation of Cursor

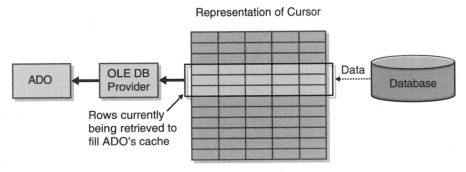

Figure 7-2 *The static cursor.*

Changes made by other users to the data in the database that corresponds to the results of the query will not be visible. You also won't see new records added by other users that satisfy your query criteria, nor will you see that another user has deleted a record that exists in your cursor. If your query retrieved customer account information into a static cursor, you won't see changes that another user has made to the customer's balance due. Again, the data in your static cursor is static.

Static cursors are traditionally defined as read-only. All client-side Recordsets are marked as "static," but we'll talk about this scenario a little later in this chapter in the section "Client-Side Cursors."

If you use an ADO Recordset that communicates using a static cursor, you can use all of the different *Move* methods to navigate through the Recordset. ADO will fetch the number of records specified by the CacheSize property. As you navigate through the Recordset, ADO will fetch more data from the cursor any time you step outside the data currently cached.

Keyset Cursors

While a static cursor is similar to a forward-only cursor in nature, a keyset cursor is a much more complicated construct. Not only does a keyset cursor allow you to update data, but it also lets you see changes made by other users.

As mentioned in the previous section, the query processor will completely populate a static cursor when you submit your query. For a keyset cursor, the query processor initially retrieves only the data required to locate the records in your tables that will satisfy the results of your query, as shown in Figure 7-3. Generally this data corresponds to the primary key in your tables and is often referred to as the keyset.

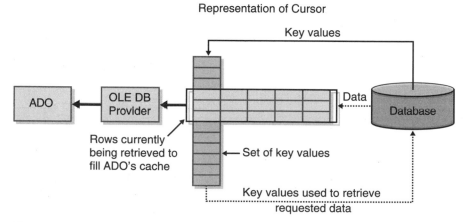

Figure 7-3 *The keyset cursor.*

The data in the keyset serves two purposes. First, the query processor uses this data to locate the records that satisfy your query. Second, if you update data in any of the records in your keyset cursor, the keyset data enables the query processor and/ or the database system to locate that record in the table and update it.

You can open a keyset cursor as read-only or updatable. In addition, changes made by other users will be visible in your keyset cursor. As it does with the static cursor, ADO stores the number of records in its local cache specified by the CacheSize property. Each time ADO requests data from the keyset cursor to fill the cache, the query processor locates the appropriate entries in the database based on the keyset data.

For example, if you open a keyset cursor on the contents of the Customers table, the query processor will store the CustomerID field in the keyset. Then every time ADO refills the cache, the query processor will use the CustomerID to return the latest information from the database to the keyset cursor. If another user has changed a particular customer's balance due, you'll see that change the next time you fetch that customer's record.

Although you can see changes made by another user after you've opened your keyset cursor, you can't see new records added by other users that satisfy the criteria of your query. The data in the keyset (remember that this is the set of key values, not the cursor itself) is static.

Records deleted by other users will be removed from your keyset cursor the next time you refresh the cache. Be sure to do some testing with your particular OLE DB provider or ODBC driver. Depending on the behavior of that provider or driver, you might receive a trappable run-time error if you attempt to navigate to a deleted record. For example, if you move to a deleted record in a keyset cursor by setting the Bookmark property on your Recordset, you'll receive a run-time error if you're using the SQL Server ODBC driver but not if you're using the OLE DB provider. I'd love to tell you that the behavior you'll see will be consistent, but that's not the case.

Dynamic Cursors

The dynamic cursor behaves a lot like the keyset cursor. Initially, the query processor retrieves the key field information for the records that satisfy the search criteria, just like a keyset cursor. Also, the query processor returns the initial set of records to fill the client's cache. But this is where any similarity ends. If you are using a dynamic cursor, the next time the client requests another set of records the query processor will reexamine the contents of the database and rebuild the keyset before returning more records to the client application, as shown in Figure 7-4.

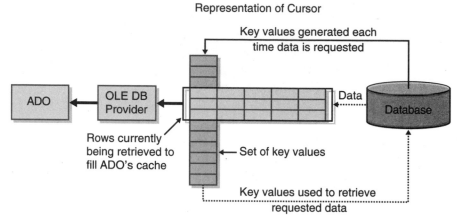

Figure 7-4 *The dynamic cursor.*

This functionality means that a dynamic cursor can contain records that other users have added since you initially submitted the query. Say you move to the beginning of your Recordset object and count the number of records in the Recordset by counting the number of times you need to call *MoveNext* until EOF is True. There's no guarantee that you'll come up with the same number of records in the Recordset if you call *MoveFirst* and loop through its contents again.

Mixed Cursors

The mixed cursor, a hybrid of the keyset and dynamic cursors, is seldom used and is not supported in ADO.

Client-Side Cursors

If you request a client-side recordset and then check the CursorType property, ADO will report that you're using a static cursor. This is not the "classic" use of a static cursor as described earlier in the "Static Cursors" section, and it's worth discussing how this cursor behaves.

When you request a client-side recordset, ADO passes your query to the OLE DB provider and retrieves the results through a firehose cursor. ADO stores the results of the query in its own Cursor Engine, as shown in Figure 7-5. At this point, you can scroll back and forth through your Recordset object, and ADO will retrieve the requested data from the Cursor Engine.

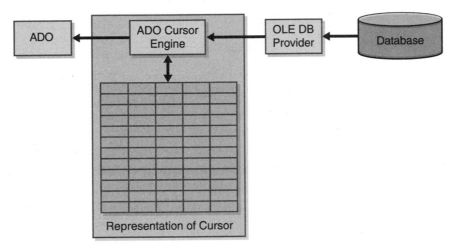

Figure 7-5 *Client-side cursor.*

So, as you navigate through your recordset you will not see changes made to the database by other users. Because the cursor supports scrolling, and because changes made by other users are not visible, the behavior of a client-side recordset most closely resembles that of a static cursor.

However, a client-side recordset can be updatable, a fact that seems to cause more confusion for experienced database developers than for novices. While discussing customers' applications with them, I found that quite a few experienced developers were basing their Recordset objects on server-side keyset cursors. They were doing this because more often than not they required an updatable Recordset and they understood that the ADO Cursor Engine only supports static cursors, which are read-only.

How are these static cursors updatable? We'll cover this topic in more depth in the next chapter, but here's a quick overview. ADO lets you modify the contents of the cursor. However, because this static cursor is maintained by the ADO Cursor Engine rather than by the database system, changing the contents of the cursor does not automatically update the corresponding records in your database. When you modify your client-side recordset and ask ADO to update the database, by means of the *Update* or *UpdateBatch* method, ADO interprets the changes you've made to the Recordset object and attempts to update the database by using action queries that reflect these changes.

Client-side cursors scale well because the ADO Cursor Engine stores the results of your query and lets your database system do what it was designed to do—maintain your data and process your queries.

DATABASE-SPECIFIC CURSOR CONSIDERATIONS

Many client/server database books purport that "cursors are evil," but you've probably realized by now that this isn't your typical client/server database book. Cursors are not inherently bad; in some cases, they're actually appropriate. Part of the problem is that they're widely misunderstood. "Cursors are evil" is an easy message to convey—and it's generally true of server-side cursors—but it's a little simplistic. I'd rather cover the pros and cons of cursors in different scenarios and let you make your own choices.

The terms server-side and client-side can be misleading when applied to cursors and Recordset objects. The terms are simple, but the concepts are not. Rather than asking, "Where is the data in a server-side cursor stored?" perhaps a better way to phrase the question is, "Am I storing the results of my query in the ADO Cursor Engine or not?" It's simple, direct, and to the point.

We recently touched on the subject of client-side Recordsets and how the ADO Cursor Engine maintains your data. Explaining where the cursor in a server-side cursor is located isn't quite as simple. It depends on what type of OLE DB provider or ODBC driver you're using. Let's cover the three most common databases used with ADO—SQL Server, Microsoft Access, and Oracle—and look at what it really means to use a server-side cursor when you work with a Recordset in these databases. I'll also explain where the data in the server-side cursor is located in each one.

Server-Side Cursors with SQL Server

The SQL Server database system supports cursors. When you use a server-side cursor with the SQL Server OLE DB provider or ODBC driver, you're using a cursor that's maintained by SQL Server itself. This is a very powerful feature. There are times when you want to process the results of a query in such a way that you absolutely can't live without an updatable cursor. But most of the time you can, and should, live without using SQL Server's cursors. Here are a few reasons why.

Imagine that SQL Server is an extremely important employee of yours—perhaps the person you ask to analyze large amounts of business data to generate reports for major presentations. Let's call her Syd. You want Syd to work within her specialty. You don't want her to spend her time organizing past reports in file cabinets and managing the library where they're stored. That wouldn't be wise use of Syd's time. Let someone else take care of the grunt work.

Similarly, you don't want SQL Server to get bogged down storing the results of your queries unless absolutely necessary. Think about a simple query in your application that returns a couple hundred records. Perhaps your application needs to continually work with the results of five such queries. A thousand employees, perhaps up to five hundred at any one time, will use your application. This puts a heavy usage load on the database. It makes much more sense for your database system to do what it's designed to do—store your data and process queries—rather than expend its resources storing the results of your queries.

Don't forget that if you're using server-side cursors in your application, you need a live connection to the database as you navigate through your Recordset. Are you sure you want to incur network round-trips each time your code or your user decides to scroll through the recordset? Another consideration is that this type of application doesn't scale well. As you add more users, you add more connections to your database at a linear rate, and the same instance of SQL Server needs to maintain the cursors for each user. Plus, you'll be unable to move to a multitiered application using technologies such as Component Services or Microsoft Transaction Server (MTS). Most multitiered applications require that the middle-tier objects maintain no state. In other words, your clients should not have live connections to your database.

If you're still not convinced that making widespread use of server-side cursors in your ADO and SQL Server application is a bad idea, check with your database administrator. Just prepare to be convincing when you say, "I was just kidding—I wanted to see how you'd react," if you want your database administrator to trust your judgment ever again. Experience has proven that basing your application on server-side cursors with SQL Server causes poor performance and scaling, and may also lead to hair loss and unemployment.

Server-Side Cursors with Access

Both the Access OLE DB provider and the Access ODBC driver support server-side cursors. They're implemented differently from SQL Server's cursors, however. The term "server" is a little misleading when it comes to server-side cursors in Access.

With SQL Server, the database server maintains the cursor while the OLE DB provider and ODBC driver simply access that cursor. With Access, the OLE DB provider and ODBC driver have to do a great deal more work: they have to examine the database file and generate the results of the query. While the database file might be central to your application, each client is directly accessing the database file by means of the OLE DB provider or ODBC driver.

This architecture scales better than SQL Server's cursors. Now don't overreact—I'm not saying you should use an Access database rather than SQL Server. Access databases aren't designed for high-stress, multiuser applications. The point is that as you add more users with this type of architecture, the Access database file and lock file are much busier but you're not tying up the server with the results of cursors. The cursors are maintained in the same process as ADO.

During the ADO 2.0 beta testing, one user noted that his large queries returned much faster with Data Access Objects (DAO) than with ADO, but only with Access databases. It turns out the difference in performance was actually between server-side and client-side cursors. By default, DAO stores the results of queries in what's essentially a server-side cursor. Opening a server-side ADO Recordset took the same amount of time as opening a DAO Recordset. So, why does it take longer to open a client-side ADO Recordset?

When using a client-side cursor with an Access database, you're essentially moving data from the Access cursor engine to the ADO Cursor Engine. (As mentioned earlier, ADO processes the results of the query from a firehose cursor and stores that data in its own Cursor Engine.) This process is more complicated than simply copying a block of memory. The Jet 4.0 OLE DB Provider or ODBC driver processes the query, generates the results, and then has to pass all of this data to the ADO Cursor Engine one record at a time. This process accounts for the difference in performance.

So should you simply not use client-side cursors with Access databases? Not so fast. Some of ADO's functionality (for instance, the ability to persist a Recordset to a file, the batch updating feature, the ability to sort your Recordset, and hierarchies) is available only with client-side Recordsets. Plus, if you're using a keyset or dynamic cursor to store the results of your Access queries, the OLE DB provider or ODBC driver still needs to examine the database every time you step outside the number of cached records specified by the Recordset's CacheSize property.

While you might see a difference in performance between client-side and server-side cursors when you open the Recordset, as the beta tester in our example did, that's not a comprehensive test. When you consider what you do with the cursor during its lifetime—scrolling back and forth, updating, and so forth—you're normally going to see similar performance between the two cursors. I myself generally use client-side cursors with Access databases.

Server-Side Cursors with Oracle

Recently, Oracle added support for cursors outside of a stored procedure. However, to the best of my knowledge, there are no OLE DB providers or ODBC drivers that take advantage of this new feature of Oracle databases. Yet the Microsoft ODBC driver for Oracle has always supported cursors. You can open up a Recordset object with a CursorLocation property value of adUseServer and get a keyset cursor with the Microsoft ODBC driver for Oracle. How is this possible?

The Microsoft ODBC driver for Oracle actually implements the cursor in a way that is somewhat similar to how the Access OLE DB provider and ODBC driver implement cursors. For a keyset cursor, the Microsoft ODBC driver for Oracle requests keyset information for the records that satisfy the query's criteria and then retrieves those records whenever the Recordset requests more data.

This architecture places less stress on the database server than does SQL Server's implementation of cursors. The data in the cursor is cached in the Microsoft ODBC driver for Oracle, and the Oracle server does what it does best—it maintains data and processes queries.

As of Microsoft Data Access Components (MDAC) 2.1, the Microsoft OLE DB Provider For Oracle does not implement cursors. You can only retrieve data out of a firehose cursor. If you need a Recordset that supports scrolling and/or updating, you can still use the Microsoft OLE DB Provider For Oracle if you use the ADO Cursor Engine to provide that functionality.

YOU CAN'T ALWAYS GET WHAT YOU WANT

Back-end databases, OLE DB providers, ODBC drivers, CursorLocation, CursorType, LockType, CommandType, oh my! What's a database developer to do? With a little experience and a lot of reading, you'll develop a good feel for which combinations are possible and which aren't. But what happens if you do request a particular combination that's impossible? What if you request an updatable server-side static cursor? What happens if you request a client-side dynamic cursor?

As you're charting this new territory, you'll probably explore different options and experiment with code, and along the way you'll inadvertently discover the answers to questions such as these. There's one aspect of this discussion that relates to a bad joke about the difference between Microsoft Visual Basic and Visual C++ programmers: Visual Basic programmers get excited when their applications run without generating an error; Visual C++ programmers get excited when their applications simply compile. There's a kernel of truth here: it's comparatively easy to get Visual Basic code to run. But keep in mind that just because your Visual Basic code runs without generating an error, don't assume that you're getting what you asked for.

"Why didn't I get an error if I didn't get what I asked for?" you might wonder.

No, this is not a Microsoft conspiracy to placate developers. Imagine you're building an application that will access a variety of different databases. Perhaps your application will actually be an ad hoc query tool in which the user supplies the connection string, the query string, the cursor type, and so forth. In such a case, you'd probably prefer not to be required to repeatedly request a Recordset, asking for slightly less functionality each time, until you get the exact Recordset you want. You'd have a much easier time developing your code if you could pass a request to ADO for a particular type of Recordset and then examine what you actually received. This is precisely what happens.

If you ask for a client-side dynamic cursor, you'll get a static cursor without generating an error. If you ask for an updatable server-side static cursor, you'll get an updatable keyset cursor if the OLE DB provider or ODBC driver can support one. Otherwise, you'll receive a read-only cursor. Programmers with experience using RDO or the ODBC API are already familiar with this behavior.

Check the CursorType property on the Recordset after you've opened it to find out if you got the cursor type you requested. It's up to the component that's implementing the cursor to specify what type of cursor you receive.

RecordCount and Bookmarks

When displaying data, many developers want to do two things as soon as they open their Recordset—display the results in a grid and display the number of records returned by the query. Depending on the cursor type, you might not be able to do either. You might find that the Recordset object's RecordCount property returns −1 and that you get an error when you try to bind your Recordset to your grid.

Why Does the RecordCount Property Return −1?

Not all cursors provide the functionality required to report how many records they contain. While developers who have a lot of experience with cursors might find this obvious, others are initially amazed—they find this behavior absurd. An ADO Recordset is unable to provide a definite value for RecordCount when using forward-only or dynamic cursors, while static and keyset cursors have a well-defined RecordCount.

With a static cursor, the data remains the same; changes made by other users will not be visible. If you scroll back and forth through the cursor, you'll always see the same number of records unless you're using a client-side cursor, in which case you're the only one adding or removing records. For this reason there is a well-defined number of records in a static cursor at all times. While keyset cursors allow you to see changes made by other users to the records that make up the cursor, membership in the cursor is still static. Thus, keyset cursors also contain a well-defined number of records.

Forward-only cursors are more concerned with performance than with functionality. You generally ask for data in a forward-only cursor if you want to retrieve data as quickly as possible. Forward-only cursors do not support a record count and the RecordCount property is set to −1 to reflect this. If you need to know how many records the query returned with a forward-only cursor, count the records as you fetch them. Alternatively, most database systems support a COUNT function that you can use to simply return the number of records retrieved by a query.

```
strSQL = "SELECT Count(CustomerID) FROM Customers"
Set rsNumCustomers = cnDatabase.Execute(strSQL, , adCmdText)
lngNumCustomers = rsNumCustomers(0).Value
rsNumCustomers.Close
```

Keep in mind that between the time you issue the query to retrieve the record count and the time you issue the query to retrieve the contents of the Customers table, the number of records in the table might have changed.

Dynamic cursors are geared more toward functionality than performance, but a dynamic cursor never contains a definite number of records. As discussed earlier, you can move to the first record of a dynamic cursor and examine each record to the end of the cursor in order to count them, but there's no guarantee that you'll find the same number of records if you perform that operation again. With a dynamic cursor, the query processor examines the data in the database to determine which records satisfy the query's criteria each time ADO requests more data to fill its cache. For this reason, when using a dynamic cursor, the RecordCount property returns –1 rather than reporting potentially misleading information.

What Do You Mean, "The rowset is not bookmarkable"?

This common but somewhat confusing error message might be familiar to some programmers. Let's talk about why this error message occurs and what you can do when you encounter it.

When envisioning the results of a query, many developers automatically imagine a nice, orderly grid of data. Grids are a great way to represent data, but only to a point. Not all grids are created equal. In Visual Basic 6, for example, the Hierarchical FlexGrid control can display the contents of some Recordsets that the DataGrid control cannot. If you try to bind the Hierarchical FlexGrid to a forward-only cursor, the grid will display the contents of the Recordset, while if you try to bind the DataGrid to a forward-only cursor, the grid will report an error saying, "The rowset is not bookmarkable."

The Hierarchical FlexGrid reads the contents of the Recordset into its own area of memory and displays that information in the grid. It's not really a bound control in the traditional sense. When you click on a particular record in the grid, you're not navigating to that record in the Recordset object. Once the Hierarchical FlexGrid reads the contents of the Recordset into its own internal data structures, it no longer interacts with the Recordset object. The grid is unaware of changes made to the Recordset, and vice versa.

With the DataGrid, on the other hand, clicking on a particular row in the grid automatically moves you to that row in the Recordset object to which the DataGrid is bound. While this may not seem impressive, it requires some functionality from the Recordset that's not supported for all cursors: the bookmark.

Think of a bookmark in the traditional sense—as a placeholder you put in a book to mark the page you want to return to later. You assume that the page you return to will be identical to the page you bookmarked. A bookmark in a cursor provides similar functionality. When you click on a record in the DataGrid, there must be some way of uniquely identifying each record in the cursor so that you can be sure you're moving to the correct record in the Recordset.

It's not enough to say, "Move to the fourth record in the cursor" if the membership in the cursor is not fixed (as in a dynamic cursor) or if the records in the cursor can be reordered (by changing the Sort property on a client-side Recordset). The records in the cursor must be uniquely identified in order to support bookmarks. This functionality is supported by the same cursor types that support the RecordCount property—static and keyset—since their membership is fixed.

Forward-only cursors cannot support bookmarks; since there's no way to move back to a particular record in a forward-only cursor, a bookmark serves no purpose. Dynamic cursors do not support bookmarks, because there is no guarantee that the record you want to mark will be in the cursor later.

QUESTIONS THAT SHOULD BE ASKED MORE FREQUENTLY

Q. *What type of cursor should I use?*
A. Whatever is appropriate in your application.

In most cases, what's appropriate is what will perform well with large numbers of simultaneous users. The simplest advice I provide to customers is to use client-side cursors because of the functionality they provide and because they don't put undue stress on the database system.

Q. *Why shouldn't I use the dynamic cursors? They seem to provide the most functionality, and I like functionality.*
A. You pay for the functionality you get.

With forward-only cursors, you're asking the database system to provide minimal functionality. If you want to scroll back and forth through your data, you need to store it on your own or in the ADO Cursor Engine. The more functionality you ask your database server to provide in the cursor, the more work it needs to perform. Remember that every time ADO asks for more data to fill its cache, the query processor reexamines the tables referenced by the query, determines which records satisfy the query criteria, and then generates the requested records in the cursor. Sure, a dynamic cursor provides more functionality, but there's a heavy price to pay for that functionality.

Chapter 8

Updating Your Database

Life would be simple if the data accessed by your application was strictly read-only. However, designing and implementing your application becomes more complex once you add the ability to update your database. Fortunately, incorporating the ability to add, delete, and modify data in your database is relatively simple compared to handling scenarios in which multiple users attempt to modify the same data at the same time.

How do you want your application to behave if multiple users try to modify a single record in your database? Should the first user to submit changes succeed and the second user receive an error message? What to do, what to do?

Before we dive into those questions, let's examine the four techniques you can use with ADO to modify data in your database: action queries, stored procedures, updatable server-side Recordsets, and updatable client-side Recordsets. We'll talk about the pros and cons of each of these methods. Each technique has trade-offs based on execution time, development time, flexibility, and control. It's up to you to decide which way is right for you. First we'll cover the two "do-it-yourself" methods— action queries and stored procedures—before moving on to the more RAD (rapid application development) methods of using server-side or client-side updatable Recordsets.

DOING IT YOURSELF

Many programmers hate relying on code written by anyone else. It's as much a matter of control as it is of trust. They want to retain as much control as possible over exactly how they're updating data in their database. There are two main vehicles that these developers use to update their databases—action queries and stored procedures.

Action Queries

Before the Microsoft empire was even a glint in Bill Gates's glasses, developers relied on action queries as the tried-and-true method of modifying data. Data access developers from all walks of life have used action queries, which are sometimes referred to as query-based updates (QBU). The following is an example of an action query:

```
UPDATE Customers SET BalanceDue = 100 WHERE CustomerID = 7
```

Don't discount this method of updating your database simply because it's not a trendy or sexy concept. Action queries offer a great deal of flexibility and control. Some large companies have built multitiered applications that perform all updates through action queries. What's so impressive about this feat? All the data about the structure of the database used to build these action queries lies in an area of the database rather than in the application itself. Now that takes some planning.

The flexibility and control of action queries stem from the fact that you specify exactly how—and whether—the information in the database should be updated. For example, the previous action query simply sets the BalanceDue field for a particular customer. Suppose that the balance due is $50 and you want to increase it $50 by setting it to $100. However, you don't want to change the balance due for that customer if someone else changes it between the time you retrieve the record and the time you try to update it. Assuming the CustomerID has a value of 7, you could issue the following query:

```
UPDATE Customers SET BalanceDue = 100
     WHERE CustomerID = 7 AND BalanceDue = 50
```

If another user has changed this customer's BalanceDue field, this query won't find the record it's requesting and, as a result, won't update that record in the table.

If you simply want to add $50 to the current balance due, you could issue this query instead:

```
UPDATE Customers SET BalanceDue = BalanceDue + 50 WHERE CustomerID = 7
```

It's easy to execute action queries using the ADO object model. Just use the *Execute* method on either the Connection or Command object. Here's an example that uses the Connection object:

```
Dim cnDatabase As ADODB.Connection
⋮
strSQL = "UPDATE Customers SET BalanceDue = 100 WHERE CustomerID = 7"
cnDatabase.Execute strSQL, intRowsAffected, _
                adCmdExecuteNoRecords + adCmdText
MsgBox intRowsAffected & " record(s) affected."
```

For more information on executing action queries, see the information on the Connection and Command objects in Chapters 3 and 5, respectively.

ACTION QUERIES AND THE ADO CURSOR ENGINE

I'll let you in on a little secret. The ADO Cursor Engine creates action queries to perform updates. Even if you're planning to write your own action queries to update your database, you can still learn a lot from reading Chapters 10 and 11 on how the ADO Cursor Engine builds and handles action queries. You might get some great ideas. You might also realize that it's more difficult than you thought to build a multiuser application that utilizes action queries to update your database. Perhaps those of you who once scoffed at the thought of letting someone else's code handle your database updates will look at everything the ADO Cursor Engine does and decide to use it instead of doing all that work yourself.

Pros and cons of using action queries

What are the pros and cons of using action queries to modify data in your database? First, let's look at the pros.

One reason for using action queries is that they are extremely flexible. You can accomplish just about any modification to a record by implementing one or more action queries. Another reason is that almost all database systems support standard SQL action queries. If you decide to change back-end databases, you might not need to change the structure of your action queries at all.

Finally, action queries can simplify the process of handling updates from multiple users. You can specify values in your WHERE clause that ensure you're not overwriting another user's changes. If the query doesn't update any records, you can create additional queries to determine why.

The one major drawback of updating your database by creating action queries is that you need to write a great deal of code. You'll need to store the query results in your application and maintain all the data necessary to build your action queries. What's so difficult about that?

Your first instincts for building large, multiuser applications might be to wrap data in your own easy-to-manage objects. For example, rather than using an ADO Recordset object to store the contents of the Customers table, you'd create a collection of Customer objects along with all the supporting properties and methods. Populating that collection based on the results of a query isn't difficult—it's only a simple loop.

Building the action query to submit changes made to a Customer object to your database is more of a challenge. If you want to avoid overwriting changes made by other users, you'll want to use previously retrieved values or a timestamp value in the WHERE clause of your query. If you want to modify a field that contains character data, you'll need to delimit the strings in your queries and probably check the strings you're submitting to see whether that delimiter is in the string. If you need to submit BLOB (binary large object) data, you'll probably need to create a parameterized query.

Suffice it to say, this work is far from trivial. However, once you've built one application to handle the complexities involved, you might find yourself using similar routines in other applications. Perhaps you'll create your own objects to handle the bulk of this work and use them in multiple applications. Maybe, just maybe, you'll build something similar to the ADO Cursor Engine.

Stored Procedures

Like action queries, stored procedures offer a great amount of flexibility and control. Many database administrators (DBAs) allow users to perform updates only through stored procedures because of the level of control they offer.

WORKING WITH YOUR DBA

In some cases, the DBA is also the person developing the database application. If you're the application developer and you aren't the DBA, be sure to talk to the DBA before you start writing any code. You don't want to spend countless hours developing your database application, expecting to use action queries or updatable Recordsets to modify your data, only to learn that your DBA won't allow modifications through anything other than stored procedures.

It's always a good idea to talk to your DBA about how to design your application. The DBA will probably want to know what you're up to, especially if you plan to put any undue stress on the server.

When you use a stored procedure to update your database, you pass the information needed to modify the database into the stored procedure. As with action queries, you can control how your database performs the update by how much information you provide. You can also return information from the stored procedure to help explain the results of the update attempt: success, failure, or other information.

Microsoft SQL Server allows you to pass query results back from the stored procedure. Oracle doesn't provide such functionality. However, the Microsoft ODBC driver for Oracle and the OLE DB Provider For Oracle can retrieve an array from an Oracle stored procedure and transform that data into a structure that ADO will use to create a Recordset object. (For more information about using this feature of the Microsoft ODBC driver and OLE DB Provider For Oracle, see article Q176086 in the Microsoft Knowledge Base at *http://support.microsoft.com/support/kb/articles/Q176/0/86.asp*.) If you're looking for more information about building stored procedures, you'll find plenty of books on the topic written about each of the major database systems.

Stored procedures are generally faster than action queries because the database system can compile the better part of the query ahead of time. You can also use stored procedures to isolate business rules from your application. For example, you can add logic to your stored procedure to send e-mail to the purchasing department when the number of widgets in stock drops below a certain level. Because the database system is responsible for executing the stored procedure, the amount of functionality you can add to your stored procedure depends on your choice of database system.

> **CAUTION** Don't move all your logic to stored procedures if you're unsure of the possible consequences. Although stored procedures are fast, flexible, and powerful, you can code yourself into a corner by relying on them too heavily. What happens if you rely on functionality that's particular to the stored procedures of one database system and you later migrate your database or need access to two different database systems? Granted, this scenario probably doesn't occur frequently, but it is one you should be aware of.

Don't assume that because it's possible to modify a stored procedure without changing the code in your application, you'll always be able to do so successfully. You can make modifications to a stored procedure such as adding an optional parameter, adding a business rule that doesn't affect the parameters or data returned by the stored procedure, or retrieving data from a different table—all without changing the code in your application. However, if you add a required parameter to your stored procedure, you'll obviously need to modify the code in your application. As a general rule, think of your stored procedure as a COM component. If you change the server interface, you might not be binary compatible anymore, in which case you'll need to recompile your client code.

Here's a brief example of the ADO code required to call a stored procedure in SQL Server that sets the BalanceDue field for a particular customer:

```
strSQL = "CALL SetBalanceDue('ALFKI', 150.00)"
cnDatabase.Execute strSQL, , adCmdText + adExecuteNoRecords
```

And here's the SQL Server stored procedure that was called from the ADO code:

```
CREATE PROCEDURE SetBalanceDue
(@CustomerID varchar(5), @BalanceDue money) AS
UPDATE Customers SET BalanceDue = @BalanceDue
            WHERE CustomerID = @CustomerID
```

If you want to run the query multiple times, you can use a parameterized Command object.

This example is overly simplistic. If you plan to use stored procedures to update your database, you should be prepared to handle the same multiuser optimistic updating scenarios mentioned in the previous section on action queries. In this sample stored procedure, if two users retrieve the same customer's balance due and each handles an order and attempts to modify the balance due, each user's update will succeed without generating an error. This obviously isn't a desirable scenario. The changes made by the first user will be overwritten by the second user. In this case, the following stored procedure would be a better choice:

```
CREATE PROCEDURE SetBalanceDue
(@CustomerID varchar(5), @Delta money) AS
UPDATE Customers SET BalanceDue = BalanceDue + @Delta
            WHERE CustomerID = @CustomerID
```

Now if multiple users call the stored procedure, the change in the balance due is registered rather than the new balance due.

But even this stored procedure is simplistic. Does your application need to know the balance due for the customer after the update is complete? How will you elegantly handle it if the customer no longer exists in your table? In this stored procedure, if no such customer exists, no error occurs. The query in the stored procedure simply does not modify any records in the table.

Let's talk about updating a Customers table with stored procedures. Suppose you're interested in updating 10 fields in a table. You could create a separate stored procedure to update each field based on the primary key value. Another option is to use a single stored procedure to update all fields, which seems like a much more palatable solution. But how do you handle optimistic concurrency scenarios with this stored procedure? You could accept two values—the original value and the new value—for each field as parameters on the stored procedure. You would then use the parameters in an action query such as the following:

```
UPDATE Customers SET Field1 = @NewValue1, Field2 = @NewValue2, ...
            WHERE Field1 = @OldValue1 AND Field2 = @OldValue2 AND ...
```

Of course, the more fields your table contains, the more complex this stored procedure becomes.

A more elegant approach is to use a timestamp field in the table. You can then use this value—along with the primary key value in your WHERE clause—rather than the original values for the fields in the table. The query in your stored procedure would look like this:

```
UPDATE Customers SET Field1 = @NewValue1, Field2 = @NewValue2, ...
    WHERE KeyField = @KeyValue AND TimestampField = @TimestampValue
```

Now that you've simplified the process of passing data into the stored procedure by reducing the amount of data you need to pass, you must examine what data the stored procedure needs to return. You'll probably want to use the return parameter on your stored procedure to indicate the success or failure of the update attempt. If the update attempt fails—possibly as the result of a business rule or because another user has updated or deleted the record since you last fetched it—you can use an output parameter to return an error number or message.

You might also want to return data from the desired record. For example, if the update is based on a timestamp value, you might want to return that new timestamp value, thereby enabling your application to update that same record in the future. Or if the update attempt fails because another user has modified the record, you might want to return the current contents of the record. Regardless of why you want to return data from the record you're updating, you can specify that the parameters corresponding to the fields in your table will support the return of data. Or you can return the current contents of the record through a query—if your database system supports returning query results from a stored procedure.

Here's an example of a SQL Server stored procedure that uses timestamp values to prevent users from unexpectedly overwriting each other's changes. If the update succeeds, the procedure returns the new timestamp value. If the update fails, it returns an error message indicating that the record was either modified or deleted. If the record was modified, the stored procedure returns its current contents.

```
CREATE PROCEDURE ModifyCustomer
(@ID int, @Company varchar(64) OUTPUT, ... @ErrorMsg varchar(64) OUTPUT)
AS
SET NOCOUNT ON
UPDATE Customers SET Company = @Company, Contact = @Contact, ...
    WHERE CustomerID = @ID AND TSField = @TSField
/* Execute action query using new values from parameters. */
IF @@ROWCOUNT = 1
    /* If the query updated one row, the update was successful. */
    BEGIN
        /* Return the new timestamp value for the modified record
           in the timestamp parameter. */
        SELECT @TSField = TSField FROM Customers WHERE CustomerID = @ID
        RETURN 0
    END
```

(continued)

```
    ELSE
        /* If the action query did not update one record, we know it
            updated zero records because of our primary key. Now we must
            determine why the query updated no records. */
        BEGIN
            DECLARE @NumRows int
            /* Determine whether the record still exists in the table. */
            SELECT @NumRows = Count(CustomerID) FROM Customers
                                WHERE CustomerID = @ID
            IF @NumRows = 1
                /* The record exists in the table. Therefore, the update
                    failed because the record has been modified since last
                    fetched. */
                BEGIN
                    /* Explain why the update failed, and return the current
                        contents of the record in the parameters. */
                    SELECT @ErrorMsg = 'Record was modified by another user'
                    SELECT @Company = Company, @Contact = Contact, ...
                            FROM Customers WHERE CustomerID = @ID
                END
            ELSE
                /* The record does not exist in the table. Explain why the
                    update failed using the error message output
                    parameter. */
                SELECT @ErrorMsg = 'Record was deleted by another user'
            RETURN -1
        END
RETURN
```

Pros and cons of using stored procedures

Let's take a look at the arguments for and against using stored procedures to update
a database. First we'll examine the advantages:

- Because you generally use an action query inside a stored procedure,
  stored procedures are as flexible as action queries.

- Many database systems allow you to take advantage of added features
  inside a stored procedure. For example, SQL Server has built-in extended
  stored procedures you can call to send e-mail.

- Most client/server database systems support some form of stored procedures.

- Stored procedures are often faster than action queries because the database server can compile the query ahead of time.

- As a security measure, many database administrators allow updates only
  through stored procedures.

■ In some cases, you can modify a stored procedure to change business logic without having to modify the application.

■ A stored procedure is like a shared COM component: you can call it from different applications.

Now let's take a look at the flip side of using stored procedure calls to update a database:

■ Stored procedure code is generally back-end specific. If you move from Oracle to SQL Server, or vice versa, you will need to rewrite your stored procedures. There's also no guarantee that one database system will support all the functionality available in stored procedures written for another database system.

■ Stored procedures give you one more set of components to maintain. This might seem like a picky complaint, but I've spoken with several developers who've called support saying, "My application worked just fine the other day and now…" The reason is usually that another developer who maintains the stored procedure had modified it slightly to change the business logic and didn't alert the developer who was using the stored procedure in his Microsoft Visual Basic and ADO code.

■ Stored procedures require you to learn another programming language. Another picky point. However, if your application relies heavily on stored procedures and you have little experience with them, you should adjust your ship schedule to accommodate the time you'll need to learn the stored procedure language of that database system.

■ Stored procedures require a lot of work. Just as with using action queries in your application, you'll have to write a lot of code for stored procedures. Essentially, you're looking at the same amount of code with either option. When using stored procedures to perform your updates, you need to build the stored procedures that your application will call. Furthermore, you still need to store the results of queries, call the stored procedures, and handle the results in your code.

Using Updatable Recordsets

Updatable Recordset objects are definitely a RAD concept. Forget about having to fetch data from a Recordset object and into your own data structures, such as Variant arrays, collections, business objects, user-defined types (UDTs), and eXtensible Markup Language (XML) tags! No longer do you have to create and call stored procedures or generate your own action queries! Say goodbye to writing a bunch of code! Decrease the amount of time required to build the database connectivity layer of your application! Why, you can even leverage a plethora of data-bound controls, which can reduce the time you spend developing the user interface layer!

I intentionally worded the previous paragraph to make updatable Recordsets sound as sensational as an infomercial would. (What scares me is that the spelling checker didn't blink at my use of "infomercial.") You might be wondering whether updatable Recordsets will let you scramble an egg while it's still inside its shell. Used properly, updatable Recordsets can save you more time than anything sold in an infomercial. Plus, there's no shipping or handling costs. And just look how this code can cut a tin can in half and still remain sharp enough to slice a tomato!

```
strSQL = "SELECT * FROM Customers"
Set rsCustomers = New ADODB.Recordset
rsCustomers.Open strSQL, cnDatabase, adOpenKeyset, _
                adLockOptimistic, adCmdText
rsCustomers("BalanceDue").Value = rsCustomers("BalanceDue").Value + 50
rsCustomers.Update
```

Somewhere between the marketing hype (marketers who say that you can build a multiuser database application in five minutes missed their calling as used car salespeople) and the stubborn and sometimes fanatical developers who'd rather perish than use someone else's code (trust no one...else's code) lies the middle ground where you'll find the truth. Let's take a brief look at updatable server-side and client-side Recordsets and examine their pros and cons.

Updatable Server-Side Recordsets

Chapter 7 covered keyset cursors and dynamic cursors—the types of server-side cursors that support updating. In this section, you'll see how to use the Recordset object to interact with these cursors.

When you modify the Value property of the various Field objects in your Recordset and then call the Recordset's *Update* method, ADO passes that information to the server-side cursor through the OLE DB provider or ODBC driver. But who updates the database? Basically, whoever manages the cursor handles that job.

Remember that when you work with SQL Server, the OLE DB provider and ODBC driver communicate with the database and allow you to access the data in the cursor. SQL Server actually manages the cursor. SQL Server also updates data in your database as you modify the contents of the cursor.

The Access OLE DB provider and ODBC driver manage the cursor and directly communicate with the database as well as let you interact with the cursor. Therefore, they're also responsible for updating your database based on the changes made to the cursor.

The Microsoft ODBC driver for Oracle exposes and manages the cursor. (Perhaps someday the related OLE DB provider will do this too.) As you change data in the cursor, the ODBC driver interprets these changes and tells the Oracle database server how to modify the underlying data in your database.

Pros and cons of using server-side Recordsets

What are the pros and cons of using server-side Recordsets to update your database? Let's look at the advantages first:

- You don't have to write as much code as you would using action queries or stored procedures. You can use the Recordset object to interact with the server-side cursor that maintains the results of your query. You don't need to write code to determine how to update your database. Instead, you simply access and modify your data through the Recordset object.

- You can take advantage of ADO features that apply to server-side cursors, such as searching and filtering.

- If you're working with a SQL Server database, you're keeping less data in your application. The Recordset's CacheSize property controls how many records of data are cached in the ADO libraries.

- You can use the features of a keyset cursor or a dynamic cursor.

- You can take advantage of data-bound controls. Visual Basic, for example, ships with data-bound controls (text boxes, list boxes, combo boxes, and grids) that you can bind to your Recordset to decrease the amount of code you need to write.

Now let's examine the disadvantages of updating your database by using server-side Recordsets:

- Server-side Recordsets require a live connection to your database. As you navigate through the Recordset, you will likely incur network round-trips—even if the data in your cursor has not changed.

- Server-side Recordsets sometimes scale poorly in multiuser situations. (See the discussion of server-side cursors in Chapter 7 beginning on page 168.)

- Because of the requirement of a live connection to your database, you cannot effectively use server-side Recordsets in a Component Services or Microsoft Transaction Server (MTS) component.

■ Because server-side Recordsets rely on the database system, the OLE DB provider, or the ODBC driver to actually update the database, you might need to develop code that is specific to the type of database you're using. For example, Microsoft Access and SQL Server do not handle optimistic updates from live cursors the same way.

Updatable Client-Side Recordsets

Client-side Recordsets offer a middle ground between action queries and server-side Recordsets. When it comes to modifying the Recordset object, client-side Recordsets behave the same as server-side Recordsets. However, instead of communicating with a cursor that's maintained by the database, the OLE DB provider, or the ODBC driver, ADO retrieves the results of your query and stores that data in its own Cursor Engine.

The data in your Recordset is static, meaning you won't see changes other users make to the data in the database. Once the ADO Cursor Engine has retrieved the results of your query, you can disconnect your Recordset and you won't need to communicate with your database until you're ready to modify its contents or retrieve more data.

The ADO Cursor Engine examines the changes you make to the Recordset and translates those changes into action queries. Based on the number of records modified by those action queries, the Cursor Engine determines whether the action query successfully updated the data in your database. The next few chapters will explore this process in much more depth.

Pros and cons of using client-side Recordsets

Now let's examine the advantages and disadvantages of using client-side Recordsets to update your database. First, we'll take a look at the advantages:

■ As with server-side Recordsets, the biggest benefit of using client-side Recordsets is that you don't have to write as much code as you would with action queries and stored procedures.

■ Since the ADO Cursor Engine maintains the Recordset results, client-side Recordsets scale better than server-side Recordsets.

■ ADO offers a great deal of functionality for client-side Recordsets: searching, filtering, sorting, batch updating, persistence, hierarchical Recordsets, and the ability to pass a client-side Recordset object across process boundaries.

■ As with server-side Recordsets, you can use data-bound controls.

There's only one significant drawback to using client-side Recordsets to update your database. By allowing the ADO Cursor Engine to maintain the results of your queries and update your database, you still give up some control.

QUESTIONS THAT SHOULD BE ASKED MORE FREQUENTLY

Q. *So what's the best way for me to update my database? Should I write all the code myself, or should I use updatable Recordset objects throughout my application? Should I believe the marketing hype, or should I believe the gurus who say that if you want a job done right you must do it yourself?*

A. The simple answer is that there's no simple answer. You can go to either extreme, or you can look for some middle ground. Keep an open mind, and try a variety of techniques.

One recommendation: try new techniques, but give yourself time to experiment with them. If you plan ahead and design your application well, you might be able to move from one method to another. For example, you could build an initial version of your application that passes Recordset objects across process boundaries in a three-tiered application and uses the ADO Cursor Engine to modify data in your database. In later releases, you could use the Recordset objects to interact with the user and store changes he makes. Then you could examine those changes and call your own stored procedures to update the database. You could later modify your components to use two-dimensional arrays, Variants, or UDTs to store the results of queries and maintain data. Almost anything is possible.

The more you experiment with the different ways to update your database, the better equipped you'll be to decide what's right for you. Think about what you need in functionality and performance. Then figure out a way to determine whether a particular approach will give you what you need.

In Part II of this book, we'll discuss features of the ADO Cursor Engine. As you read about these features, you'll discover what the ADO Cursor Engine has to offer—and you might decide to use it in your applications. Or you might develop a clearer understanding of how to implement similar features in your own libraries.

Part II

Working with the ADO Cursor Engine

Chapter 9

ADO Cursor Engine Overview

Of all the libraries included with the Microsoft Data Access Components (MDAC), the Microsoft ADO Cursor Engine is my favorite. There, I've said it. And I don't mind admitting it.

Some of the most vocal pundits in the software development community gravitate toward one of two extremes. Some will tell you the tools they recommend are so easy that you won't have to write a line of code. Others believe that it's a bad idea to use anyone else's components. They'd sooner write their own compiler than rely on someone else's code.

I like to think that most developers lie somewhere in the middle—they're happy to use someone else's tools if they understand the tools and if the tools work well, but they're also comfortable relying on their own programming skills when necessary. When it comes to ADO, I see utilization of the ADO Cursor Engine as that middle ground.

The ADO Cursor Engine has some powerful features, although it's not perfect. The more experience you gain, the more clearly you'll see the benefits and drawbacks of using the ADO Cursor Engine. This chapter will provide you with an overview of the Cursor Engine features that we'll discuss in the coming chapters.

THE RECORDSET AS A DATA CONTAINER

One of the simplest features of the ADO Cursor Engine is its ability to store the results of your queries. Of course you can also use a server-side cursor to store query results, but in most cases, as we discussed in Chapter 7, you want to avoid server-side cursors.

Using a client-side Recordset object to work with the results of your query can save a great deal of coding. You don't have to move the data from the recordset to your own data structure. You also have a wealth of rapid application development (RAD) features available to you when you use the Recordset object. Bound controls are among the more obvious and traditional RAD features.

Bound Controls

Traditionally, bound controls in Microsoft Visual Basic have gotten a bad rap. But I'm much more impressed with the bound controls included with Visual Basic 6 than I was with previous versions of the controls. With version 6, you can bind controls more easily and dynamically at run time. Using bound controls with ADO Recordset objects doesn't incur as much overhead—such as network activity and additional database connections—as using them with the Recordset objects' DAO (Data Access Objects) counterparts. Visual Basic 6 makes it possible to format your data (including currency and Null data) with the DataFormat property on most bound controls. As you can see, bound controls are a more attractive option than they were in the past.

However, by using bound controls you still give up a great deal of flexibility. Displaying data in a bound grid is simple, but interacting with that data the way you want can pose a challenge. In many cases, you'll probably want more control over data manipulation in your application than bound controls offer. For example, when a user enters a product number into an order, you might want to perform a lookup and display the name, price, and availability for that product as soon as the user leaves the product number field. Sometimes you can implement this type of functionality with bound controls; sometimes you can't.

Bound controls often have limitations and bugs that you don't discover until you're halfway through the process of building your application. I've spoken with quite a few Visual Basic developers who had to give up using the DataEnvironment object in their applications because binding controls to the DataEnvironment became more trouble than it was worth.

I use the DataEnvironment object occasionally, but I avoid binding controls to it. The DataEnvironment doesn't properly broadcast events to controls. Controls are not notified of critical events such as when you're requerying your Recordset or navigating through a hierarchical Recordset. As a result, you would have to write so much code to repeatedly bind your controls to the DataEnvironment that you might decide to forego using the DataEnvironment in future projects.

Interacting with bound controls is hardly groundbreaking, however. Both DAO and RDO (Remote Data Objects) can do that, but with an ADO client-side Recordset you can do so much more.

Filtering and Searching

Have you ever wanted to display only certain records in your Recordset based on a particular criterion? For example, suppose you retrieve all your customers but, based on user input, want to display only the customers located in a particular region.

You could examine the customer data on your own and decide which data to display. You could also submit a new query to your database to retrieve only the customers in that region. ADO offers another option—you can simply apply a filter to your Recordset, like this:

```
rsCustomers.Filter = "State = 'MA'"
```

Now only customers living in the state of Massachusetts will be visible in your Recordset.

ADO also lets you search for a record in your Recordset using a similar syntax. Suppose that instead of applying a filter to your data, you simply want to locate a record that satisfies a certain criterion—for example, the customer must live in the state of Massachusetts. In this case, you can use the *Find* method on the Recordset:

```
rsCustomers.Find "State = 'MA'"
```

Although we discussed the Filter property and the *Find* method in Chapter 4, two points are worth discussing further here. First, you should be aware that ADO's filtering and searching features aren't available only in client-side Recordsets. These features also work if you use a Recordset based on a server-side cursor. However, I don't recommend using these features unless you're using a client-side Recordset.

When you use a client-side Recordset, the data in the Recordset won't change unless you modify it. Therefore, ADO can build temporary indexes to aid in filtering and searching. ADO can't build a temporary index when you use server-side cursors because it needs to continually refetch data from the cursor to locate the desired record or records. Data in server-side keyset cursors and dynamic cursors can change based on other users' modifications to the database. And what happens when another user adds a new record to your database that satisfies the criteria for the filter you applied to your dynamic server-side cursor? When does that new record appear in your cursor, if at all? Wait, wait—don't tell me. I really don't want to know.

This brings me to my second point: to be brutally honest, I have mixed feelings about ADO's filtering and searching features. They're quite limited. For example, you can't specify multiple criteria when you use the Recordset object's *Find* method. And the support for wildcards in character fields leaves something to be desired. The filtering and searching features also seem to choke if you use multiple delimiter characters (', ", and so on) in the criteria.

Don't get me wrong. I like the fact that these features were added in ADO 2.0, but they're simplistic and limited when compared to the same features in DAO. While the ADO documentation doesn't claim that these features are as robust as their DAO counterparts, it doesn't go out of its way to point out these shortcomings. I'd like to say that the development team plans to improve on these features, but as of ADO 2.5, this doesn't seem to be the case.

With all that said, if you use simple criteria, searching and filtering in ADO does work well. I do recommend using these features—as long as you're aware of their limitations and you know that those limitations won't affect your application. We won't discuss filtering and searching again in this book. For more information on the use and limitations of these features, see Chapter 4 and the Web site for Microsoft's on-line Knowledge Base (*http://support.microsoft.com/search*).

Sorting

Sometimes it's nice to sort data based on a field (column) or multiple fields. This functionality is available in most applications. Open a directory in Microsoft Windows Explorer, and you can click any of the column headers to sort the files and directories by their name, date, and so on. You can implement similar functionality by using the Sort property on the Recordset object.

For example, suppose you want to sort your customers by a BalanceDue field and see the customers who owe you the most money first. You could simply add the following line of code:

```
rsCustomers.Sort = "BalanceDue DESC"
```

No need for me to warn you about any issues here. Sorting is not nearly as complex as filtering and searching. For more information on sorting, see the discussion of the Sort property in Chapter 4.

UPDATES: SIMPLE AND BATCHED

Of course, the ADO Cursor Engine wouldn't be widely accepted unless you could use it to update the data in your database. You can update your database by simply modifying the appropriate field in the recordset and calling the Recordset object's *Update* method, as follows:

```
strSQL = "SELECT CustomerID, CustomerName, BalanceDue FROM Customers"
rsCustomers.CursorLocation = adUseClient
rsCustomers.Open strSQL, cnDatabase, adOpenStatic, adLockOptimistic
rsCustomers.Fields("BalanceDue") = rsCustomers.Fields("BalanceDue") + 50
rsCustomers.Update
```

The ADO Cursor Engine also includes the ability to cache updates you make to your Recordset object and send them to your database in a batch at a later time by calling the *UpdateBatch* method. You'll notice that the previous code used the adLockOptimistic constant in the call to the Recordset's *Open* method. The following code uses adLockBatchOptimistic in the call to *Open* so the database isn't updated until *UpdateBatch* is called. For more information, see the "LockType Property" section in Chapter 4.

```
strSQL = "SELECT CustomerID, CustomerName, BalanceDue FROM Customers"
rsCustomers.CursorLocation = adUseClient
rsCustomers.Open strSQL, cnDatabase, adOpenStatic, adLockBatchOptimistic
rsCustomers.Fields("BalanceDue") = rsCustomers.Fields("BalanceDue") + 50
rsCustomers.Update
rsCustomers.MoveNext
rsCustomers.Fields("BalanceDue") = _
                rsCustomers.Fields("BalanceDue") + 125
rsCustomers.Update
rsCustomers.UpdateBatch
```

In Chapter 10, you'll see in much greater detail how ADO updates the data in your database.

UPDATE RESYNC

As you'll see in the next chapter, the ADO Cursor Engine uses action queries to submit the changes stored in your Recordset to your database. Action queries are similar to a one-sided conversation—that is, the action query does a lot of talking and almost no listening.

At times you'll want to know more than just whether your update succeeded, however. For example, perhaps you want to retrieve some values generated by your server, such as timestamps, defaults, and auto-incrementing fields. Recordsets that utilize the ADO Cursor Engine expose a dynamic property called Update Resync that you can use to retrieve such data. We'll cover Update Resync—how it works and how to use it—in more detail in Chapter 11.

DISCONNECTED RECORDSETS

What do you need to consider when you communicate with your database infrequently? For example, let's say that when your application starts up you want to retrieve data from your database but that you might not need to communicate with the database again during the lifetime of your application.

You might not want to keep a connection to your database open during long stretches of time when you're not actively using it. When using the ADO Cursor Engine, you can simply set the ActiveConnection property on your Recordset object to Nothing, and then close your Connection object and still have access to the data in your Recordset object. In fact, you can use the Cursor Engine's batch updating functionality and modify the contents of your Recordset object without a live connection to your database. You can later reopen your Connection object, reset the ActiveConnection property on the Recordset object, and call the object's *UpdateBatch* method to submit the changes to your database. This process is demonstrated in the following code:

```
strSQL = "SELECT CustomerID, CustomerName, BalanceDue FROM Customers"
rsCustomers.CursorLocation = adUseClient
rsCustomers.Open strSQL, cnDatabase, adOpenStatic, adLockBatchOptimistic
Set rsCustomers.ActiveConnection = Nothing
cnDatabase.Close
:

'Modify your Recordset object while it's off line.
:
'Reconnect to the database.
cnDatabase.Open
Set rsCustomers.ActiveConnection = cnDatabase
rsCustomers.UpdateBatch
```

It's that easy. We won't discuss this feature, per se, in later chapters. However, we will talk about ways to use it more effectively in the chapters on updating your database with the ADO Cursor Engine (Chapter 10), handling optimistic updating conflicts (Chapter 12), and persisting your Recordset (Chapter 13).

DEALING WITH OPTIMISTIC UPDATE CONFLICTS

Chances are that multiple users will be running your application simultaneously. It's possible that more than one user will want to modify the same record of data in your database at the same time. To deal with this situation, most developers employ an optimistic updating scheme rather than a pessimistic updating scheme.

Optimistic updating greatly decreases the likelihood that data your users are trying to access is locked. The drawback to using optimistic updating is that you generally need to write a lot of code to handle the cases in which a user's updates to a record fail because another user changed the same record.

The ADO Cursor Engine helps simplify the process of handling these situations. ADO notifies you of such conflicts and provides several ways for you to determine why the update failed so that you can take the appropriate action. In Chapter 12, we'll discuss detecting and handling conflicts in greater detail.

PERSISTING YOUR DATA

A salesman walks into a psychiatrist's office and says, "Doc, you *have* to help me!" No, wait, that's not it....

A salesman walks into the MIS director's office and says, "Fred, you *have* to help me! The order entry system is wonderful, but I need you to modify it slightly so that I can load it onto my laptop. I want to enter new customers and orders while I'm out on the road, save them on my hard drive, and load them into the database when I'm done playing golf...I mean when I'm back in the office."

Those clever programmers on the ADO team thought of this exact scenario (even though programmers, by trade, tend not to get along with salespeople). You can save a client-side Recordset to a file and reopen it at a later time, as shown in the following code snippet. If you choose, you can even send that persisted recordset as an e-mail attachment and have another user or application open it.

```
strSQL = "SELECT CustomerID, CustomerName, BalanceDue FROM Customers"
rsCustomers.CursorLocation = adUseClient
rsCustomers.Open strSQL, cnDatabase, adOpenStatic, adLockBatchOptimistic
Set rsCustomers.ActiveConnection = Nothing
cnDatabase.Close
rsCustomers.Save strPathToFile
⋮
cnDatabase.Open
rsCustomers.Open strPathToFile, Options:=adCmdFile
Set rsCustomers.ActiveConnection = cnDatabase
rsCustomers.UpdateBatch
```

In Chapter 13, we'll talk more about how to use persisted recordsets, what data is saved, and the different formats you can use to save your data.

HIERARCHICAL RECORDSETS

Data doesn't exist in a vacuum. If you build an order entry system and the user requests data for a particular order, you'll probably include information from more than one table. Maybe you'll want to display the information from the Customers table about the customer who placed the order, as well as the items from the Orders table that make up the order.

The ADO Cursor Engine includes functionality that lets you organize data from separate tables into a hierarchy. You can issue a single query that retrieves information such as customer, order, and order detail into different levels of a hierarchy. As you navigate through the customer level of the hierarchy, you'll see only the orders that apply to that customer. And as you look at a particular order, you'll see only those items that the order includes.

In Chapter 14, you'll see how ADO organizes this data and synchronizes it in your hierarchy. The query syntax to build the hierarchy is somewhat confusing. We'll look at some examples of this syntax without going into too much depth. The topic of hierarchical query syntax could fill an entire book. The goal in Chapter 14 is to help you understand how this feature works so that you can use it intelligently and avoid coding yourself into a corner.

PASSING RECORDSETS ACROSS PROCESS BOUNDARIES

You've probably heard that two-tiered client/server applications are passé and that Component Services (Microsoft Transaction Server) and Microsoft Internet Information Services (IIS) are now the tools of choice for building large, multiuser applications. Maybe you know a little bit about the inner workings of COM as well as its distributed counterpart, DCOM, but you're not sure how to proceed with your development.

The ADO Cursor Engine makes passing Recordset objects across process boundaries amazingly simple. From a programming standpoint, you can treat the Recordset object almost like a standard data type, such as an integer.

We'll cover some of the basics of passing Recordset objects across process boundaries in Chapter 15. But be forewarned: this is a fairly advanced topic in COM, and while I cover many of the inner workings of ADO, the inner workings of COM are beyond the scope of this book. I strongly recommend picking up a book or two on the topic such as *Understanding ActiveX and OLE,* by David Chappell [Microsoft Press, 1996], or *Inside COM,* by Dale Rogerson [Microsoft Press, 1997].

REMOTE DATA SERVICE

As if passing a Recordset object and all of its contents across process boundaries using DCOM weren't impressive enough, the ADO Cursor Engine also helps you pass Recordsets across the Internet by means of HTTP (or HTTPS), using a set of libraries called Remote Data Service (RDS).

You can use RDS with any Microsoft Visual Studio language to develop applications that communicate over the Internet almost as easily as you can develop applications that communicate over your intranet. We'll cover RDS in more detail in Chapter 16.

BENEFITS OF USING THE ADO CURSOR ENGINE

Some of the greatest advantages of using the ADO Cursor Engine are that you can save time, simplify your code, and write code that is database independent.

Saving Time

The biggest benefit of using the ADO Cursor Engine is the time you can save by leveraging the libraries created by the ADO development team.

If you're an accomplished programmer, there is nothing that the ADO Cursor Engine does that you can't do yourself—given enough time. But that's the catch. How many programmers have enough time to develop such a flexible, powerful set of libraries?

Notice that I said "accomplished programmer." As you'll see in the upcoming chapters, most of the features of the ADO Cursor Engine are nontrivial. While they're not perfect, they are rather well thought out. It takes a great deal of planning and expertise to develop such a helpful set of features. I fancy myself a decent programmer, and I know better than to criticize developers in the Microsoft Data Access Group. They could probably do my job. But I don't think I could handle theirs.

While I would never tell a programmer *not* to try to develop a set of libraries similar to the ADO Cursor Engine, I'd wish him luck and hope he has a backup plan or an impressive résumé.

Simplifying Your Code

Using the ADO Cursor Engine can also simplify your code. Some of the most impressive developers I've worked with, both inside and outside of Microsoft, write code that is disorganized and difficult to follow. The biggest drawback to such spaghetti code—code that works but which no one but its creator can understand—is that it can become impossible to maintain.

As a support professional, I spend a good portion of my time reviewing code written by customers and coworkers. You can follow another programmer's code much more easily if the programmer relies on components that you're already familiar with, such as those of the ADO Cursor Engine.

Writing Database-Independent Code

Have you ever developed an application to interact with an Access database only to discover later that the plans have changed? Perhaps someone within your company has decided that the next version of your application must instead work with a client/server database such as SQL Server, Oracle, Sybase, Informix, or DB2.

If your application relies on features available in the Access driver or provider's server-side cursors, you'll have a lot of code to rewrite if your new database doesn't expose server-side cursors or has functionality that's different from that of Access databases. If you initially designed your application to use the ADO Cursor Engine, however, you'll be able to use most of your code to communicate with the new type of database.

The features of the ADO Cursor Engine are designed to be database independent, allowing you to use the same code against any database.

DRAWBACKS OF USING THE ADO CURSOR ENGINE

I won't try to tell you that the ADO Cursor Engine doesn't have drawbacks or limitations. I've yet to see a set of RAD libraries that doesn't. However, I won't give you the laundry list of these disadvantages here. For the most part, I'll point them out while discussing the Cursor Engine's features so that you're aware of them ahead of time, rather than finding out about them three quarters of the way through your development cycle.

Performance Issues

ADO is essentially an ad hoc query tool. It has to gather data about your database fields and tables in order to let you update the data. Most of the time, you already have the information that ADO is looking for. But ADO doesn't have interfaces to allow you to supply that information. As a result, the ADO Cursor Engine queries your database for that information.

For example, suppose you know the data type you've chosen for the BalanceDue field in your Customers table. You also know the fields that are part of that table's primary key. ADO gathers all this data each time you issue a query to generate an updatable Recordset with the ADO Cursor Engine. If you write your own code at the OLE DB or ODBC API level, you can avoid much of the overhead involved in an ad hoc query tool such as ADO. But generally, few applications benefit from the slight increase in performance, and few programmers have the requisite time and expertise to implement such code.

Limited Flexibility

During the ADO 2.0 development cycle, the program managers talked about using the *GetString* method of the Recordset object to build HTML tables. This sounded like a great idea to me, and I was surprised when I noticed the feature was dropped. (As of ADO 2.5, it still hasn't been added.) I later found out why—there was no way to implement the feature that would satisfy a significant percentage of users.

No matter how much flexibility the ADO development team considered putting into the feature, a fairly significant percentage of the users would inevitably say things like, "But I want the negative values to appear in a bold, red, italic font with a mauve background." There will always be limitations.

The ADO Cursor Engine is not infinitely flexible, but in most cases there's enough built-in flexibility to get the job done. I'll do my best to point out the limitations to you throughout the rest of the book. Since I don't list all the limitations here, you'll have to read on to learn about them as I discuss the major features and uncover the way in which many of them work.

Read-Only Fields

OK, scratch that, I will tell you about one specific limitation here. When the ADO Cursor Engine marks a field as read-only, there's no way you can programmatically modify that data in the Recordset.

Fields are usually marked as read-only for one of two reasons. First, an OLE DB provider might indicate that you're not allowed to update a particular field in a table. Since the ADO Cursor Engine will attempt to update the table based on changes you make to the associated Recordset, ADO won't allow you to update a field in the Recordset that corresponds to the read-only field in the table.

Second, ADO will not allow you to modify calculated fields in your Recordset. If you use the following query to generate a Recordset

```
SELECT Au_ID, Au_FName + ' ' + Au_LName AS Author_Name FROM Authors
```

you'll receive a field called Author_Name that's the concatenation of the Au_FName and Au_LName fields in the table. While you might be able to understand how to translate a change to this calculated field into appropriate values for the author's first and last name, the ADO Cursor Engine does not know how to accomplish this feat. As a result, this field is read-only in the Recordset.

If you retrieve a new timestamp value from your database and want to merge that data into an open Recordset, you're out of luck. It's unlikely that you'll run into such a situation in your application. However, there are similar scenarios in which you might find yourself coded into a corner if you don't know how the ADO Cursor Engine works. If you want to avoid such problems, read on—it builds character.

QUESTIONS THAT SHOULD BE ASKED MORE FREQUENTLY

Q. *The ADO Cursor Engine sounds great! How do I make sure I'm using it?*
A. Simply set the CursorLocation property on your Connection or Recordset object to adUseClient before opening your Recordset. For more information, see the discussion of the CursorLocation property of the Connection object (Chapter 3) or Recordset object (Chapter 4).

Q.   *If the Cursor Engine is so powerful and flexible, why isn't adUseClient the default value for the CursorLocation property?*

A.   Backward compatibility. The initial release of ADO used only server-side cursors. In order to ensure that code written for ADO 1.0 continues to run the same way with each successive version of ADO, the default is still to use server-side cursors. New components that use ADO, such as the ADO Data Control and the DataEnvironment, are not subject to those backward-compatibility issues, and they use the Cursor Engine by default.

Chapter 10

How the ADO Cursor Engine Updates Your Database

Whenever developers ask me why they're getting errors when they use a client-side Recordset to update their data, I ask them if they understand how ADO tries to update their data. I'm sometimes surprised by their reaction to that question. The most common response is, "Why should I care what ADO is doing? I just want my code to work."

Unfortunately, I can't send customers to their rooms, and telling them I'm disappointed in them rarely generates much of a response. The less you know about how ADO updates your database when you use a client-side cursor, the slimmer the chances that your application will work reliably. That statement usually gets a programmer's attention.

Let's look at a quick and dirty example of an update operation:

```
strSQL = "SELECT CustomerID, CompanyName, BalanceDue FROM Customers"
rsCustomers.CursorLocation = adUseClient
rsCustomers.Open strSQL, cnDatabase, adOpenStatic, _
                adLockOptimistic, adCmdText
rsCustomers.Find "CustomerID = 7"
rsCustomers.Fields("BalanceDue") = rsCustomers.Fields("BalanceDue") + 50
rsCustomers.Update
```

You can run this code and successfully add $50 to the balance due for the customer with a CustomerID of 7. But what really happened?

Let's start with a little bit of background. I used to be an Xbase programmer. In Xbase, it's easy to tell that the record you're accessing programmatically is the actual record in the actual table in the actual database file.

Microsoft Access is a little more complex. The Jet engine keeps its own copy of the results of your query. But when you modify a record in your Data Access Objects (DAO) Recordset (or your server-side ADO Recordset), the Jet engine physically locates and modifies the desired record.

The ADO Cursor Engine doesn't work like Jet or like Xbase. Remember that the data in a client-side cursor is inherently disconnected from the database. ADO retrieves the results of the selection query and copies the data into the ADO Cursor Engine. After you make changes to your Recordset, the ADO Cursor Engine translates those changes into an action query and submits that query to your database through the OLE DB provider or ODBC driver.

Referring back to our example, you can see that ADO retrieves records into the Recordset based on the results of the query in the *strSQL* string. Now let's say that the customer's balance due prior to running this code was $125. When you modify that data, the ADO Cursor Engine builds a new query to update the customer's balance due:

```
UPDATE Customers SET BalanceDue = 175
              WHERE CustomerID = 7 AND BalanceDue = 125
```

If instead of modifying the balance due you deleted or added a customer by using the Recordset's *Delete* or *AddNew* method, the respective action queries created by the ADO Cursor Engine would look like this:

```
DELETE Customers WHERE CustomerID = 7
```

and

```
INSERT INTO Customers (CustomerID, CompanyName, BalanceDue)
    VALUES (7, 'Seventh Heaven', 175)
```

Voilà! It's not quite magic, but it's still pretty impressive if you ask me.

Keep in mind that when you write query statements, you have a distinct advantage over ADO: You (should) know the name of the table you're modifying as well as the name of the field or fields that constitute the primary key. But we didn't set any properties on the Field or Recordset object to provide this information to ADO when we modified the Recordset. So how did the ADO Cursor Engine know how to construct this query? Through the use of metadata.

HOW ADO GATHERS METADATA

Metadata is a term that we use a lot in product support. Essentially "metadata" means data about data. The ADO Cursor Engine needs very little metadata to retrieve the results of your query—only the data type and the name of the field. But to build the action queries needed to modify the data in the database, the ADO Cursor Engine needs more information.

Base Table and Field Names

In order to update your database, the ADO Cursor Engine needs to know which table (or tables) you want to modify. There is no way you can programmatically supply that information to ADO. The ADO Cursor Engine also needs to know the names of the fields in the tables you want to modify. But can't the Cursor Engine get that information? Doesn't the Name property for each Field object in the Recordset correspond to the actual field in the table?

Not always. Maybe your query calls a stored procedure, or maybe you use a different name for a field in the results by using an alias. The name of a field in your query results is not necessarily the name of the corresponding field in your table.

So where does the table and field information come from? From the same place the data came from—your OLE DB provider. Just before retrieving the results of your query, the ADO Cursor Engine asks your OLE DB provider (or ODBC driver) for the metadata it needs to build the action queries that update your database.

The ADO Cursor Engine requests this information from the OLE DB provider immediately after retrieving the names and data types of each field, just prior to retrieving the results of your query. However, many providers and drivers do not support returning this information along with the results of the initial query. But the ADO Cursor Engine doesn't give up that easily.

If the OLE DB provider or ODBC driver doesn't support returning the base table and field names, ADO will attempt to determine the table names by parsing the query in the *strSQL* string. The Cursor Engine then retrieves information about the different fields in those tables by issuing a *SELECT * FROM TableName* query and storing metadata about the fields in the query's result set (and discarding the data returned by the query). This method is neither efficient nor foolproof, but it's still the best option short of allowing the developer to supply this metadata.

If the OLE DB provider or ODBC driver returns inaccurate data or the ADO Cursor Engine can't gather the base table and field names, you'll likely receive the "Insufficient base table information for updating" error message when you try to update your database.

Locating the Record to Modify

You've supplied the new data for the record you want to modify by changing the Recordset object. You now understand how the ADO Cursor Engine determines the base table and field information. But how does the ADO Cursor Engine locate the correct record to update?

For a moment, forget about the fact that ADO is essentially an ad hoc query tool. If you wanted to build a table of customer data and use action queries to modify its contents, how would you set up the table so that you could easily specify in your action queries which record you want to update?

I hope that your answer is, "Dave, I can't believe you'd ask me such a simple question. In fact, I'm a little insulted. Any database developer worth her salt knows that you should build a primary key into your tables." (If that wasn't your answer, take a database implementation class for your database of choice.) There are isolated cases in which you might not want a primary key but have the need to update data through ADO. However, these instances are few and far between.

So—you have a primary key on your table. As you might have noticed earlier in our example, the primary key field, CustomerID, was one of the fields that the ADO Cursor Engine used in the WHERE clause of the action query to update the database. Like the base table and field names metadata, the ADO Cursor Engine asks the OLE DB provider or ODBC driver for information about the primary key for each table it needs to update. If the table you want to update does not contain a primary key, the ADO Cursor Engine will try to locate a unique index instead.

This series of API calls is one of the more expensive sets of calls that ADO makes (which is why I'm hopeful that a future release will offer a programmatic way to supply such metadata). These calls are expensive because the OLE DB provider and ODBC driver query the database's tables to retrieve the primary key information. The Microsoft SQL Server OLE DB provider and ODBC driver implement an optional feature that returns the primary key data rather efficiently by stating whether a particular field in the results is considered a key field. Those are the only components I'm aware of that implement such a feature, however. With other OLE DB providers and ODBC drivers, the ADO Cursor Engine must query the database to retrieve information on the primary key for each table in your query, and then determine whether your query retrieved the fields that make up the primary key. Though the ADO Cursor Engine's logic here is sound and its code is efficient, the requests it must make to retrieve this information are still expensive.

There is an exception to this costly process of retrieving primary key data for a given table that's worth mentioning. The Microsoft OLE DB Provider For Oracle avoids this process by requesting the row ID and using that row ID, rather than the primary key value, in the action query. This feature alone has significantly improved performance in applications that use the ADO Cursor Engine to modify data in Oracle databases, and it has convinced many Oracle programmers to migrate to the Microsoft OLE DB Provider For Oracle.

In ADO 2.5, you can force the Microsoft OLE DB Provider For Oracle to use key fields in the ADO Cursor Engine's query-based updates by setting the value of the Determine Key Columns For Rowset dynamic property on the Recordset object, as shown in the following code. This dynamic property is targeted to a small group of Oracle "power users" who might not want to use row ID values in the ADO Cursor Engine's query-based updates.

```
strSQL = "SELECT * FROM Customers"
Set rsCustomers = New ADODB.Recordset
With rsCustomers
    'Make the connection to the Oracle database the active connection.
    Set .ActiveConnection = cnOracle
    'Set the cursor location to use a server-side cursor.
    .CursorLocation = adUseServer
    'Set the dynamic property to use key fields in the query-based
    ' updates.
    .Properties("Determine Key Columns For Rowset") = True
    'Reset the cursor location to use a client-side cursor.
    .CursorLocation = adUseClient
    .Open strSQL, , adOpenStatic, adLockBatchOptimistic, adCmdText
    MsgBox .Fields("CustomerID").Properties("KeyColumn")
    .Close
End With
```

> **NOTE** The code example for the OLE DB Provider For Oracle looks a little odd, but it's the only way I've found to use the Determine Key Columns For Rowset dynamic property successfully as of ADO 2.5. The property is available in the Recordset object's Properties collection only after you set the Recordset's ActiveConnection property to a Connection object that's using the Microsoft OLE DB Provider For Oracle, and only if the Recordset's CursorLocation property is set to adUseServer. Don't ask me why the restriction on the CursorLocation exists, since this property is designed for the ADO Cursor Engine. Once you set the dynamic property, set the Recordset's CursorLocation property to adUseClient and open the Recordset object using the parameters shown in the example. Leave the ActiveConnection parameter empty or you'll reset the Recordset's connection-specific properties, thereby undoing the change you went to great lengths to make.

If you insist on using a table that does not contain a primary key or a unique index, ADO has no reliable way to locate the record you want to modify. So the ADO Cursor Engine gives it the old college try. Rather than considering a field or group of fields to constitute a unique way to locate the desired record, the ADO Cursor Engine uses all the objects in your Recordset's Fields collection in the WHERE clause of the action query.

Where Is This Metadata Stored?

Each of the Field objects in your Recordset contains dynamic properties to store this metadata: BaseColumnName, BaseTableName, BaseCatalogName, BaseSchemaName, and KeyColumn. I've spoken with a few developers who were building ad hoc query applications and wanted to rely on ADO to report this metadata. The ADO Cursor Engine populates the values for these properties only if you request an updatable Recordset. If you request a read-only Recordset, the ADO Cursor Engine doesn't bother to retrieve this metadata. These properties are still available on client-side Recordsets that are not updatable, but the properties will not return valid values. Sorry.

CONCURRENCY CONTROL

Let's quickly recap. Suppose you write this code:

```
strSQL = "SELECT CustomerID, CompanyName, BalanceDue FROM Customers"
With rsCustomers
    .CursorLocation = adUseClient
    .Open strSQL, cnDatabase, adOpenStatic, _
                  adLockOptimistic, adCmdText
    .Find "CustomerID = 7"
    .Fields("BalanceDue") = .Fields("BalanceDue") + 50
    .Update
End With
```

The ADO Cursor Engine will then build the following action query to modify the data in your database:

```
UPDATE Customers SET BalanceDue = 175
                WHERE CustomerID = 7 AND BalanceDue = 125
```

You now know where the table name, field names, and primary key data came from. There's only one piece of this action query that we haven't covered—the fact that the original value for the modified field appears in the WHERE clause along with the value of the primary key field. Why is that piece of information in the action query? The reason has to do with the difficulties involved in concurrent updates.

The Importance of Being Polite

It's relatively simple to develop database applications that will be used by only a single user at a time. But once you add a second user, things become much more complex.

Take our simple example as, well, an example. Say that the application is designed for telephone operators to take orders over the phone. When the customer calls and reaches an operator, that operator enters the customer's ID into your application and retrieves that customer's information. Toward the end of the call, the operator enters a $50 order for the customer, and your code increases the customer's balance due from $125 to $175 by modifying the appropriate Field object in the Recordset.

Now suppose that, unbeknownst to the operator, an employee in the billing department accesses the same database and processes a $100 check from that same customer between the time that your application retrieves the customer data for the operator and the time that the operator tries to enter the order. When the operator received the call, the customer's balance due was $125, but by the time the operator tries to submit the order, the customer's balance due has changed to $25.

How should your application handle this situation? That's open to discussion. Ultimately, I would want the system to accept the customer's order and set the balance due to $75. If you're building your own action queries and not relying on the features available through an updatable Recordset, you could simply issue a query such as the following:

```
UPDATE Customers SET BalanceDue = BalanceDue + 50
            WHERE CustomerID = 7
```

However, the ADO Cursor Engine is a bit like a doctor: Its first imperative is to do no harm. It does not want to unintentionally overwrite changes made by another user. Therefore, the ADO Cursor Engine uses the original value for the modified fields in the WHERE clause of the action query.

Determining Whether an Update Succeeds

As I said earlier, this is the action query that the ADO Cursor Engine built to submit a change to the database:

```
UPDATE Customers SET BalanceDue = 175
            WHERE CustomerID = 7 AND BalanceDue = 125
```

Since, in this particular case, the BalanceDue for the record was updated to 25 before this call was made, ADO would raise the following error:

```
"The specified row could not be located for updating: Some values may
 have been changed since it was last read."
```

Perfect! This is exactly what you need. If the update attempt had succeeded, the operator would've changed the balance due to $175, unknowingly overwriting the changes made by the employee in the billing department. But how did ADO know to generate this error?

If you took the previous action query and programmatically submitted it to the database, the query would not generate such an error. In fact, it would not generate an error at all. Instead, you'll see that the query modified no records, if you know where to look. For instance, if you submitted this action query by using the *Execute* method on the Connection or Command object, you could check the value returned in the *RecordsAffected* parameter to determine the number of records modified by the query.

The ADO Cursor Engine uses similar mechanisms to determine whether the attempt to update your database succeeded. If the action query modifies no records, the Cursor Engine returns the previous error message. If the action query modifies one record, the ADO Cursor Engine interprets this as a successful update.

Using the Primary Key

You should treat primary keys with the utmost respect, leaving them read-only if at all possible. If you allow users to modify the value of the primary key field, it's possible for the action query to modify one record, but that record might not be the one you intended to modify. Also, if you don't have a primary key or a unique index on your table, the action query that the ADO Cursor Engine generates might modify more than one record. In such a case, the ADO Cursor Engine will interpret this result as a failure and generate the following error:

```
"Insufficient or incorrect key column information; too many rows
 affected by update."
```

However, even though ADO raised an error, it's too late. The damage is done. ADO has already updated the database and can't undo it. Pressing Ctrl+Z or Ctrl+U won't save you now. You have only one method of recourse when you trap such an error: if you wrapped the changes in a transaction, you can roll them back.

But you won't run into such a problem. You'll have a primary key on your tables, and you'll include the fields that make up that primary key in your Recordset. Right?

Controlling the Criteria in the WHERE Clause

An updatable client-side Recordset has a dynamic property named Update Criteria that you can set to specify which fields, along with the key fields, are used in the WHERE clause for the action queries. You can set this property to any value in the ADCPROP_UPDATECRITERIA_ENUM enumerated data type, shown in the following table.

ADCPROP_UPDATECRITERIA_ENUM VALUES

Constant	Value	Description
adCriteriaKey	0	Uses only the values of the key fields in the WHERE clause of the query-based update
adCriteriaAllCols	1	Uses the original values of the fields in the WHERE clause of the query-based update
adCriteriaUpdCols	2	Default; uses the original values of the modified fields as well as the values of the key fields in the WHERE clause of the query-based update
adCriteriaTimeStamp	3	Uses the value of the timestamp field as well as the values of the key fields in the WHERE clause of the query-based update

By default, this property is set to adCriteriaUpdCols. Since the key fields and the original values for modified fields are included in the WHERE clause, your update will fail if another user has modified one of the fields you were trying to update. If another user modifies a field in the Recordset that you did not modify and that is not considered a key field, your update will succeed.

You can set this property to adCriteriaAllCols if you want to specify the original value for all fields in the WHERE clause of the action query. This ensures that if another user modifies any field in your Recordset, your update attempt will fail.

If you have a timestamp field in your table and in the results of your query, you can set the Update Criteria property to adCriteriaTimeStamp. This setting instructs the ADO Cursor Engine to use the original values for key fields and the value in your timestamp field. When a user modifies a record that contains a timestamp field, the database updates that field with a new value. Therefore, if a user modifies the record you're trying to update, your update will now fail—even if that user modified a field that isn't included in the results of your query.

The last available value is adCriteriaKey. While this setting can come in handy, it can cause serious problems if used incorrectly. If you set the Update Criteria property to adCriteriaKey, the ADO Cursor Engine will use only the values of the key fields in the WHERE clause. Although you generally want to avoid overwriting other users' changes, in some cases, that's the desired result. If you're writing code for such a scenario, this is the setting for you.

WHAT HAPPENS AFTER MY UPDATE ATTEMPT?

If the attempt to update your database is successful, the ADO Cursor Engine takes some simple steps to try to let you update that same record again with your same Recordset object. Remember that in our example, the ADO Cursor Engine built and submitted the following query to the database:

```
UPDATE Customers SET BalanceDue = 175
            WHERE CustomerID = 7 AND BalanceDue = 125
```

Suppose that the update attempt succeeds and you want to modify that same record of data in your database again without reexecuting your initial query. For example, the customer places a second order worth $80 while on the phone with the operator who's using your application. Ultimately, you want the ADO Cursor Engine to generate and submit the following query:

```
UPDATE Customers SET BalanceDue = 255
            WHERE CustomerID = 7 AND BalanceDue = 175
```

In short, you want the ADO Cursor Engine to store the data it uses to successfully update the record in your table so that it can use that data during future update attempts. It's no coincidence that this is exactly what happens. When your update succeeds, the ADO Cursor Engine will change the OriginalValue property on the Field objects that you modified to reflect the change made to the record in your database.

> **NOTE** The fact that the value of the OriginalValue property changes when you update your database means that the name of the OriginalValue property was a bit of a misnomer. However, this value makes it possible (in most cases) to modify the same record in your Recordset object multiple times without having to refetch the current contents of the record from your database. In Chapter 11, we'll examine some cases in which this repeated modification isn't possible.

Your update attempt might fail for several reasons. When an update attempt fails because another user has modified the same record, it's considered an optimistic updating conflict. Chapter 12 will cover this type of problem in more detail.

Update attempts that fail because of unacceptable data, violations of primary or foreign key constraints, and so on are not considered conflicts because they technically are not failures caused by another user modifying the same record. I recommend that, while designing your application, you intentionally cause such a violation. Then find a way to trap for the problems you expect and resolve them accordingly.

JOINS

In a perfect world—or a perfect data access object model—you could update data based on a join that you design however you see fit. You'd have enough control to tell the object model exactly what it means to insert, modify, or delete a record in your Recordset. But as I'm sure you've noticed, this is not a perfect world and ADO is not a perfect data access object model. Although queries that use joins are fine for read-only data, updating a Recordset based on a join query is not as easy as you might think.

Let's take a look at a simple update example. Suppose that you want to retrieve customer and order information into a single recordset by joining information, as in the following query:

```
SELECT * FROM Customers, Orders
        WHERE Customers.CustomerID = Orders.CustomerID
```

Obviously if you want to modify order data in this recordset, that change would correspond to a single record in the Orders table. Simple enough. But what if you change the value of fields from both tables? Say that the CompanyName field exists in the Customers table and that the OrderTotal field exists in the Orders table:

```
rsOrdersAndCustomers("CompanyName").Value = "Some New Customer Name"
rsOrdersAndCustomers("OrderTotal").Value = 1500
```

What does this code mean?

ADO understands that this code requires changes to both tables. The Cursor Engine builds separate action queries to submit to each of the tables. If that's what you want to happen, great! Wonderful! So what's the problem? If you're only worried about a single isolated update such as this, there is no problem.

However, what if you want to modify the record to indicate that the order belongs to a different customer? If you modify fields that correspond to fields in the Customers table, the ADO Cursor Engine will generate an action query to modify the record in the Customers table. This can be a problem if you wanted the changes in the record to update only the unique table produced by the join.

As a general rule, no matter what fields you modify in your recordset, the ADO Cursor Engine will attempt to update the tables associated with them.

Insertions

What if you want to enter a new record into this recordset? If you simply want to create a new order, you'll have to set the Value property on only the Field objects that correspond to the Orders table. Once you commit the change to the database, the ADO

Cursor Engine will generate an action query to insert your new record into the Orders table. But if you set the Value property on Field objects corresponding to the Customers table, the ADO Cursor Engine will also try to insert a record into the Customers table.

Deletions

Deletions are a little simpler. If you try to delete a record from this recordset, the ADO Cursor Engine will build action queries to delete the order from the Orders table as well as the customer from the Customers table. If that's what you intended to do, you should be just fine.

If you wanted to delete only the record from the unique table (in this case the Orders table), you would need to use another dynamic property on the Recordset object that's exposed by the Cursor Engine: Unique Table.

```
strSQL = "SELECT * FROM Customers, Orders " & _
                "WHERE Customers.CustomerID = Orders.CustomerID"
rsCustomersAndOrders.CursorLocation = adUseClient
rsCustomersAndOrders.Open strSQL, cnDatabase, adOpenStatic, _
                adLockOptimistic, adCmdText
rsCustomersAndOrders.Properties("Unique Table").Value = "Orders"
rsCustomersAndOrders.Delete
```

By setting the Unique Table dynamic property on the Recordset object to *Orders*, you're telling the ADO Cursor Engine to delete only the record from the Orders table and ignore the other tables referenced by the query. This dynamic property exists on all client-side Recordset objects but is helpful only to deletions in joins. Currently, ADO ignores the Unique Table dynamic property and the related Unique Schema and Unique Catalog dynamic properties for modifications and insertions with joins.

RESYNC COMMAND DYNAMIC PROPERTY

In ADO 2.1, the Cursor Engine introduced a new dynamic property called Resync Command to help make updating Recordsets based on joins simpler. In order to use this property, you must also set the Unique Table dynamic property on the Recordset. In the case of the query we've been using, the unique table is the Orders table. To update a join, set the Unique Table property to the unique table in your join. Then set the Resync Command property to the query you want to use to resynchronize the data in your join-based Recordset. Use parameter markers (?) in the WHERE clause to denote the key columns in the unique table.

A couple of examples will help to clarify how useful this feature can be. Let's revisit our customers and orders query and look at how you can use Resync Command to simplify modifying or inserting records in Recordsets based on joins.

```
SELECT Customers.CustomerID AS [Customers.CustomerID],
       Customers.CompanyName, Customers.ContactName, Orders.*
FROM Customers, Orders WHERE Customers.CustomerID = Orders.CustomerID
```

> **NOTE** In this code, I aliased the CustomerID field from the Customers table, which makes the query string more complex but simplifies the ADO code. See the "Questions That Should Be Asked More Frequently" section at the end of this chapter for a brief explanation.

So, the query string we would use for the Resync Command property is

```
SELECT Customers.CustomerID AS [Customers.CustomerID],
       Customers.CompanyName, Customers.ContactName, Orders.*
FROM Customers, Orders WHERE Customers.CustomerID = Orders.CustomerID
                       AND Orders.OrderID = ?
```

This is simply the original query with the key column for the unique table in a WHERE clause.

We're going to cover two scenarios with our example. The first scenario involves changing the customer referenced by the order and getting the appropriate customer data into our Recordset. The second scenario entails adding a new order and getting the appropriate customer data into our Recordset.

Changing the Customer Referenced by an Order

The problem with changing the customer referenced by an order is that we want to modify only the data in the Orders table. To do that, we can simply modify the value of the CustomerID field (that refers to the Orders table) in our Recordset. Submitting that change to the database will have the desired effect—in our database. The fields in the Recordset object that correspond to the Customers table will not automatically reflect this change.

This is where programmers start to run into problems. They want to see the appropriate customer data in the join. If you requery the Recordset, you will see the appropriate customer data, but that involves reexecuting the entire query, and most programmers don't want to incur that expense.

Calling *Resync* won't help in this case (yet) because the ADO Cursor Engine will resynchronize each half of the join separately and will resynchronize the fields corresponding to the Customers table based on the old ID field it has for that record. So, calling *Resync* at this point would simply refetch the old customer information.

The other avenue that programmers pursue is programmatically changing the data in the customer side of the join. ADO interprets this as a change to the actual customer data, and will build an action query to locate that customer and modify that record of the Customers table to reflect the changes you make to the Recordset. Generally, this is not what you want to do.

Here's where the Resync Command property comes in handy. We can use the following code to retrieve the results of a join on the Customers and Orders tables and modify the customer that the order references. Then we can call the *Resync* method to resynchronize the record in the Recordset based on the query string in the Resync Command property. Once we do that, the appropriate customer data appears in our Recordset.

```
'Create the initial query.
strSQL = "SELECT Customers.CustomerID AS [Customers.CustomerID], " & _
        "Customers.CompanyName, Customers.ContactName, Orders.* " & _
        "FROM Customers, Orders " & _
        "WHERE Customers.CustomerID = Orders.CustomerID"
Set rsCustomersAndOrders = New ADODB.Recordset
rsCustomersAndOrders.CursorLocation = adUseClient
rsCustomersAndOrders.Open strSQL, cnDatabase, adOpenStatic, _
                          adLockOptimistic, adCmdText

'Specify values for the Unique Table and Resync Command properties.
rsCustomersAndOrders.Properties("Unique Table") = "Orders"
strSQL = "SELECT Customers.CustomerID AS [Customers.CustomerID], " & _
        "Customers.CompanyName, Customers.ContactName, Orders.* " & _
        "FROM Customers, Orders " & _
        "WHERE Customers.CustomerID = Orders.CustomerID " & _
        "AND Orders.OrderID = ?"
rsCustomersAndOrders.Properties("Resync Command") = strSQL

'Update the CustomerID field that corresponds to the Orders table.
rsCustomersAndOrders!CustomerID = "ANTON"
rsCustomersAndOrders.Update
'Resynchronize the record to retrieve the proper data from the
' Customers table.
rsCustomersAndOrders.Resync adResyncCurrent
```

Generating a New Order and Displaying the Correct Customer Data

Similar to updating records in a Recordset that is based on a join, adding new records to a Recordset based on a join can pose a problem. In this scenario, we want to create a new order, supply a value for the CustomerID field, and ultimately see the appropriate customer data in our Recordset.

NOTE Using the Northwind database for SQL Server or Access adds a complexity. The OrderID field is an auto-incrementing field generated by the database system. We'll talk more about working with this type of field in Chapter 11. For now, we're going to supply that OrderID value programmatically as if the Orders table did not use an auto-incrementing field.

If we simply supply the order information and leave the fields that correspond to the Customers table blank, we successfully create the new order but we don't get the customer data we're looking for. Calling *Requery* might not be desirable, since it reexecutes the entire query. Without setting the Resync Command property, the *Resync* method will actually generate an error since the field that corresponds to the CustomerID field and references the Customers table is still empty.

Once again, the Resync Command property comes to our rescue. We can successfully retrieve the desired customer data by setting the Unique Table and Resync Command properties as follows:

```
'Create the initial query.
strSQL = "SELECT Customers.CustomerID AS [Customers.CustomerID], " & _
         "Customers.CompanyName, Customers.ContactName, Orders.* " & _
         "FROM Customers, Orders " & _
         "WHERE Customers.CustomerID = Orders.CustomerID"
Set rsCustomersAndOrders = New ADODB.Recordset
rsCustomersAndOrders.CursorLocation = adUseClient
rsCustomersAndOrders.Open strSQL, cnDatabase, adOpenStatic, _
                          adLockOptimistic, adCmdText

'Specify values for the Unique Table and Resync Command properties.
rsCustomersAndOrders.Properties("Unique Table") = "Orders"
strSQL = "SELECT Customers.CustomerID AS [Customers.CustomerID], " & _
         "Customers.CompanyName, Customers.ContactName, Orders.* " & _
         "FROM Customers, Orders " & _
         "WHERE Customers.CustomerID = Orders.CustomerID " & _
         "AND Orders.OrderID = ?"
rsCustomersAndOrders.Properties("Resync Command") = strSQL

'Add a new row to the Recordset and populate the fields
' that correspond to the Orders table.
rsCustomersAndOrders.AddNew
rsCustomersAndOrders!OrderID = 12345
rsCustomersAndOrders!EmployeeID = 1
rsCustomersAndOrders!OrderDate = Date
rsCustomersAndOrders!ShipVia = 1
rsCustomersAndOrders!CustomerID = "ANTON"
rsCustomersAndOrders.Update
'Resynchronize the record to retrieve the proper data from the
' Customers table.
rsCustomersAndOrders.Resync adResyncCurrent
```

Compound Keys

In the previous examples, the unique table contains a primary key based on a single field. What if your table uses a compound primary key and you want to use the Resync Command property?

Let's say that the Orders table has a compound primary key that consists of two fields: ID1 and ID2. In that case, our Resync Command property looks like this:

```
SELECT Customers.CustomerID AS [Customers.CustomerID],
     Customers.CompanyName, Customers.ContactName, Orders.*
FROM Customers, Orders WHERE Customers.CustomerID = Orders.CustomerID
                  AND Orders.ID1 = ? AND Orders.ID2 = ?
```

Notice that there's no difference in the parameter markers. You might need to play with the order of the key fields in your initial query string and your Resync Command query. My advice is to make sure the key fields appear in the same order in the Recordset as in the WHERE clause of the query in the Resync Command property.

I'm extremely impressed with how the ADO development team implemented the Resync Command and Unique Table properties to make updating Recordsets based on joins simpler. However, these properties are best used in live (nondisconnected) Recordsets that use simple optimistic locking. These properties aren't very helpful for disconnected Recordsets or for Recordsets that utilize the ADO Cursor Engine's batch updating features.

Comparatively speaking, the ADO Cursor Engine does a great job of handling joins. If you use the same join query against a SQL Server database and use a server-side cursor, you'll receive an error if you try to update any field that corresponds to a field in the Customers table. SQL Server marks those fields as read-only. The Resync Command property can make updating Recordsets based on join queries possible in some cases, but I prefer opening such Recordsets as read-only.

QUESTIONS THAT SHOULD BE ASKED MORE FREQUENTLY

Q. *What if I don't include the key field or fields for my table in my initial query? Will I still be able to update my database with the Recordset object?*
A. Short answer: Don't do this. (Why would you ever do this? Bad programmer!) Include the key field or fields in your query.

Long answer: I have to admit, I've done some testing of this scenario because I was curious and I've had people ask about it before. In my tests, I watched a trace of the action queries passed by ADO to my SQL Server database through SQL Server Profiler. It turns out that ADO included primary key values in the action queries, even though I didn't include the primary key field in my query. However, that field didn't show up in the trace as being part of the query. What happened?

The SQL Server OLE DB provider (and ODBC driver) returned this data in a hidden field. I discovered this by checking the Recordset's Hidden Columns dynamic property. Sure enough, it was set to 1. Needless to say, I was impressed. This functionality seems similar to the Microsoft OLE DB Provider For Oracle having the sense to retrieve row ID data to facilitate updating. But don't rely on this functionality.

Why ask ADO, the OLE DB provider, or the ODBC driver to do all this work when you could simply include the key field or fields in your query? Don't be lazy. Besides, not all providers and drivers retrieve this data. When I ran this test with the Jet OLE DB Provider, it didn't retrieve the key field or fields, but it still allowed me to update my database. How? From some painful testing, I deduced that it simply used data from all the fields in the Recordset to form some sort of mock key.

In short, if you don't include the key field or fields in your query, you might still be able to update your database, but how that's accomplished depends on your OLE DB provider or ODBC driver—then again, you really shouldn't be doing this in the first place. Instead, just say no.

Q. *What happens if I don't have a live connection to my database and I call* **Update** *or* **UpdateBatch***?*

A. The ADO Cursor Engine assumes you have good reason to do this and pretends it successfully updated your database. There might be times when you want to make use of this particular behavior. Just be sure to keep this behavior in mind if you disconnect your Recordset from your database. If you call the *UpdateBatch* method while your Recordset is disconnected, those changes will no longer be marked as pending. When you reconnect the Recordset, those changes will not be transmitted to your database.

Q. *I'm having problems with my joins. With some back-end databases, I can't tell what table a particular field references because both tables in my join contain that same field name. What should I do, and why does this problem occur only with particular back-end databases?*

A. ADO simply uses the field names that the OLE DB provider or ODBC driver returns. If the OLE DB provider or ODBC driver doesn't return the field names the way you want, try using aliases in the query string so that you can tell the fields apart in the Recordset object.

Chapter 11

Update Resync

Let's briefly recap how the ADO Cursor Engine performs updates. When you write code such as the following

```
strSQL = "SELECT CustomerID, CustomerName, BalanceDue " & _
        "FROM Customers"
With rsCustomers
    .CursorLocation = adUseClient
    .Open strSQL, cnDatabase, adOpenStatic, _
            adLockOptimistic, adCmdText
    .Fields("BalanceDue") = 150
    .Update
End With
```

ADO executes an action query that modifies the data in your database based on the changes you've made to your Recordset. In this case, the action query looks like this:

```
UPDATE Customers SET BalanceDue = 150
        WHERE CustomerID = 7 AND BalanceDue = 100
```

To determine whether the query succeeded in updating the appropriate data, ADO examines the number of records affected by the action query. If at least one record was affected, ADO interprets this as a successful update. If no records were updated, ADO interprets this as a failed update because of a change made by another user. That record might have been deleted, or the value of the BalanceDue field might have changed. Such is the nature of optimistic updating.

You'll sometimes need more than just an action query, however. In some situations you'll want to retrieve data immediately after submitting a change to the database.

WHEN A SIMPLE ACTION QUERY ISN'T ENOUGH

There are times when the simple action queries generated by the ADO Cursor Engine don't supply enough information to perform the updates you require. Action queries essentially function like a one-way street: they tell the database how to modify the record but don't return the new contents of that record. However, in reaction to the changes made by ADO, the database system might need to make a number of other changes to the record because of elements such as auto-incrementing identity fields, timestamps, and default values. You usually don't need to be aware of this data. However in some cases, without this data you might encounter problems when you try to change a single record in your Recordset more than once.

You might be asking yourself, "Why would I ever want to update the same record twice in a single session? That's inefficient." Maybe, but often it's necessary based on user actions. For example, it's possible that the user would try to update the same record more than once. (Did you consider that scenario when designing or testing your application?) Let's look at some cases you might not have considered that could cause problems if you had no information from the updated record.

Auto-Incrementing Identity Field

Suppose that your primary key is based on an auto-incrementing identity field. Prior to version 2.1 of ADO, if you used client-side Recordsets, you had no way to retrieve the new value when adding a new record to the database. The ADO Cursor Engine would insert the new record but would not retrieve the new primary key value generated for the record. After the update, the identity column in the Recordset remained set to Null, and any subsequent attempt to update that record would fail. (You'll recall from Chapter 10 that the ADO Cursor Engine needs the primary key value to generate the action query to update a record.) Any attempt to retrieve the new identity value by calling the *Resync* method of the Recordset would fail because the ADO Cursor Engine needs that primary key value to determine which record in the table to use to resynchronize the current record in the Recordset.

Timestamp-Based Updates

Perhaps you're using timestamp fields to control your updates. When you initially retrieve a particular record, you're retrieving the current value of that timestamp field. The ADO Cursor Engine uses that value in the action query. But when the database system receives that action query and modifies that record, the system generates a new value for the timestamp field.

Again, the action queries performed by the ADO Cursor Engine act like a one-way street. This newly generated timestamp value is not retrieved and placed into your Recordset. Instead, the modified record in your Recordset contains the outdated timestamp value that the ADO Cursor Engine retrieved when you opened the Recordset. Therefore, a subsequent attempt to update this same record will fail.

Default Values

Database developers often use default values when defining a table. If you add a new record to your Recordset and leave the value of a field empty, that field will be set in your database to Null or to the default value (if one exists for that field). However, since that default value is generated by the database and action queries don't return information, that default value does not (by default) appear in your Recordset when you submit the record to the database.

UPDATE RESYNC TO THE RESCUE!

ADO 2.1 introduced a dynamic property to the Recordset object called Update Resync, which is used with client-side Recordsets to aid developers who encounter scenarios such as those just described. Depending on the value that you specify for this property, ADO executes queries to refetch the record that you just updated (or attempted to update) in the database.

If you're using optimistic updating mode, ADO issues these queries when you call the *Update* method on the Recordset, immediately after the ADO Cursor Engine issues the action query. If you're using batch optimistic updating mode, ADO issues these queries when you call *UpdateBatch*. The Update Resync property can contain values from the CEResyncEnum data type, shown in the following table:

CERESYNCENUM VALUES

Constant	Value	Description
adResyncNone	0	Retrieves no data after modifications
adResyncAutoIncrement	1	Default; retrieves auto-incrementing value for new records
adResyncConflicts	2	Retrieves underlying values for records whose updates fail because of optimistic updating conflicts
adResyncUpdates	4	Retrieves the current contents of records after their updates have been submitted to the database
adResyncInserts	8	Retrieves the current contents of new records after they have been submitted to the database
adResyncAll	15	Performs actions associated with adResyncAutoIncrement, adResyncConflicts, adResyncUpdates, and adResyncInserts

To access this property, you must set the CursorLocation property to adUseClient on either the Recordset object or the Connection object prior to opening the Recordset, as shown, respectively, in the following code:

```
With rsCustomers
    .CursorLocation = adUseClient
    .Open strSQL, cnDatabase, adOpenStatic, _
        adLockReadOnly, adCmdText
    .Properties("Update Resync") = adResyncUpdates
End With
```

or

```
cnDatabase.CursorLocation = adUseClient
With rsCustomers
    .Open strSQL, cnDatabase, adOpenStatic, _
        adLockOptimistic, adCmdText
    .Properties("Update Resync") = adResyncUpdates
End With
```

The Update Resync property is a bitmask—which means you can also use the sum of different constants for the property:

```
rsCustomers.Properties("Update Resync") = _
        adResyncAutoIncrement + adResyncInserts
```

Let's take a closer look at the behavior associated with each of the available constants.

adResyncNone

Using this constant turns off the Update Resync functionality. The ADO Cursor Engine will not issue any queries to retrieve information about the record that it just updated.

adResyncAutoIncrement

This constant is extremely helpful when you want to use a client-side Recordset to insert new records into a table that uses an auto-incrementing identity field. Many developers who are accustomed to using Microsoft Access to insert records have come to expect this functionality—as soon as they add a new record, they expect to see the new value for the identity field. As a result, adResyncAutoIncrement is the default value for the Update Resync property on client-side Recordsets.

To understand how the processing works with this constant assigned to the Update Resync property, let's take a look at some code:

```
strSQL = "SELECT CustomerID, CustomerName, BalanceDue " & _
        "FROM Customers"
With rsCustomers
    .CursorLocation = adUseClient
    .Open strSQL, cnDatabase, adOpenStatic, _
        adLockOptimistic, adCmdText
    .Properties("Update Resync") = adResyncAutoIncrement
    .AddNew
    .Fields("CustomerName") = "Acme Widgets"
    .Fields("BalanceDue") = 100
    .Update
End With
```

When you call the *Update* method on the Recordset object, the ADO Cursor Engine builds the following query to insert the new record into the table in the database:

```
INSERT INTO Customers (CustomerName, BalanceDue)
        VALUES ('Acme Widgets', 100)
```

The database uses this query to insert the record and informs the ADO Cursor Engine that the insertion was successful. Then the Cursor Engine issues the following query:

```
SELECT @@IDENTITY
```

The ADO Cursor Engine uses this query to retrieve the database-generated, auto-incrementing identity value for the newly inserted record and places that information into the appropriate field in the client-side Recordset object.

There are a few caveats you should keep in mind about using this feature with different database products:

- **Microsoft SQL Server** As of ADO 2.5, this feature works with both the SQL Server OLE DB provider and ODBC driver. As of ADO 2.1, this feature worked with the SQL Server OLE DB provider but not the SQL Server ODBC driver.

- **Access** This feature works with version 4 of the Jet OLE DB Provider but only for Jet 4 with Access 2000–formatted databases. This feature does not work with the Access ODBC driver because the driver doesn't support the *SELECT @@IDENTITY* query.

- **Oracle** Oracle has no notion of an identity field whose value is generated at the time of insertion. Instead, Oracle uses a concept called sequences that adds an extra step but avoids this scenario. For more information on sequences, see your Oracle documentation.

The *SELECT @@IDENTITY* query returns the last identity value generated on the connection, but the value might not be what you expect. If the INSERT command updates the record and then fires a trigger that inserts another record in a different table that includes an auto-incrementing identity field, you'll retrieve the value from this second table rather than the value of the identity field in the record you actually inserted. (A trigger is a special class of stored procedure that runs when an INSERT, UPDATE, or DELETE statement is issued.)

There are three main reasons you might want or require the newly generated identity value. First, it's helpful to have this information in your Recordset as soon as you pass the new record to the database. For example, if the auto-incrementing identity field is the OrderID field, a user who's taking orders from customers might need to read back a new order ID to a customer.

Second, most identity fields are the primary key field for the table—information that can come in handy. The ADO Cursor Engine uses the primary key value in building action queries. If you want to modify the newly inserted customer information but don't have the value of the CustomerID field for that customer, ADO can't build an action query to modify the appropriate record in the table.

Third, the ADO Cursor Engine uses the primary key value when you call the *Resync* method. For example, you might have a rule in your trigger for generating another piece of information that you want to retrieve immediately after adding the customer—for example, typing the zip code might generate the city and state. You might also need to retrieve the value of the server-generated timestamp field in order to handle subsequent updates.

> **NOTE** The ability to retrieve newly generated auto-increment values was one of the most popular requests for ADO in the 2.0 time frame. This feature was available in DAO/Jet, but no comparable feature existed in either RDO or ADO. In an attempt to persuade the development team, Don Willits (author of the MSDN white paper "Implementing ADO with Various Development Languages: The ADO Rosetta Stone") and I pledged to purchase a keg of good beer for the ADO development team if they could deliver such a feature. Although Don and I later discovered that the development team already had such a feature in the specs for ADO 2.1, we were still happy to fulfill our promise. It was nice to see some of the programmers, testers, and program managers in a relaxed atmosphere. As one of the program managers became very relaxed, he asked what features I'd like to see in the next version. I'm extremely impressed with this feature and want to congratulate the development team on such a helpful and well-designed feature.

adResyncInserts

There are times—such as when you're basing your updates on a timestamp field—when you want to know what the database server did to the record you just inserted into your table. For a newly inserted record, you need to retrieve the value that the server generated for that field in order to perform a subsequent update on that record. For example, perhaps you have a trigger that sets a value for your BalanceDue field, in which case you need to retrieve and/or modify that value immediately after inserting the new record.

If you're using a primary key based on an auto-incrementing identity field, you need to combine the adResyncAutoIncrement and adResyncInserts constants to retrieve the contents of the newly inserted record. As we discussed in the previous section, adResyncAutoIncrement will retrieve the new auto-increment value. The ADO Cursor Engine then uses this value to retrieve the contents of the newly inserted record. Here's an example that utilizes this feature to insert a new record into a table containing an auto-incrementing identity field and then performs a subsequent update to that same record based on the timestamp field:

```
strSQL = "SELECT CustomerID, CustomerName, BalanceDue, LastModified" & _
        " FROM Customers"
With rsCustomers
    .CursorLocation = adUseClient
    .Properties("Update Criteria") = adCriteriaTimeStamp
    .Properties("Update Resync") = adResyncInserts + _
                                   adResyncAutoIncrement
    .Open strSQL, cnDatabase, adOpenStatic, _
         adLockOptimistic, adCmdText
    .AddNew
    .Fields("CustomerName") = "Acme Widgets"
    .Update
    .Fields("BalanceDue") = 100
    .Update
End With
```

The ADO Cursor Engine executes the following queries the first time the *Update* method is called:

```
INSERT INTO Customers (CustomerName)
        VALUES ('Acme Widgets')

SELECT @@IDENTITY

SELECT CustomerID, CustomerName, BalanceDue, LastModified
    FROM Customers WHERE CustomerID = n
    (n = the value retrieved in the previous SELECT query)
```

The first query inserts the record into the table. The second query retrieves the value generated by the server for the auto-incrementing identity field. Utilizing the data returned by the second query, the third query retrieves the contents of the newly inserted record.

In this scenario, the LastModified field contains a timestamp. When you modify the BalanceDue field and call the *Update* method the second time, the ADO Cursor Engine builds the following action query to handle the modification:

```
UPDATE Customers SET BalanceDue = 100
        WHERE CustomerID = <retrieved value> AND BalanceDue = 0
            AND LastModified = <retrieved value>
```

Because you're using a timestamp field to handle the updates, the initial value that SQL Server generates for the timestamp field is required for this action query to succeed. However, another attempt to update this record will fail because the database generated a new timestamp value when you made this update, but you didn't retrieve this new value when calling *Update* the second time. To handle that scenario, you can use the adResyncUpdates constant.

adResyncUpdates

Just as adResyncInserts retrieves data from the record you just inserted, adResync-Updates retrieves data from the record you just modified. In the previous example, the code successfully updates a record it had just inserted because, thanks to adResyncInserts, the timestamp field was retrieved immediately after the insertion. When that record is updated, the database generates a new value for the timestamp field, and that data is not returned to the Recordset, leaving the field in the Recordset outdated. Therefore, another attempt to update that same record would fail.

By using the adResyncUpdates constant, you can tell the ADO Cursor Engine that after you update an existing record by calling the *Update* method, you want to resynchronize the data in that record of the Recordset. The following example uses this feature:

```
strSQL = "SELECT CustomerID, CustomerName, BalanceDue, LastModified" & _
        " FROM Customers"
With rsCustomers
    .CursorLocation = adUseClient
    .Properties("Update Criteria") = adCriteriaTimeStamp
    .Properties("Update Resync") = adResyncUpdates
    .Open strSQL, cnDatabase, adOpenStatic, _
        adLockOptimistic, adCmdText
```

```
    .Fields("BalanceDue") = 150
    .Update
    .Fields("CustomerName") = "Acme Widgets"
    .Update
End With
```

When you call the *Update* method the first time, ADO builds this next action query to update that record in the table:

```
UPDATE Customers SET BalanceDue = 150 WHERE
        CustomerID = 7 AND BalanceDue = 100
                AND LastModified = 0x0...
```

Because you have set the Update Resync property to adResyncUpdates, the ADO Cursor Engine also issues the following query to retrieve the contents of the record that it just updated:

```
SELECT CustomerID, CustomerName, BalanceDue, LastModified
        FROM Customers WHERE CustomerID = 7
```

The ADO Cursor Engine then places the returned information into the corresponding fields for the current record in the Recordset. Therefore, when you attempt to update that same record again, the second update will succeed because ADO retrieved the new timestamp value for the LastModified field that the database generated during the previous update. Similarly, subsequent updates will also succeed.

You should be aware of one issue regarding adResyncUpdates: when the ADO Cursor Engine retrieves information about the record in the database after you've performed your update, you might see that fields you hadn't modified have new values in your Recordset.

Let's look at a scenario in which the updates are based on only the fields being modified. The following code simply modifies the BalanceDue field for a particular customer:

```
strSQL = "SELECT CustomerID, CustomerName, BalanceDue " & _
        "FROM Customers"
With rsCustomers
    .CursorLocation = adUseClient
    .Properties("Update Criteria") = adCriteriaUpdCols
    .Properties("Update Resync") = adResyncUpdates
    .Open strSQL, cnDatabase, adOpenStatic, _
            adLockOptimistic, adCmdText
    .Fields("BalanceDue") = 150
    .Update
End With
```

If another user modifies the CustomerName field for that customer between the time you open the Recordset and the time you perform the update, there won't be a conflict. Why? Because the ADO Cursor Engine generates the following action query:

```
UPDATE Customers SET BalanceDue = 150
    WHERE CustomerID = 7 AND BalanceDue = 100
```

The CustomerName field isn't involved in this action query. The Update Criteria property is set to a value (adCriteriaUpdCols) indicating that the ADO Cursor Engine will specify only the updated fields (and the primary key field, of course) in the action query.

Let's quickly recap. You retrieved information about a particular customer. You modified the BalanceDue field and were about to update that customer information when another user modified the customer name. When you call the *Update* method, the update will succeed. Because you specified that you want to resynchronize the record after the update, you'll see the new value for the customer name in the Value property for that field.

adResyncConflicts

The action queries that ADO builds are considered optimistic update attempts because you're (optimistically) assuming that no one else has modified the data in the desired record. When you attempt to update a record that another user has since modified, ADO will still issue an action query such as the following:

```
UPDATE Customers SET BalanceDue = 150
    WHERE CustomerID = 7 AND BalanceDue = 100
```

But sometimes ADO will receive notification from the OLE DB provider and ODBC driver that no records were updated. This situation is called a conflict, and it generally occurs when another user has modified the value of one or more of the fields in the WHERE clause of the UPDATE query. (We'll cover trapping for and handling conflicts in more depth in Chapter 12.) If your optimistic update fails because of a conflict, ADO will pass the following error message to you:

```
"The specified row could not be located for updating: Some values may
have changed since it was last read."
```

Setting the Update Resync property to adResyncConflicts causes the ADO Cursor Engine to retrieve the current contents of the record you're attempting to modify if the update fails because of a conflict. The retrieved data is stored in the UnderlyingValue property for each Field in the Recordset object. You can use the data stored in the Value, OriginalValue, and UnderlyingValue properties to determine how to handle such a conflict. As I mentioned, we'll cover conflicts in more detail in the next chapter.

adResyncDeletes

I was just checking to see whether you're paying attention. There is no adResync-Deletes constant. Why? There's no need for one. If your attempt to delete succeeds, the record is removed from the table. There's no need to retrieve information about the record.

If the deletion fails because of a conflict, use adResyncConflicts to determine why the conflict occurred. If the deletion failed for another reason, such as referential integrity constraints (for instance, trying to delete a record from the Customers table when the customer has orders in the Orders table), you'll receive a trappable error.

adResyncAll

If you take a look at the values that are associated with the different constants in the CEResyncEnum enumeration, you might notice that the value of adResyncAll is the sum of the other constants. Setting the Update Resync property to adResyncAll combines the functionality of all the other constants in the data type but saves you the time of typing them all individually.

QUESTIONS THAT SHOULD BE ASKED MORE FREQUENTLY

Q. *Since adResyncAutoIncrement is the default value for this property, does that mean that the ADO Cursor Engine issues the* **SELECT @@IDENTITY** *query after every insert? If so, if I want to ensure that I get the best possible performance and if my Recordset doesn't contain an identity field, should I set the Update Resync property to adResyncNone?*

A. The ADO Cursor Engine retrieves enough metadata to determine whether your Recordset contains an identity field. If your Recordset doesn't have an identity field, the ADO Cursor Engine will not submit a *SELECT @@IDENTITY* query after inserting the new record into your table. In other words, the answer to both questions is no.

Q. *Why don't I see the value for the identity field in the new record I just inserted into my Access database?*

A. Remember, this functionality was added to version 4 of the Jet OLE DB Provider and works only with Jet 4 with Access 2000–formatted databases.

Chapter 12

Detecting and Handling Conflicts

As you know, multiple users often want to change the same data in your database at the same time. If users would simply agree not to do this, developing multiuser database applications would be much easier. Of course, you can prevent users from changing the same data at the same time by utilizing pessimistic locking in your database, but that's overly restrictive in comparison to optimistic locking. Besides, pessimistic locking is for lazy programmers.

So rather than take the easy way out and write an application that's too restrictive, you choose optimistic locking. You decide to start working with a small application that simulates multiple users trying to update a single record, and you encounter the following error message when the second user tries to perform an update:

```
"The specified row could not be located for updating: Some values may
have been changed since it was last read."
```

You might have had a hunch that the second user's update would fail, but when it did you probably asked yourself, "Now what?"

NOW WHAT?

I hear this question a lot from programmers who call Microsoft Developer Support wanting to know what to do when their optimistic update attempts fail. Just as there's no simple answer to the question, "How do I handle errors in my application?"

there's no simple answer here. And yet, it's not overly complicated to handle failed optimistic update attempts. You simply have to figure out what went wrong, why it happened, and what to do about it. That's not so difficult, right?

A lot of programmers I speak with about handling failed optimistic update attempts are surprised when I ask them, "Well, once you understand what went wrong, how do you want your code to react?"

When I explain error handling of optimistic updates to customers, I tend to go back to the same example each time—the same snippet of code we've used throughout most of the book:

```
strSQL = "SELECT CustomerID, CompanyName, BalanceDue " & _
         "FROM Customers WHERE CustomerID = 7"
rsCustomers.Open strSQL, cnDatabase, adOpenStatic, _
                 adLockBatchOptimistic, adCmdText
rsCustomers!BalanceDue = rsCustomers!BalanceDue + 50
rsCustomers.Update
rsCustomers.UpdateBatch
```

You know from previous chapters that if your code retrieves the customer's balance due and another user enters an update for that same customer before you enter your update, your update attempt fails. There are two common ways to handle this scenario.

The first is to let the user know that the update to the customer's balance due failed and explain why it happened. Provide some way for the user to decide what to do: cancel the order, add the cost of the order to the customer's new balance due, or set the balance due to another amount.

Another possible solution is to programmatically resolve the conflict and inform the user about the conflict and how it was resolved. In this case, you could write code to retrieve the customer's new balance due from the database and simply add the cost of the new order to that balance due. Then you could inform the user that the order was added successfully and the customer's balance due was modified appropriately, but that the new balance due might not be what he or she expected because of a change made by another user.

In either case, you'd have to determine the cause of the update conflict. In this chapter, we'll talk about what features ADO offers to help you determine the cause of the conflict. But first, we'll discuss some general error-handling information.

ERROR HANDLING AND TESTING

Before examining how you can use ADO to determine why your update attempt failed, let's briefly discuss error handling and testing.

Error Handling in General

Thorough error handling is the key to dealing with update problems, but while I have a lot of experience programming in Microsoft Visual Basic, I don't spend my days writing components or applications that need to handle a wide variety of potential problems. The sample code used in this chapter utilizes simplistic error handling. Writing effective, complex error-handling routines is beyond the scope of this book.

I strongly recommend that you pick up a book on programming your language of choice to learn the best way to write error-handling routines. For Visual Basic programmers, I definitely recommend *Advanced Microsoft Visual Basic 6.0, Second Edition,* by The Mandelbrot Set (International) Limited [Microsoft Press, 1998], specifically the chapter titled "On Error GoTo Hell."

Even though I don't need to write a lot of error-handling routines, I've learned this much so far: You simply can't write a generic routine to handle all errors. You must determine what particular problems your application might need to handle and write routines to trap these errors. If you can determine the cause of the error, you should handle it appropriately and allow the user to continue using the application. Furthermore, your application should fail as elegantly as possible when you receive an unexpected error.

Becoming Your Own Worst User

The best way to see how your code will react to a particular problem is to cause that problem and watch what happens. Figure out how to use the interactive debugging mode of your programming language of choice, or write an error-logging routine to log unhandled errors. Then cause the problem you want to handle, determine what code you need to add to trap for that error, and handle it appropriately.

When you're testing your application, keep in mind that you should never overestimate the intelligence of your users. Otherwise, they might surprise you with the different problems they cause in your application. Let's look at an example.

I hate mornings. I am not a morning person. One morning a former coworker woke me up at about 5:30 A.M. with a phone call. Apparently, the main report generated by an application I'd written wouldn't print. Eventually I gained consciousness, and we found that the reporting routine was caught in an infinite loop. Why? The user had entered an order into the system and specified the number of items to build and ship as a negative number.

I'm still not clear on why this user thought entering a negative number of items was a good idea, but I wound up rewriting some code later to prevent users from entering such orders and to allow the printing routine to run successfully even if a negative number did manage to work its way into the database. The moral of the story is: unless you like being woken up at odd hours, do what you can to handle as many problems as possible in the initial implementation of your application.

GATHERING INFORMATION FROM ADO

Let's look at the error information ADO provides and what features ADO offers programmers to help them determine why an optimistic update attempt failed. The ADO object model contains some properties and methods you can use to determine the type of modification made to the record that contains pending changes and why your update attempt failed.

ADO's Error Information

One of ADO's major drawbacks is that it often provides little information through the Error object about what happened. It sometimes returns the message, "Errors occurred," which doesn't help you determine why the error occurred. Trust me, the ADO development team is aware of programmers' frustrations with this error.

The Record and Stream objects, both new to ADO 2.5 and covered in more depth in Chapter 6, provide more detailed error information. The development team had similar code in the works for the other ADO objects, but they were concerned about the possibility of creating compatibility problems with existing code. However, the team hasn't given up, and they're currently investigating ways to improve on the current error handling in the next release of ADO, after 2.5. So for now, ADO objects that existed prior to 2.5 will still generate the same error information in ADO 2.5 that they did in ADO 2.1 to maintain backward compatibility.

> **NOTE** Maintaining backward compatibility can be quite a burden. If you developed a Microsoft Internet Information Services (IIS) and Active Server Pages (ASP) application using ADO 2.1 and built error handlers to trap for optimistic updating errors or other problems that generated the "Errors occurred" error, you might have to rewrite your application if installing a newer version of ADO generated different error messages when running the same code. This makes it difficult for the ADO development team to improve on the "Errors occurred" message.

What sort of error information does ADO generate when optimistic updates fail? Generally, you'll see your old friend:

```
"The specified row could not be located for updating: Some values may
have been changed since it was last read."
```

But it depends on what else went wrong. If you have optimistic updating conflicts as well as referential integrity violations when you call *Recordset.UpdateBatch*, you might receive an error that refers to only the referential integrity violations. And as I mentioned, in some cases ADO simply returns, "Errors occurred." What's a poor programmer to do?

Filter Property

You can set the Filter property on the Recordset object so that the only visible records in the Recordset are those whose updates failed as a result of conflicts with the current information in the database. Set the Filter property to adFilterConflictingRecords, and then check the RecordCount property on the Recordset object. The RecordCount property will return either a positive number indicating the number of records whose updates failed as a result of conflicts, or 0 if no conflicts occurred. An update that failed as a result of a referential integrity violation or other database constraint won't be visible through this filter because such failures are not deemed as conflicts.

You can also set the Filter property to adFilterPendingRecords to see only the records that contain pending updates. Because records in a Recordset whose updates fail due to optimistic updating conflicts still contain pending updates, they're visible through this filter. However, records whose updates fail because of referential integrity violations or other database constraints will also be visible because their updates are still marked as pending.

Status Property

As its name implies, the Status property on the Recordset object indicates the status of the current record. You can check this property to determine whether the record contains pending changes (as well as the types of changes) and whether the attempt to submit the record's pending changes failed because of an optimistic updating conflict. The Status property returns a combination of the following values for a particular record:

- **adRecUnmodified** If the update attempt succeeded and no pending changes exist

- **adRecNew** If the record contains a pending insert

- **adRecModified** If the record contains a pending modification

- **adRecDBDeleted or adRecDeleted** If the record contains a pending deletion

- **adRecConcurrencyViolation** If the record contains a pending change because the update attempt failed as a result of an optimistic updating conflict

NOTE The documentation for adRecDBDeleted states that this value corresponds to a record that has been deleted from the database, while adRecDeleted indicates that the record has been deleted from the Recordset. My experience with the Status property has been that it returns adRecDeleted for a pending deletion prior to submitting that change to the database with *UpdateBatch*. If the attempt to delete that record in the database fails because of a conflict, the Status property changes to adRecDBDeleted + adRecConcurrencyViolation. Your results can vary; I recommend that you run tests using your OLE DB provider (or ODBC driver) and database.

ADO 2.5 introduced a Status property on the Field object. This property is implemented only on the Field object exposed by the Record object; if you return the Status value of a Field object that's exposed by a Recordset object, that value is always 0. Perhaps in the next release of ADO, this property will return information that you can use to determine which fields were modified locally in the Recordset and which fields changed in the database to cause the optimistic updating conflict.

Value and OriginalValue Properties

Once you've used the Filter and/or Status properties on the Recordset object to determine which records' update attempts failed, you'll want to figure out which pending changes those records contain. You might want to report this information to the user, and if you plan on resolving the optimistic updating conflict programmatically, you'll need this information to determine what the failed update attempt was supposed to do to the database.

For example, if your failed update attempt contains a modification, you can compare the Value property to the OriginalValue property on each Field object. If the pending update is a failed deletion, you can use the OriginalValue property on the Field object or objects that correspond to the field or fields in the primary key to determine which record in the database your code intended to delete.

Resync Method and Update Resync Property

Once you've determined which pending change a record contains, you'll want to examine the corresponding record in your database to understand why the update attempt failed. You can use either the *Resync* method or the Update Resync dynamic property on the Recordset object to retrieve the current contents of that record.

If you set the Update Resync dynamic property in the Recordset's Properties collection to adResyncConflicts, the ADO Cursor Engine will automatically retrieve the current contents of the record you're attempting to update if a conflict occurs. You can also call the *Resync* method on the Recordset object to retrieve this data on a record with pending changes. This method will retrieve data for only the records in your Recordset that contain pending changes and that satisfy the criteria of the value used in the *AffectRecords* parameter.

UnderlyingValue Property

For each of the records containing a failed update attempt, you'll generally want to compare the contents of the record you initially retrieved from the database, the changes you made to the data in your local Recordset object, and the current contents of that record in the database. All this information is available through the Field object. You've already seen that the local changes are stored in the Value property of the Field object and that the data initially retrieved from the database is stored in the OriginalValue property. When you use the Update Resync property on the Recordset object, the current contents of that record in the database are placed in the UnderlyingValue property of the Field object.

Just as you can compare the OriginalValue and Value properties on each Field object to determine which changes were made to the local Recordset, you can compare the OriginalValue and UnderlyingValue properties to determine which changes were made to the record in the database since you opened the Recordset.

If you want to use the *Resync* method rather than the Update Resync property, you'll need to set the *ResyncValues* parameter on the method to adResyncUnderlying-Values, in order to store the current contents of the record into the UnderlyingValue property on each Field object. Keep in mind that you can use the *Resync* method to retrieve data this way only on a Recordset object that uses batch optimistic locking. If your Recordset object uses simple optimistic locking, the *Resync* method will generate an error if the record contains a pending change. The Update Resync property does not enforce such a restriction.

Detecting "Holes" in Your Recordset

When we covered keyset cursors in Chapter 7, we briefly talked about "holes" that can occur in your Recordset object when a record that initially existed in the results of your query is deleted from the database. You can discover these holes if you try to examine the Value property or the UnderlyingValue property of one of the Field objects of a record you've deleted in your Recordset.

With either of these properties you'll receive the following error:

```
"A given HROW referred to a hard- or soft-deleted row."
```

You can accurately determine whether the optimistic updating conflict occurred because the record the ADO Cursor Engine tried to modify was deleted from the database by trapping for this error. You can trap this error by retrieving the current contents of the conflicting record from the Update Resync property or the *Resync* method and checking the UnderlyingValue property or the Value property on any of the Field objects.

If you call the *Resync* method on the Recordset object and the ADO Cursor Engine cannot locate the corresponding record in the database because it was deleted, you'll receive the following trappable error:

```
"The key value for this row has been changed or deleted at the data
source. The local row is now deleted."
```

Contrary to the error message, the record hasn't actually been removed from your Recordset.

One last note: If another user modifies the value of the primary key in the database, the ADO Cursor Engine will react as though the record no longer exists in the table. An attempt to resynchronize a record whose update failed because another user modified the primary key for that record will retrieve no data because the ADO Cursor Engine has no way of locating that record.

> **NOTE** I don't recommend letting your users modify the primary key value for records in your database. Given how much the ADO Cursor Engine relies on the primary key value, you should avoid this scenario if at all possible. Say an optimistic update attempt fails because another user modified the primary key for the corresponding record in the database. ADO will react as though the user deleted that record from the database. If you need to know whether that record was really deleted or whether the problem was due to another user changing the value of the primary key, you're probably out of luck. There's no reliable way to locate the corresponding record in this scenario. Therefore, I won't discuss this scenario in the following sections. In this case, you're on your own.

IDENTIFYING POSSIBLE CONFLICTS

I've yet to see a list of the different types of optimistic updating conflicts, so I've compiled one of my own. I've also included a sample on the CD entitled "Detecting Conflicts" that allows you to cause and log conflicts. It's described in more detail in Appendix B. For now, let's take a brief look at the different types of conflicts.

Simple Conflicts

The conflict I described earlier in the chapter is an example of a simple conflict. You want to modify a field or fields in a particular record, but after you retrieve the record and before you modify it, another user changes at least one of the fields you want to modify. You can trap for a conflict and determine whether it represents a simple conflict by resynchronizing the conflicting record and comparing the Value, Original-Value, and UnderlyingValue properties of each Field object. If the OriginalValue property of at least one Field object is set to a value that differs from both its Value and UnderlyingValue properties, you have a simple conflict.

The Status property on a record that represents a simple conflict will return adRecModified + adRecConcurrencyViolation when the conflict occurs.

Cross Conflicts

I invented the term "cross conflict" to suit this scenario: you want to modify a field or fields in a record in your database, but your update fails because another user has modified that record—but the other user did not modify any of the fields that you want to modify.

If you base your updates on timestamp values, this type of conflict is certainly possible. This scenario can make it difficult for you to determine how the other user modified that record because the other user might have modified a field that doesn't even appear in the results of your query. Resynchronizing the record in your Recordset will simply retrieve the same data in all fields, except the timestamp field, that you already had. Instead of resynchronizing on your original query you could retrieve the contents of the entire record into a new Recordset object, but you'd be unable to determine what field changed because that data did not appear in your original Recordset. Realistically, all you can do is inform your user that another user has modified that record in the database. Whether the user can continue will depend on the requirements of your application.

You can also generate a cross conflict if you use all the fields in your recordset in the WHERE clause of the action queries generated by the ADO Cursor Engine. This will occur if your table lacks a primary key (but you won't try to update such a table using the ADO Cursor Engine, right?) or if you set the Update Criteria dynamic property on the Recordset object to adCriteriaAllCols.

In this situation, you can determine that you've encountered a cross conflict by resynchronizing the record and comparing the OriginalValue and UnderlyingValue properties on each Field object to locate which field or fields were modified by another user. Then compare the Value and OriginalValue properties on that Field object or objects to determine whether they were also modified in the local Recordset object.

For cross conflicts, as for simple conflicts, the Status property will report adRecModified + adRecConcurrencyViolation.

Modifying a Deleted Record

You can't modify a record that no longer exists in your database. Until you resynchronize the record you attempted to modify, this scenario will look like a simple conflict or a cross conflict. In other words, after the update attempt fails, the Status property on the Recordset object will return adRecModified + adRecConcurrencyViolation.

You'll be able to determine why the update attempt failed after you've resynchronized the record. If you attempt to examine the UnderlyingValue property on any of the Field objects, you'll receive the following trappable error:

```
"A given HROW referred to a hard- or soft-deleted row."
```

At this point, you can let the user know why the update attempt failed and, if possible, allow him or her to continue as appropriate.

Deleting a Modified Record

This type of conflict is similar to both the modifying a deleted record conflict and the cross conflict. You can treat this conflict just like a cross conflict in terms of trying to determine how the record you want to delete has been changed. After the deletion attempt fails, this conflict will result in a Recordset Status value of adRecDBDeleted.

If your table has no primary key (bad idea), or if you set the Update Criteria dynamic property on the Recordset object to adCriteriaAllCols, the ADO Cursor Engine will use the value of all fields in your Recordset in the WHERE clause of the action query to delete the record from the database. If another user modifies one or more of those fields in the database between the time you initially retrieve the record and the time you try to delete the record from the database, your attempt to delete that record will fail. Resynchronize the record, and compare the OriginalValue and Underlying-Value properties on each Field object in the Recordset to determine what information in the record has changed. Then inform the user of the problem, and continue as appropriate.

If you set the Update Criteria dynamic property on the Recordset to adCriteria-Timestamp, any change made to the record you want to delete will cause a conflict. However, as with a cross conflict, you won't be able to determine how the record changed if another user has changed a field that does not appear in the results of your query.

Deleting a Deleted Record

Attempting to delete a record that another user has deleted from the database will fail. After the deletion attempt fails, the Recordset will contain a Status value of adRecDeleted + adRecConcurrencyViolation.

As with trying to modify a deleted record, resynchronizing the record and then checking the UnderlyingValue property on any Field object in the Recordset will generate the trappable error letting you know that the data corresponds to a deleted record.

How your application reacts to this error will depend on what's appropriate for that application. Even though ADO reports a conflict, you might decide that the user doesn't need to know that another user actually deleted the record from the database—since the result is the same no matter who deleted the record. Of course, you might want your application to let the user know that the attempt to delete the record from the database failed and why this failure occurred.

FAILED UPDATE ATTEMPTS THAT AREN'T CONSIDERED CONFLICTS

There are plenty of times when an update attempt fails for reasons other than optimistic updating conflicts. A database that preserves referential integrity might reject a user's attempt to delete a record from the Customers table for a customer who has open orders. An error will also occur if the user tries to place more data into a field than the database can store. The user could also violate a field constraint in the database by trying to set a customer's balance due to a negative number.

The ADO Cursor Engine doesn't consider these types of failed updates to be conflicts. Your best bet is to anticipate which changes your users might request that would fail because of such problems, and then develop error-handling code that can detect and resolve such problems appropriately.

IF AT FIRST YOU DON'T SUCCEED, TRY, TRY AGAIN...INTELLIGENTLY

So far, you've learned how to detect which records contain updates that failed because of optimistic updating conflicts, what type of modifications are contained in each of those records, and why those conflicts occurred. The only problem left is determining how to resolve those conflicts.

Actually, the way in which you resolve conflicts will depend on your application. One solution is to resubmit changes for records in your Recordset, which ADO allows you to do.

Attempting to Update After Resynchronizing Your Data

It's time to go back to our original optimistic updating conflict example. We retrieved data about a particular customer. Let's say that the customer's balance due was initially $75 and we tried to add $50:

```
strSQL = "SELECT CustomerID, CompanyName, BalanceDue " & _
         "FROM Customers WHERE CustomerID = 7"
```

(continued)

```
rsCustomers.Open strSQL, cnDatabase, adOpenStatic, _
                   adLockBatchOptimistic, adCmdText
rsCustomers.Properties("Update Resync") = adResyncConflicts
rsCustomers!BalanceDue = rsCustomers!BalanceDue + 50
rsCustomers.Update
rsCustomers.UpdateBatch
```

Based on this code, the ADO Cursor Engine built the following action query to update the data in the database:

```
UPDATE Customers SET BalanceDue = 125
    WHERE CustomerID = 7 AND BalanceDue = 75
```

Meanwhile, back in the jungle...Between the time this user retrieved the customer's balance due and the time the user submitted the information for the new order, another user entered a $65 order for the same customer. The first user's update attempt failed, and with a little code, we figured out why the conflict occurred.

In this situation, the best way to handle the problem is to let the user know that a conflict occurred and why, and then ask the user if he or she wants to change the balance due to the newly retrieved balance due plus the cost of the order. Even if your code didn't store the cost of the order, you can calculate it by subtracting the amount in the OriginalValue property from the amount in the Value property on the BalanceDue field. Then you simply add the result to the value in the UnderlyingValue property and assign that result to be the new Value of the BalanceDue field:

```
Dim curCostOfOrder As Currency
With rsCustomers.Fields("BalanceDue")
    curCostOfOrder = .Value - .OriginalValue
    .Value = .UnderlyingValue + curCostOfOrder
End With
rsCustomers.Update
```

Now the Recordset contains the data you want to submit to the database. If only you could simply call *Recordset.UpdateBatch* at this point and submit that data to the database.

Actually, it's that simple. Most of the time, that's all you need to do. Let's look at why calling *UpdateBatch* at this point usually succeeds and why it might fail.

Why the update usually succeeds

In the previous example, we used the Update Resync dynamic property to automatically resynchronize the record when a conflict occurred. When we changed the value of the BalanceDue field, and then called *Update* and *UpdateBatch*, the ADO Cursor Engine built and submitted the following action query:

```
UPDATE Customers SET BalanceDue = 190
      WHERE CustomerID = 7 AND BalanceDue = 140
```

You know where the new value for the BalanceDue field came from. That's the field you calculated using the contents of the Value, OriginalValue, and UnderlyingValue properties on the Field object. The other difference between this action query and the one that the ADO Cursor Engine built when you attempted to submit your initial changes to the database is the value of the BalanceDue field in the WHERE clause. Where did this information come from?

In the initial action query, the ADO Cursor Engine used the contents of the OriginalValue property on the modified field in the WHERE clause. This time the ADO Cursor Engine uses the data stored in the UnderlyingValue property. This isn't really a change in the Cursor Engine's logic. In each case, it uses the most recently retrieved value for the modified field. Thus, your second attempt to update this record in the database will probably succeed.

Why the update might fail

Why might the second attempt to update this record in the database fail? That's still part of the nature of optimistic updating. When you resynchronize the record with the pending changes, you aren't preventing other users from changing the contents of that corresponding record in the database. It's possible that another user could modify that record between the time you retrieve its contents and the time you make another attempt to update it. It's unlikely, but it is possible.

No Error Handling Is Still Better than Bad Error Handling

There's one small drawback to the fact that the ADO Cursor Engine makes it fairly easy to resubmit a pending change to the database.

Think back to the example I've used throughout the chapter. You can trap for the error that occurs when you call the *UpdateBatch* method. If you resynchronize the conflicting record by calling the *Recordset.Resync* method or by using the Update Resync property, the next attempt to submit your update will likely succeed for reasons we just discussed. Make sure you determine the cause of the conflict in order to plot the proper course of action, before making another attempt to submit the pending change to the database. Why? In our example we adjusted the BalanceDue field before we resubmitted the update based on data we retrieved when we resynchronized the record. Had we not adjusted the Value property of the BalanceDue field first, we would have lost the change made by the other user that caused the conflict, and the BalanceDue field in the database would not reflect that user's order.

QUESTIONS THAT SHOULD
BE ASKED MORE FREQUENTLY

Q. *I can handle optimistic updating conflicts once, but I don't want to continually trap for them. Is there any way I can make sure that my second update attempt succeeds?*

A. You can use transactions to accomplish this if you're working with a transactional database. This will prevent other users from changing the record while you resync and update. The following code begins a transaction before resynchronizing the records whose updates failed because of conflicts:

```
rsCustomers.Filter = adFilterConflictingRecords
cnDatabase.BeginTrans
rsCustomers.Resync adAffectGroup, adResyncUnderlyingValues
'Resolve conflicts.
⋮
rsCustomers.UpdateBatch
cnDatabase.CommitTrans
```

After resynchronizing those conflicts, resolve your conflicts within the Recordset object, and then call *Recordset.UpdateBatch* to submit the changes and *Connection.CommitTrans* to commit the transaction. Because you retrieve the current contents of the conflicting records within a transaction, that data is locked for the lifetime of the transaction and can be modified only within that transaction. As a result, there is no chance of another user modifying that data and causing conflicts when you call *UpdateBatch* this second time. Keep in mind that the greatest benefit in using transactions is also the greatest drawback: the data is locked for the lifetime of the transaction. See Chapter 3 for more on using transactions.

Q. *I think I found a way to avoid conflicts. I set the Update Criteria property to adCriteriaKey, and now I rarely see update conflicts. But I'm a little worried. Was this a good idea?*

A. Probably not. You're correct in assuming that by setting Update Criteria to adCriteriaKey you'll avoid generating conflicts. However, you're likely to overwrite changes made by other users. Reread the section "Controlling the Criteria in the WHERE Clause" in Chapter 10 (page 210) to make sure you understand *why* you'll avoid generating conflicts by using the property this way. Generally, you don't want to overwrite other users' changes.

Chapter 13

Persisting Your Recordset

There will probably be times when your users want to save the current contents of a recordset, disconnect from the server, and still have access to the information in that recordset. A salesperson going on the road is the perfect example of such a user. You want your salesperson to be able to view product and customer information and to create orders while he is on a sales call. This requires that the salesperson save the recordset data to a file—just as you'd save a Microsoft Word document or a Microsoft Excel spreadsheet to a file for later use—on the hard drive of his portable computer. When the salesperson is finished drumming up business, he can reconnect to the database and submit the new orders stored in the files on the hard drive. This ability to retain recordset information after a database or server connection has been closed is called persistence.

Personally, I love this feature. In some of the test applications I've written, I store data in a persisted recordset rather than storing settings in the Microsoft Windows Registry. Not that I have anything against using the Registry, but when I use persisted recordsets, I can put the test application on a server and use the same settings to run the application without having to change the settings of the machine I'm using.

A BRIEF HISTORY OF PERSISTENCE IN ADO

In ADO 2.0, the ADO development team added a *Save* method to the Recordset object so that you could write code that looks like this:

```
strSQL = "SELECT * FROM Orders"
rsOrders.CursorLocation = adUseClient
rsOrders.Open strSQL, cnDatabase, adOpenStatic, _
            adLockBatchOptimistic, adCmdText
'Disconnect from the database.
Set rsOrders.ActiveConnection = Nothing

'Modify the data.
⋮

'Save the modifications and close the Recordset.
rsOrders.Save strPathToFile, adPersistADTG
rsOrders.Close

'At this point the user closes and reopens the application.
⋮

'Open the Recordset, reset the connection, and update the database.
rsOrders.Open strPathToFile, , adOpenStatic, _
            adLockBatchOptimistic, adCmdFile
Set rsOrders.ActiveConnection = cnDatabase
rsOrders.UpdateBatch
```

This code performs the following actions:

1. Retrieves data from the Orders table in the database

2. Disconnects the Recordset object from the Connection object

3. Modifies the data in the Recordset

4. Saves the data to a file, and closes the Recordset

5. Reopens the Recordset from the modified file

6. Reassociates the Recordset with the Connection object

7. Submits the pending changes to the database

Of course, you'd want to create separate code modules to group specific actions, but I think you get the idea: ADO saves you time by simplifying this potentially complex scenario.

In ADO 2.1, they added a second format for the data: eXtensible Markup Language (XML). Simply use the optional *PersistFormat* parameter on the *Save* method to store your data in XML format, as shown here:

```
rsOrders.Save strPathToFile, adPersistXML
```

Now how much would you pay? Don't answer yet. Just look what else you get! ADO 2.5 brings even more functionality to the *Save* method. No longer do you need to store your data in a file; you can now save the data in a stream. You can use the *Save* method with the new ADO Stream object or with the Response object, which is available through the Active Server Pages (ASP) object model. Implementation examples using the Stream and Response objects, respectively, are shown here:

```
'Use the ADO Stream object with the Save method.
Set stmData = New ADODB.Stream
rsOrders.Save stmData, adPersistADTG

'Use the ASP Response object with the Save method.
rsOrders.Save Response, adPersistADTG
```

WHAT YOU NEED TO KNOW ABOUT PERSISTENCE

ADO makes persisting data fairly simple and straightforward. You don't have to use the OLE DB provider to implement persistence; you can simply use the *Save* and *Open* methods. Once you've used these methods to store and retrieve data, there's little else you need to know about this feature—except for a few small details, which we'll discuss now.

What Data Gets Stored?

When you call the *Save* method on the Recordset object, ADO examines the contents of the Recordset and stores most of that data in a file or a Stream object. You can later ask ADO to turn that data back into a Recordset object, but you don't wind up with a carbon copy of your original Recordset object. So how does the resulting Recordset object differ from the original?

If you set the Filter property on your Recordset to an array of bookmarks or to one of the constants in FilterGroupEnum, when you call the *Save* method ADO will store all the records in your Recordset to the file or the Stream object. If you set the Filter property to a string-based filter, ADO will store only the records visible through that filter.

Calling the *Save* method on a hierarchical recordset will cause ADO to store data from that chapter and subsequent child chapters. (As you'll recall, a chapter is a set of records in a hierarchy that are associated with the current row in a parent-child relationship.) Data from parent and sibling chapters will not be stored. For example, if you open a hierarchy with customers' orders and order details and call the *Save* method on the orders level recordset of the hierarchy, ADO will store only the currently visible orders and their associated order details. Customer data, data for orders from other customers, and the details associated with those orders will not be stored. Figure 13-1 shows the contents of the hierarchy. The data highlighted is written to disk when you call the *Save* method on the orders level of the hierarchy. We'll discuss hierarchical recordsets in more detail in Chapter 14.

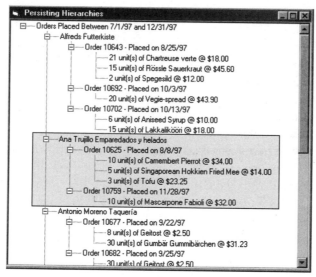

Figure 13-1 *An example of data stored when you persist a hierarchical Recordset.*

You'll probably want to use batch optimistic locking with persisted recordsets so that you can modify data off line and submit those changes later. If you open an updatable client-side Recordset, the ADO Cursor Engine retrieves the metadata required to support updating, such as base column names, base table names, and primary key data.

The value of the Field object's UnderlyingValue property for each field of each record is not stored as part of the metadata. If you resynchronize your Recordset object and store data in this property, the data will be lost when you persist your Recordset. Therefore, if you persist that Recordset, reopen it later, and attempt to resubmit a pending change, ADO will act as though this were the first update attempt and will again use the values in the OriginalValue properties of the Field objects in the WHERE clause of the action query.

Another piece of metadata ADO doesn't store with your file or stream is the current position in the recordset. Regardless of which record you were viewing prior to persisting the recordset, when you reopen your Recordset object, you'll see the first record. Similarly, data such as the original value of the Source property is lost when you persist and reopen your Recordset. This means that an attempt to call the *Requery* method on the reopened Recordset will fail. Maybe in a future version of ADO this data will be stored to make this functionality possible.

Which Format Should You Use: ADTG or XML?

Prior to the release of ADO 2.1, there was only one format that you could use to persist your data: Advanced Data TableGram (ADTG), which is a proprietary data format. But, as mentioned earlier, ADO 2.1 made the XML format available for persistence.

XML is a hot topic in the programming community for a number of reasons— it's self-describing, it's generally associated with web-based applications, and all you need to use it is a parser.

But that doesn't mean you should always persist your Recordset object in XML rather than in ADTG. Yes, XML is much more flexible, but that flexibility comes with a performance penalty. When you ask ADO to reopen a Recordset object that has been persisted to a file or a stream in XML format, ADO uses the Microsoft Internet Explorer XML parser to convert the data. When a Recordset has been persisted in ADTG format, ADO converts the data back into a Recordset object without using an external parser. For small recordsets, the difference in performance is negligible. However, for large recordsets, it can become an issue for two reasons: you're moving data through an extra component in the XML parser, and the XML format is generic text-based data while the ADTG format is designed specifically for Recordsets.

There is more than one way to self-describe the data stored in a Recordset object. One of my colleagues who works closely with the ADO product group explained that you could use ADO to retrieve data with a firehose cursor, persist that data in XML format, and then manipulate that data and insert the metadata that the ADO Cursor Engine requires to support updating into the XML file. I thought this was a great idea and was able to make it work, but then found that my code wasn't behaving as I expected when I used ADO 2.5. That's when I noticed that the XML format ADO uses changed from ADO 2.1 to ADO 2.5. This means that if you write code to manipulate the XML data that ADO generates, your code might work only for a specific version of ADO. C'est la vie. So keep in mind that there's no guarantee the ADO development team will continue to use the same XML format in future versions of ADO.

QUESTIONS THAT SHOULD BE ASKED MORE FREQUENTLY

Q.   *After I call the* Save *method, will my cursor be positioned at the same record as it was prior to calling this method?*

A.   No. ADO moves you to the first record in the Recordset after you've called the *Save* method.

Q.   *When I call the* Requery *method on the Recordset object I opened from a file or a stream, the method fails. Have I done something wrong?*

A.   You've done nothing wrong, but there's nothing more you can do. As of ADO 2.5, you can't call the *Requery* method when you reopen a persisted Recordset. Perhaps a future release will provide a way to do this. However, you can still call the *Resync* method successfully.

Q.   *When I try to open a Recordset from a Stream object, I receive an error message stating that the arguments are the wrong type. Why is that?*

A.   I noticed behavior that I found surprising when opening a Recordset from a Stream object. Leave the ActiveConnection parameter on the Recordset's *Open* method blank. Then set the ActiveConnection property on your Recordset object to an open Connection object or a valid connection string, and you should be fine.

Q.   *Why can't I persist a parameterized hierarchical Recordset?*

A.   You're getting ahead of yourself a bit. As of ADO 2.5, there's no way to persist such a Recordset. In Chapter 14, we'll examine hierarchical Recordsets in more depth and explain why this limitation currently exists. (Don't worry if this question throws you for a loop.)

Q.   *Do I need to work with a client-side Recordset in order to use persistent data?*

A.   No. ADO will let you save the contents of your Recordset even with a server-side cursor. However, if you reopen your Recordset from a file or a stream, that data will be stored by the ADO Cursor Engine.

Q.   *What does ADO do when I call the* Save *method on a firehose cursor?*

A.   When you use a firehose cursor, ADO doesn't store the contents of the records you've already examined. If your cursor has moved beyond the first record in the Recordset, ADO will reexecute your query when you call the *Save* method. In the first question in this section, I noted that when you call *Save*, ADO will move your cursor to the first record of the Recordset. For a firehose cursor, this means ADO will reexecute your query in order to move back to the first record after persisting the Recordset. Keep this behavior in mind if you plan to persist data from a firehose cursor, especially if you want to call a stored procedure to generate your data.

Q. *Can I reopen my Recordset asynchronously?*

A. As of ADO 2.5, yes. Prior to ADO 2.5, your asynchronous request would have been ignored and would have opened synchronously.

Chapter 14

Hierarchical Recordsets

Data does not exist in a vacuum. Most of the data in your database is probably interconnected. Take a look at the referential integrity constraints in the Northwind database that ships with Microsoft Visual Basic, Microsoft Access, and Microsoft SQL Server. Most of the tables exist as either the parent or the child in a relationship.

In your applications, you're likely to encounter scenarios in which you'll want to retrieve data from two or more related tables in your database. With other object models such as Data Access Objects (DAO) and Remote Data Objects (RDO), you could retrieve such data in one of two ways: into separate result sets, or into one or more result sets using join operations.

As I alluded to in Chapter 10, recordsets based on join queries can be difficult to maintain and update. While the ADO Cursor Engine has features that can simplify these problems, most programmers avoid using join queries on tables that contain updatable data and one-to-many relationships, such as a Customers table and an Orders table. In addition to the problems with updating data, a join query results in a waste of memory; your application must store a single set of data in multiple memory locations. For example, every record of a Recordset object based on a join query between the Customers table and the Orders table contains a different order, but the customer information is duplicated for customers with multiple orders.

If you retrieve data into separate Recordset objects rather than performing a join, you'll need to write additional code to keep the Recordsets synchronized. For example, if you're viewing customer and order data, you'll want to apply a filter to the orders Recordset so that the only visible orders are those for the currently bookmarked customer.

To avoid these problems with joins and separate objects, the ADO development team introduced in version 2.0 the concept of a hierarchical Recordset. Based on a concept used in early versions of Microsoft FoxPro, a hierarchical Recordset is similar to many related Recordset objects. You can create a single query, such as the following, to retrieve data from multiple tables:

```
strSQL = "SHAPE {SELECT * FROM Customers} AS Customers " & _
         "APPEND ({SELECT * FROM Orders} AS Orders " & _
         "RELATE CustomerID TO CustomerID) AS Orders"
```

You can use this query in the following code to retrieve the data into a hierarchical Recordset object and access the different levels—also known as chapters—of the hierarchy:

```
'Open the customers hierarchical Recordset object.
rsCustomers.Open strSQL, cnNorthwind, adOpenStatic, _
                 adLockBatchOptimistic, adCmdText
'Reference the orders from the customers hierarchical Recordset object
' in the orders Recordset object.
Set rsOrders = rsCustomers.Fields("Orders").Value
```

Now as you move your cursor through the *rsCustomers* Recordset object, only the orders for the customer at the current cursor location are visible in the *rsOrders* Recordset object.

Let's first take a look at how to load the OLE DB provider that helps generate hierarchical Recordsets. Then we'll look at the two main types of hierarchies—standard and parameterized—as well as the hierarchical query syntax.

USING THE DATA SHAPE PROVIDER

Microsoft Data Access Components (MDAC) includes a number of OLE DB providers that are considered "service providers." Rather than communicating directly with a database, you utilize the services of these providers. One prime example of such a service provider is the OLE DB provider for data shaping—often referred to as MSDataShape. In this text, I'll also refer to the provider as the "data shape provider."

The features described throughout this chapter require the use of the MSDataShape provider. To use the functionality exposed by this provider, you have to reference the provider when you connect to your database. Luckily, referencing this provider requires only a small change in your connection string. If your normal connection string was

```
strConn = "Provider=SQLOLEDB;Data Source=ScepHome;" & _
          "Initial Catalog=Northwind;"
```

you would change it to

```
strConn = "Provider=MSDataShape;Data Provider=SQLOLEDB;" & _
          "Data Source=ScepHome;Initial Catalog=Northwind;"
```

to use the MSDataShape provider. Simply put, what you normally used as your provider is now the "data provider"—the OLE DB provider that MSDataShape will use to communicate with your database.

If you use properties exposed by the Connection object to connect to your database rather than using a connection string to do so, the Connection object will expose a Data Provider property in its dynamic Properties collection after you set the Provider property to MSDataShape. Thus, instead of connecting with code such as

```
cnNorthwind.Provider = "SQLOLEDB"
cnNorthwind.Properties("Data Source") = "ScepHome"
cnNorthwind.Properties("Initial Catalog") = "Northwind"
```

you would use code such as

```
cnNorthwind.Provider = "MSDataShape"
cnNorthwind.Properties("Data Provider") = "SQLOLEDB"
cnNorthwind.Properties("Data Source") = "ScepHome"
cnNorthwind.Properties("Initial Catalog") = "Northwind"
```

Once you've connected to your database using the MSDataShape provider, you can continue to run your standard nonhierarchical queries as you normally would.

How the Data Shape Provider Works

When you submit a query on a connection that loads the data shape provider, the provider parses the query string to determine whether that string includes keywords that the provider uses to build hierarchical recordsets. If no such keywords are used, the data shape provider passes the query string to the OLE DB provider you've specified as the data provider.

Parsing a Hierarchical Query String

If the data shape provider finds keywords, it breaks the query string into distinct queries, passes those queries along to the data provider, processes the results, and organizes the data into the hierarchy you requested. For example, let's take a look at the query string used earlier in the chapter:

```
strSQL = "SHAPE {SELECT * FROM Customers} AS Customers " & _
         "APPEND ({SELECT * FROM Orders} AS Orders " & _
         "RELATE CustomerID TO CustomerID) AS Orders"
```

This query is composed of two simple query strings that retrieve the contents of two separate tables (Customers and Orders), and it specifies how to relate the results of the two queries. In this case, you're asking the data shape provider to relate the two queries based on the contents of the CustomerID field for each query. Thus, only the records from the Orders table that have the same CustomerID value as the current record returned by the Customers query will be visible.

The SHAPE keyword invokes the data shape provider's logic. The APPEND keyword tells the data shape provider to add a field to the initial recordset. With this added field, the orders for each customer appear to be contained in a Field object in the resulting Recordset object. The following code prints all orders for each customer:

```
rsCustomers.Open strSQL, cnNorthwind, adOpenStatic, _
                adLockBatchOptimistic, adCmdText
Set rsOrders = rsCustomers.Fields("Orders").Value
Do While Not rsCustomers.EOF
    Debug.Print rsCustomers!CustomerID & " - " & rsCustomers!CompanyName
    Do While Not rsOrders.EOF
        Debug.Print vbTab & rsOrders!OrderID & " - " & rsOrders!OrderDate
        rsOrders.MoveNext
    Loop
    rsCustomers.MoveNext
Loop
```

Each time you move to the next record in the *rsCustomers* Recordset, only those orders for the current customer are visible in the *rsOrders* Recordset. While the query syntax is rather complicated, examining the data in the hierarchical Recordset is fairly simple. In this example, I refer to the customer data as the "parent data" and the orders data as the "child data."

Using Grid Controls with Hierarchical Recordsets

Microsoft Visual Basic 6 includes a control designed to display the results of hierarchical queries: MSHFlexGrid, which is the Microsoft Hierarchical FlexGrid Control 6.0 (OLEDB). When you use this control to display the contents of a hierarchical

Recordset, the parent data resembles the results of a standard query and is displayed in a simple grid, similar to a Microsoft Excel spreadsheet. The child data is displayed in an additional column or columns in the grid. In this example, the orders for each customer appear as a grid within a grid in a kind of tree structure as shown in Figure 14-1. You can use the symbol to the left of the customer information to expand or hide the order information.

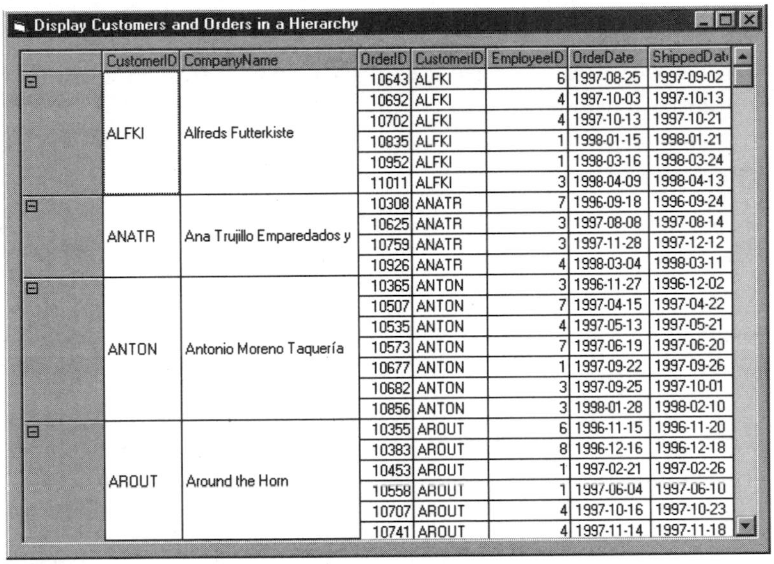
Display Customers and Orders in a Hierarchy

CustomerID	CompanyName	OrderID	CustomerID	EmployeeID	OrderDate	ShippedDat
ALFKI	Alfreds Futterkiste	10643	ALFKI	6	1997-08-25	1997-09-02
		10692	ALFKI	4	1997-10-03	1997-10-13
		10702	ALFKI	4	1997-10-13	1997-10-21
		10835	ALFKI	1	1998-01-15	1998-01-21
		10952	ALFKI	1	1998-03-16	1998-03-24
		11011	ALFKI	3	1998-04-09	1998-04-13
ANATR	Ana Trujillo Emparedados y	10308	ANATR	7	1996-09-18	1996-09-24
		10625	ANATR	3	1997-08-08	1997-08-14
		10759	ANATR	3	1997-11-28	1997-12-12
		10926	ANATR	4	1998-03-04	1998-03-11
ANTON	Antonio Moreno Taquería	10365	ANTON	3	1996-11-27	1996-12-02
		10507	ANTON	7	1997-04-15	1997-04-22
		10535	ANTON	4	1997-05-13	1997-05-21
		10573	ANTON	7	1997-06-19	1997-06-20
		10677	ANTON	1	1997-09-22	1997-09-26
		10682	ANTON	3	1997-09-25	1997-10-01
		10856	ANTON	3	1998-01-28	1998-02-10
AROUT	Around the Horn	10355	AROUT	6	1996-11-15	1996-11-20
		10383	AROUT	8	1996-12-16	1996-12-18
		10453	AROUT	1	1997-02-21	1997-02-26
		10558	AROUT	1	1997-06-04	1997-06-10
		10707	AROUT	4	1997-10-16	1997-10-23
		10741	AROUT	4	1997-11-14	1997-11-18

Figure 14-1 *A hierarchical recordset in the Hierarchical FlexGrid Control.*

While this method of envisioning the hierarchy makes sense and is how you want to display the data, it's not how ADO stores the data. Let's take a closer look at the two main types of hierarchies and how ADO maintains the data in each case.

How MSDataShape Stores Data and Maintains Hierarchies

There are two main types of hierarchies: standard and parameterized. While they can use similar queries to retrieve the same data, they differ in how and when they retrieve that data. In this section, we'll take a look at both types of hierarchies.

Standard Hierarchies

The example discussed in the previous section is a standard hierarchy. The data shape provider parses the query string and passes each separate query contained in that string to the data provider.

ADO maintains the results of each query (in the case of our example, the customers query and the orders query) separately, in structures similar to Recordset objects. When you request the contents of the Orders field in the customers Recordset, ADO applies a filter to the results of the query on the Orders table, which is the data you see.

Many features available through the data shape provider make the query string and the resulting Recordset complex. We'll still categorize those complex hierarchies as standard hierarchies to reflect how the data is stored and maintained. In short, any hierarchy that isn't parameterized—a capability we'll cover momentarily—is considered standard.

Parameterized Hierarchies

A parameterized hierarchy is more than a hierarchical query that uses parameters. With a standard hierarchy, the data shape provider submits one query per level of the hierarchy to the OLE DB provider that communicates with the database. Parameterized hierarchies work differently and use a slightly different syntax. A query string similar to the string discussed on page 258, but using a parameterized hierarchy, looks like this:

```
strSQL = "SHAPE {SELECT * FROM Customers} AS Customers APPEND " & _
         "({SELECT * FROM Orders WHERE CustomerID = ?} AS Orders " & _
         "RELATE CustomerID TO PARAMETER 0) AS Orders"
```

The child query within the query string uses the standard parameter marker, ?, in a WHERE clause, and I've changed the syntax slightly in the RELATE clause. Instead of retrieving all order data in a single query, the data shape provider builds a parameterized query that retrieves all orders for a particular customer. Thus, after retrieving the contents of the customers query, the data shape provider executes the parameterized query once for each customer retrieved.

But not all this data is retrieved immediately. Although the data shape provider retrieves all the customer data when you open your hierarchical Recordset, it doesn't retrieve any order data until you request it.

Choosing a parameterized hierarchical design has its pros and cons. The major benefits are that your code runs more quickly because you're not retrieving as much data initially and that you're not going to retrieve "orphaned" data, a topic I'll cover shortly. The major drawback is that this type of hierarchy requires a live connection to your database. You cannot persist a parameterized hierarchical Recordset to a file or stream by calling the Recordset object's *Save* method, nor can you pass such a Recordset across process boundaries. (We'll talk about passing Recordsets out of process in Chapter 15.) You also cannot reshape—a feature we'll discuss shortly—

parameterized hierarchies. Hopefully, a future release of ADO will allow programmers to retrieve all data for the hierarchy and allow ADO to disconnect parameterized hierarchical Recordsets to pass them across process boundaries or persist them to files.

Comparing Standard Hierarchies with Parameterized Hierarchies

There's another major difference between the way standard hierarchies and parameterized hierarchies work: how ADO stores the contents of the hierarchy. With a standard hierarchy, ADO executes one query per level of the hierarchy and stores each level in a separate structure. Our standard hierarchy example stores the customers data in one structure and the orders data in another structure. ADO then applies a filter to the orders data so that only the orders for the current customer are visible. With the parameterized hierarchy, ADO executes a separate query to retrieve the orders for each customer. ADO stores the results of each query in separate structures. As you move from one customer to the next, you view the results of each separate query to retrieve order data.

Because the orders for each customer in a parameterized hierarchy are contained in separate structures, you might see some slightly different behavior than if you'd used a standard hierarchy. The next example is a major stretch, but it probably provides the clearest demonstration of how ADO stores the hierarchical data and what that means to you. Suppose that in your customers and orders hierarchy, you realize that the user made a couple of mistakes when entering the orders: one order was entered for customer B instead of customer A, while a second order was entered for customer A instead of customer B.

So, a supervisor uses a maintenance application that you've developed for such a case. Your code retrieves the customers and orders into a hierarchical Recordset. The supervisor uses your application to make the necessary changes and saves the data. The data in your database is now accurate.

However, depending on how you created your hierarchical Recordset, that supervisor might see some odd results displayed in your application. If you used a standard hierarchy, the orders for customer A and customer B will appear as they should in the hierarchy once the supervisor has completed the changes. The newly corrected orders will be linked to the appropriate customers in the hierarchy. When you re-reference each customer, ADO reapplies the filter to the order data and the supervisor sees the appropriate customers. With parameterized hierarchies, the orders now contain the correct information, but they're still associated with the same customers they were associated with before the supervisor made the corrections, as shown in Figure 14-2.

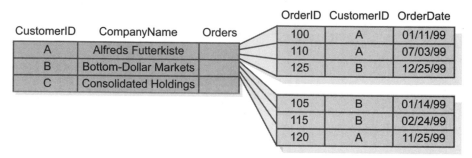

Figure 14-2 *Parameterized hierarchy after switching customer IDs for two orders.*

Which Type of Hierarchy Should You Use?

I use standard hierarchies rather than parameterized hierarchies so that I can persist my Recordsets to files or pass them across process boundaries. One of the drawbacks of standard hierarchies is that you can wind up retrieving and storing "orphaned" data (child data that doesn't correspond to any row at the parent level) in the hierarchy. For example, say that you wanted to retrieve the customers from a particular country and the orders for those customers in a hierarchy. You could use a query like this:

```
strSQL = "SHAPE {SELECT * FROM Customers WHERE Country = 'Germany'} " & _
         "AS Customers APPEND ({SELECT * FROM Orders} AS Orders " & _
         "RELATE CustomerID TO CustomerID) AS Orders"
```

The problem is that the query the data shape provider will submit to your database will retrieve all records in the Orders table, regardless of whether they correspond to customers located in Germany.

The simple solution is to use the following parameterized query:

```
strSQL = "SHAPE {SELECT * FROM Customers WHERE Country = 'Germany'} " & _
         "AS Customers APPEND " & _
         "({SELECT * FROM Orders WHERE CustomerID = ?} AS Orders " & _
         "RELATE CustomerID TO PARAMETER 0) AS Orders"
```

Now you'll retrieve orders only for the customers located in Germany because the data shape provider retrieves orders in a separate query for each customer and will submit queries only for the customers retrieved in the parent query.

But what if you want to limit the amount of data you retrieve—meaning you don't want to retrieve any orphaned data—without facing the limitations of parameterized hierarchical Recordsets? There is another alternative.

Forget about hierarchies for a moment. What if you want to create a query that will retrieve only the orders for customers located in Germany? The orders are in one table, and the field that contains the location of the customer is in another table. SQL

Server and Access support all the following syntaxes, each of which will retrieve the desired data:

```
SELECT Orders.* FROM Orders, Customers
WHERE Orders.CustomerID = Customers.CustomerID
    AND Customers.Country = 'Germany'

SELECT * FROM Orders WHERE CustomerID IN
(SELECT CustomerID FROM Customers WHERE Country = 'Germany')

SELECT * FROM Orders WHERE EXISTS
(SELECT * FROM Customers WHERE CustomerID = Orders.CustomerID
                              AND Country = 'Germany')
```

Run some tests and see which of the syntaxes will provide the best performance. Suppose you find that the first syntax works best for you. You could then use that query in your hierarchy:

```
SHAPE {SELECT * FROM Customers WHERE Country = 'Germany'} AS Customers
    APPEND ({SELECT Orders.* FROM Orders, Customers
            WHERE Orders.CustomerID = Customers.CustomerID
            AND Customers.Country = 'Germany'} AS Orders
            RELATE CustomerID TO CustomerID) AS Orders
```

FUNCTIONALITY AND SYNTAX

Hierarchical recordsets are powerful and flexible. While I'll include examples of some of the syntax options shortly, they will not be exhaustive by any means. The documentation on the SHAPE syntax was initially lacking but has improved in the MDAC 2.1 and MDAC 2.5 releases. Take a look at the documentation in the Data Access SDK and the online Knowledge Base at the Microsoft Web site (*http://support.microsoft.com/search*) for more information.

The Data Environment Designer

The Data Environment designer included with Visual Basic 6 and Microsoft Office 2000 Developer Edition is a helpful tool for building hierarchical queries.

I don't actually use the Data Environment designer in the applications I build. But if I ever need to generate a hierarchical query, I build it using the Data Environment designer and then look at the query string the designer generated. Once I realized I could right-click the top level of the hierarchical query in the Data Environment designer and see the syntax it generated, I decided I didn't need to learn the syntax by heart.

Reshaping

Earlier, you learned that different internal structures contain different levels of standard hierarchies. In the customers and orders standard hierarchy example, all the orders are kept in the same structure. Starting with version 2.1 of ADO, you can access the different levels of the hierarchy as though they were separate Recordset objects.

If you use the following code to open your customers and orders hierarchy

```
strSQL = "SHAPE {SELECT * FROM Customers} AS Customers " & _
         "APPEND ({SELECT * FROM Orders} AS Orders " & _
         "RELATE CustomerID TO CustomerID) AS Orders"
Set rsCustomers = New ADODB.Recordset
rsCustomers.CursorLocation = adUseClient
rsCustomers.Open strSQL, cnNorthwind, adOpenStatic, _
                 adLockBatchOptimistic, adCmdText
Set rsOrders = rsCustomers.Fields("Orders").Value
```

the *rsOrders* Recordset will contain the orders for the first customer in the *rsCustomers* Recordset.

But if you change the code slightly, you can view orders in the *rsOrders* Recordset for all the customers. Rather than set the *rsOrders* Recordset to the Orders field in the *rsCustomers* Recordset, you can use the following code:

```
Set rsOrders = New ADODB.Recordset
rsOrders.CursorLocation = adUseClient
rsOrders.Open "SHAPE Orders", cnNorthwind, adOpenStatic, _
              adLockBatchOptimistic, adCmdText
```

Note the syntax. Use the SHAPE keyword, and specify the name of the hierarchy level you want to examine. This is the same name you specified in the AS clause of the query string you used to generate the hierarchy.

Reshaping the data this way provides additional means of referencing the same data structures. If you were to use the previous code snippet to view all orders and then you change a value in a field in the *rsOrders* Recordset, you would see that change in the hierarchy as well.

Hierarchy Examples

Let's build a fairly large hierarchy by following a series of steps. To save space and make the query readable, we'll mainly use the concise but lazy *SELECT * FROM* full-table queries.

Basic hierarchical query

Start by retrieving the orders for a particular customer:

```
SELECT * FROM Orders WHERE CustomerID = 'ALFKI'
```

Now add the order details in a parameterized hierarchy, but only for the returned orders. Use a parameterized query here so that you don't retrieve the order details for orders that aren't in the parent level of the Recordset. (You could do that in a nonparameterized query as described earlier, but it's worth seeing the parameterized query syntax in this large example.) Then define a calculated field that contains the cost of that particular order item. Here's the simple (nonhierarchical) parameterized query to retrieve this data:

```
SELECT [Order Details].*, Quantity * UnitPrice AS ItemTotal
FROM [Order Details] WHERE OrderID = ?
```

When you add this query to a hierarchical query, you get the following:

```
SHAPE {SELECT * FROM Orders WHERE CustomerID = 'ALFKI'} AS Orders
APPEND ({SELECT [Order Details].*, Quantity * UnitPrice AS ItemTotal
FROM [Order Details] WHERE OrderID = ?} AS OrderDetails
RELATE OrderID TO PARAMETER 0) AS OrderDetails
```

The SHAPE keyword lets the data shape provider know that this is a hierarchical query. Enclose the parent level of the hierarchy in curly braces, and then name that hierarchy level (Orders) with the AS clause. Use this name whenever you want to reshape the hierarchy. The APPEND keyword notes that you're adding a field to the Recordset. In this case, the new field contains the order details. You need to surround the definition of this field with parentheses.

The first step in defining this field is to enter the query that defines the data and enclose it in braces. Name the hierarchy level—in this case, OrderDetails—with the AS keyword. Use the RELATE keyword to define the relationship between the parent and child levels of the hierarchy, with the field from the parent query listed first. You use PARAMETER 0 here rather than a field from the child query because you're using a parameterized query. That's the end of the definition for the field added by the APPEND keyword, so you should add the closing parenthesis and name the field with the AS clause.

Now that we've covered most of the pieces of the SHAPE query, let's add more levels, one at a time, and show the new query in each case.

Adding fields

In the OrderDetails level of the hierarchy, there's a field that contains the total cost (Quantity * UnitPrice) of each order. Add a field to the Orders level of the hierarchy that contains the total cost of all the orders for this customer. You can also add a field that contains the number of orders for this customer. Your new hierarchical query should look like this:

```
SHAPE {SELECT * FROM Orders WHERE CustomerID = 'ALFKI'} AS Orders
APPEND ({SELECT [Order Details].*, Quantity * UnitPrice AS ItemTotal
FROM [Order Details] WHERE OrderID = ?} AS OrderDetails
```

(continued)

```
RELATE OrderID TO PARAMETER 0) AS OrderDetails,
SUM(OrderDetails.ItemTotal) AS OrderTotal,
COUNT(OrderDetails.OrderID) AS NumItems
```

The syntax for these new fields is straightforward. For each function (*SUM* and *COUNT*), specify the function name and include the field on which to base the calculation as the parameter. This parameter contains the name of the hierarchy level as well as the field in that level.

Adding a sibling

Now let's add a field to the Orders level of the hierarchy that contains information about the shipping company used for this order. This is considered a sibling chapter to the order details data because it's at the same level in the hierarchy. Your hierarchical query now looks like this:

```
SHAPE {SELECT * FROM Orders WHERE CustomerID = 'ALFKI'} AS Orders
APPEND ({SELECT [Order Details].*, Quantity * UnitPrice AS ItemTotal
FROM [Order Details] WHERE OrderID = ?} AS OrderDetails
RELATE OrderID TO PARAMETER 0) AS OrderDetails,
SUM(OrderDetails.ItemTotal) AS OrderTotal,
COUNT(OrderDetails.OrderID) AS NumItems,
({SELECT * FROM Shippers} AS Shipper RELATE ShipVia TO ShipperID)
AS Shipper
```

Note that this syntax is similar to the syntax you used earlier when adding order details. In the RELATE clause of the Shipper hierarchical level, the field names aren't the same. In this case, that's because the Orders and Shippers tables have different names for fields that contain the same data. The name of the field (ShipVia) in the parent level (Orders) of the relationship is on the left side of the TO clause, while the name of the field (ShipperID) in the child level (Shipper) is on the right.

Grouping data

Now let's take this hierarchy and group the data by employee. This grouping will partition the order details into sections—each group of orders placed by a particular employee:

```
SHAPE (SHAPE {SELECT * FROM Orders WHERE CustomerID = 'ALFKI'} AS Orders
APPEND ({SELECT [Order Details].*, Quantity * UnitPrice AS ItemTotal
FROM [Order Details] WHERE OrderID = ?} AS OrderDetails
RELATE OrderID TO PARAMETER 0) AS OrderDetails,
SUM(OrderDetails.ItemTotal) AS OrderTotal,
COUNT(OrderDetails.OrderID) AS NumItems,
({SELECT * FROM Shippers} AS Shipper RELATE ShipVia TO ShipperID)
AS Shipper) AS Orders COMPUTE Orders BY EmployeeID
```

In this code, you added another SHAPE keyword, enclosed the entire query in parentheses, and then named the field that contains the data—in this case, Orders.

Then you entered the COMPUTE keyword to specify that you plan to group the data; you specified the name of the hierarchy level that you'll perform the grouping on, followed by the BY keyword; and finally you entered the name of the field on which to group.

Adding fields to groups

Let's complete this hierarchy by displaying the number of orders for each employee and the total cost of the orders each employee entered into the system:

```
SHAPE (SHAPE {SELECT * FROM Orders WHERE CustomerID = 'ALFKI'} AS Orders
APPEND ({SELECT [Order Details].*, Quantity * UnitPrice AS ItemTotal
FROM [Order Details] WHERE OrderID = ?} AS OrderDetails
RELATE OrderID TO PARAMETER 0) AS OrderDetails,
SUM(OrderDetails.ItemTotal) AS OrderTotal,
COUNT(OrderDetails.OrderID) AS NumItems,
({SELECT * FROM Shippers} AS Shipper RELATE ShipVia TO ShipperID)
AS Shipper) COMPUTE Orders, COUNT(Orders.OrderID) AS NumOrders,
SUM(Orders.OrderTotal) AS EmployeeTotal BY EmployeeID
```

Whew. In Appendix B, we'll discuss the Huge Hierarchy sample that further builds on this hierarchy to display product information for each line item in each order. We'll also add information about the employees (such as name and title) to the hierarchy.

Adding blank fields

Another feature of the data shape provider is that you can add blank fields to a query. For example, say you wanted to add a Comments field to your customers query that doesn't correspond to a field in the Customers table. What I like about this feature is that you can modify the contents of this field and the data shape provider will ignore these changes. You can use the field like a scratch pad, knowing that ADO won't try to force those changes into your database. Here's an example of the syntax:

```
SHAPE {SELECT * FROM Customers} AS Customers
    APPEND NEW adVarChar(64) AS Comments
```

You specify the NEW keyword to tell the data shape provider to add a blank field. Then you state the data type for the field and use the AS keyword to name it.

You can even build a hierarchy without a connection to a database. Here's a hierarchy that uses the NEW keyword to create blank fields in both a parent level and a child level:

```
SHAPE APPEND NEW adInteger AS ParentID, NEW adVarChar(32) As ParentName,
((SHAPE APPEND NEW adInteger AS ChildID, NEW adInteger AS ParentID,
NEW adVarChar(32) AS ChildName) RELATE ParentID TO ParentID) AS Child
```

Note that the child query is enclosed in parentheses rather than curly braces.

Working without a connection

How do you use the data shape provider in your connection string without connecting to your database? Set the Data Provider argument of the connection string to None, as shown here:

```
Provider=MSDataShape;Data Provider=None;
```

QUESTIONS THAT SHOULD
BE ASKED MORE FREQUENTLY

Q.   *How does the StayInSync property on the Recordset object work? I can never make it work the way I want.*

A.   The StayInSync property controls whether a reference to a child level of a hierarchy will remain synchronized with the current position of its parent level. Say you open a customers and orders hierarchy with the customer data as the parent and obtain a reference to the orders level of the hierarchy. By default, as you navigate through the customer data, the orders Recordset object variable will always contain the orders for the current customer. Suppose you want to reference orders for a customer without the contents of the orders object variable changing when you move to another customer. You can set the StayInSync property on the customers Recordset to False before obtaining a reference to the orders level of the hierarchy, as shown here:

```
rsCustomers.Open strHierarchicalQuery, cnDatabase, adOpenStatic, _
                 adLockReadOnly, adCmdText
rsCustomers.StayInSync = False
Set rsOrders = rsCustomers.Fields("Orders").Value
```

For more information on the Recordset's StayInSync property, see Chapter 4.

Q.   *I want to base the relationship of a hierarchy on an auto-incrementing field, but I'm having problems when adding new records to the parent and child. What should I do?*

A.   This is a fairly common question, so I created a sample named Identity In Hierarchy to address it. The sample uses the Orders and Order Details tables in the SQL Server Northwind database. You can view this sample on the companion CD and learn more about it in Appendix B.

Q.   *When programming in Visual Basic, do I need to use the Value property on the Field object when referencing a child level of a hierarchical Recordset?*

A. Yes. The following code makes use of the fact that the default property on the Field object is the Value property. The Value property on the CompanyName Field object will be stored in the *strCompanyName* string variable:

```
Dim strCompanyName As String
strCompanyName = rsCustomers.Fields("CompanyName")
```

The following code, however, will fail with a type mismatch error:

```
Dim rsOrders As ADODB.Recordset
Set rsOrders = rsCustomers.Fields("CompanyName")
```

Why? Using the Set keyword means you want to reference an object, so this code will actually try to set a Recordset object variable to a Field object. Thus, you need to write your code as shown here:

```
Dim rsOrders As ADODB.Recordset
Set rsOrders = rsCustomers.Fields("CompanyName").Value
```

Chapter 15

Passing Your Recordset Out of Process

More and more programmers are moving from using traditional client/server applications to using multitiered applications. Component Services (which is based on Microsoft Transaction Server) and Microsoft Internet Information Services (formerly known as Internet Information Server) are server-based technologies that provide much of the "plumbing" programmers need to develop multitiered applications in the Microsoft Windows environment. Component Object Model (COM) is another piece of the puzzle that can simplify the interprocess communication required in multitiered applications.

When it comes to developing multitiered applications, working with ADO offers some advantages over working with its predecessors, Data Access Objects (DAO) and Remote Data Objects (RDO). The ADO development team built libraries that work in conjunction with COM to package your recordset, pass its contents across a process boundary, and unpackage that stream of data into a Recordset object in the receiving process.

With the functionality built into COM and ADO, it's almost too easy to develop a multitiered application using any of the languages in the Microsoft Visual Studio suite. So why dedicate an entire chapter to the topic of passing recordsets across process boundaries? Although COM and ADO hide much of the complexity involved in communicating across process boundaries, you need to understand how COM and ADO handle this situation so that you can avoid coding yourself into a corner.

> **NOTE**   This is a fairly complex topic that involves some of the behaviors of COM, as well as of ADO. If you're interested in learning more about COM and interprocess communication, I strongly recommend reading *Understanding ActiveX and OLE,* by David Chappell [Microsoft Press, 1996], and *Inside COM,* by Dale Rogerson [Microsoft Press, 1997].

HOW COM SIMPLIFIES INTERPROCESS COMMUNICATION

Shortly after the release of Visual Studio 6, I attended a technical conference and saw people at a booth handing out T-shirts and other trinkets emblazoned with fluorescent flowers and hearts and the slogan, "COM Is Love." The giveaways weren't only designed to appeal to psychedelic programmers; they were also promoting that company's COM books and training programs. While I can neither confirm nor deny that COM is in fact love, I can explain how COM simplifies interprocess communication between objects.

Passing Parameters

Let's take a small step back and discuss calling procedures and passing parameters. Most languages provide two ways to pass parameters to procedures: by value and by reference. Passing a parameter by value is somewhat self-explanatory—you pass a value, or a copy of the data, into the procedure. If you pass a parameter by reference, a pointer to the data is passed into the procedure. When you pass by reference, you generally pass less data (you pass only a pointer to an area in memory), and the changes you make to the data within the procedure are visible outside the procedure.

When communicating among different applications or processes, passing simple parameters by value is fairly easy, while passing parameters by reference is more complex. In Windows, an application can modify the contents of memory allocated to its process. However, an application is not allowed to modify data stored in memory that's been allocated to other processes. So how can you call a procedure in another process and pass parameters by reference? Let COM do the dirty work.

How COM Passes Parameters

When you call a method on a COM component that's running in a separate process, COM handles the interprocess communication by packaging your parameter data and passing it across the process boundary. Packaging data in this fashion is called marshaling. If you want to pass a parameter by reference, COM initially treats your parameter as though you wanted to pass it by value—COM marshals your data across the process boundary so that the procedure has a copy of your data. But once the procedure completes, COM marshals the data in your parameter back to you. The result is that the procedure that resides in a separate process has accessed and modified data contained in the calling process.

Passing standard data types such as integers and strings is fairly straightforward. COM can easily package these data types, pass that data across process boundaries, and unpackage it in another process. User-defined types (UDTs) are more difficult to marshal, but COM recently acquired the ability to pass UDTs that are made up of standard data types (such as strings and integers) across process boundaries.

COM Objects and Process Boundaries

COM objects are much more complex than UDTs, and you cannot easily pass a COM object to another process. There's much more to an instance of a class than the values of its properties. COM objects have methods, and COM objects generally encapsulate data in internal structures that aren't exposed to other applications. You can, however, pass pointers or references to a COM object to another process. Whether you specify in your application to pass object variables by reference or by value, in both cases you're essentially passing a pointer to the COM object. Thus, COM objects are always passed by reference.

This is what occurs when you try to pass DAO's Recordset object and RDO's rdoResultset object across process boundaries. You simply get a pointer to the original object that still resides in its initial process.

This behavior is the default because COM can't generically package all the contents of an object to re-create it in another process. Programmers using the COM object can't override this default behavior. However, the developer of the COM object can build custom libraries to handle the interprocess communication so that the other process receives a distinct, and (hopefully) nearly identical, copy of the original object. Servers that handle this interprocess communication on their own have custom marshaling routines.

How ADO Further Simplifies Interprocess Communication

ADO Recordset objects are more flexible than most COM objects. When you pass a Recordset object variable to a procedure, two results are possible: the procedure will receive a reference (or pointer) to the same Recordset object (as with most COM objects), or the procedure will receive a separate Recordset object that contains the same data. The result of passing a Recordset object variable from one procedure to another depends on many factors, such as whether the procedure call crosses a process boundary, whether the Recordset contents are stored in the ADO Cursor Engine, whether the procedure you're calling can accept the Recordset object variable by reference or by value, and so on. Let's take a closer look at some of these factors and the behaviors associated with them.

Passing Recordsets Within a Process

When you pass a Recordset object variable between procedures within the same process, ADO passes a reference to the object. This means that you'll have multiple references to the same Recordset object. The changes you make to the Recordset in the called function—such as modifying records and navigating—will affect all references to the Recordset.

You cannot pass a Recordset object variable by value within a single process and get a separate copy of your data. However, you can use the Recordset object's *Clone* method to get separate bookmarks. (See the discussion of the *Clone* method in Chapter 4.) Another option is to persist the Recordset (as discussed in Chapter 13) to a file or a stream and then reopen it.

Passing Recordsets Across Process Boundaries

Of course, I wouldn't have mentioned custom marshaling routines if ADO didn't utilize this feature of COM. The way in which ADO marshals Recordset objects across process boundaries is based on whether you use the ADO Cursor Engine to store the results of your query.

Server-side Recordsets
With a server-side cursor, the database and/or the OLE DB provider manage the results of the query. In order to access that particular cursor, you need to maintain a single physical connection to the database. For this reason, ADO passes a pointer to the Recordset object across the process boundary. Therefore, whether you pass by value or by reference, server-side Recordsets are always passed by reference.

Let's talk about the repercussions of passing Recordset object variables in this fashion. Imagine building a business object in a Microsoft ActiveX EXE and using that EXE as a middle-tier server that communicates with your database. (Although an ActiveX DLL running in Component Services, Microsoft Transaction Server, or Internet Information Services would be a more scalable approach, the ActiveX EXE offers a simpler illustration of this point.)

In this scenario, your client application is installed on multiple machines, and each client communicates with the business object on a separate machine using DCOM, which then communicates with your database. To retrieve data, the client calls a function within your business object that submits a query to the database, stores the results in a server-side cursor, and passes the Recordset object variable to the client.

The client application doesn't receive the data inside the Recordset object; it receives only a reference to the Recordset, which continues to reside on the server machine, as shown in Figure 15-1. As a result, each time your client accesses the Recordset object to examine its contents, it makes network calls to communicate with the business object running on the server.

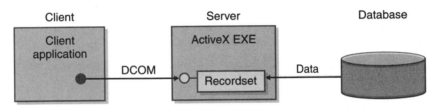

Figure 15-1 *A client communicating across a process boundary with a server-side Recordset.*

This application architecture works quite well for a small number of users, but it scales poorly. The business object in this architecture is considered "stateful," meaning it must maintain data on behalf of the client. Because it contains client-specific data, a separate instance of the business object must exist for each instance of a running client. Business objects that are "stateless" retain no data for the client, so the server can use one object to communicate with multiple clients. The result is that stateless objects scale well.

A middle-tier server that serves up stateful business objects must store data for each client. The more data each business object needs to maintain, the more memory that server uses for each client accessing it. The more memory each client requires on the server, the fewer clients that server can support. Because of the constant network traffic required and the limited scalability of this architecture, it's not suitable for applications that accommodate more than a handful of users.

NOTE   If you're going to employ such an architecture, I recommend using your own ActiveX EXE as the server rather than Component Services or Internet Information Services. Those high-powered servers are most helpful if you're using stateless objects. Also, by using your own ActiveX EXE as the server, you have a little more control over how your server manages its state.

Client-side Recordsets

When you pass a client-side Recordset object variable across process boundaries, the ADO libraries are loaded in the client and server processes. Suppose that you have a business object running on a separate server. Your client calls a function on the business object that returns a Recordset object. The ADO libraries on the server marshal the Recordset data from the ADO Cursor Engine running on the server to the ADO libraries on the client. The ADO libraries on the client machine unmarshal the data in the client's Cursor Engine and create a new local Recordset object to access that data.

Once the call to the function on your business object completes, your client application will have its own local Recordset object, rather than a pointer to a Recordset object that's actually maintained by your business object. The business object can now close or release its Recordset object without affecting the client application's Recordset object.

The result of this process is that your client receives Recordsets served up by your business objects but stores all the Recordset data locally. The business object is now stateless. Your client will not incur network round-trips when you access the data in your Recordset, and you can take advantage of the ADO Cursor Engine's batch updating features. Because your data is in a Recordset object rather than in your own data structures, you can use bound controls to interact with your data.

Passing client-side Recordsets by reference and by value

Unlike server-side Recordsets, when you pass client-side Recordsets across process boundaries, the resulting objects will behave differently depending on whether you pass the object variable by reference or by value.

Earlier we talked about how COM passes standard data types, such as integers and strings, across process boundaries. If you pass an integer by value, COM passes the value of the integer across the process boundary into an integer variable in the process of the procedure that you're calling. If you pass an integer by reference, COM follows those same steps but, at the end of the procedure call, passes that value back into the integer variable in the calling process.

You'll see similar behavior when you pass your client-side Recordset across process boundaries. Let's say that your client application has a Recordset object that was returned by a business object running on a separate machine in your network. Because you used the ADO Cursor Engine to handle the results of the query and specified adLockBatchOptimistic as the LockType when you opened your Recordset, the client application stores all the data locally. You built your client application so that the user can modify the data in the Recordset. Now you want to pass those changes to the database.

So you build a function on your business object that takes a Recordset object as a parameter. This function opens a connection to your database, associates that connection with the Recordset object, and then submits the pending changes in the Recordset by calling the Recordset's *UpdateBatch* method. Calling *UpdateBatch* changes the data in the Recordset slightly—the successful updates are no longer marked as pending records.

If you build the function so that the Recordset object variable is passed by value, you'll see the behavior described earlier: ADO passes data into the function so that the function receives its own copy of the Recordset object. Similar to when you pass an integer by value, the changes made to the Recordset object in the function will not affect the Recordset object in the client application.

If you build the function so that the Recordset object variable is passed by reference, the changes made to the Recordset object in the function will also affect the Recordset object in the client application. When the function call completes, the ADO libraries pass the modified Recordset data in the business object to the client application. Thus, when you pass your client-side Recordset object variable by reference across process boundaries, ADO marshals the data in the Recordset object to the function and back again. Microsoft Visual Basic programmers should keep in mind that parameters are, by default, passed by reference.

HOW ADO MARSHALS CLIENT-SIDE RECORDSETS

In Chapter 13, we talked about ADO's ability to persist the contents of a Recordset object to a file. ADO creates that file in such a way that it can later reopen the file and turn the data inside back into a Recordset object.

ADO's custom marshaling routine uses similar logic. The routine examines the contents of the Recordset and packages that data in the same format used to write to a file. But instead of writing this data to a file on your hard drive, ADO passes it to the ADO libraries running in another process. These ADO libraries turn that data into a new Recordset object.

Chronologically speaking, this functionality was introduced before ADO gained the ability to save a Recordset to a file. Shortly after ADO was introduced, Microsoft's data access development team created an add-on technology originally called Advanced Data Connector (ADC). The ADC libraries could pass ADO Recordsets between local processes through COM, between machines on a network using DCOM, and between machines over the Internet through HTTP. This technology was later renamed Remote Data Service (RDS); the ability to pass Recordsets between processes using COM or DCOM is now built into ADO. We'll discuss the RDS object model as well as its ability to pass Recordset objects over the Internet in Chapter 16.

WHICH DATA IS MARSHALED WITH A CLIENT-SIDE RECORDSET?

When you pass a client-side Recordset across process boundaries, the new Recordset is not an exact duplicate of the original. This is not the same concept as photocopying a document and getting a slightly blurrier copy of the original. You'll definitely receive all the values for all currently visible records and fields. Let's take a closer look at what is and is not copied into your new Recordset object.

Metadata to Support Updating

The ADO Cursor Engine's batch updating functionality is one of the more compelling reasons to use client-side Recordsets. The Cursor Engine passes all the metadata it needs to support batch updating. The base table names, base column names, and primary key information are included in the stream of data. The ADO Cursor Engine also includes the value stored in the OriginalValue property of each Field in each record of your Recordset.

However, the data stored in the UnderlyingValue property is not included. If you pass a Recordset back to your business object to submit pending changes to your database and any updates fail because of conflicts, you can resynchronize your Recordset to try to determine why the updates failed. But if you marshal the contents of the Recordset to the client application, the data you retrieved into the UnderlyingValue property for each Field object will not be included with the rest of the data, so at that point you won't be able to determine how to deal with the conflict.

Filters

Here's one area in which marshaling a Recordset object across process boundaries yields different results than saving the Recordset to a file. If you use the Filter property on a client-side Recordset to control which records are visible in the Recordset and then call its *Save* method, only the currently visible records will be stored in the file or stream.

When you pass a Recordset across process boundaries, all records—not only those currently visible—are included in the new Recordset. Keep this behavior in mind; otherwise, you might anger your network administrator by wasting bandwidth and upset your database administrator by accidentally passing sensitive data that the user wasn't meant to see. (But at least you'd make some new contacts in the human resources group—in your upcoming exit interview.)

Hierarchies

What if you're passing a hierarchical Recordset across process boundaries? (Don't forget that you can't marshal parameterized hierarchies.) Which levels and chapters of the hierarchy will appear in your new Recordset object?

Let's use a hierarchy that contains customers, orders, and order details. Say that you have a reference to a particular chapter of the orders level of the hierarchy. Only the orders for the current customer are visible in the orders Recordset. But if you pass this Recordset across a process boundary, ADO will include all orders—rather than only including the orders for the current customer. ADO will also include all order detail information, but it won't include customer information. In short, ADO will pass all chapters for the referenced level of the hierarchy, as well as all data in child levels of the hierarchy, across the process boundary.

MarshalOptions Property

You can use the MarshalOptions property on the Recordset object to control which records in your client-side Recordset are marshaled out of process. By default, this property is set to adMarshalAll, which means that all records in the Recordset will be marshaled. You can set this property to adMarshalModifiedOnly so that only the records containing pending changes will be passed across the process boundary. Using this property can decrease network traffic when you're passing a Recordset from your client application to your business object in order to submit the pending changes to your database. (For more information on the MarshalOptions property, see Chapter 4.)

QUESTIONS THAT SHOULD BE ASKED MORE FREQUENTLY

Q. *I remember someone telling me once that ADO marshaled large Recordsets asynchronously. Is that true?*

A. That was true for a brief period of time. In version 2.0, ADO marshaled large (8 KB or larger) client-side Recordsets asynchronously. You could turn off this feature by setting a key in the Registry. The ADO development team later decided that this feature's drawbacks outweighed its benefits. Starting with version 2.1, large Recordsets are once again marshaled synchronously by default. For more information on this feature, see Microsoft's Knowledge Base.

Q. *I'm using client-side Recordsets with batch optimistic locking in a three-tiered application. I can modify a record in the Recordset object in my client application and successfully submit that change to the database by passing the Recordset object to my business object, reconnecting it to the database, and calling the* **UpdateBatch** *method. But if I try to modify that same record again in my client Recordset object, the update fails when I try to submit that change to the database. I get an error saying, "The specified row could not be located for updating." Why am I having this problem?*

A. You're running into one of the minor drawbacks of passing your Recordset to the business object by value. Let's look at the changes you're making to the Recordset object in your client application. Suppose you change a customer's balance due from $75 to $125 in your client-side Recordset. When you send that Recordset to the business object to submit the update, ADO generates the following action query:

```
UPDATE Customers SET BalanceDue = 125
      WHERE CustomerID = 7 AND BalanceDue = 75
```

Because you passed your Recordset object to the business object by value, the changes that occur to the record when you call *UpdateBatch* on the business object recordset are not returned to the Recordset object in your client application. That Recordset object is essentially unaware that you've submitted a pending change to the database. If you now change that same customer's balance due from $125 to $200 and pass the Recordset to the business object to submit the change, ADO will generate the following action query:

```
UPDATE Customers SET BalanceDue = 200
      WHERE CustomerID = 7 AND BalanceDue = 75
```

Because the Recordset object in the client application is unaware that the business object submitted the initial change (from $75 to $125) to the database, it still sees the original value of the balance due as $75.

To solve this problem you could pass the Recordset object by reference instead of by value in order to keep the client's Recordset object aware of the changes it already submitted to the database. Another option is to reexecute the initial query and return this "fresher" Recordset each time you call the business object. This way, ADO will use the recently retrieved data in each action query it generates. A third option is to call the *UpdateBatch* method on the disconnected client Recordset once you've successfully submitted the pending changes. When you call *UpdateBatch* on a disconnected Recordset, ADO assumes you know what you're doing and marks the pending changes as successfully submitted to the database. While this option looks like a hack, it's pretty effective.

Q. *As a follow-up to the previous question, I decided to pass Recordset objects by reference from the client to the business object in order to give my client the ability to repeatedly modify the same record. Then I decided to set the MarshalOptions property to adMarshalModifiedOnly to decrease the amount of data passed across the network. Now I've run into a new problem. The Recordset that the business object returns contains only the records that previously had pending changes. The Recordset initially had 20 records. I modified three records, deleted one, and added two. After the call to the business object, the Recordset contained 5 records (3 modified + 2 added) rather than the 21 I expected. What can I do?*

A. Unfortunately, there's no way to make this work the way you want. When you set MarshalOptions to adMarshalModifiedOnly, this is exactly the behavior you should expect. The real question is, "Can I merge the Recordset that my business object returned with my original one?" The answer is no.

I'd love to see the ADO Cursor Engine add functionality that makes this scenario more palatable, but I don't expect that to happen for two main reasons:

■ It would take some serious internal design changes and a lot of new code to make this possible. I won't go into detail about this; just trust me when I say it's easier said than done.

■ Few programmers design their applications in such a way that they would need this functionality.

I'll never say never, but I won't hold my breath waiting for this feature. If you must make this scenario work, you'll need to write a lot of code to handle it yourself.

Chapter 16

Remote Data Service

Since its initial release, Microsoft has touted ADO as the data access model of choice for Internet programmers. In the 1.0 release, ADO was a server-side technology designed for programmers of Active Server Pages (ASP). Shortly after the initial release of ADO, Microsoft released a technology called Advanced Data Connector (ADC), which has since been renamed Remote Data Service (RDS). In this chapter, we'll cover the RDS object model and look at how RDS can help you build applications designed to work over the Internet.

WHAT IS RDS?

RDS is a series of components that allow client applications anywhere on the Internet to communicate with business objects running on internal servers. When you use RDS in a client application to instantiate a business object running on another server, you don't get the object itself. Instead, you receive what amounts to a pointer to that object. The actual object will continue to reside on the server. RDS then acts as a middleman. When your client code accesses the pointer to your business object, RDS receives the request, packages it, and sends it to the RDS server components. Then the RDS server components access the business object, package the results, and return them to your client code. This process is shown in Figure 16-1.

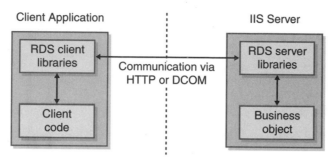

Figure 16-1 *Client/server communication through RDS.*

Two RDS components run on the client: the DataControl object, which we'll discuss momentarily, and the DataSpace object, which we'll cover later in the chapter. If you want to run a query against a database, you can assign a connection string and a query string to the DataControl object, and the DataControl object will return an ADO Recordset object with the desired data. If you want to access a business object running on your Internet Information Services (IIS) server, you can use the DataSpace object to return a pointer to that business object.

RDS also includes a server component called the DataFactory object, which you'll learn about in the second half of this chapter. The DataFactory object provides functionality similar to the DataControl object. The library for the RDS server component is called RDSServer to differentiate it from the client components.

Another RDS feature we'll discuss is that it allows you to use handlers to control data access through the DataControl object. You can use handlers to restrict access to your database and to simplify your code.

Finally, as an alternative to using the RDS objects, Microsoft Data Access Components (MDAC) includes an OLE DB provider that provides functionality that closely resembles the DataControl object.

Let's take a closer look at the first of these features, the DataControl object.

RDS DATACONTROL OBJECT

The RDS DataControl object is similar to the data controls included with Microsoft Visual Basic except that it's not a visible control. It's simply an object, just like the ADO Connection and Recordset objects.

The DataControl object's most compelling feature is that it can greatly simplify the process of querying a database on an internal network and sending the results, in the form of a Recordset object, to a client application anywhere on the Internet.

The DataControl object was designed primarily for use on web pages. Microsoft Internet Explorer supports binding controls to the DataControl. You can use the DataControl object on a web page or in a client application written in Visual Basic,

Microsoft Visual C++, and other languages that support COM objects, but you can't bind controls directly to the DataControl in the forms packages of these languages.

RDS DataControl Object Properties

Let's take a closer look at the properties exposed by the DataControl object, as described in the following table.

PROPERTIES OF THE RDS DATACONTROL OBJECT

Property Name	Data Type	Description
Connect	String	Specifies the string the object uses to connect to a database.
DataSpace	String	Ignore; exists for backward compatibility. We won't discuss this property.
ExecuteOptions	Integer	Controls whether the query is run asynchronously.
FetchOptions	Integer	Controls whether the results of a query are fetched asynchronously.
FilterColumn	String	Specifies the name of the field in the recordset on which you want to apply a filter.
FilterCriterion	String	Specifies the filter criterion (<, >, =, and so on).
FilterValue	String	Specifies the value you want to use in the filter.
Handler	String	Indicates the name of the custom handler to use when connecting.
InternetTimeout	Long	Specifies the time, in milliseconds, that RDS should wait before timing out.
ReadyState	Long	Indicates the current state of the query.
Recordset	Recordset object	Contains the results of a query.
Server	String	Specifies the name of the IIS server and communications protocol to use.
SortColumn	String	Specifies the name of the field on which you choose to sort your data.
SortDirection	Boolean	Specifies the direction to use for the sort.
SourceRecordset	Recordset object	Allows you to specify the Recordset whose changes you want to submit to the database.
SQL	String	Specifies the query string you want to submit to your database.
URL	String	Specifies the URL for an ASP page that will return a Recordset.

Connect property

The Connect property on the RDS DataControl object is similar to the ConnectionString property on the ADO Connection object. To use this property, supply the connection string you want to use to connect to your database. You can use the Connect property in conjunction with an RDS handler, which we'll discuss later in the chapter.

Keep in mind that the Connect property tells the RDS server components how to connect to your database. If you want to describe how the DataControl will connect to a machine running IIS, use the Server property.

ExecuteOptions property

The ExecuteOptions property accepts an integer to specify whether the query should be submitted synchronously or asynchronously. You can use either value from ADCExecuteOptionEnum, listed in the following table.

ADCEXECUTEOPTIONENUM VALUES

Constant	Value	Description
adcExecSync	1	Submits a query synchronously
adcExecAsync	2	Default; submits a query asynchronously

FetchOptions property

The FetchOptions property accepts an integer that controls how the results of a query are fetched. You can use a value from ADCFetchOptionEnum, listed in this next table.

ADCFETCHOPTIONENUM VALUES

Constant	Value	Description
adcFetchUpFront	1	Fetches all records in a recordset before returning control to your code.
adcFetchBackground	2	Fetches the records, beyond the initial set specified by the Recordset's CacheSize property, in the background. After the initial set of records has been fetched, control is returned to your application. If you attempt to access a record that hasn't been fetched, your code will be blocked until that record is fetched. This behavior is similar to that of ADO's adAsyncFetch constant in the ExecuteOptionEnum enumeration.
adcFetchAsync	3	Default; fetches the records, beyond the initial set specified by the Recordset's CacheSize property, in the background. After the initial set of records has been fetched, control is returned to your application. If you attempt to access a record that hasn't been fetched, your code will not be blocked. This behavior is similar to that of ADO's adAsyncFetchNonBlocking constant in the ExecuteOptionEnum enumeration.

FilterColumn, FilterCriterion, and FilterValue properties

You can use these three properties together to apply a string-based filter to the results of a query. Each property accepts a string and can be used as shown here:

```
DataControl.FilterColumn = "City"
DataControl.FilterCriterion = "="
DataControl.FilterValue = "Seattle"
```

The FilterCriterion property accepts =, >, <, >=, <=, and <>. It does not accept LIKE. You cannot use wildcards with the FilterValue property.

> **NOTE** If you change the value of the FilterColumn, FilterCriterion, or FilterValue property, the changes won't be applied to the Recordset returned by the DataControl object until you call the DataControl's *Reset* method.

If you want to clear the current filter, set the FilterColumn or FilterCriterion property to an empty string and then call the *Reset* method with a value of False in the *fRefilter* parameter.

Handler property

The Handler property accepts a string to specify the name of the RDS handler to use to enforce security on a server. This property defaults to an empty string.

InternetTimeout property

The InternetTimeout property accepts a long integer value to control the number of milliseconds that RDS will wait before timing out an attempt to connect to an IIS server. The property defaults to 300,000 milliseconds (5 minutes). The InternetTimeout property affects only connection attempts using HTTP or HTTPS.

ReadyState property

The ReadyState property on the RDS DataControl object is similar to the State property on the ADO Connection and Recordset objects. You can use the ReadyState property to determine the current state of a query. The ReadyState property returns a long integer value from ADCReadyStateEnum, as described in the following table.

ADCReadyStateEnum Values

Constant	Value	Description
adcReadyStateLoaded	2	The current query is still executing.
adcReadyStateInteractive	3	RDS has fetched the initial set of records from a query, but there are more records to fetch.
adcReadyStateComplete	4	The query has completed, and all records have been fetched.

The DataControl object's *onReadyStateChange* event will fire when the value of the ReadyState property changes.

Recordset and SourceRecordset properties

The Recordset property on the DataControl object contains the results of your query. This property is read-only:

```
Set MyRecordsetObject = DataControl.Recordset
```

If you've been working with a separate Recordset and want to use it with the DataControl, use the SourceRecordset property, which is write-only:

```
Set DataControl.SourceRecordset = MyRecordsetObject
```

Server property

The Server property controls which server the DataControl object will connect to in order to interface with the RDS components that run in IIS on that machine. The setting for this property also controls the protocol (such as HTTP or DCOM) that RDS will use to communicate with its server-side components:

```
'Connect to internal server through DCOM.
DataControl.Server = "MyWebServer"

'Connect to internal server through HTTP.
DataControl.Server = "http://MyWebServer"

'Connect over the Internet through HTTP.
DataControl.Server = "http://www.microsoft.com"
```

> **NOTE**   The Server property does not specify the server where your database is located. That information should be provided in the Connect property (described earlier in this section).

SortColumn and SortDirection properties

To sort the results of a query based on a particular field, set the SortColumn property to the name of that field. The SortDirection property accepts a Boolean value to specify whether RDS should sort the data in ascending or descending order. By default, this property is set to True, which indicates that RDS should sort the data in ascending order. A setting of False specifies a sort in descending order.

> **NOTE**   If you change the value of the SortColumn and SortDirection properties, you must call the DataControl object's *Reset* method before they will affect the Recordset returned by the DataControl.

SQL property

The SQL property contains the query that RDS will submit to your database. This property accepts a string and is similar to the CommandText property of the Command object and the Source property of the Recordset object.

URL property

The URL property is a string that can be set to a valid URL. Typically, the URL property is set to a URL for an ASP page that returns a recordset in its Response object. The URL property was added in RDS 2.5, allowing you to use the DataControl with XML data.

RDS DataControl Object Methods

Now let's examine the methods of the DataControl object, which are shown in the following table.

METHODS OF THE RDS DATACONTROL OBJECT

Method Name	Description
Cancel	Cancels an asynchronous operation
CancelUpdate	Cancels the pending changes for a record
CreateRecordset	Creates a new, empty Recordset object with the structure you request
Refresh	Connects to an IIS server, executes a query, and retrieves the results
Reset	Resets the sort or filter on a Recordset object
SubmitChanges	Submits the pending changes in a Recordset object to your database

Cancel method

Use the *Cancel* method to cancel an asynchronous action on the DataControl object. If you call the *Cancel* method while RDS is still executing a query, the DataControl will return without generating an error. The *onReadyStateChange* event will fire, the ReadyState property will return adcReadyStateComplete, and the Recordset object will contain a null pointer.

You can also call the *Cancel* method to terminate the asynchronous fetching of results for a query. Using the *Cancel* method in this fashion still won't generate an error. The *onReadyStateChange* event will fire, the ReadyState property will return adcReadyStateComplete, and the Recordset property will return a valid Recordset object containing the records that RDS fetched before you called the *Cancel* method.

CancelUpdate method

Use the *CancelUpdate* method to cancel pending changes in the Recordset.

When you call the *CancelUpdate* method, all pending changes in the Recordset are discarded. The Recordset will then contain the data retrieved the last time you called the DataControl object's *Refresh* method.

CreateRecordset method

You can use the *CreateRecordset* method to generate a new, empty Recordset. *CreateRecordset* accepts a single parameter:

■   ***varColumnInfos***   This parameter holds a Variant array that contains information about the structure of the Recordset that you want to create.

You can generate this parameter in one of two ways. The first technique is easier to follow but requires more code. The second is easier to write but can be a bit confusing until you understand the structure of the parameter. Let's take a look at the first technique:

```
'Create the fixed-length Variant arrays.
Dim aColumns(2), c0(3), c1(3), c2(3)
'The c0 array represents the first (or 0th) column.
'The initial entry in the array corresponds to
' the column's name and accepts a string.
c0(0) = "CustomerID"
'The second entry corresponds to the column's data type.
'CreateRecordset requires that this information be stored in an
' integer. ADO uses a long integer for its data types. If you're using
' the ADO constants rather than the explicit value, you'll need to use
' CInt.
c0(1) = CInt(adInteger)
'The third entry corresponds to the column's size. If you're using data
' types that handle various sizes (char, varchar, binary, varbinary),
' specify the size here. Otherwise, use -1.
c0(2) = -1
'The fourth and final entry controls whether the column accepts
' null values.
c0(3) = False
'Generate the arrays for the other two columns.
c1(0) = "CustomerName"
c1(1) = CInt(adVarChar)
c1(2) = 64
c1(3) = False
c2(0) = "BalanceDue"
c2(1) = CInt(adCurrency)
c2(2) = -1
```

```
c2(3) = False
'Store each column array as an element in the aColumns array.
aColumns(0) = c0
aColumns(1) = c1
aColumns(2) = c2
'Now call CreateRecordset.
Set Recordset = DataControl.CreateRecordset(aColumns)
```

Once you have a handle on the structure of the *varColumnInfos* parameter, you can use the second technique, which takes advantage of dynamic arrays and the *Array* function of Visual Basic for Applications (VBA). With the second technique, you use the *Array* function to build and populate dynamic Variant arrays—rather than the static Variant arrays used in the first technique.

```
'Create the structures as dynamic Variant arrays.
Dim aColumns(), c0(), c1(), c2()
'Create each column array using the Array function, specifying
' the column's name, data type, size, and whether it accepts null
' values.
c0 = Array("CustomerID", CInt(adInteger), -1, False)
c1 = Array("CustomerName", CInt(adVarChar), 64, False)
c2 = Array("BalDue", CInt(adCurrency), -1, False)
'Create the aColumns array, supplying each of the column arrays.
aColumns = Array(c0, c1, c2)
Set Recordset = DataControl.CreateRecordset(aColumns)
```

This feature is similar to ADO's creatable Recordsets that allow you to populate the Fields collection using the *Fields.Append* method, which is discussed in Chapter 4 on pages 105 and 106.

Refresh method

Call the *Refresh* method on the DataControl object when you want to refresh the information you retrieved from a query. The *Refresh* method will create a connection to an IIS server, open a connection to your database, and submit a query. The *Refresh* method takes no parameters.

Reset method

Use the *Reset* method when you want the changes you've made to the DataControl object's sorting and filtering properties to take effect. The *Reset* method accepts a single parameter:

■ *fRefilter* This optional parameter defaults to 1. A value of 1 indicates that you want the changes to the filtering and sorting information to apply to the currently filtered data. This parameter can help create compound filters.

For example, let's say you want to view only customers whose names begin with the letter "D." You can't use wildcards, but you could use a compound filter by setting the filter properties twice, as shown here:

```
Dim rdsDC As RDS.DataControl
    ⋮
With rdsDC
    .FilterColumn = "CompanyName"
    .FilterCriterion = ">="
    .FilterValue = "D"
    .Reset False
    .FilterColumn = "CompanyName"
    .FilterCriterion = "<"
    .FilterValue = "E"
    .Reset True
End With
```

This code uses the *fRefilter* parameter in the calls to the *Reset* method. Initially, you simply want to show the records whose CompanyName field contains a value greater than or equal to "D". When you call the *Reset* method, you use False as the value for the *fRefilter* parameter because you want to remove any previous filters before applying this one. Then you want to show the records whose CompanyName field contains a value less than "E". But you want the records to satisfy the previous filter criteria as well, so you use a value of True for the *fRefilter* parameter.

If you want to clear the current filter, set the FilterColumn or FilterCriterion property to an empty string and then call the *Reset* method with a value of False for the *fRefilter* parameter.

SubmitChanges method

The DataControl object's *SubmitChanges* method takes no parameters and is similar to the *UpdateBatch* method on the Recordset object. You use it to submit the changes pending in the Recordset to your database.

If you have changes pending in records that aren't visible because of the current filter setting, those pending changes will not be submitted. The changes that are submitted are bundled in a transaction. If any of the update attempts fail, the entire transaction is rolled back and none of the changes will be committed to your database.

RDS DataControl Object Events

Finally, let's look at the two events that the DataControl object exposes, shown in the following table.

RDS DATACONTROL EVENTS

Event Name	Description
onError	An error has occurred.
onReadyStateChange	The value of the ReadyState property has changed.

onError event

The *onError* event fires when the DataControl object encounters an error. You can use the *onError* event to handle errors generated by the DataControl. This event supports four parameters:

- **SCode**   An integer value that indicates the status code of the error.

- **Description**   A string that describes the error.

- **Source**   A string that contains the query or command that generated the error.

- **CancelDisplay**   A Boolean value that you can set to control whether the error will display a dialog box. This parameter is False by default, meaning a dialog box will be displayed.

onReadyStateChange event

The *onReadyStateChange* event fires when the value of the DataControl object's ReadyState property changes. This event uses no parameters. You can use this event to determine when the results of your query have been fetched, as shown here:

```
Private Sub rdsDC_onReadyStateChange()
    'Test the ReadyState property to see whether the operation has
    ' completed.
    If rdsDC.ReadyState = adcReadyStateComplete Then
        'Retrieve the Recordset.
        Set rs = rdsDC.Recordset
        'Test to see whether an uninitialized Recordset was returned.
        If Not rs Is Nothing Then
            Set gridResults.DataSource = rs
            gridResults.Visible = True
        Else
            MsgBox "No Recordset was returned"
        End If
    End If
End Sub
```

RDS DATASPACE OBJECT

While the DataControl object simplifies communicating with databases across the Internet, the DataSpace object provides comparable functionality for business objects. The DataSpace object isn't nearly as complex as the DataControl object because it exposes only one property and only one method. However, that property and method provide all the flexibility you need to access business objects running on your server.

InternetTimeout Property

The InternetTimeout property on the DataSpace object is identical to the Internet-Timeout property on the DataControl object. For more information, see page 287.

CreateObject Method

Use the *CreateObject* method to instantiate a business object on your IIS server. This method accepts two string parameters:

- ■ *bstrProgID*   This required parameter specifies the ProgID for the business object.

- ■ *bstrConnection*   This required parameter tells RDS where to create the object and which protocol to use.

The syntax for the *CreateObject* method differs slightly depending on the protocol you're using. Here are examples of using this method with the possible protocols.

```
'Instantiate the object through HTTP.
'You can reference an IIS server on your local network or over the
' Internet.
Set MyObject = DataSpace.CreateObject("MyServer.MyClass", _
                        "http://www.microsoft.com")


'Instantiate the object through HTTPS.
'You can reference an IIS server on your local network or over the
' Internet.
Set MyObject = DataSpace.CreateObject("MyServer.MyClass", _
                        "https://www.microsoft.com")


'Instantiate the object through DCOM.
'This syntax works only when you're connected to your network.
Set MyObject = DataSpace.CreateObject("MyServer.MyClass", _
                            "MyIISServer")
```

```
'Instantiate the object locally.
'Use this syntax if you have your business object installed
' on the machine where you're running your code.
Set MyObject = DataSpace.CreateObject("MyServer.MyClass", "")
```

RDSSERVER DATAFACTORY OBJECT

The DataFactory object is an RDS component that runs on your IIS server. In fact, the DataControl object passes the connection and query strings to the DataFactory component on the server that you've specified.

> **NOTE** I've found that if you use the DataSpace object in Visual Basic, you should dimension your business object variable as Object rather than use early binding.

You can use the DataFactory object to query and update your database. You can also convert Recordsets to MIME strings and generate empty Recordsets.

Think of the DataFactory object as a generic business object designed to help you communicate with your database through queries. DataFactory acts as the default server-side object of RDS. When you use the DataControl object to query your database, RDS instantiates a hidden DataFactory object on your server to submit the query. Let's take a closer look at the methods available through the DataFactory object, shown in the following table.

METHODS OF THE RDSSERVER DATAFACTORY OBJECT

Method Name	Description
ConvertToString	Converts the Recordset to a MIME-encoded string.
CreateRecordset	Creates a new, empty Recordset with the structure you request.
Execute	Interacts with the RDS DataControl. Not intended for external use.
Query	Connects to your database, executes a query, and retrieves the results.
SubmitChanges	Submits the changes in the specified Recordset to the database associated with a connection string.
Synchronize	Interacts with the RDS DataControl. Not intended for external use.

ConvertToString Method

The *ConvertToString* method accepts a Recordset object and returns its contents in a MIME-encoded string. This method is designed for ASP programmers who want to embed the contents of a Recordset in an HTML page.

The *ConvertToString* method is already somewhat antiquated. There are better ways to send data to your client application. Rather than using MIME-encoded strings, you might want to consider marshaling the object itself through a business object, using the DataSpace object or the *Execute* or *Query* method on the DataFactory object. Another option is to store the contents of a Recordset in XML format using the ASP Response object and to use the DataControl object's URL property to retrieve the contents.

CreateRecordset Method

The DataFactory object's *CreateRecordset* method is identical to the *CreateRecordset* method of the DataControl object. For more information, see the section "*CreateRecordset* method" on page 290.

Query Method

The DataFactory object's *Query* method returns a Recordset object based on a query string. This method accepts three parameters:

- **bstrConnection**   This required parameter is the connection string that the DataFactory will use to communicate with your database.

- **bstrQuery**   You specify the query string you want to submit to your database in this required parameter.

- **IMarshalOptions**   This optional parameter accepts a long value from ADCFetchOptionEnum. For information on these values, see the section "FetchOptions property" on page 286.

SubmitChanges Method

The DataFactory object's *SubmitChanges* method is similar to the *SubmitChanges* method of the DataControl object. The *SubmitChanges* method on the DataFactory object accepts two required parameters:

- **bstrConnection**   Supply the connection string for your database in this parameter.

- **pRecordset**   Supply the Recordset object that has pending changes you want to submit to the database in this parameter.

One difference between this method and its DataControl namesake is that with the DataFactory object's *SubmitChanges* method, pending changes in records that aren't visible because of the filter applied to the Recordset are still submitted to your database. The DataFactory object still wraps these changes in a transaction so that if any of the pending changes fail, the entire batch of changes fails.

RDS HANDLERS

Now that you've seen what RDS has to offer, you might be a little nervous about security. With the DataControl or DataFactory object, a user could access your database by simply submitting any connection string and any query string. If that doesn't scare you, consider the queries that a user could submit:

```
SELECT * FROM Employees
UPDATE Employees SET Salary = 1000000 WHERE EmployeeID = 42275
DELETE FROM Employees WHERE EmployeeID = 1
DROP TABLE Employees
DROP DATABASE MyBusiness
```

Now do you care?

NOTE Of course, you don't have to worry about queries like these because you've set up a secure database. A user could never submit queries like these unless he or she had the appropriate privileges, right?

To help tighten the security of your RDS applications, you can use a handler. RDS includes a simple handler in the form of an .ini file that lets you control access to connections, queries, and logging errors. This file is MSDFMap.ini, and its contents might look something like this:

```
[connect default]
;Do not allow access to connections that don't have an entry in the
; handler.
Access=NoAccess

[connect CustomerDatabase]
;Allow read/write access to the customer database
; by substituting the connection string below.
Access=ReadWrite
Connect="Provider=SQLOLEDB;Data Source=ScepHome;  ⇁
Initial Catalog=Northwind;User ID=RDSUser;Password=RDSPassword;"

[sql default]
;Do not allow access to queries that don't have an entry in the handler
; by supplying any invalid query.
sql="InvalidQuery"

[sql GetAllCustomers]
;Allow access to the customer table with the query below.
sql="SELECT * FROM Customers"
```

(continued)

```
[sql GetACustomer]
;Allow access to the customer table with the parameterized query below.
sql="SELECT * FROM Customers WHERE CustomerID = ?"
```

> **NOTE** There's more information on the options available for the MSDFMap.ini file in the Data Access Services portion of the Platform SDK. Look for the topic "Understanding the Customization File."

If you use this handler with your RDS code, you must supply a connection string and query string from the lists in the file (CustomerDatabase, GetAllCustomers, and so on). To retrieve a specific customer with RDS and this handler, use this code:

```
With DataControl
    .Server = "http://MyServer"
    .Handler = "MSDFMap.Handler"
    .Connect = "CustomerDatabase"
    .SQL = "GetACustomer('ALFKI')"
    .Refresh
End With
```

Notice that you're using a parameterized query and treating it almost the same way you would a function by supplying the customer's name—including the string delimiter—as a parameter to that function.

The Data Access portion of the Platform SDK covers RDS handlers at length. You'll find documentation on which features are available in the connect, sql, userlist, and logs sections of the DataFactory handler (also called a customization file). The SDK also shows how you can build your own customized handler objects in Visual Basic and Visual C++.

If you plan to use a handler other than the MSDFMap.ini file, be sure that you check the SDK to see how to mark the handler as "safe for scripting" to ensure secure Internet access.

If you want to force all RDS code to use a handler in order to prevent users from running any query against any database, you can place the following entry in the specified key in the Microsoft Windows Registry for your IIS server:

```
HandlerRequired=1
HKEY_LOCAL_MACHINE\SOFTWARE\Microsoft\DataFactory\HandlerInfo
```

In fact, to tighten security, Windows 2000 automatically places this entry in the Registry when you install it. This means that by default, you cannot use the RDS DataControl or RDSServer DataFactory object with Windows 2000 without specifying a handler. You can manually change the Registry key to HandlerRequired=0 in order to remove this restriction.

Installing MDAC 2.5 on a machine running Microsoft Windows NT 4 will not impose this restriction.

MICROSOFT OLE DB REMOTING PROVIDER

There's another way you can execute remote queries using the RDS technology—by using the Microsoft OLE DB Remoting Provider, known as MS Remote. Instead of using a DataControl object or a DataSpace object and a DataFactory object to retrieve a Recordset, you can use the ADO Connection object and a connection string that references the MS Remote provider. You can supply a connection string and a query string to the MS Remote provider as shown here:

```
strConn = "Provider=MS Remote;Remote Server=http://scep;" & _
          "Remote Provider=SQLOLEDB;Data Source=Gilliam;" & _
          "Initial Catalog=Northwind;User ID=sa;Password=;"
Set cnNorthwind = New ADODB.Connection
cnNorthwind.Open strConn

strSQL = "SELECT * FROM Customers"
Set rsCustomers = New ADODB.Recordset
rsCustomers.Open strSQL, cnNorthwind, adOpenStatic, _
                adLockBatchOptimistic, adCmdText
```

Notice that the connection string is similar to the connection string you'd use with straight ADO while running on the local network. MS Remote is now your provider, and the provider you want to use to connect to your database is now the Remote Provider. (This is similar to what happens when you use the MSDataShape provider and call it the Data Provider.) Specify the IIS server and protocol you want to use in the Remote Server argument. You can also use an Internet Timeout argument to specify a value that you'd otherwise use in the InternetTimeout property of the RDS DataControl or DataSpace object.

If you want to use the MS Remote provider with a handler, you can use code such as the following. Note that you substitute a connection string and query string as specified in the handler's settings:

```
strConn = "Provider=MS Remote;Remote Server=http://scep;" & _
          "Handler=MSDFMap.Handler;Data Source=CustomerDatabase;"
Set cnNorthwind = New ADODB.Connection
cnNorthwind.Open strConn

strSQL = "GetAllCustomers"
Set rsCustomers = New ADODB.Recordset
rsCustomers.Open strSQL, cnNorthwind, adOpenStatic, _
                adLockBatchOptimistic, adCmdText
```

I'll admit that, initially, I preferred using the DataControl and DataFactory objects. But the more I used the MS Remote provider, the more it felt like a logical extension of ADO to the Internet.

QUESTIONS THAT SHOULD
BE ASKED MORE FREQUENTLY

Q.   *Why can't I instantiate my business objects on my IIS server with the RDS DataSpace object's* CreateObject *method?*

A.   You'll need to change some Registry settings in order to allow access to these objects. MDAC does not enable this feature on installation for security reasons. You'll need to run RegEdit and then look for the following Registry key:

```
HKEY_LOCAL_MACHINE\System\CurrentControlSet\Services\W3SVC\  →
Parameters\ADCLaunch
```

Now add the ProgID for each business object you want to expose through RDS. For a more in-depth explanation, see the topic "Registering a Custom Business Object" in the Data Access Services portion of the Platform SDK Help.

Q.   *Does using handlers make RDS safe across the Internet?*

A.   That's an important question to ask but a tough one to answer. While I have a lot of experience building two-tiered and three-tiered database applications with ADO, I don't have much Internet programming experience. If you want more information on Internet security, read up on IIS and HTTPS.

I strongly recommend requiring RDS to use a handler to limit users' access to your database. Handlers keep the location of your database and the query string out of the client code. This allows you to modify or move your database, and you need to modify only the appropriate connection and/or query strings. You'll also keep your users from obtaining information about what sort of database you're using, where it's located, and so on.

Sometimes setting up anonymous users is helpful and appropriate. It simplifies coding and lets you take advantage of OLE DB session pooling. However, it's still anonymous.

You might decide that you need to store information about each customer in your database and provide each customer with a password. You can require that users supply their customer ID and password with their orders so that you can track the orders appropriately. Now you only need to make sure that you're using a secure connection through HTTPS so that no one else on the Internet can access the password supplied by the user.

Part III

Appendixes

Appendix A

ADOX and JRO

Version 2.1 of Microsoft Data Access Components (MDAC) introduced two new libraries that complement ADO to provide functionality for Microsoft Access databases previously available only in Data Access Objects (DAO): Microsoft ActiveX Data Objects Extensions for Data Definition Language and Security (ADOX) and Microsoft Jet and Replication Objects (JRO). ADOX allows users to view, create, and modify database structures. JRO includes Jet database replication features, as well as features previously available in the DAO DBEngine object.

ADOX

ADOX adds data definition language features previously available only in DAO. You can use ADOX objects to create, modify, or examine tables, queries, and security settings for databases. Rather than having to create tables with action queries such as

```
CREATE TABLE Customers
        (CustomerID varchar(5) NOT NULL CONSTRAINT PK_Customers PRIMARY KEY,
        CompanyName varchar(40), BalanceDue money)
```

you can use code such as the following:

```
'Create a new Table object.
Set tblCustomers = New ADOX.Table
With tblCustomers
    .Name = "Customers"
    'Specify column information.
    .Columns.Append "CustomerID", adVarChar, 5
    .Columns.Append "CompanyName", adVarChar, 40
    .Columns.Append "BalanceDue", adCurrency
    'Add the primary key.
    .Keys.Append "PK_Customers", adKeyPrimary, "CustomerID"
End With
'Add the new table to your database.
catDatabase.Tables.Append tblCustomers
```

What a Great Idea!

I don't mind admitting it. I love the concept of ADOX. That might not sound like the most glowing recommendation, but in a moment, you'll see some of the benefits and limitations of the ADOX implementation.

Some of the Microsoft Visual Studio 6 development tools allow you to generate new tables, views, and stored procedures for Microsoft SQL Server and Oracle databases. The database tools, including the DataView window, allow you to fill out a grid with information about each column and generate a CREATE TABLE query to your database that creates the table. Users often ask why these features don't work with other databases.

Each database has its own data definition language quirks. For example, a text field in SQL Server is called a long field in Oracle and a memo field in Access. These differences make it difficult to build a generic tool to generate DDL queries that work on all databases. The DataView window must include SQL Server–specific and Oracle-specific code that accepts input and generates the appropriate DDL query. But wouldn't it be easier if you could generate database-independent code to build tables and queries?

ADOX is designed to let you do exactly that. You don't have to know what SQL Server, Oracle, and Access call their large text fields. You simply have to remember what ADO calls them: adLongVarChar. But wait! When you use ADOX, who generates the database-specific DDL queries? ADOX doesn't inherently know all the DDL idiosyncrasies of each database, and ADOX isn't like the Visual Studio database tools that are designed to create and modify objects in just two databases— SQL Server and Oracle.

It's actually the OLE DB provider that generates the DDL queries. Think of ADOX as a simple standard that asks the OLE DB provider to generate DDL queries. ADOX is merely a middleman. That's why I think ADOX is such a great idea. It provides the structure but leaves it up to the OLE DB provider to offer the functionality.

Now for the Bad News

Unfortunately, this means that in order to use ADOX to interact with your database, you need to use an OLE DB provider that supports ADOX interfaces. At the time of this writing, only two OLE DB providers support a significant portion of the features available in ADOX: the OLE DB Provider For SQL Server and the Jet 4.0 OLE DB Provider.

The Jet 4.0 OLE DB Provider supports almost all of ADOX. You can use this provider with ADOX to create an Access 2000 database and populate it with tables, queries, users, and groups. However, you cannot add Access-specific objects such as reports, forms, and modules by using ADOX. There's a sample titled Make Northwind on the companion CD that creates an Access 2000 database using ADOX and the Jet 4.0 OLE DB Provider. This sample is nearly identical to the Northwind database included with Access and Microsoft Visual Basic, except that it doesn't include the forms, reports, and modules. Discounting those objects, I'd say that using the Jet 4.0 OLE DB Provider with ADOX allows you to create about 95 percent of the functionality of an Access 2000 database. The only significant feature the Jet 4.0 OLE DB Provider with ADOX lacks is the ability to create new security databases (.mdw).

The SQL Server OLE DB provider supports a smaller subset of the ADOX features. I've yet to find definitive documentation stating exactly which ADOX features this provider does support or outlining any plans to add more ADOX functionality to the provider. However, here's what I have learned through my own experiences:

■ You cannot access the Users, Groups, and Views collections, and you cannot create Catalogs (databases).

■ Using ADOX with the SQL Server OLE DB provider lets you access about two-thirds of the functionality of a SQL Server database.

ADOX Object Model

Unless you plan to interact with only Access databases, I don't recommend using ADOX. For that reason, I won't cover every property and method of every object in the ADOX hierarchy. Instead, I'll cover the highlights of each object and collection in the ADOX object model, shown in Figure A-1. Version 2.5 of the ADOX objects can be accessed in Visual Basic by selecting Microsoft ADO Ext. 2.5 For DDL And Security in the References dialog box.

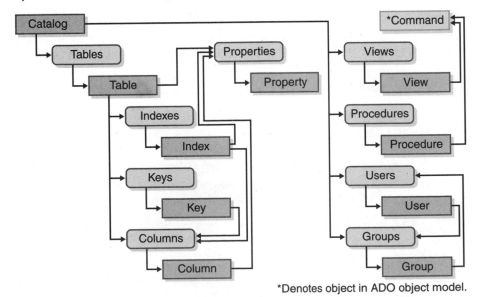

*Denotes object in ADO object model.

Figure A-1 *The ADOX object model.*

Catalog object

The ADOX Catalog object corresponds to your database. To connect to an existing database, use the Catalog's ActiveConnection property just as you would for the Connection object. Set the property to a valid connection string or a Connection object.

You can use the Catalog object to create new Access databases with the Jet 4.0 OLE DB Provider. Call the *Create* method on the Catalog object and supply a connection string that includes the path to the Access database you want to create, as shown here:

```
strPathToFile = "C:\Windows\Desktop\New.mdb"
strConn = "Provider=Microsoft.Jet.OLEDB.4.0;" & _
          "Data Source=" & strPathToFile & ";"
Set cat = New ADOX.Catalog
cat.Create strConn
```

By default, the Jet 4.0 OLE DB Provider will create an Access 2000 database (Jet 4.0). You can specify that you want to create a Jet 3.*x* (Access 95 and Access 97) database by using the Jet OLEDB:Engine Type property in the connection string, as follows:

```
strPathToFile = "C:\Windows\Desktop\New97.mdb"
strConn = "Provider=Microsoft.Jet.OLEDB.4.0;" & _
          "Data Source=" & strPathToFile & ";" & _
          "Jet OLEDB:Engine Type=4;"
Set cat = New ADOX.Catalog
cat.Create strConn
```

You can use the Catalog object to determine and specify which user owns an object by calling the *GetObjectOwner* and *SetObjectOwner* methods, as shown here:

```
'Display the current owner of the Customers table.
MsgBox cat.GetObjectOwner("Customers", adPermObjTable)

'Set JoeUser to the owner of the Customers table.
Call cat.SetObjectOwner("Customers", adPermObjTable, "JoeUser")
```

> **NOTE** Keep in mind that when you're using ADOX security features (the User and Group objects and the *GetObjectOwner* and *SetObjectOwner* methods) you'll need to specify the location of the system database file, which is usually named system.mdw.

The Catalog object also exposes the Tables, Views, Procedures, Users, and Groups collections.

Table object and Tables collection

As its name indicates, the Table object refers to a table in your database. The Table object exposes the Columns, Indexes, Keys, and Properties collections. There are two properties of the Table object that you should be aware of: Name and Type.

Before you try to append a Table object to a Catalog's Tables collection, be sure you set the Name property on the Table object. You might find more entries in a Catalog object's Tables collection than expected. Items in the collection can include views and system tables. To determine which type of object an item is, check the Table object's Type property, which will return a string. Checking the Access Northwind database, you'll see Table objects whose Type property returns TABLE, VIEW, SYSTEM TABLE, and ACCESS TABLE.

To see some sample code that shows how to create a Table object, check out the "Property object and Properties collection" section on page 309.

Column object and Columns collection

The Column object corresponds to a column in your table. It exposes many of the same properties that the ADO Field object exposes: Attributes, DefinedSize, Name, NumericScale, Precision, and Type.

The Column object's RelatedColumn property is applicable only to Column objects in the Columns collection of a Key object and is designed for foreign keys. You'll see how to use the RelatedColumn property shortly when we cover the Property object and the Properties collection.

The SortOrder property applies only to Column objects in the Columns collection of an Index object and controls whether entries in an Index object are stored in ascending or descending order.

There are two ways to use a Table object's Columns collection to append a Column object. First you can create a Column object, set its properties, and then append it to the Columns collection, as shown here:

```
Set colCustomerID = New ADOX.Column
colCustomerID.Name = "CustomerID"
colCustomerID.Type = adVarWChar
colCustomerID.Size = 5
tblCustomers.Columns.Append colCustomerID
```

The *Append* method on the Columns collection accepts a Variant as its first parameter. You can pass a Column object into this parameter as just shown.

A second way to append a Column object is by passing to the *Append* method a string that contains the name of the new Column object you want to create, as shown here:

```
tblCustomers.Columns.Append "CustomerID", adVarWChar, 5
```

When you use the *Append* method in this fashion, use the second parameter to specify the data type for the new Column object. The third parameter is optional and is used to specify the size of the new column if it's a variable-sized data type such as a character or binary field.

Key object and Keys collection

The Key object corresponds to a primary, unique, or foreign key (or constraint) on a table. The Type property controls what type of key the object is. The Key object's Columns collection contains the Column object that the key references.

For foreign keys, the RelatedTable property refers to the name of the related table. Use the DeleteRule or UpdateRule property to control what occurs when you delete or modify the primary key value of a row in the parent table of a relationship. The DeleteRule and UpdateRule properties are updatable only before you append the Key object to the Keys collection.

The *Append* method on the Keys collection is similar to the Columns collection's *Append* method. You can append a Key object to the Keys collection with code such as

```
Set keyPrimary = New ADOX.Key
    ⋮
tblOrders.Keys.Append keyPrimary
```

You can also use the *Append* method to create a new Key object and add it to the Keys collection in one call, as shown here:

```
tblOrders.Keys.Append "PK_Orders", adKeyPrimary, "OrderID"
```

The first parameter specifies the name of the Key object. The second parameter corresponds to the Key object's Type property, and the third parameter corresponds to the name of the Column object referenced by the Key object. This syntax comes in handy when you're creating a primary key or a unique key.

But if you plan to create a foreign key, you'll need to specify the related table and corresponding column. Use the fourth and fifth parameters on the *Append* method to supply this information, as shown here:

```
tblOrders.Keys.Append "FK_Orders_Employee", adKeyForeign, "EmployeeID", _
                "Employees", "EmployeeID"
```

Index object and Indexes collection

To add an index to a table, create an Index object. You can control whether Null values are allowed in the index by setting the IndexNulls property to a value in AllowNullsEnum. The default value for IndexNulls is adIndexNullsDisallow. The

Clustered property accepts a Boolean value that controls whether the index is clustered; this property is False by default. To control whether the entries in the index are unique, set the Unique property on the Index object. This property is set to False by default. The Clustered and Unique properties are read-only once you've appended the Index object to the Indexes collection.

The Index object exposes two collections, Columns and Properties. The Columns collection contains references to the columns that make up the index. The Properties collection contains database-specific properties for the index.

Like the *Append* method on the Columns and Keys collections, the *Append* method on the Indexes collection has the ability to create a new Index object and add it to the Indexes collection. This code passes an Index object to the Indexes collection's *Append* method:

```
Set idx = New ADOX.Index
    ⋮
tbl.Indexes.Append idx
```

To create a new Index object and add it to the Indexes collection in a single call, supply the name of the new Index object as the first parameter and the name of the Column object that it references as the second parameter:

```
tbl.Indexes.Append "IndexName", "ColumnName"
```

If you want to create an Index object that references multiple Column objects, pass a Variant array that contains the column names for the second parameter, as shown here:

```
tbl.Indexes.Append "IndexName", Array("Column1", "Column2", ... "ColumnN")
```

Property object and Properties collection

Like the ADO object model, the ADOX object model exposes database-specific properties through the Properties collection. The Table, Column, and Index objects each have a Properties collection. For example, you might want to specify that a column in a table is auto-incrementing. This database-specific property is available in the Column object's Properties collection, rather than as a direct property of the Column object.

If you want to access a database-specific property of a Column object through its Properties collection, make sure that you've set the ParentCatalog property on the Column object or its parent Table object.

The following code creates the Orders table in the Northwind database. Note that the code sets the ParentCatalog property on the Table object to access the dynamic AutoIncrement property on the OrderID column.

```
'Create a new Table object.
Set tbl = New ADOX.Table
'Set the ParentCatalog property on the Table
' to expose the database-specific properties.
Set tbl.ParentCatalog = cat
tbl.Name = "Orders"
'Add the Columns to the table.
tbl.Columns.Append "OrderID", adInteger
tbl.Columns("OrderID").Properties("AutoIncrement") = True
tbl.Columns.Append "CustomerID", adWChar, 5
⋮
'Create the primary key.
tbl.Keys.Append "PK_Orders", adKeyPrimary, "OrderID"
'Create the foreign key.
'You must explicitly create the key this way to set the
' DeleteRule property.
Set fk = New ADOX.Key
fk.Name = "FK_Orders_Customers"
fk.Type = adKeyForeign
fk.RelatedTable = "Customers"
fk.Columns.Append "CustomerID"
fk.Columns("CustomerID").RelatedColumn = "CustomerID"
fk.UpdateRule = adRICascade
tbl.Keys.Append fk
⋮
'Create the indexes.
tbl.Indexes.Append "IDX_Orders_Customers", "CustomerID"
⋮
'Add the table to the database.
cat.Tables.Append tbl
```

View and Procedure objects and Views and Procedures collections

The View object and the Procedure object have identical structures. They each expose a Name property as well as the DateCreated and DateModified properties. Both the View and Procedure objects make the structure of their queries available through a property called Command, which contains a Command object.

See the "Questions That Should Be Asked More Frequently" section at the end of this appendix for some peculiarities that occur when creating and interacting with Access QueryDefs, the Access term for stored queries.

User and Group objects and Users and Groups collections

The User object represents a user's account in the database, while the Group object corresponds to a group of users. Each object has a Name property as well as methods for setting and checking permissions on an object. The User object also has a method for changing the user's password, aptly named *ChangePassword*.

The User and Group objects are linked together in the ADOX object model. Because a user can be a member of many groups, the User object has a Groups collection that lists the groups of which that user is a member. Similarly, a group can contain multiple users, and the Group object has a Users collection that lists its members.

You can add a user to or remove a user from a group by using the User object's Groups collection. For example, the following code might be helpful if an employee is promoted:

```
cat.Users("Joe").Groups.Delete "Engineers"
cat.Users("Joe").Groups.Append "Managers"
```

You could also accomplish the same task by using the Users collection of the Group object, as shown here:

```
cat.Groups("Engineers").Users.Delete "Joe"
cat.Groups("Managers").Users.Append "Joe"
```

ADOX Security Sample

The following code sample helped me grasp the concept of using Jet security through the ADOX object model. This code creates a new Access database with an Orders table. The code then creates several new users and groups. Some of the users are placed in the Sales group, while one is placed in the Guests group. The Sales group is given read, insert, and update (but not delete) permissions to the Orders table, while the Guests group has no permissions on the table. The sample then uses ADO code to simulate each user logging in and trying to perform an action in order to demonstrate that the permissions were set up properly.

> **NOTE** Database security is not a minor topic that we can cover thoroughly in a couple of pages. Jet programmers who want to learn about Jet security (if you're reading this portion of the appendix, this probably applies to you) should read Chapter 10, "Managing Security," of the *Microsoft Jet Database Engine Programmer's Guide, Second Edition,* by Dan Haught and Jim Ferguson [Microsoft Press, 1997].

```
Dim strPathToMDB As String, strPathToMDW As String
Dim strConn As String, strSQL As String
Dim cat As ADOX.Catalog, tblOrders As ADOX.Table
Dim cn As ADODB.Connection, rs As ADODB.Recordset
```

(continued)

```
'Initialize path to the new database.
strPathToMDB = "C:\Windows\Desktop\Secure.mdb"
'Initialize path to an existing Access 2000 security database.
strPathToMDW = "D:\Office\Access2000\Office\System.MDW"
strConn = "Provider=Microsoft.Jet.OLEDB.4.0;" & _
          "Data Source=" & strPathToMDB & ";" & _
          "Jet OLEDB:System Database=" & strPathToMDW & ";"

If Dir(strPathToMDB) <> "" Then Kill strPathToMDB
Set cat = New ADOX.Catalog
cat.Create strConn & "User ID=Admin;Password=;"

Set tblOrders = New ADOX.Table
With tblOrders
    Set .ParentCatalog = cat
    .Name = "Orders"
    .Columns.Append "OrderID", adInteger
    !OrderID.Properties("AutoIncrement") = True
    .Columns.Append "OrderDate", adDate
    .Columns.Append "OrderAmt", adCurrency
    .Keys.Append "PK_Orders", adKeyPrimary, "OrderID"
End With
cat.Tables.Append tblOrders

'Create users.
cat.Users.Append "Al", ""
cat.Users.Append "Beth", ""
cat.Users.Append "Charles", ""
cat.Users.Append "Zed", ""

'Create groups.
cat.Groups.Append "Sales"
cat.Groups.Append "Guests"

'Add users to groups.
cat.Groups("Sales").Users.Append "Al"
cat.Groups("Sales").Users.Append "Beth"
cat.Groups("Sales").Users.Append "Charles"
cat.Groups("Guests").Users.Append "Zed"

'Set permissions on Orders table for groups.
'Allow the people in sales to modify the contents of the Orders table.
'Prevent guests from viewing the contents of the table.
cat.Groups("Sales").SetPermissions "Orders", adPermObjTable, _
    adAccessGrant, adRightRead + adRightInsert + adRightUpdate
```

```
cat.Groups("Guests").SetPermissions "Orders", adPermObjTable, _
    adAccessDeny, adRightNone

'Close this connection.
cat.ActiveConnection.Close
Set cat = Nothing

strSQL = "SELECT * FROM Orders"
'Log in as someone in sales and add an order.
Set cn = New ADODB.Connection
cn.Open strConn, "Al", ""
Set rs = New ADODB.Recordset
rs.Open strSQL, cn, adOpenKeyset, adLockOptimistic, adCmdText
rs.AddNew Array("OrderDate", "OrderAmt"), _
        Array(Date, "100.00")
rs.Close
cn.Close

'Log in as someone in sales, and modify an order.
cn.Open strConn, "Beth", ""
rs.Open strSQL, cn, adOpenKeyset, adLockOptimistic, adCmdText
rs.Update Array("OrderAmt"), _
        Array("200.00")
rs.Close
cn.Close

'Log in as someone in sales, and try to delete an order.
'According to the permissions we've set, this should fail.
cn.Open strConn, "Charles", ""
rs.Open strSQL, cn, adOpenKeyset, adLockOptimistic, adCmdText
On Error Resume Next
rs.Delete
If Err.Number <> 0 Then
    Err.Clear
    cn.Errors.Clear
    rs.CancelUpdate
Else
    MsgBox "Oops. This user should not have been able to delete a " & _
        "row in the Orders table."
End If
On Error GoTo 0
rs.Close
cn.Close

'Log in as a general user, and query the Orders table.
'According to the permissions we've set, this should fail.
```

(continued)

```
cn.Open strConn, "Zed", ""
On Error Resume Next
rs.Open strSQL, cn, adOpenKeyset, adLockOptimistic, adCmdText
If Err.Number <> 0 Then
    Err.Clear
    cn.Errors.Clear
Else
    MsgBox "Oops. This user should not have been able to view the " & _
        "Orders table."
    rs.Close
End If
On Error GoTo 0
cn.Close
```

> **NOTE** Be sure to check out the "Questions That Should Be Asked More Frequently" section at the end of this appendix if you have trouble running this code a second time.

JRO

JRO includes Jet database replication features and provides the ability to compact Jet databases and refresh the data in the Jet engine's cache. The JRO object model includes three main objects: the JetEngine object, the Replica object, and the Filter object. First I'll cover the JetEngine object, and later in this appendix I'll discuss the Replica object. Version 2.5 of the JRO objects can be accessed in Visual Basic by selecting Microsoft Jet And Replication Objects 2.5 Library in the References dialog box.

JetEngine Object

The JRO JetEngine object exposes two methods—*CompactDatabase* and *Refresh-Cache*—that provide the ADO and Jet programmer with features previously available only through the DAO DBEngine object. Let's take a brief look at each of these methods.

CompactDatabase method

When you delete a row in an Access table, that row is "lost"—in other words, you can no longer view the row. However, that data is not removed from the physical database file. As a result, continued use of an Access database causes the file to grow.

Access has the ability to "compact" a database. When you compact a database, you recover its lost space. The Jet engine essentially copies the database's structure and the contents of its tables into a new copy of the database. The engine does not copy deleted rows. Thus, the new copy of the database is smaller than the original copy that contained deleted rows.

The *CompactDatabase* method also allows you to control attributes of the new database, including its format (Access 2000, Access 97, and so on), database password, and locale. For more information on each of these options, see the documentation on the *CompactDatabase* method in the Jet and Replication Objects portion of the Platform SDK.

Here's an example that uses *CompactDatabase* to compact a database:

```
strConnOriginal = "Provider=Microsoft.Jet.OLEDB.4.0;" & _
                  "Data Source=D:\Program Files\MyApp\Orig.MDB;"
strConnNew = "Provider=Microsoft.Jet.OLEDB.4.0;" & _
             "Data Source=D:\Program Files\MyApp\New.MDB;"
Set jroEngine = New JRO.JetEngine
jroEngine.CompactDatabase strConnOriginal, strConnNew
```

RefreshCache **method**

Before I describe the *RefreshCache* method of the JetEngine object, let me first discuss an extremely important concept about the Jet architecture—in my estimation, a concept that eludes too many Jet programmers.

You can build a database application and have multiple users simultaneously reading from and writing to your database. Figure A-2 shows multiple clients accessing a data server. Applications that use SQL Server and Oracle databases employ this type of architecture regardless of whether the application uses a traditional two-tiered or an *n*-tiered approach. While the database engine caches data to improve performance by decreasing the number of times it communicates with the hard drive, all clients receive their data from the same database engine. The important point to take away from Figure A-2 is that all clients access data through the same database engine.

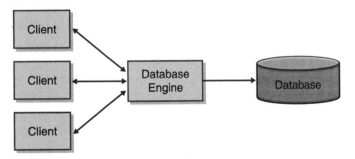

Figure A-2 *Multiple clients accessing a database through a single database engine.*

Multiuser Jet database applications look a little different, regardless of whether you use DAO or ADO. Each client loads its own copy of the Jet engine into its process. Each copy of the Jet engine reads and writes to the database file, as shown in Figure A-3.

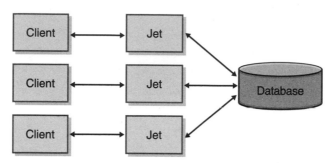

Figure A-3 *Multiple clients accessing a Jet database.*

There's more than a simple structural difference between the Jet architecture and that of a central database engine such as SQL Server or Oracle. In the Jet architecture, each copy of the Jet engine caches data. When you ask the Jet engine to modify a row of data, that change is initially made only in the Jet engine's cache. The change is not written to the database file until later.

Say you add a row to a table in an Access database. Other users won't see that row until your copy of the Jet engine flushes its cache and writes the new row to the database file. You can force the Jet engine to write changes to the database file by wrapping them in a transaction. For more information on the intricacies of the Jet engine's cache and how you can fine-tune its behaviors, see the *Microsoft Jet Database Engine Programmer's Guide, Second Edition.*

Armed with some knowledge of the Jet architecture, let's move on to the *RefreshCache* method. When you run a query against an Access database, the Jet engine caches some data. A change made by another user that has been written to the Access database file after you've run your query might not be visible even after you requery your Recordset object. Here's an example:

```
'Connect to your database.
Set cn = New ADODB.Connection
cn.Open strConn

'Create a table for testing purposes.
cn.BeginTrans
strSQL = "CREATE TABLE CacheTest (ID int " & _
        "CONSTRAINT PK_CacheTest PRIMARY KEY, Description varchar(20))"
cn.Execute strSQL, , adCmdText + adExecuteNoRecords

'Insert a row into the new table.
strSQL = "INSERT INTO CacheTest (ID, Description) " & _
        "VALUES (1, 'First Record')"
cn.Execute strSQL, , adCmdText + adExecuteNoRecords

'Force the Jet engine to write the new row and table to the database file.
cn.CommitTrans
```

```
'Run a query to check the number of rows in the table.
strSQL = "SELECT COUNT(*) FROM CacheTest"
Set rs = cn.Execute(strSQL, , adCmdText)
Debug.Print rs(0)

'Use another connection to simulate a second user adding
' a row to the same table.
Set cnOtherUser = New ADODB.Connection
cnOtherUser.Open strConn
cnOtherUser.BeginTrans
strSQL = "INSERT INTO CacheTest (ID, Description) " & _
         "VALUES (2, 'Second Record')"
cnOtherUser.Execute strSQL, , adCmdText + adExecuteNoRecords

'Force the Jet engine to write the new row to the database file.
cnOtherUser.CommitTrans

'Requery to determine the current number of rows in the table.
rs.Requery
Debug.Print rs(0)
```

Although this code forces the Jet engine to write the row added by the second user to the database file, a requery of the Recordset object does not see the second row. To force the Jet engine to refresh the data in its cache, use the JetEngine object's *RefreshCache* method:

```
'Force the Jet engine to write the new row to the database file.
cnOtherUser.CommitTrans

'Force the Jet engine to refresh the cache on the main connection.
Set jroEngine = New JRO.JetEngine
jroEngine.RefreshCache cn

'Requery to determine the current number of rows in the table.
rs.Requery
Debug.Print rs(0)
```

Now, when the code requeries the Recordset, you'll see the new row in the table.

Jet Replication

Replication is a process by which a database is duplicated, usually on different machines, and synchronized when changes are made. Like Jet security, Jet replication is a topic that we can't cover in nearly enough detail here. To develop a strong understanding of Jet replication, I highly recommend reading Chapter 7, "Database Replication," of the *Microsoft Jet Database Engine Programmer's Guide, Second Edition*. Consider this portion of the appendix an overview that will make the material in Chapter 7 of the programmer's guide a little easier to digest.

When you mark a database for replication, the Jet engine creates a number of system tables that track which changes must be replicated to other databases. To mark a database as "replicable," create a JRO Replica object and call its *MakeReplicable* method, as shown here:

```
Set jroReplica = New JRO.Replica
jroReplica.MakeReplicable strPathToMasterMDB, False
```

The first parameter specifies the location of the database you want to mark as replicable. The second parameter controls the granularity of the tracking of changes. The default value for this parameter, which is True, indicates that you want to track changes by each column. This way, if two users change the same row but don't modify the same column in that row, both changes will succeed when replicated. A value of False would generate a conflict in the same scenario, similar to an optimistic updating conflict with Recordsets that use the ADO Cursor Engine's batch updating features.

You might not want all objects in a database to participate in replication. To control whether an object will participate in replication, call the Replica object's *SetObjectReplicability* method. The following code specifies that the table named LocalTable will not be replicated:

```
jroReplica.SetObjectReplicability "LocalTable", "Tables", False
```

The first parameter of the method specifies the object, and the second parameter specifies the type of object you want to control. The third parameter accepts a Boolean value that denotes whether you want the object to participate in replication. The Replica object also has a *GetObjectReplicability* method that you can use to programmatically determine whether an object in the database is targeted for replication. This method's syntax, shown in the following code, is nearly identical to the syntax of *SetObjectReplicability*:

```
MsgBox jroReplica.GetObjectReplicability("LocalTable", "Tables")
```

Once you've set the "replicability" of all the objects in the master database, you can create the replica databases by calling the *CreateReplica* method of the Replica object:

```
jroReplica.CreateReplica strReplicaMDB, "JROTest", _
                    jrRepTypeFull, jrRepVisibilityLocal
```

Supply the location of the new replica in the first parameter and a description of this replica in the second parameter. The third parameter indicates which type of replica you want to create and accepts a value from ReplicaTypeEnum. The *CreateReplica* method allows you to create full and partial replicas. A partial replica uses a filter to determine which data in the parent database it will receive. This parameter is optional and defaults to jrRepTypeFull, which is a full replica. The fourth parameter specifies the value for the Visibility property of the replica you're creating. This property affects how conflicts are handled when changes in the replica that are submitted to the parent database cause conflicts.

The *CreateReplica* method also accepts optional fifth and sixth parameters to control the priority of the changes in the replica and whether the data in the replica is updatable. By default, the new replica's Priority property will be 90 percent of its parent, and the data in the replica will be updatable.

To control which data a partial replica will receive, use a JRO Filter object. The code that follows creates a partial replica based on a master database, generates a filter for the partial replica, and then calls the Replica object's *PopulatePartial* method to populate the partial replica:

```
'Create the JRO Replica object.
Set jroReplica = New JRO.Replica
'Connect to the master database.
jroReplica.ActiveConnection = "Provider=Microsoft.Jet.OLEDB.4.0;" & _
                              "Data Source=" & strMasterMDB & ";"
'Create a partial replica.
jroReplica.CreateReplica strPartialMDB, "JROPartial", _
                jrRepTypePartial, jrRepVisibilityGlobal
'Close the connection to the master database.
jroReplica.ActiveConnection.Close
strConn = "Provider=Microsoft.Jet.OLEDB.4.0;" & _
          "Data Source=" & strPartialMDB & ";" & _
          "Mode=Share Exclusive;"
'Connect to the partial replica.
jroReplica.ActiveConnection = strConn
'Specify a filter for the partial replica.
jroReplica.Filters.Append "Customers", jrFilterTypeTable, _
                "[State]='MA' or [State]='WA'"
'Populate the partial replica.
jroReplica.PopulatePartial strMasterMDB
```

Now that you understand how to create full and partial replicas and you've read Chapter 7 of the *Microsoft Jet Database Engine Programmer's Guide, Second Edition,* (nudge, nudge) to determine a replication topology, you need to understand how to synchronize the replicas.

The JRO Replica object has a *Synchronize* method that you can use to transmit changes from one database to another. The following code connects to the master database and then transmits the changes to a replica database:

```
Set jroReplica = New JRO.Replica
Set jroReplica.ActiveConnection = strConnMaster
jroReplica.Synchronize strPathToReplicaMDB, jrSyncTypeExport, _
                jrSyncModeDirect
```

The *Synchronize* method accepts three parameters. The first parameter indicates the location of the database with which you want to synchronize the current replica. In this case, you've connected the master database and you're submitting the location of one of the replica databases in this parameter. The second parameter controls the direction of the synchronization and accepts a value from SyncTypeEnum. Here you're exporting changes, which means changes stored in the master database are transmitted to the replica. You can also specify that changes are only imported (jrSyncTypeImport) or both imported and exported (jrSyncTypeImpExp), which is the default. The third parameter controls the synchronization mode and accepts a value from SyncModeEnum. Jet supports direct replication (jrSyncModeDirect); indirect replication (jrSyncModeIndirect), which is the default; and Internet replication (jrSyncModeInternet). Let's briefly discuss synchronization modes before discussing synchronization directions.

Direct synchronization is the simplest synchronization mode. With this mode, the Jet engine has a direct connection between the two databases being synchronized. With indirect synchronization, as its name implies, no direct connection exists between the databases. Imagine that you want to indirectly export changes from one database to another. You could examine one database's changes, log those changes in a small file, and close the connection to that database. Later, you could connect to the other database and modify its contents based on entries in the log file. This, in a nutshell, is how indirect synchronization works. Internet synchronization is similar to direct synchronization, except two copies of the Jet engine are used over HTTP. Microsoft Office 2000 Developer edition is required for Internet synchronization and includes more documentation on the topic.

When you call the *Synchronize* method, the second parameter, *SyncType*, controls the synchronization direction. You can export changes in your current database to the database with which you are synchronizing. You can also import changes, or both import and export changes. If only the master database is updatable, you'll need to transmit changes in one direction only: from the master to the replicas. If you make the replicas updatable, you'll need to transmit changes in both directions when synchronizing.

Two-way synchronization poses challenges similar to using batch optimistic locking in ADO Recordsets. By the time you transmit your updates to the central database, another user might have modified the same data in such a way that your updates fail. Unlike batch optimistic locking in ADO, Jet replication does not provide much information if a conflict occurs. The conflicts are logged in a separate system table. When you call the *Synchronize* method of the JRO Replica object, you can determine whether conflicts occurred by checking the ConflictTables property on the Replica object.

The ConflictTables property returns an ADO Recordset object. The first Field object in this Recordset contains the name of the table that contained a conflict. The second Field object in this Recordset contains the name of the system table in which that conflict has been stored. If you synchronize two databases and conflicts occur, and then you open either database with Access, Access will inform you that conflicts occurred and the Microsoft Replication Conflict Viewer will prompt you to resolve the conflicts.

The following code shows a simplistic example of how to examine and resolve conflicts programmatically:

```
Set jroReplica = New JRO.Replica
jroReplica.ActiveConnection = "Provider=Microsoft.Jet.OLEDB.4.0;" & _
                              "Data Source=" & strMasterMDB & ";"
jroReplica.Synchronize strReplicaMDB, jrSyncTypeImpExp, jrSyncModeDirect
If jroReplica.ConflictTables.EOF And jroReplica.ConflictTables.BOF Then
    MsgBox "No conflicts"
Else
    Set rsConflicts = New ADODB.Recordset
    Do While Not jroReplica.ConflictTables.EOF
        'Build a query to examine the conflicts logged in the system table.
        strSQL = "SELECT * FROM " & jroReplica.ConflictTables(1)
        'Examine the conflicts logged in the master database.
        rsConflicts.Open strSQL, cnMaster, adOpenKeyset, _
                    adLockOptimistic, adCmdText
        Do While Not rsConflicts.EOF
            'Resolve the conflict.
            rsConflicts.Delete
            rsConflicts.MoveNext
        Loop
        rsConflicts.Close
        'Examine the conflicts logged in the replica database.
        rsConflicts.Open strSQL, cnReplica, adOpenKeyset, _
                    adLockOptimistic, adCmdText
        Do While Not rsConflicts.EOF
            'Resolve the conflict.
            rsConflicts.Delete
            rsConflicts.MoveNext
        Loop
        rsConflicts.Close
    Loop
    Set rsConflicts = Nothing
End If
```

QUESTIONS THAT SHOULD BE ASKED MORE FREQUENTLY

Q. *Does an Access QueryDef correspond to an ADOX View or Procedure object?*

A.   Access considers all queries to be QueryDefs, but many database systems categorize queries as either views or stored procedures. So, is an Access QueryDef a view or a stored procedure? The general rule is that the QueryDef is a view unless it's an action query (UPDATE, DELETE, INSERT, and so on), or unless it accepts parameters, in which case it's considered a stored procedure. If you add a QueryDef to an Access database, you can use *Views.Append* or *Procedures.Append* regardless of whether the QueryDef corresponds to a view or a stored procedure. In the Make Northwind sample on the companion CD, I add all QueryDefs to the database through *Views.Append*.

Q. *I can't seem to add a QueryDef to my Access database. I don't get any errors, so I think I'm creating it correctly, but I don't see the QueryDef when I open my database in Access. Am I doing something wrong?*

A.   In this case, if you're not generating an error, you're not doing anything wrong. This behavior is the result of a problem in the Jet 4.0 OLE DB Provider. This problem is not isolated to ADOX. If you generate your own action query to create a QueryDef, you will not see the new QueryDef when you open the database in Access. However, the QueryDef does exist. You can see it in the Visual Basic DataView window, and you can call the QueryDef with ADO.

Q. *The sample code in the "ADOX Security Sample" section of this appendix was handy, but I'm having problems with it. I was able to run it once, but when I ran it a second time, I got errors saying that the account name already exists. What went wrong?*

A.   Actually, nothing went wrong. The behavior is by design, but it's also worth explaining. Let's take a quick look at the first line of code that generates this error:

```
cat.Users.Append "Al", ""
```

In this code, it appears that you're adding a user to your database. However, what's actually happening is that you're adding the user to the Jet security database. When you run the code a second time, you've already deleted and re-created your database, but you're not deleting and re-creating the Jet security database. For that reason, the account still exists in the security database and you receive an error.

If you are simply using the sample code to learn a little about Jet security but don't plan to use it in your application, this answer is probably sufficient. But if you want to use Jet security in your application, let me again recommend that you read Chapter 10 of the *Microsoft Jet Database Engine Programmer's Guide, Second Edition.*

Q. *Replication seemed like a great idea to me until I came to the end of the section on replication in this appendix. It seemed like you left out the resolution that would help me understand how to resolve conflicts easily. Did I miss something?*

A. The replication discussion in this appendix ends abruptly because replication that involves two-way synchronization (in which the replica databases allow updates) is extremely complex. If a simple solution to resolving conflicts existed, I would have included it. My advice is to use two-way synchronization only if you can structure your database and your application in such a way that conflicts can be avoided or easily resolved.

For example, allowing the replica databases to modify a balance due field in a customer table would be unwise if you plan to use two-way synchronization. Say that you have a number of phone operators, each entering orders into a local replica of your main database. If two operators receive orders for the same customer, log their orders in an orders table, and update the customer's balance due locally, at least one of these changes will generate a conflict when the operators synchronize their databases. A better architecture for this scenario would be to have no balance due field in the customer table. The balance due could be generated instead by a query that examines the customer's order and payment histories.

Q. *When I marked my database for replication, the auto-incrementing field started to behave differently. It looks like it's now generating random numbers rather than generating sequential numbers. Why is that?*

A. The auto-incrementing field is behaving this way to prevent primary key violations. If the database continued to generate new values in the standard sequence (1, 2, 3, and so on), you would run into serious problems if you employed two-way synchronization and based the table's primary key on the auto-incrementing field. Suppose you create a master database and two replicas. And suppose you have an Orders table that uses an auto-incrementing field as the primary key. If you place a new row in the Orders table of each replica, each new row will have the same value for its primary key field, and the second database to submit its changes to the master database will generate a primary key violation. To decrease the chances of such violations occurring, Jet automatically changes auto-incrementing fields to use random numbers instead of linear sequences.

Appendix B

Companion CD Sample Code

As I mentioned in Chapter 1, I designed the sample code on the companion CD to help you learn more about ADO. I'm all for "best practice" code samples, but what works best for a single-user Microsoft Jet database application won't work best for a multiuser, multitiered application accessing an Oracle or Microsoft SQL Server database.

I wrote the code included on the companion CD using Microsoft Visual Basic 6 for a few reasons. Sample code written in Visual Basic is fairly simple to follow compared to code written in Microsoft Visual C++ or Microsoft Visual J++. Also, Visual Basic code doesn't require Microsoft Internet Information Services to run—unlike programming Active Server Pages (ASP) using Microsoft Visual InterDev. The last reason is that Visual Basic is the language I'm most comfortable with. I'd love to see better Visual C++ and Visual J++ samples that show how to use ADO, but I'm not the person to write those samples. While the code on the companion CD won't help someone who is new to Visual C++ or Visual J++ understand how to instantiate ADO objects or COM objects in general, it will help programmers who are experienced in those and other languages discover more about ADO.

WHAT'S MY CONSTANT?

While this sample probably won't help you to learn more about ADO directly, I've leveraged this code as a tool in other projects and samples.

How many times have you checked the value of a property only to realize that you don't know what constant or combination of constants that value represents? If you were to check the Status property of the current record of the Recordset object to try to determine the cause of a conflict, would you rather see 2052 or adRecConcurrency-Violation + adRecDeleted?

The What's My Constant sample doesn't contain any forms. Instead, the sample is a series of class modules that you can compile into an ActiveX DLL. Once you have compiled the project, you can use the classes in your own projects. For example, say you had trapped for an optimistic updating conflict in your code and you wanted to understand what constant (or combination of constants) that value corresponds to. You could use this dynamic-link library in your project by adding a reference to the WhatsMyConstant library and then adding the following code:

```
Set objTranslateConstant = New WhatsMyConstant.ADOConstants
MsgBox objTranslateConstant.GetRecordStatus(rs.Status)
```

Now, rather than knowing only that the Status property returned a value such as 2052, you would know the constant or combination of constants in the enumeration that correspond to that value. In this case the code would display the string "adRecConcurrencyViolation + adRecDeleted" in a dialog box.

The What's My Constant sample contains separate class modules for ADO, ADOX, JRO, and RDS constants. Each function within a class accepts a value from a particular constant enumeration and returns the name of the constant (or combination of constants) that the value passed into the function represents.

As someone who has learned a lot about ADO by trying to answer my own questions, I've found this code quite helpful. In fact, you'll see portions of the code in this sample appear in other samples on the companion CD. You're welcome to compile the library and use it in your own projects or simply copy portions of the code from the sample.

CURSORS

Chapter 7 teaches you about the different cursor types and some of their properties. The two main forms in the Cursors sample—frmGoFish and frmSeeChanges—can help you build on that knowledge.

Remember the game Go Fish? In this simple card game, you ask another player for a specific card such as an ace or a king. If that player does not have that card in his or her hand, you must "go fish" by taking a card from the deck. If you're lucky, the card you draw from the deck will be the card you asked for.

Many programmers run into cursor-related problems when they do not receive the type of cursor they asked for. I often hear programmers say they're experiencing unexpected behavior when they open a particular type of cursor. Because I usually wind up asking questions such as, "I know you requested a keyset cursor, but did you get what you asked for?" I decided to name one of the forms in this sample frmGoFish. You can use this form, shown in Figure B-1, to supply a connection string and a query string, as well as values for the Recordset's CursorLocation, CursorType, and LockType properties. After you run the query, the form will indicate the resulting values for the Recordset's CursorLocation, CursorType, LockType, and Record-Count properties, as well as whether the Recordset supports bookmarks.

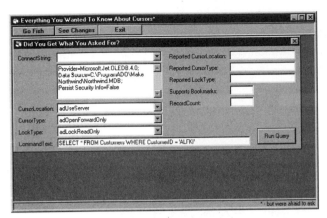

Figure B-1. *Click the Go Fish button to bring up the frmGoFish form, titled Did You Get What You Asked For?*

The other main form in the project, frmSeeChanges, will help you understand which changes made by other users will be visible in your Recordset. Because providing this functionality is quite an undertaking, I've tried to make this sample helpful without making it overly complex. Consider it a starting point on which you can build.

With this form, shown in Figure B-2, you can specify a connection string, as well as values for the Recordset's CursorLocation, CursorType, LockType, and CacheSize properties. When you click the Run Query button, the form's code connects to the specified database and creates a sample table, populates that table with 20 rows, retrieves those rows into a Recordset, and then simulates changes made by other users by modifying, deleting, and inserting rows in the database (but not in the Recordset). You can then navigate through the Recordset with a simplistic data control to see whether some of those changes are visible.

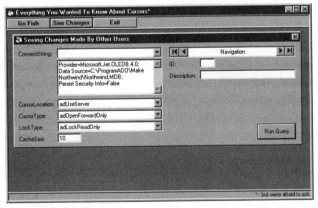

Figure B-2. *Click the See Changes button to bring up the frmSeeChanges form, titled Seeing Changes Made By Other Users.*

The table that this form's code creates, SeeChanges, is simple. It has an integer field named ID, which serves as its primary key, and a Description field. When the code opens the Recordset object, the table contains 20 rows with ID values of 1–20 and a description of "Original Entry". After the code opens the Recordset, it modifies some rows by setting the description of rows 2, 3, 5, 7, 11, 13, 17, and 19 to "Modified By Another User". The code also deletes rows with IDs of 1, 4, 9, and 16, and it creates new rows with IDs of 21–24 and the description "Entered By Another User".

Both frmGoFish and frmSeeChanges use code copied from the What's My Constant sample to display the names of constants associated with values retrieved from the Recordset's CursorLocation, CursorType, and LockType properties. This code appears in the module named modADOConstants.

These two forms also use a common form called frmManageConnectionStrings, shown in Figure B-3, that allows the user to manipulate and store multiple connection strings for the form. You access this form by selecting <Manage Connection Strings> from the ConnectString drop-down list box. The user interface for frmManageConnectionStrings is fairly simplistic, but it lets you add, edit, and delete connection strings and make them available on the frmGoFish and frmSeeChanges forms in the ConnectString drop-down list box. There is one highlight of the code for this form that I'd like to point out. If you double-click the connection string text box while you're in Edit mode, the code invokes the Data Link Properties dialog box to help you edit the connection string. The frmGoFish and frmSeeChanges forms in this sample use similar code. I also use the frmManageConnectionStrings form in the Detecting Conflicts sample.

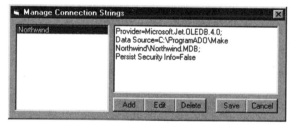

Figure B-3. *The frmManageConnectionStrings form, titled Manage Connection Strings.*

NOTE   There's one minor "gotcha" to using the Data Link Properties dialog box in these sample applications. By default, if you enter a password in the dialog box, that password will not be returned with the rest of the connection information. Check the Allow Saving Password check box to return the password in the connection string.

There's a module called modSettingsFile that I use to store and retrieve settings for a particular application. But this code doesn't store this information in the Microsoft Windows Registry. Instead, this code persists a Recordset to store data in a settings file where the application resides. Why store settings this way? Not only to familiarize myself with using ADO's persistence functionality, but also because I work on a number of different computers on the same network. I like the idea of copying the executable and the settings file to another computer so that I can use the same settings on that computer. You'll also find this module in the Detecting Conflicts sample.

DETECTING CONFLICTS

Chapter 12, which discusses batch updating conflicts, might make the process of detecting and resolving conflicts seem more complex than it really is. The chapter examines the features of the ADO object model that you can utilize when you encounter batch updating conflicts, and I felt a sample application that demonstrates how to use these features would be helpful.

The Detecting Conflicts sample lets you select which types of conflicts you want to learn more about and then causes them to occur. When you click the Cause Conflicts button in the Detecting Conflicts window, the sample code executes a number of steps that cause the conflicts to occur and records information about those conflicts in a log file. Let's examine these steps now.

First the sample connects to your database by using the connection string the user supplies. Then the sample creates and populates its own table, named Conflict-Test, in the database. Next the contents of this table are retrieved into a Recordset object. The code modifies the contents of the Recordset and then records the pending changes (the contents of each record and the value of the Status property) in the log file. The sample then modifies the contents of the table to simulate the changes another user would make, causing the conflicts to occur. Finally the sample submits the pending changes to the database and logs information about any conflicts that occurred.

I wanted this sample to be simple and flexible, but those two traits are often mutually exclusive. In order to allow the user to select which types of conflicts to cause, I had to come up with a way to handle those selections dynamically. So I created a user-defined type (UDT) called udtConflict (defined in the modDetecting-Conflicts module) that contains information about each type of conflict. Actually, I call these items "conflicts" for lack of a better term. Some of these items, such as a successful update, do not constitute a conflict. Take a look at the comments with the UDT declaration and at the *InitConflicts* procedure in the module. This information should make the purpose of the UDT's different attributes fairly clear.

Before the sample submits the pending changes to the database, it loops through the Recordset and records information about those pending changes in the log file. Why did I add this code to the sample? As I mentioned in the answer to the last question in the "Questions That Should Be Asked More Frequently" section of Chapter 8, you can use the ADO Cursor Engine to store pending changes and then call stored procedures based on those changes. This portion of the code demonstrates how you can use the Status property of a pending change to determine which type of change it represents: insertion, deletion, or modification. Assuming you'll need different stored procedures for each type of change, you can use this information to determine which stored procedure to call. Or you can generate and submit your own action query instead.

After the sample logs the pending changes and modifies the table, it submits those changes by calling the *UpdateBatch* method on the Recordset. It then logs information about any conflicts that occurred. The code records the value of the Status property for each record that contains a conflict, as well as information about the Value, OriginalValue, and UnderlyingValue properties for each Field object. Note that the code traps for errors when trying to access these properties in case the record or its counterpart in the database has been deleted. Once the sample has logged information about the conflicts, it displays the contents of the log file in Notepad. Using this information, you should be able to determine how to resolve your conflicts.

The Detecting Conflicts sample uses a copy of the same form that the Cursors sample uses to manage connection strings (frmManageConnectionStrings), as well as a copy of the module for interacting with the settings file (modSettingsFile) and a procedure copied from the What's My Constant sample (*GetRecordStatus*).

Huge Hierarchy

Although Chapter 14 covers hierarchical recordsets in some depth, I wanted to build a sample that illustrates how helpful they can be in certain situations. The Huge Hierarchy sample retrieves information from the sample Northwind database into, well, a huge hierarchy.

Before we talk about the structure of the hierarchy, let's briefly talk about how the code connects to your database. The Huge Hierarchy sample uses a copy of the modSettingsFile module to interact with a local settings file. The connection string that was last used successfully is stored in this settings file. If you are running this sample for the first time or if you couldn't connect to your database the last time you ran this sample, the initialization code displays the familiar Data Link Properties dialog box, prompting you to indicate the location of a Northwind database. (If you don't have SQL Server 7 or Microsoft Data Engine [MSDE] installed and you don't have a copy of the sample Microsoft Access database, you can create your own copy with the Make Northwind sample described later in this appendix.) You don't have to specify in the Data Link Properties dialog box that you plan to use MSDataShape (the OLE DB provider for data shaping). The code in the sample handles that for you.

Once you connect to a Northwind database, the Huge Hierarchy sample displays a multiple-document interface (MDI) parent form that lists the available customers in a drop-down list box. Select a customer, and click the Go button to display the hierarchy of information on the customer's orders in a new MDI child form, as shown in Figure B-4.

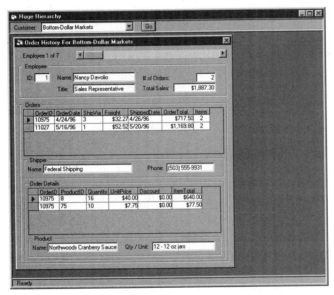

Figure B-4. *Hierarchy containing a customer's orders.*

Now let's talk about the hierarchy itself. This sample retrieves all order information for a customer into a hierarchical recordset and displays that data on a form. That customer's orders are grouped first by the employee who took the order. For each employee, you can see information about that employee, the number of orders that the employee placed for this customer, and the combined total for those orders. You can navigate through the employees who placed orders for this customer by using the horizontal scroll bar that appears above the employee information.

Below the employee information, the sample displays in a grid each of the orders the employee placed for this customer. This information includes the total cost of the order and the total number of items in the order—information that does not appear in the Northwind database's Orders table. The data shape provider's aggregation features let you gather this information from each order's child data, pulled from the Order Details table. Because each order can be sent through a different shipper, information about the shipper that's handling the selected order appears beneath the grid of orders. The sample also displays the items in each order in a grid beneath the shipper information, as well as information about the product ordered.

The MDI child form that displays all this information is called frmHugeHierarchy, and the code that generates the hierarchical Recordset is located in the form's *Load* event. Figure B-5 breaks down this mammoth query, making it easier to follow.

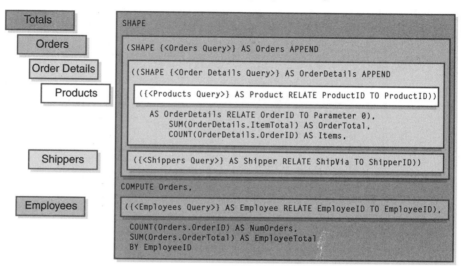

Figure B-5. *Hierarchical query and its syntax.*

Figure B-5 uses the shorthand <Orders Query>—rather than including that portion of the query—to save space and make the hierarchical query easier to follow. Here are those queries, copied from the *Form_Load* procedure:

```
strOrdersQuery = "SELECT OrderID, CustomerID, OrderDate, " & _
                "EmployeeID, ShipVia, Freight, ShippedDate " & _
                "FROM Orders WHERE CustomerID = '" & CustomerID & "'"

strOrderDetailsQuery = "SELECT OrderID, ProductID, Quantity, " & _
                "UnitPrice, Discount, " & _
                "((Quantity * UnitPrice) - Discount) " & _
                "AS ItemTotal FROM [Order Details] " & _
                "WHERE OrderID = ?"

strProductsQuery = "SELECT ProductID, ProductName, " & _
                "QuantityPerUnit FROM Products"

strShippersQuery = "SELECT ShipperID, CompanyName, Phone FROM Shippers"

strEmployeesQuery = "SELECT EmployeeID, FirstName + ' ' + LastName " & _
                "AS EmployeeName, Title FROM Employees"
```

I used a parameterized query for the order detail information so that I retrieve only the details in the orders for the customer, thus improving performance and minimizing the amount of data to store in the hierarchy. For the queries to retrieve product, shipper, and employee information, I simply retrieved the entire table. Why? I could have used parameterized queries for this information. However, I estimated that a large percentage of the data in the Products, Shippers, and Employees tables would be retrieved in each hierarchy, and therefore I would see no benefit in using the parameterized syntax.

Once the code executes the query to generate the hierarchical recordset, all that's left to do is bind controls to the different levels of the hierarchy. As I've mentioned elsewhere in this book, I'm generally not a big fan of bound controls. However, in this sample they're used only to display the contents of the recordset, and they've greatly simplified the code in the application.

While the hierarchical query itself is very complex, the code in the form is incredibly simple: open a hierarchical recordset, obtain references to the different levels of the hierarchy, and bind controls to those levels. That's it. Look at the amount of information on that form, and then think about how little code it took to retrieve and display it all. And that's the point of the sample—in some situations, hierarchical recordsets can greatly simplify your code.

IDENTITY IN HIERARCHY

The programmers I've spoken to who have worked with hierarchical recordsets have been pleased, overall, with their experiences. However, they frequently ask about one specific scenario: how do you build a hierarchy that uses a relationship based on an auto-incrementing identity field if you need to add new records to that hierarchy?

For example, imagine a hierarchy involving the Orders and Order Details tables in the Northwind database. The logical field on which to base a relationship is the OrderID field. Unfortunately, you'll encounter problems if you place new orders and details for those orders into this hierarchy. The Identity In Hierarchy example is designed to help you understand why this scenario has problems and to offer an alternative solution.

The Identity In Hierarchy sample works with the SQL Server OLE DB provider and ODBC driver with a Northwind database from SQL Server 7 or MSDE, or with the Jet 4.0 OLE DB Provider and a Northwind database in Access 2000 format. An important part of the sample will not work with databases created using previous versions of Access; the ADO cursor engine will be unable to retrieve the newly generated auto-increment identity values.

Like the Huge Hierarchy sample, the Identity In Hierarchy sample uses the modSettingsFile module to try retrieving the last successful connection string from a settings file. If this attempt fails, the sample displays the Data Link Properties dialog box to request a valid connection string to connect to a Northwind database and then saves that string in the settings file for future use.

Once the sample successfully connects to a Northwind database, it displays an MDI parent form with three menu options: Bad Hierarchy, Good Hierarchy, and Order Entry. If you click the first option, the sample displays a form called frmBadHierarchy, shown in Figure B-6. The code in this form opens a small orders and order details hierarchy—pulling the contents of two existing orders from the Northwind database and adding to the hierarchy two new orders (with two line items per order). Two bound grids display the two levels of the hierarchy. When the form appears, everything looks great. So why does the form name imply that this is a "bad" hierarchy?

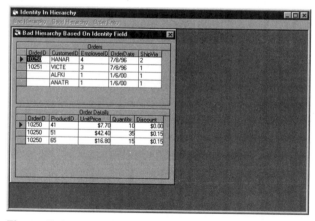

Figure B-6. *Select Bad Hierarchy to display the frmBadHierarchy form, titled Bad Hierarchy Based On Identity Field.*

Let's look at the line items for the two new orders. Because these orders are pending in the hierarchy, they do not have a value for the OrderID field yet. If you're working with a SQL Server or an MSDE database and you click either of the pending orders, you'll notice the same four line items appear in the lower grid for both orders. If you're using the Jet 4.0 OLE DB Provider, selecting either pending order will display a blank line in the lower grid. (The difference in the behavior here is due to a difference in how the providers handle comparisons with null values.) Here's why: When you move to a new record in the orders level of the hierarchy, the data shape provider looks at the value of the OrderID field for the order and then makes visible the records in the order details level of the hierarchy with the same value in the OrderID field. Because these pending orders do not have a value for the OrderID field, there is no way for the data shape provider to locate only their line items. So what should you do? If only you could add a new field to each level of the hierarchy and base the relationship between the levels on that field. Fortunately, you can.

If you close the Bad Hierarchy form and click the Good Hierarchy menu option, the sample will display a form with a hierarchy that has a similar structure to the bad hierarchy. You'll quickly notice that each level of the hierarchy has a new field that contains a globally unique identifier (GUID). Now move to the pending orders and make sure that two line items are visible for each pending order. The sample uses this new field, which I call PseudoKey, rather than the OrderID field to set the relationship for the hierarchy.

NOTE I chose a GUID field because you can request a GUID from Windows and know that you'll receive a unique value. You could base the relationship on an integer instead and simply keep track of the values you've used.

This is the query string that the "bad" hierarchy uses to retrieve its order data:

```
SHAPE {SELECT OrderID, CustomerID, EmployeeID, OrderDate, ShipVia
FROM Orders WHERE OrderID = 10250 OR OrderID = 10251}
AS Orders
```

And here's the query string that the "good" hierarchy uses:

```
SHAPE {SELECT OrderID, CustomerID, EmployeeID, OrderDate, ShipVia
FROM Orders WHERE OrderID = 10250 OR OrderID = 10251}
AS Orders APPEND NEW adGUID AS PseudoKey
```

Essentially, it's the same query with a blank field for handling GUID values. The entire query looks like this:

```
SHAPE (SHAPE {SELECT OrderID, CustomerID, EmployeeID, OrderDate, ShipVia
FROM Orders WHERE OrderID = 10250 OR OrderID = 10251} AS Orders
APPEND NEW adGUID AS PseudoKey) APPEND ((SHAPE {SELECT OrderID,
ProductID, UnitPrice, Quantity, Discount FROM [Order Details]
WHERE OrderID = 10250 OR OrderID = 10251} AS OrderDetails
APPEND NEW adGUID AS PseudoKey) RELATE PseudoKey TO PseudoKey)
AS OrderDetails
```

Inserting new orders and line items into the hierarchy requires one additional step: generating a new GUID value for each order. Actually, that's the easy part. This type of hierarchy is great for adding new orders because you can supply a new value for the PseudoKey field. But the orders and line items that this query initially retrieves from the database have no value for the PseudoKey field.

After the code opens the hierarchical Recordset, it loops through the orders and supplies a value for the PseudoKey field based on the OrderID field. The code also loops through all the order details in the hierarchy (using the reshaping feature covered in Chapter 14) and supplies the appropriate value for the PseudoKey field in the order details as well. Without this (somewhat laborious) code, you would have problems viewing the line items of an existing order.

Only one small challenge remains. How do you submit new orders and line items? If you call the *UpdateBatch* method on a reference to the orders level of the hierarchy, you'll submit the new orders. But if you try to do the same thing with a reference to the order details level of the hierarchy, you'll receive an error because you haven't supplied values for the OrderID field of the new line items.

The third menu option on the MDI parent form is Order Entry. Click this menu option, and you'll see a simple form that displays four orders: two that already exist and two that are pending. You can view or edit the orders and add new orders. (Forgive the simplistic user interface for editing and adding orders.) This important code in this part of the sample appears in the *Click* event for the Submit Changes button. After submitting the changes in the orders level of the hierarchy, this code locates the newly submitted orders and then loops through the line items for each of these orders to set the value for the OrderID field.

> **NOTE**   If you're wondering how ADO retrieves the value for the OrderID field of the new orders, go back to Chapter 11 and read the section on adResyncAutoIncrement. And don't even think about collecting $200 on your way there.

And with that, our quest is at an end. By clicking the Submit Changes button you now can see the new OrderID values for the orders you've added in the grid of orders. Click the Display Order button to see the line items for the order. The new orders won't appear in your database. The code wraps the calls to *UpdateBatch* in a transaction that it then rolls back, allowing you to run the sample over and over again.

NO CHUNKS

This simple sample demonstrates how to move the contents of a file to and from a database using the Stream object. Using the sample should be straightforward.

When you run the sample the form in Figure B-7 appears, displaying only one enabled button: Connect. If you click this button, the sample invokes the Data Link Properties dialog box to prompt you for a connection string.

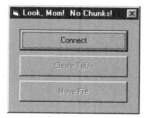

Figure B-7. *The No Chunks sample on initial startup.*

Once you've built a valid connection string, the sample connects to your database, disables the Connect button, and enables the Create Table button. Clicking this button creates in your database a table that's designed to store the contents of files. I wrote the sample to work with SQL Server, which calls its large binary data type "image." If you're using a database program other than SQL Server, this query might fail; you'll need to check the documentation for your database software and change this query in order to properly create the table. As long as you don't change the field names, the rest of the sample should run just fine.

> **NOTE** Don't try to store files in text fields. I don't believe I've ever seen this clearly stated in product documentation, but it needs to be said. Even text files contain binary data. Most database systems have separate data types for large amounts of text and binary data. Binary data is not subject to international localizations or ANSI/Unicode conversions, but text data is. So give unto text data types what is text and give unto binary data types what is binary, and there will be much rejoicing.

Once the sample creates the table in which it can store file contents, you'll see the Move File button enabled. Click this button, and the sample will prompt you for a file to move. Select the file, and the code uses the Stream object to move the contents of the file into your database.

Once this operation completes, the code deletes your file and displays a dialog box that lets you know the file has been deleted. At this time you can open Windows Explorer and confirm that the file has been deleted. Close the dialog box, and the sample retrieves the file from your database and informs you when the operation completes. You can then access the file to confirm that it's identical to the original.

Take a look at the code in the *Click* event for the Move File button. The ADO code is much simpler than any sample code using the *AppendChunk* and *GetChunk* methods. (See Chapter 4 for a description of these methods.)

MY WEB SITE

The My Web Site sample shows how you can use the ADO object model—especially its two new objects, Record and Stream—in conjunction with the OLE DB Provider For Internet Publishing to build a simple tool to access files residing on a web server. This OLE DB provider is not actually distributed with Microsoft Data Access Components (MDAC). However, it's included in the full install of Microsoft Internet Explorer 5.

I built this sample to communicate with Internet Information Services (IIS) 5 running on Windows 2000 Server, but I was able to use the sample with Internet Information Server 4 running on Microsoft Windows NT 4.0 Server as well, and with

Personal Web Server running on Windows NT 4.0 Workstation. The OLE DB provider uses WebDAV—a standard that most web servers support—to communicate with the web server.

For security reasons, web servers generally require that you have administrator rights to the areas of the web site that you want to access. Unfortunately, I am not an IIS security guru, so I'm not sure exactly which settings you might need to use. I didn't change any security settings on my computer running Windows 2000 Server and was able to run the code successfully from it as well as from other computers on the internal network at my office. Once you can connect successfully, you should be able to run the sample without any problems.

When you run the sample, it immediately displays a simple dialog box prompting you for the location of the web site you want to manage. The sample then connects to that web server using the OLE DB Provider For Internet Publishing and displays the contents of the web site in tree view.

From there you can copy, delete, move, and download files by right-clicking them and selecting the appropriate action from the context menu. You can also upload new files by right-clicking a folder and selecting Upload File. Right-clicking a folder also lets you copy, delete, or move that folder and all its contents.

The code in this sample is simple and straightforward—which is why I created it. Using ADO and the OLE DB Provider For Internet Publishing, you can manage the contents of your web servers with some very simple code.

MAKE NORTHWIND

This project uses ActiveX Data Objects Extensions for Data Definition Language and Security (ADOX) to create a database with tables and queries that are nearly identical to the sample Northwind database that ships with various versions of Visual Basic, Access, and other Microsoft products. You might find this sample helpful if you want to learn more about creating Access databases with ADOX, or if you simply want to create a database similar to the Northwind sample.

The modCreateStructure module creates the new database file as well as the tables and QueryDef objects. (Keep in mind that QueryDefs created with the Jet 4.0 OLE DB Provider are not visible through the Access 2000 user interface.) If you're having problems creating tables or queries with ADOX, take a look at this portion of the code.

This sample's folder includes a subdirectory named Data. The files in this subdirectory correspond to the contents of the tables in the Northwind database. After the sample uses the modCreateStructure module to create the new database's structure, it uses the modInsertData module to populate the new database's tables based on the contents of these files. I've left the contents of the Northwind database's BLOB (binary large object) fields out of these data files to save some space and simplify the code in the sample.

Although the sample does not utilize the modLogData module, I've included it with the project so you could see the code I used to generate the files in the Data subdirectory.

REPLICATION

The Replication sample is designed to serve as an introduction to using the replication and synchronization features of Jet and Replication Objects (JRO), discussed in Appendix A. This sample creates three new Access 2000 databases in the sample code's directory: Master.mdb, Replica.mdb, and Partial.mdb. The first database acts as the master database in the replication topology. The second database represents a full replica, and the third represents a partial replica.

The first step is to create and populate the master database. The sample code uses ADOX to create a table that will participate in replication, and then uses ADO to insert three rows into the table before marking the database as replicable. You might not want all the tables in your database to participate in replication, so the sample also creates a table named Local, which it marks as nonreplicable.

The sample then uses the master database to create the new full and partial replica databases. Once that's done, the code connects to the partial replica database and sets up a filter to determine which data from the master database gets replicated to the partial replica.

To demonstrate JRO's synchronization features, the sample modifies two rows in both the master and the full replica, and then synchronizes both databases. Note that there's an overlap—one row (CustomerID = 3) is modified in both databases. This will cause a conflict when the databases are synchronized.

After synchronizing these two databases, the sample code checks for conflicts. If conflicts occurred, the code displays a dialog box asking whether you want to resolve the conflicts. Jet stores information about conflicts in special system tables. If you indicate that you want to resolve the conflicts programmatically, the code loops through these system tables and deletes their contents.

Although this doesn't realistically constitute resolving the conflicts, the Jet engine assumes that if you clear the contents of these tables, you've resolved the conflicts. If you tell the sample that you don't want to resolve the conflicts programmatically, the next time you open the databases in Access 2000, Access will display dialog boxes indicating that conflicts occurred.

As I explained in the "Questions That Should Be Asked More Frequently" section of Appendix A, resolving conflicts is not easy. Actually, I intentionally based the Replication sample on a scenario I felt was a common but unwise one. If at all possible, you should avoid using replication in scenarios where such conflicts occur.

Index

Page numbers in italics refer to figures, illustrations, code samples, and tables.

Special Characters

<> (not equal to) operator used with
FilterCriterion property on RDS
DataControl objects, 64, 287

* (asterisk) used as wildcard character when
setting Filter property, 64

= (equals) operator
used with *Criteria* parameter of *Find*
method, 81
used with Filter clauses, 64
used with FilterCriterion property on RDS
DataControl objects, 287

\> (greater than) and >= (greater than or equal
to) operators, 64, 287

< (less than) and <= (less than or equal to)
operators, 64, 287

% (percent) sign used as wildcard character
when setting Filter property, 64

(pound) symbols as delimiter character
when setting Filter property, 65

? (question marks) as parameter markers in
WHERE clauses, 214–15, *214*, 260

" (quotes) as delimiter character when setting
Filter property, 193

' (single quotes) as delimiter character when
setting Filter property, 65, 193

[] (square brackets) as delimiter character
when setting Filter property, 64

A

AbsolutePage property on Recordset objects,
55–56

AbsolutePosition property on Recordset
objects, 56

Access. *See* Microsoft Access; Microsoft
Access 2000

ActiveCommand property on Recordset
objects, 13–14, 56

ActiveConnection parameter of *Open* method
on Record objects, 147, 252

ActiveConnection parameter of *Open* method
on Recordset objects, 88

ActiveConnection property on ADOX Catalog
objects, 306

ActiveConnection property on Command
objects, 13, 120

ActiveConnection property on Record objects,
140

ActiveConnection property on Recordset
objects
avoiding generating multiple Connection
objects using, 16–17, *16,* 18–19, *18*
avoiding long open connections, 196, *196*
errors produced when opening Recordsets
from Stream objects, 252
overview, 56–57

ActiveX EXE. *See* Microsoft ActiveX EXE used
as middle-tier server

ActualSize property on Field objects
DefinedSize property and, 108
getting prior to calling *GetChunk* method,
115
returns number of bytes not number of
characters in field, 116

ADCExecuteOptionEnum values, *286*

ADCFetchOptionEnum values, *286*

ADCPROP_UPDATECRITERIA_ENUM values,
210–11, *211*

ADCReadyStateEnum values, *287*

AddNew method on Recordset objects,
74–75, *75*

ADO. *See* Microsoft ActiveX Data Objects
(ADO); *specific topics in this index*

ADO Cursor Engine. *See* Cursor Engine

ADOX. *See* Microsoft ActiveX Data Objects
Extensions for Data Definition
Language and Security (ADOX)

ADTG (Advanced Data TableGram),
persisting data using, 251

Advanced Data Connector. *See* Remote Data
Service (RDS)

DAVID SCEPPA

David Sceppa grew up in the town of Westwood, Massachusetts, where he learned right (Red Sox, Celtics) from wrong (Yankees, Lakers) and idolized John Cleese. He was fortunate to live in a town with a public school system that encouraged him to develop strong mathematical and computer programming skills. While in high school, David worked part-time on a Paradox database system at Enterprise Leasing of New England, where he never thought the company would outgrow its (then) enormous 20-MB hard drive.

David attended Princeton University, earning a degree in mathematics and participating in the teacher preparation program. He spent summers developing and maintaining a FoxPro database system for a company that assembled circuit boards.

After graduation, David moved to the other end of Interstate 90—Seattle—where he briefly attended the University of Washington as a graduate student before accepting a job as a Microsoft FoxPro support professional. He later joined the Microsoft Visual Basic database support team and now acts as a technical lead, interacting with customers and development teams within Microsoft. David is also a Microsoft Certified Solution Developer.

David has recently discovered that he likes bebop jazz and that he can't keep a straight face while writing about himself in the third person. His long-term goals are to complete a marathon, teach mathematics to high school students, win an award for his world-famous chili, and see the Red Sox win a World Series.

The manuscript for this book was prepared using Microsoft Word 2000. Pages were composed by Microsoft Press using Adobe PageMaker 6.52 for Windows, with text in Garamond and display type in Helvetica Black. Composed pages were delivered to the printer as electronic prepress files.

Cover Graphic Designer
Girvin Strategic Branding & Design

Cover Illustrator
Glenn Mitsui

Interior Graphic Artist
Rob Nance

Principal Compositor
Barb Runyan

Technical Copy Editor
Shawn Peck

Principal Proofreader/Copy Editor
Melissa Bryan

Indexer
Kari Kells

The *bible* for *Visual Basic* *data access*

U.S.A. **$49.99**
U.K. £32.99 [V.A.T. included]
Canada $71.99
ISBN 1-57231-848-1

The HITCHHIKER'S GUIDE TO VISUAL BASIC® AND SQL SERVER,™ Sixth Edition, is the definitive guide for developers who want to use Visual Basic to access SQL Server. Whether you're using earlier versions or the new Visual Basic 6.0 and the completely reengineered SQL Server 7.0 (which now runs on Microsoft® Windows® 95 and Windows 98), this book will help you decide which of the constantly evolving data access options is best for your situation. Author William Vaughn provides the same depth and breadth of coverage that have made earlier editions of this book indispensable. Plus, he introduces innovations that may well change the way you think about data access!

Microsoft Press® products are available worldwide wherever quality computer books are sold. For more information, contact your book or computer retailer, software reseller, or local Microsoft® Sales Office, or visit our Web site at mspress.microsoft.com. To locate your nearest source for Microsoft Press products, or to order directly, call 1-800-MSPRESS in the U.S. (in Canada, call 1-800-268-2222).

Prices and availability dates are subject to change.

Microsoft®

mspress.microsoft.com

MICROSOFT LICENSE AGREEMENT

Book Companion CD

IMPORTANT—READ CAREFULLY: This Microsoft End-User License Agreement ("EULA") is a legal agreement between you (either an individual or an entity) and Microsoft Corporation for the Microsoft product identified above, which includes computer software and may include associated media, printed materials, and "online" or electronic documentation ("SOFTWARE PRODUCT"). Any component Included within the SOFTWARE PRODUCT that is accompanied by a separate End-User License Agreement shall be governed by such agreement and not the terms set forth below. By installing, copying, or otherwise using the SOFTWARE PRODUCT, you agree to be bound by the terms of this EULA. If you do not agree to the terms of this EULA, you are not authorized to install, copy, or otherwise use the SOFTWARE PRODUCT; you may, however, return the SOFTWARE PRODUCT, along with all printed materials and other items that form a part of the Microsoft product that includes the SOFTWARE PRODUCT, to the place you obtained them for a full refund.

SOFTWARE PRODUCT LICENSE

The SOFTWARE PRODUCT is protected by United States copyright laws and international copyright treaties, as well as other intellectual property laws and treaties. The SOFTWARE PRODUCT is licensed, not sold.

1. **GRANT OF LICENSE.** This EULA grants you the following rights:

   a. **Software Product.** You may install and use one copy of the SOFTWARE PRODUCT on a single computer. The primary user of the computer on which the SOFTWARE PRODUCT is installed may make a second copy for his or her exclusive use on a portable computer.

   b. **Storage/Network Use.** You may also store or install a copy of the SOFTWARE PRODUCT on a storage device, such as a network server, used only to install or run the SOFTWARE PRODUCT on your other computers over an internal network; however, you must acquire and dedicate a license for each separate computer on which the SOFTWARE PRODUCT is installed or run from the storage device. A license for the SOFTWARE PRODUCT may not be shared or used concurrently on different computers.

   c. **License Pak.** If you have acquired this EULA in a Microsoft License Pak, you may make the number of additional copies of the computer software portion of the SOFTWARE PRODUCT authorized on the printed copy of this EULA, and you may use each copy in the manner specified above. You are also entitled to make a corresponding number of secondary copies for portable computer use as specified above.

   d. **Sample Code.** Solely with respect to portions, if any, of the SOFTWARE PRODUCT that are identified within the SOFTWARE PRODUCT as sample code (the "SAMPLE CODE"):

      i. **Use and Modification.** Microsoft grants you the right to use and modify the source code version of the SAMPLE CODE, *provided* you comply with subsection (d)(iii) below. You may not distribute the SAMPLE CODE, or any modified version of the SAMPLE CODE, in source code form.

      ii. **Redistributable Files.** Provided you comply with subsection (d)(iii) below, Microsoft grants you a nonexclusive, royalty-free right to reproduce and distribute the object code version of the SAMPLE CODE and of any modified SAMPLE CODE, other than SAMPLE CODE, or any modified version thereof, designated as not redistributable in the Readme file that forms a part of the SOFTWARE PRODUCT (the "Non-Redistributable Sample Code"). All SAMPLE CODE other than the Non-Redistributable Sample Code is collectively referred to as the "REDISTRIBUTABLES."

      iii. **Redistribution Requirements.** If you redistribute the REDISTRIBUTABLES, you agree to: (i) distribute the REDISTRIBUTABLES in object code form only in conjunction with and as a part of your software application product; (ii) not use Microsoft's name, logo, or trademarks to market your software application product; (iii) include a valid copyright notice on your software application product; (iv) indemnify, hold harmless, and defend Microsoft from and against any claims or lawsuits, including attorney's fees, that arise or result from the use or distribution of your software application product; and (v) not permit further distribution of the REDISTRIBUTABLES by your end user. Contact Microsoft for the applicable royalties due and other licensing terms for all other uses and/or distribution of the REDISTRIBUTABLES.

2. **DESCRIPTION OF OTHER RIGHTS AND LIMITATIONS.**

   - **Limitations on Reverse Engineering, Decompilation, and Disassembly.** You may not reverse engineer, decompile, or disassemble the SOFTWARE PRODUCT, except and only to the extent that such activity is expressly permitted by applicable law notwithstanding this limitation.

   - **Separation of Components.** The SOFTWARE PRODUCT is licensed as a single product. Its component parts may not be separated for use on more than one computer.

   - **Rental.** You may not rent, lease, or lend the SOFTWARE PRODUCT.

   - **Support Services.** Microsoft may, but is not obligated to, provide you with support services related to the SOFTWARE PRODUCT ("Support Services"). Use of Support Services is governed by the Microsoft policies and programs described in the user manual, in "online" documentation, and/or in other Microsoft-provided materials. Any supplemental software code provided to you as part of the Support Services shall be considered part of the SOFTWARE PRODUCT and subject to the terms and conditions of this EULA. With respect to technical information you provide to Microsoft as part of the Support Services, Microsoft may use such information for its business purposes, including for product support and development. Microsoft will not utilize such technical information in a form that personally identifies you.

- **Software Transfer.** You may permanently transfer all of your rights under this EULA, provided you retain no copies, you transfer all of the SOFTWARE PRODUCT (including all component parts, the media and printed materials, any upgrades, this EULA, and, if applicable, the Certificate of Authenticity), **and** the recipient agrees to the terms of this EULA.

- **Termination.** Without prejudice to any other rights, Microsoft may terminate this EULA if you fail to comply with the terms and conditions of this EULA. In such event, you must destroy all copies of the SOFTWARE PRODUCT and all of its component parts.

3. **COPYRIGHT.** All title and copyrights in and to the SOFTWARE PRODUCT (including but not limited to any images, photographs, animations, video, audio, music, text, SAMPLE CODE, REDISTRIBUTABLES, and "applets" incorporated into the SOFTWARE PRODUCT) and any copies of the SOFTWARE PRODUCT are owned by Microsoft or its suppliers. The SOFTWARE PRODUCT is protected by copyright laws and international treaty provisions. Therefore, you must treat the SOFTWARE PRODUCT like any other copyrighted material **except** that you may install the SOFTWARE PRODUCT on a single computer provided you keep the original solely for backup or archival purposes. You may not copy the printed materials accompanying the SOFTWARE PRODUCT.

4. **U.S. GOVERNMENT RESTRICTED RIGHTS.** The SOFTWARE PRODUCT and documentation are provided with RESTRICTED RIGHTS. Use, duplication, or disclosure by the Government is subject to restrictions as set forth in subparagraph (c)(1)(ii) of the Rights in Technical Data and Computer Software clause at DFARS 252.227-7013 or subparagraphs (c)(1) and (2) of the Commercial Computer Software—Restricted Rights at 48 CFR 52.227-19, as applicable. Manufacturer is Microsoft Corporation/One Microsoft Way/Redmond, WA 98052-6399.

5. **EXPORT RESTRICTIONS.** You agree that you will not export or re-export the SOFTWARE PRODUCT, any part thereof, or any process or service that is the direct product of the SOFTWARE PRODUCT (the foregoing collectively referred to as the "Restricted Components"), to any country, person, entity, or end user subject to U.S. export restrictions. You specifically agree not to export or re-export any of the Restricted Components (i) to any country to which the U.S. has embargoed or restricted the export of goods or services, which currently include, but are not necessarily limited to, Cuba, Iran, Iraq, Libya, North Korea, Sudan, and Syria, or to any national of any such country, wherever located, who intends to transmit or transport the Restricted Components back to such country; (ii) to any end user who you know or have reason to know will utilize the Restricted Components in the design, development, or production of nuclear, chemical, or biological weapons; or (iii) to any end user who has been prohibited from participating in U.S. export transactions by any federal agency of the U.S. government. You warrant and represent that neither the BXA nor any other U.S. federal agency has suspended, revoked, or denied your export privileges.

DISCLAIMER OF WARRANTY

NO WARRANTIES OR CONDITIONS. MICROSOFT EXPRESSLY DISCLAIMS ANY WARRANTY OR CONDITION FOR THE SOFTWARE PRODUCT. THE SOFTWARE PRODUCT AND ANY RELATED DOCUMENTATION ARE PROVIDED "AS IS" WITHOUT WARRANTY OR CONDITION OF ANY KIND, EITHER EXPRESS OR IMPLIED, INCLUDING, WITHOUT LIMITATION, THE IMPLIED WARRANTIES OF MERCHANTABILITY, FITNESS FOR A PARTICULAR PURPOSE, OR NONINFRINGEMENT. THE ENTIRE RISK ARISING OUT OF USE OR PERFORMANCE OF THE SOFTWARE PRODUCT REMAINS WITH YOU.

LIMITATION OF LIABILITY. TO THE MAXIMUM EXTENT PERMITTED BY APPLICABLE LAW, IN NO EVENT SHALL MICROSOFT OR ITS SUPPLIERS BE LIABLE FOR ANY SPECIAL, INCIDENTAL, INDIRECT, OR CONSEQUENTIAL DAMAGES WHATSOEVER (INCLUDING, WITHOUT LIMITATION, DAMAGES FOR LOSS OF BUSINESS PROFITS, BUSINESS INTERRUPTION, LOSS OF BUSINESS INFORMATION, OR ANY OTHER PECUNIARY LOSS) ARISING OUT OF THE USE OF OR INABILITY TO USE THE SOFTWARE PRODUCT OR THE PROVISION OF OR FAILURE TO PROVIDE SUPPORT SERVICES, EVEN IF MICROSOFT HAS BEEN ADVISED OF THE POSSIBILITY OF SUCH DAMAGES. IN ANY CASE, MICROSOFT'S ENTIRE LIABILITY UNDER ANY PROVISION OF THIS EULA SHALL BE LIMITED TO THE GREATER OF THE AMOUNT ACTUALLY PAID BY YOU FOR THE SOFTWARE PRODUCT OR US$5.00; PROVIDED, HOWEVER, IF YOU HAVE ENTERED INTO A MICROSOFT SUPPORT SERVICES AGREEMENT, MICROSOFT'S ENTIRE LIABILITY REGARDING SUPPORT SERVICES SHALL BE GOVERNED BY THE TERMS OF THAT AGREEMENT. BECAUSE SOME STATES AND JURISDICTIONS DO NOT ALLOW THE EXCLUSION OR LIMITATION OF LIABILITY, THE ABOVE LIMITATION MAY NOT APPLY TO YOU.

MISCELLANEOUS

This EULA is governed by the laws of the State of Washington USA, except and only to the extent that applicable law mandates governing law of a different jurisdiction.

Should you have any questions concerning this EULA, or if you desire to contact Microsoft for any reason, please contact the Microsoft subsidiary serving your country, or write: Microsoft Sales Information Center/One Microsoft Way/Redmond, WA 98052-6399.

Proof of Purchase

0-7356-0764-8

Do not send this card with your registration.
Use this card as proof of purchase if participating in a promotion or
rebate offer on *Programming ADO*. Card must be used in conjunction with
other proof(s) of payment such as your dated sales receipt—see offer details.

Programming ADO

WHERE DID YOU PURCHASE THIS PRODUCT?

CUSTOMER NAME

Microsoft®
mspress.microsoft.com
Microsoft Press, PO Box 97017, Redmond, WA 98073-9830

OWNER REGISTRATION CARD

Register Today!

0-7356-0764-8

Return the bottom portion of this card to register today.

Programming ADO

FIRST NAME   MIDDLE INITIAL   LAST NAME

INSTITUTION OR COMPANY NAME

ADDRESS

CITY   STATE   ZIP

(   )

E-MAIL ADDRESS   PHONE NUMBER

U.S. and Canada addresses only. Fill in information above and mail postage-free.
Please mail only the bottom half of this page.

start faster
go
farther

For information about Microsoft Press®
products, visit our Web site at
mspress.microsoft.com

Microsoft®

	NO POSTAGE
---	NECESSARY
	IF MAILED
	IN THE
	UNITED STATES

BUSINESS REPLY MAIL
FIRST-CLASS MAIL   PERMIT NO. 108   REDMOND WA

POSTAGE WILL BE PAID BY ADDRESSEE

MICROSOFT PRESS
PO BOX 97017
REDMOND, WA 98073-9830